Lecture Notes
in Business Information Processing   77

Series Editors

Wil van der Aalst
Eindhoven Technical University, The Netherlands
John Mylopoulos
University of Trento, Italy
Michael Rosemann
Queensland University of Technology, Brisbane, Qld, Australia
Michael J. Shaw
University of Illinois, Urbana-Champaign, IL, USA
Clemens Szyperski
Microsoft Research, Redmond, WA, USA

Alberto Sillitti
Orit Hazzan
Emily Bache
Xavier Albaladejo (Eds.)

Agile Processes in Software Engineering and Extreme Programming

12th International Conference, XP 2011
Madrid, Spain, May 10-13, 2011
Proceedings

 Springer

Volume Editors

Alberto Sillitti
Free University of Bolzano
Piazza Domenicani, 3
39100 Bolzano, Italy
E-mail: Alberto.Sillitti@unibz.it

Orit Hazzan
Technion - Israel Institute of Technology
32000 Haifa, Israel
E-mail: oritha@techunix.technion.ac.il

Emily Bache
Bache Consulting
Flunsåsliden 25
418 71 Göteborg, Sweden
E-mail: emily@bacheconsulting.com

Xavier Albaladejo
Everis
Avda Diagonal, 605
08028 Barcelona, Spain
E-mail: xavier.albaladejo.ezequiel@everis.com

ISSN 1865-1348   e-ISSN 1865-1356
ISBN 978-3-642-20676-4   e-ISBN 978-3-642-20677-1
DOI 10.1007/978-3-642-20677-1
Springer Heidelberg Dordrecht London New York

Library of Congress Control Number: 2011925554

ACM Computing Classification (1998): D.2, K.6

Typesetting: Camera-ready by author, data conversion by Scientific Publishing Services, Chennai, India

Printed on acid-free paper

Springer is part of Springer Science+Business Media (www.springer.com)

Preface

The Agile Manifesto is now 10 years old and agile methods have changed how people develop software all over the world. The XP conference series has actively participated in promoting agility, spreading research results in the area, and getting researchers and practitioners together.

XP 2011 continued in the tradition of this conference series and provided an interesting and varied program. As usual, we had a number of different activities in the conference program including: research papers, experience reports, tutorials, workshops, lightning talks, and posters. These proceedings contain all the papers including: full research papers, short research papers, and experience reports. Moreover, we have also included in these proceedings the abstracts of the posters, the position papers of the PhD symposium, and the abstract of the workshops.

Like last year, we had two different Program Committees for evaluating research papers and experience reports. Each committee included experts in the specific area. This approach has allowed us to better evaluate the quality of the papers and provide better suggestions to the authors to improve the quality of their contributions.

All of the submitted research papers went through a rigorous peer-review process. Each paper was reviewed by at least three members of the Program Committee. Of the 56 papers submitted, only 11 were accepted as full papers (20%). All of the experience report papers also went through a rigorous selection process. We received 17 submissions; only 4 papers were accepted (23%). A committee of experts evaluated each submission looking for new experiences that would be both interesting and beneficial to be published and accessible to the agile community.

We hope that you find the proceedings of XP 2011 useful for your professional and academic activities.

Finally, we would like to thank all the people who contributed to XP 2011, including the authors, the sponsors, the reviewers, the volunteers, and the Chairs.

March 2011

Alberto Sillitti
Orit Hazzan
Emily Bache
Xavier Albaladejo

Organization

Conference Chairs

General Chair

Rachel Davies   Agile Experience Ltd., UK

Program Committee Chairs

Philippe Kruchten   University of British Columbia, Canada
Juan Garbajosa   Madrid Technical University (UPM), Spain

Research Program Chairs

Orit Hazzan   Technion, Israel
Alberto Sillitti   Free University of Bolzano, Italy

Industry Program Chairs

Emily Bache   Bache Consulting, Sweden
Xavier Albaladejo   Everis, Spain

Organizing Chairs

Juan Garbajosa   Madrid Technical University (UPM), Spain
Agustin Yagüe   Madrid Technical University (UPM), Spain

PhD Symposium Chairs

Yael Dubinsky   IBM, Israel
Jennifer Pérez   Madrid Technical University (UPM), Spain

Lightning Talks Chairs

Naresh Jain   Industrial Logic, India
Rodrigo Corral   Plain Concepts, Spain

Workshops Chairs

Lasse Koskela   Reaktor Innovation, Finland
Xiaofeng Wang   LERO, Ireland

Tutorials Chairs

Xavier Quesada   Agilar, Argentina
Ralph Miarka   Independent, Austria

Open Space Chairs

Charlie Poole   Poole Consulting, USA
Agustin Yagüe   Madrid Technical University (UPM), Spain

Special Issue Chair

Pekka Abrahamson   Free University of Bolzano, Italy

Sponsorship Chair

Erik Lundh   Compelcon, Sweden
Jorge Uriarte   Gailen, Spain

Publicity Chairs

Steven Fraser   Cisco Research Center, USA
Hironori Wazisaki   Waseda University, Japan
Jennifer Pérez   Madrid Technical University (UPM), Spain

Local Arrangements Chairs

Jessica Díaz   Madrid Technical University (UPM), Spain
Agustin Yagüe   Madrid Technical University (UPM), Spain

International Student Volunteer Chairs

Johanna Hunt   University of Sussex, UK
Angelina Espinoza   Madrid Technical University (UPM), Spain

Program Committee

Pekka Abrahamsson, Finland	Torgeir Dingsoyr, Norway	Eloy Gonzalez Ortega, Spain
Muhammad Ali Babar, Denmark	Amr Elssamadisy, USA	Gargi Keeni, India
Robert Biddle, Canada	Steven Fraser, USA	Kirsi Korhonen, Finland
Alan Brown, Spain	Lars-Åke Fredlund, Spain	Pasi Kuvaja, Finland
Luigi Buglione, Italy	Sallyann Freudenberg, UK	Stig Larsson, Sweden
Rodrigo Corral, Spain	Jorge García Peláez, Spain	José Carlos Maldonado, Brazil
Ivica Crnkovic, Sweden	Alfredo Goldman, Brazil	Michele Marchesi, Italy
Stefano de Panfilis, Italy		Yoshihiro Matsumoto, Japan
Esther Derby, USA		

Table of Contents

Research Papers

Experience Reports

Posters

Ph.D. Symposium

Workshops

Analysing the Usage of Tools
in Pair Programming Sessions

Ilenia Fronza, Alberto Sillitti, Giancarlo Succi, and Jelena Vlasenko

Free University of Bolzano-Bozen, Piazza Domenicani, 3,
I-39100 Bolzano, Italy
{Ilenia.Fronza,Alberto.Sillitti,Giancarlo.Succi}@unibz.it,
Jelena.Vlasenko@stud-inf.unibz.it

Abstract. In this study we observe the daily work of nineteen software developers of a large Italian manufacturing company for a period of ten months to determine the effects of pair programming on the use of tools. Fifteen developers are existing team members and four have recently joined the team. They practice Pair Programming spontaneously, that is, when they feel it is needed. We identify the tools the developers use, how they distribute their time among these tools when working alone and when doing Pair Programming. The data have been extracted non-invasively by means of PROM – tool for automated data collection and analysis. The preliminary results indicate that developers working in pairs devote significantly more time to programming activities than developers working alone.

Keywords: Pair Programming, Tool Usage, Agile Methods.

1 Introduction

Existing studies have reported several advantages of Pair Programming [9], [29], [16], [17], [21], [6], [30]. It has been found that developers working in pairs detect defects when typing and that the code written by pairs is significantly shorter than the code written by developers working alone. Moreover, developers working in pairs constantly exchange their knowledge and are more satisfied with their work. Unfortunately, the vast majority of the experimental studies conducted on Pair Programming have taken place in educational environments, where developers were typically computer science students, and it is known that the applicability of the results so obtained to industry is limited. Only few experiments have been carried out in an industrial environment, but they were very short in time duration (no more than few days). In addition, results obtained from different empirical studies contain contradictions.

In this study we analyse work of professional software developers of a large Italian manufacturing company from October 2007 to July 2008. The company adopts spontaneous Pair Programming, that is, developers work in pairs when feel that their task would benefit from such practice. Our goal is to investigate how Pair Programming affects the usage of tools. For this purpose we analyse how developers

A. Sillitti et al. (Eds.): XP 2011, LNBIP 77, pp. 1–11, 2011.
© Springer-Verlag Berlin Heidelberg 2011

use tools to perform their daily tasks when they work alone and when in pairs, taking into consideration their working experience in the company as such working experience can be a relevant confounding factor.

This paper is organized as follows: Section 2 discusses existing works in this area, Section 3 describes the structure of the study, Section 4 presents results of analysis of tools usage of a team of 19 developers for 10 months doing spontaneous Pair Programming, and Section 5 draws some conclusions.

2 Related Work

2.1 Research on Pair Programming

In the last 10 years a large number of studies on Pair Programming has been conducted. Mainly they are focused on the costs and benefits [9] of this technique.

Some of the studies are aimed to determine if Pair Programming has a positive effect on working skills [30], [6] and on code quality [31], [16], [30], [5]. Most of them used students as subjects of the experimentations. Therefore, the validity of these experiments is questionable and can hardly be generalized to teams of industrial developers. Only few works involved professional developers [20], [17], [8], [30], [13], [1].

Lui and Chan [20] found that pairs outperform individuals only when tasks are challenging and new to them. Hulkko and Abrahamsson [17] analysed four software projects and concluded that Pair Programming does not provide an extensive quality benefits and does not result in consistently superior productivity when comparing to solo programming. Canfora et al. [8] identified that Pair Programming decreases productivity but increases code quality. Arisholm et al. [1] conducted the largest industrial experiment so far and identified that junior pair programmers achieved a significant increase in correctness comparing to the individuals and have achieved approximately the same degree of correctness as senior programmers working alone.

2.2 Research on Tool Usage

The first statement in the agile manifesto says that more value should be given to people than to tools and processes. Still to evaluate and to improve performance of developers it is essential to understand how they work, which tools they use, and for which purposes.

Until now there has been conducted only a limited number of studies on tool usage. Table 1 gives an overview of some them.

[28] presents 4 separate studies aimed to analyze daily activities and increase productivity of software engineers. The data was collected by means of questionnaires, interviews, and observation sessions. There were also analyzed unix history files. The results indicate that the developers need a tool for code exploration.

In [19] the authors use questionnaires, interviews, observation sessions, and analysis of unix files to identify requirements for software engineering tools. The results of the study indicate that the developers need tools that allow easy and fast navigation within source code. The requirements for developing this kind of tools are proposed.

Table 1. Overview of existing studies on Tool Usage

Authors	Subjects and goal of the experiment	Results
"An Exploratory Study of Developers' Toolbox in an Agile Team," I. D. Coman and Giancarlo Succi, 2009	**Subjects:** 3 developers of a small Austrian company. **Goal:** To detect how many tools use developers, which tools are used frequently and for which purpose they serve.	Developers use 41 distinct tools. Developers use 12, 11 and 13 tools respectively. Five main activities: Documents, Navigating, Communication, Internet and Coding.
"Maintaining Mental Models: A Study of Developer Work Habits," T. D. LaToza et al., 2006	**Subjects:** 344 survey responses by Microsoft's software design engineers; Interviews with 11 Microsoft's software design engineers **Goal:** To detect which tools developers use, what their activities and practices are.	Developers use a variety of tools and search for better solutions. Developers switch frequently between tools. Developers prefer face-to-face communication than electronic one.
"An Examination of Software Engineering Work Practices," J. Singer et al., 1997	**Subjects:** Group that maintains a large telecommunication system: 6 survey responses, exploring work of 10 developers, the company's tool usage statistics. **Goal:** To provide software engineers with a toolset to improve their daily work activities.	Developers most of their time use compilers and search tools.
"Understanding Software Maintenance Tools: Some Empirical Research," T. C. Lethbridge and J. Singer, 2007	**Subjects:** Team of software engineers. **Goal:** To detect which tools developers and what should be improved to make them more productive.	Developers use more often editors and search tools than other tools

In [22] at Nokia senior developers and managers were asked to fill in questionnaires in order to identify the most useful and best implemented features in the CASE tools that were used at that moment in the company. The results indicate that the respondents in general are dissatisfied with the existing tools and that the features that were considered advanced were not as useful as expected.

In [18] the authors have conducted eleven surveys and two interviews in order to explore the tools, activities, and practices of the developers. It has been found that the developers constantly try new tools out and frequently switch between them. They also switch between tasks when interrupted.

[7] is another study that has been conducted by means of survey aiming to analyze how developers use tools and to improve user interface software development. The authors asked 370 practitioners to fill in surveys where they had to to choose among several working styles the one that was more corresponding to theirs and the tools that were mostly used to perform user interface design. The results indicate that the respondents switch frequently between working styles when they get interrupted by their colleagues and when the tool they currently use does not support their working style. As the result of the study in order to minimize switching between working styles two new tools were developed. Both of them were downloaded more than 2000 times over a period of one year. Altogether, the results from these studies are interesting but limited, and such limitation is clearly due to the difficulty of the data collection process.

A major advance in understanding better tool usage has been the introduction of AISEMA tools [11]. AISEMA allows to collect data in automated and non-intrusive way significantly increasing the reliability of the obtained results. The application of AISEMA tools is a prerequisite for the new model we propose to analyze tools data.

In [12] it was investigated how the developers working in an agile team use different tools. The data has been extracted non-invasively by means of an AISEMA tool, PROM [27]. The length of the study was 53 working days. It has been found that the developers use regularly only a small set of tools and periodically try new ones out. Developers distribute their time almost equivalently among coding, browsing Internet, and communication tools. Moreover, they prefer to replace face-to-face communication with e-mails and instant messaging.

3   The Study

As mentioned, to avoid the possible confounding effect of working experience we consider five possible working configurations:

- **experts solos:** experts working alone
- **experts pairs:** two experts working in pair
- **novices solos:** novices working alone
- **novices pairs:** two novices working in pair
- **mixed pairs:** a novice and an expert working in pair

For simplicity, following the guidelines of [Coman et al., 2009] we have focused our analysis only on the 9 tools that were used the most out of a total of 26 tools. These tools cover more than 80% of the total effort and are: Browser, Outlook, Microsoft Messenger, Microsoft Office Word, Microsoft Office Excel, Microsoft Windows Explorer, Microsoft Management Console, Remote Desktop, and Visual Studio.

3.1   The Developers

The data has been collected from a team of software developers working for a large Italian manufacturing company that prefers to remain anonymous. The developers are

Italians. All of them have university degrees in computer-related areas and programming experience from 10 to 15 years. The study has covered a time frame of 10 months from October 2007 to July 2008, during which the developers performed both maintenance and improvement tasks. The programming language in use was mainly C#. The developers used some of the Extreme Programming practices during their daily work, in particular, they used weekly iterations, Pair Programming, user stories, collective code ownership, coding standards, and test driven development. The team members used spontaneous Pair Programming, i.e., when they found it useful and appropriate. Each developer had his own workplace and workstation. The team was located in an open space what favored communication and knowledge transfers among them.

3.2 Data Collection

The data in this study represents all the activities of the developers at their computer. It has been collected non-invasively by means of PROM (PRO Metrics) [27]. PROM is a tool for automated data collection and analysis. It collects both code and process measures. PROM's architecture is based on plug-ins that collects data from the tools the developers use. Thus, PROM has information about all software application used by the developers, the time they spend in them, and the identifiers of the developers. If the developers do Pair Programming PROM will store information also about composition of pairs.

PROM was already in use when the experiment started. The developers received comprehensive information about the tool and the data it collected and participated voluntarily to the study. Each team member could access to her/his own data and also to aggregate data of other team members as a whole. Moreover, the developers had rights to look at the data stored in their own machine and to decide if they wanted to send it to the central database or to delete it. To ensure the integrity of the collected data, the developers were asked periodically to verify it.

4   Results

4.1 Time Distribution and Usage of Tools

Altogether, developers spend most of their time using three applications: Visual Studio, Browser, and Outlook (Figure 1).

Figure 2 represents the usage of Visual Studio in the five working configurations. We have found that novices and experts working alone behave very similarly and devote to programming activities about 33% of their time. Developers working in pairs spend significantly more time in programming activities than the developers working alone. Experts working in pairs spent almost twice more time in Visual Studio than experts working alone. Novices working in pairs also spend more time on programming activities than the novices working alone but the difference is less significant. Furthermore, mixed pairs spend 75% of their time on programming activities, the highest value in the study.

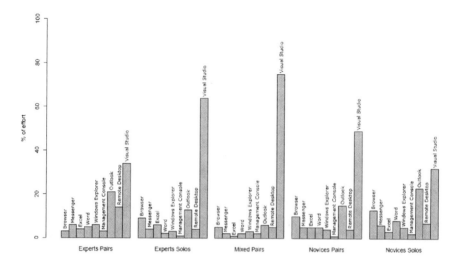

Fig. 1. Tools Usage by the developers working under different patterns

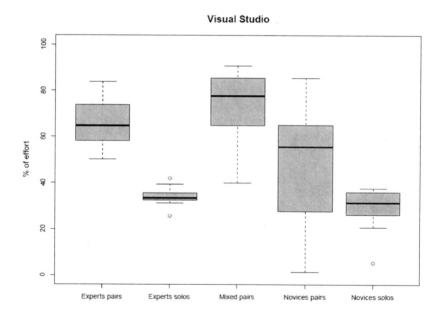

Fig. 2. Distribution of the effort spent in Visual Studio

Figure 3 represents the effort devoted by the developers to writing and reading e-mails during their working time. It is important to mention that the developers receive their tasks via e-mail and this explains the heavy usage of Outlook. It is noticeable that the developers working in mixed exhibit the lowest usage of Outlook. The pairs spend significantly less time in Outlook than solos. Experts and novices behave very similarly when they work alone. Experts working alone spend 21% of their time and the novices working alone 23%. Experts working in pairs spend a bit less time on e-mails than the novices working in pairs. Experts spend 13% of their time and novices 15%.

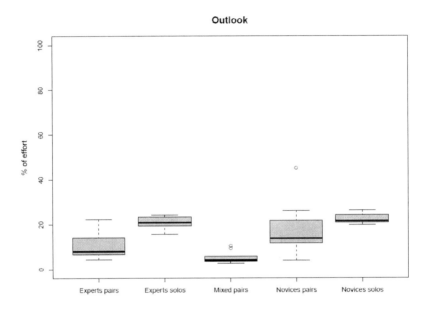

Fig. 3. Distribution of the effort spent in Outlook

Figure 4 represents the effort devoted by the developers to Browser. Novices working alone spend more time on browsing than experts working alone. Novices spend 13% and the experts spend 9% of their time on browsing the Internet. Moreover, novices working in pairs spend more time on browsing than experts working in pairs. Novices spend 10% of their time and experts only 3%. Developers working as mixed pairs spend only 5% of their time on this activity.

4.2 Analysis

Altogether, we can claim that in general the adoption of pair programming can help developers in general to concentrate on their main task – programming (Table 2).

When developers work in pairs they are more focused and devote significantly more time on programming activities than when they work alone. In particular, experts working in pairs spend 64% of their time on programming activities and when they work alone they spend only 34% of their time on programming activities. Especially effective appears to be a pair composed of one expert and one novice: during these sessions 75% of the total effort is spent in programming – possibly also to provide instruction from experts to novices.

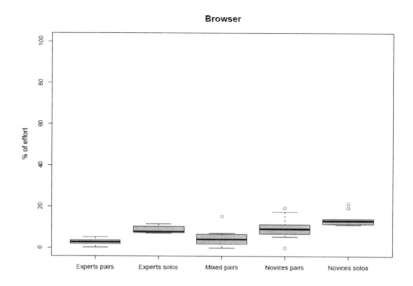

Fig. 4. Distribution of the effort spent in Browser

Table 2. Summary of the average percentage of effort spent in the three most used applications

	Visual Studio	Outlook	Browser
Experts solos	34%	21%	9%
Experts pairs	64%	13%	3%
Mixed pairs	75%	6%	5%
Novices solos	32%	23%	13%
Novices pairs	49%	15%	10%

On the other hand pairs composed of two novices appear to be less focused. Novices working alone spend 32% of their time on programming activities and when they work in pairs spend 49% of their time on programming activities what is less that spend experts working in pairs. The reason could be that novices may need to gather additional information for programming, that, for instance, can be obtained browsing suitable sites.

5 Conclusions and Future Work

The goal of this study was to observe the daily work of 19 software developers from an IT department of a large Italian manufacturing company and to investigate how they use different tools. The data was collected during a time frame of 10 months from October 2007 to July 2008. The daily work of the developers was analysed taking into consideration their working experience in the company. The developers were applying spontaneous Pair Programming, i.e., when they found it appropriate. Compared to other studies conducted on Pair Programming the observation period is significantly large what makes it important for other studies in this area.

We have found that when experts work in pairs spend 64% of their time on programming activities and when they work alone they spend only 34% of their time on programming activities. Novices working alone behave very similar to experts and spend 32% of their time on programming activities but when they work in pairs spend only 49% of their time on programming activities. In general, it can be concluded that developers working in pairs spend almost twice more time on programming activities that developers working alone.

We noticed that developers spend a noticeable part of their time browsing the Internet. In particular, developers working alone spend twice more time browsing than developers working in pairs; therefore, it could be interesting to investigate the percentage of browsing devoted for work and private purposes. This is a goal of future research.

In the future it is planned to repeat this experiment, taking also into consideration the different kind of purposes people have when using a browser, in particular, when they use it for work and when for personal reasons.

Acknowledgments

We thank Cinzia Colapinto for the valuable corrections to an earlier version of this manuscript.

References

1. Arisholm, E., Gallis, H., Dyba, T., Sjoberg, D.I.K.: Evaluating Pair Programming with respect to System Complexity and Programmer Expertise. IEEE Transactions on Software Engineering 33(2), 65–86 (2007)
2. Baheti, P., Williams, L., Gehringer, E., Stotts, D., Smith, J.M.: Distributed Pair Programming: Empirical Studies and Supporting Environments. Technical Report TR02-009, Department of Computer Science, University of North Carolina at Chapel Hill (2002)
3. Basili, V.R., Caldiera, G., Rombach, H.D.: The Goal Question Metric Approach. In: Encyclopedia of Software Engineering, pp. 528–532. John Wiley & Sons, Inc., Chichester (1994)
4. Begel, A., Nagappan, N.: Usage and Perceptions of Agile Software Development in an Industrial Context: An Exploratory Study. In: Proceedings of the First International Symposium on Empirical Software Engineering and Measurement, pp. 255–264 (2007)
5. Begel, A., Nagappan, N.: Pair programming: what's in it for me? In: Proceedings of the Second ACM-IEEE International Symposium on Empirical Software Engineering and Measurement, pp. 120–128 (2008)
6. Braught, G., Eby, L.M., Wahls, T.: The effects of pair-programming on individual programming skill. Proceedings of the 39th Special Interest Group on Computer Science Education 40(1), 200–204 (2008)

7. Campos, P., Nunes, N.J.: Practitioner Tools and Workstyles for User-Interface Design. IEEE Software 24(1), 73–80 (2007)
8. Canfora, G., Cimitile, A., Garcia, F., Piattini, M., Visaggio, C.A.: Evaluating performances of pair designing in industry. Journal of Systems and Software 80(8), 1317–1327 (2007)
9. Cockburn, A., Williams, L.: The costs and benefits of pair programming. In: Extreme Programming Examined, pp. 223–243. Addison-Wesley Longman Publishing Co., Amsterdam (2001)
10. Coman, I.D., Sillitti, A., Succi, G.: Investigating the Usefulness of Pair-Programming in a Mature Agile Team. In: Proceedings of the 9th International Conference on Agile Porcesses and eXtreme Programming in Software Engineering, pp. 127–136 (2008)
11. Coman, I.D., Sillitti, A., Succi, G.: A case-study on using an Automated In-process Software Engineering Measurement and Analysis system in an industrial environment. In: Proceedings of the 31st International Conference on Software Engineering, pp. 89–99 (2009)
12. Coman, I.D., Succi, G.: An Exploratory Study of Developers' Toolbox in an Agile Team. In: Abrahamsson, P., Marchesi, M., Maurer, F. (eds.) Agile Processes in Software Engineering and Extreme Programming. Lecture Notes in Business Information Processing, vol. 31, pp. 43–52. Springer, Heidelberg (2009)
13. Chong, J., Hurlbutt, T.: The Social Dynamics of Pair Programming. In: Proceedings of the 29th International Conference on Software Engineering, pp. 354–363 (2007)
14. Fronza, I., Sillitti, A., Succi, G.: Modeling Spontaneous Pair Programming when New Developers Join a Team. In: Proceedings of the 10th International Symposium on Empirical Software Engineering, pp. 242–244 (2009)
15. Gallis, H., Arisholm, E., Dybå, T.: An Initial Framework for Research on Pair Programming. In: Proceedings of the 4th International Symposium on Empirical Software Engineering, p. 132 (2003)
16. Heiberg, S., Puus, U., Salumaa, P., Seeba, A.: Pair-Programming Effect on Developers Productivity. In: Marchesi, M., Succi, G. (eds.) XP 2003. LNCS, vol. 2675, p. 1016. Springer, Heidelberg (2003)
17. Hulkko, H., Abrahamsson, P.: A multiple case study on the impact of pair programming on product quality. In: Proceedings of the 27th International Conference on Software Engineering, pp. 495–504 (2005)
18. LaToza, T.D., Venolia, G., DeLine, R.: Maintaining mental models: a study of developer work habits. In: Proceedings of the 28th International Conference on Software Engineering, pp. 492–501 (2006)
19. Lethbridge, T.C., Singer, J.: Understanding Software Maintenance Tools: Some Empirical Research. In: Workshop on Empirical Studies of Software Maintenance, pp. 157–162 (1997)
20. Lui, K.M., Chan, K.C.C.: When does a Pair Outperform Two Individuals? In: Marchesi, M., Succi, G. (eds.) XP 2003. LNCS, vol. 2675, pp. 225–233. Springer, Heidelberg (2003)
21. Lui, K.M., Chan, K.C.C.: Pair programming productivity: Novice-novice vs. expert-expert. International Journal on Human-Computer Studies 64(9), 915–925 (2006)
22. Maccari, A., Riva, C., Maccari, F.: On CASE tool usage at Nokia. In: Proceedings of the 17th IEEE International Conference on Automated Software Engineering, pp. 59–68 (2002)
23. McDowell, C., Werner, L., Bullock, H., Fernald, J.: The effects of pair-programming on performance in an introductory programming course. In: Proceedings of the 33rd SIGCSE Technical Symposium on Computer Science Education, pp. 38–42 (2002)

24. McDowell, C., Hanks, B., Werner, L.: Experimenting with pair programming in the classroom. In: Proceedings of the 8th Annual Conference on Innovation and Technology in Computer Science Education, pp. 60–64 (2003)
25. Nawrocki, J., Jasiñski, M., Olek, L., Lange, B.: Pair programming vs. Side-by-side programming. In: Richardson, I., Abrahamsson, P., Messnarz, R. (eds.) EuroSPI 2005. LNCS, vol. 3792, pp. 28–38. Springer, Heidelberg (2005)
26. Nawrocki, J., Wojciechowski, A.: Experimental evaluation of pair programming. In: Proceedings of the 12th European Software Control and Metrics Conference, pp. 269–276 (2001)
27. Sillitti, A., Janes, A., Succi, G., Vernazza, T.: Collecting, Integrating and Analyzing Software Metrics and Personal Software Process Data. In: Proceedings of the 29th Conference on EUROMICRO, pp. 336–342 (2003)
28. Singer, J., Lethbridge, T., Vinson, N., Anquetil, N.: An examination of software engineering work practices. In: Proceedings of the 1997 Conference of the Centre For Advanced Studies on Collaborative Research, p. 21 (1997)
29. Succi, G., Pedrycz, W., Marchesi, M., Williams, L.: Preliminary analysis of the effects of pair programming on job satisfaction. In: Marchesi, M., Succi, G. (eds.) XP 2003. LNCS, vol. 2675. Springer, Heidelberg (2003)
30. Vanhanen, J., Korpi, H.: Experiences of Using Pair Programming in an Agile Project. In: Proceedings of the 40th Annual Hawaii International Conference on System Sciences (2007)
31. Williams, L., Kessler, R.R., Cunningham, W., Jeffries, R.: Strengthening the Case for Pair Programming. IEEE Software 17(4), 19–25 (2000)
32. Williams, L., Kessler, R.R.: The Effects of 'Pair-Pressure' and 'Pair-Learning' on Software Engineering Education. In: Proceedings of the 13th Conference of Software Engineering Education and Training, p. 59 (2000)

Studying Lean-Kanban Approach Using Software Process Simulation

David Anderson[1], Giulio Concas[2],
Maria Ilaria Lunesu[2], and Michele Marchesi[2]

[1] David J. Anderson&Associates inc.,
Seattle, WA, USA
[2] DIEE - Department of Electrical and Electronic Engineering,
University of Cagliari, Piazza D'Armi,
09123 Cagliari, Italy

Abstract. We developed an event-driven simulator of the Kanban process a WIP limited pull system visualized by the Kanban board. WIP (work in process) represent the capacity in the activity to perform features simoultaneously. The simulator is fully object-oriented, and its design model reflects the objects of the Lean software development domain. We used this simulator to assess comparatively WIP-limited and unlimited processes. We also studied the optimum values of the working item limits in the activities, using a paradigmatic case of 4 activities and 100 work items. The cost function used is equal to the total time needed to complete the project, plus a weighted sum of the limits themselves. We performed an exhaustive search on all the admissible values of the solution, finding sensible optimal values, and a non-trivial behavior of the cost function in the optimization space.

This demonstrates the feasibility and usefulness of the approach.

Keywords: Kanban, Lean, software development, software process simulation.

1 Introduction

Lean software development [1] is a relatively new entry within the Agile Methodologies realm, but it is presently one of the fastest growing approaches among software professionals. Lean is derived by Lean Manufacturing [2], which strives to maximize the value produced by an organization and delivered to the customer. This is accomplished by reducing waste, controlling variability, maximizing the flow of delivered software, focusing on the whole process, and not on local improvements, all within a culture of continuous improvement. The Kanban system [3] is the latest trend in Lean software development, emphasizing a visual approach to maximize flow and spotting bottlenecks and other kinds of issues. The Lean concepts are simple, structured and yet powerful. One of the key concepts of Kanban system is that the whole development has to be optimized, avoiding local optima and striving to find global optima. The process itself is

A. Sillitti et al. (Eds.): XP 2011, LNBIP 77, pp. 12–26, 2011.

based on several parameters, and a global optimization is difficult. Moreover, these parameters are not fixed, but depend on factors such as the number and skills of developers,the specific practices used by the team, the number and effort of the features to be implemented. These factors are not only variable among different projects, but can vary also during a given project. For these reasons, an up-front, *one size fits all* study and optimization of process parameters is out of discussion. This is a typical problem where the simulation of the software process might be useful. In fact, the Kanban system is a very structured approach, and it is possible to design a software process simulator that captures most of what happens during development. Simulation is a generic term which includes a set of methods and applications that are able to represent how real systems work, typically using a general-purpose computer. Simulation has been applied to software process for more than twenty years. There are many simulation approaches, the two most used being system dynamics and event-driven simulation [4] [5]. We used the latter, which is better suited to model in detail the steps of a specific process. Kanban processes have already been extensively studied through simulation in the manufacturing context [6]. Here we quote the seminal work by Huang, Rees and Taylor [7], who assessed the issues in adapting Japanese JIT techniques to American firms using network discrete simulation. Among the many authors who studied Kanban using simulation we may quote Hurrion, who performed process optimization using simulation and neural networks [8], the data-driven simulator KaSimIR by Kchel, and Nielnder, developed using an object-oriented approach [9], the hybrid simulator by Hao and Shen [10]. The simulation approach has been also used to simulate agile development processes. While most of the work in this field was performing using system dinamics, event-driven simulators for Extreme Programming practices were introduced by Melis et al. [11], and by Turnu et al. [12]. As regards Lean-Kanban software development, the authors are only aware of a Petri-net based simulation cited by Corey Ladas in his website [13]. The mathematical formalism of Petri nets, introduced to describe state changes in dynamic systems, is simple, yet powerful. However, it is not flexible enough to describe the details of software development, including features, activities, developers, deliverables. Our simulator is fully object-oriented, so it can describe software development in a very flexible way, and it can be easily extended. The main goal of our research was to better understand the Lean-Kanban approach, to evaluate its effectiveness, and to develop methodologies to optimize its parameters.To this purpose, we developed an event-driven, object-oriented simulator of Kanban systems, both to analyze them using the simulation approach, and to optimize their parameters. Using simulation optimization, the practice of linking an optimization method with a simulation model to determine appropriate settings of certain input parameters is possible to maximize the performance of the simulated system [14].The paper is organized as follows: in Section 2, we give an overview of Kanban system and present the simulation model. In Section 3 we present and discuss the results; Section 4 concludes the paper.

2 The Lean-Kanban Approach

The Lean approach, first introduced in manufacturing in Japan between 1948 and 1975 [15], strives to deliver value to the customer more efficiently by designing out overburden and inconsistency, and by finding and eliminating waste (the impediments to productivity and quality). This is expressed in a set of principles that include optimizing flow, increasing efficiency, decreasing waste, improving learning, and using empirical methods to take decisions. In 2003, Mary and Tom Poppendieck published the first book about applying Lean principles to software development [1]. They identified seven key lean principles: eliminate waste1, build quality in, create knowledge, defer commitment, deliver fast, respect people and optimize the whole. A key Lean activity is to build a value stream map (as reported in[1] pag.9) , breaking down the process into individual steps, and identifying which steps add value and which steps do not, thus adding to the waste. Then, the goal is to eliminate the waste and improve the value-added steps. An important conceptual tool to manage how work flows is the concept of pull system (as reported in[1] pag.71), where processes are based on customer demand. The work in process (WIP) is usually made evident to the team, and to the stakeholders, using a Kanban board. In general, we can define the Kanban software process as a WIP limited pull system visualized by the Kanban board . Recently, the Kanban approach applied to software development, seem to be one of the hottest topics of Lean. In the recent 3-4 years, Kanban has been applied to software process, and is becoming the key Lean practice in this field. A correct use of the Kanban board helps to minimize WIP, to highlight the constraints, and to coordinate the team work. However, Lean is more than Kanban, and more Lean practicess hould be used, together with Kanban, to take full advantage of the application of Lean to software development. Note that the Kanban board is similar to the *information radiators* of Agile methodologies [16], but it is not the same thing. To be eligible to use the Kanban approach, the software development must satisfy the two Corey Ladas' postulates [17]:

1. *It is possible to divide the work into small value adding increments that can be indipendently scheduled.* These increments are called Features, User Stories, Stories, Work Items, or Minimum Marketable Features (MMF). The project ends when all its features are completed.
2. *It is possible to develop any value-adding increment in a continuous flow from requirement to deployment.* So, the work on each feature, from its specification to its deployment, is accomplished through a set of activities, performed in the same sequential order.

Initially, the features are put in a Backlog, from which they are pulled to be assigned to the first activity. When a feature is done in the last activity, it is automatically pulled from it, to a list of *Live* or *Released* features. The work is performed by a team of developers. Each developer has different skills related to the various activities. When the work of a developer on a feature ends, or in any case at the end of the day, he looks for another feature to work at. Kanban systems focus on a continuous flow of work, and usually do not employ fixed iterations. Work is delivered as soon as it's ready, and the team only works on very few features at a time, to limit WIP and make constant the flow of released features throughout the development. The growing interest on Kanban software development is demonstrated by the publication of various books, and by the proliferation of Web sites on the subject in the past couple of years. The most popular among these book was written by David J. Anderson [3]. Another book by Corey Ladas is about the fusion of Scrum and Kanban practices [17]. A third book on the subject was written by Kniberg and Skarin [18], and is also availabile online. The reader interested to a more detailed description of the Kanban approach should refer to these books.

3   The Kanban Model Simulator

To be able to simulate a Kanban software development process, we devised a model of the Kanban system described in the previous section, which is presented in this section. This model is simple enough to be manageable, but is able to capture all relevant aspects of the process. Moreover, the model itself and its object-oriented implementation allow to easily adding further details, if needed. The simulation is event-driven, and it records all the significant events related to the features, developers and activities during the simulation, to be able to compute any sort of statistics, and to draw diagrams, such as the cumulative flow diagram.

3.1   Features and Activities

The features the project is composed of are atomic units of work, and are not further decomposed. They are considered as already specified in a phase preceding the work simulated, and are given as inputs to the simulator. New features can be added as time proceeds. In the followings, the typical index for a feature is denoted by i, while the total number of features at time t is $N_F(t)$. Each feature is characterized by a name, a state and an estimate e_i expressing how long it will take to implement the $i - th$ feature, in man-days. The features assigned to an activity can be in three different states:

(i) just pulled but not yet assigned;
(ii) under work;
(iii) done, but not yet pulled by the next activity.

Other possible states are *Backlog* and *Released*, denoting the initial or final state, respectively. In the present model, the features are just atomic, and are not explicitly linked to a specific project. It would be possible, however, to introduce different projects, and assign the features to them. The activities represent the work to be done on the features. They can be freely configured. In the followings, the typical index for an activity is denoted by k, while the total number of activities is N_A. Each activity is characterized by:

name: the name of the activity.

maxFeatures: the maximum number of features that can be handled at any given time, including features in every possible state. It is denoted by M_K for the $k - th$ activity.

percentage: the typical percentage of the total estimated cost of a feature that pertains to the activity. For instance, is a feature has an overall estimate of 10 days, and the Design activity has a percentage of 15, the design of the feature will be estimated to be 1.5 days. The sum of the percentages of all the activities should be one. It is denoted by pk for the $k - th$ activity, with the constraint:

$$\sum p_k = 1. \tag{1}$$

When work starts on feature $i - th$ within a given $k - th$ activity, the actual effort of development of the feature in the activity is computed. If the initial total estimate of the feature is e_i, and the percentage of the total cost due to the activity is p_k, the starting estimate of the work is $x_{i,k} = e_i p_k$. The estimate $x_{i,k}$ can be randomly perturbed, by increasing or decreasing it of a percentage drawn from a given distribution D in such a way that the average of a high number of perturbations is equal to the initial estimate $x_{i,k}$. A way to obtain this behavior is to multiply $x_{i,k}$ by a random number, r, drawn from a log-normal distribution with mean value equal to 1: $y_{i,k} = x_{i,k}$, where yi, k is the actual value of the effort needed to work on feature $i - th$ in activity $k - th$. If this feature is assigned to developer $j - th$, the time to perform the work depends also on the developer's skill in activity $k - th$, $s_{j,k}$. The skill is a parameter denoting the developer's ability with respect to an "average" developer in a given activity. The estimate of the effort reflects the time to complete a task by the "average" developer. So this time,t_{ik}, expressed in days to complete an activity whose estimate is $y_{i,k}$, in function of the skill is: $t_{i,k} = \frac{y_{i,k}}{s_{j,k}}$. So, if the skill is equal to one the developer acts as an "average" developer and the time is equal to an estimate, if the skill is greater(smaller)than one the time is lower(longer). In the current implementation of the simulator, only a single developer can perform an activity on a feature in a given time (no pair-programming). Since the cost of all developers is considered equal, the actual time, t_{ik} , is directly proportional to the cost of implementing the feature. The total cost of implementing a feature is thus proportional to the sum of the development times in the various activities,t_i:

$$t_i = \sum_{k=1}^{N_A} t_{i,k}. \tag{2}$$

The sequence of activities the implementation of each feature proceeds through is fixed for each simulation. An example of activites might be: *Design, Coding, Testing, Integration*, but what really matters in the simulation is their number and their operational characteristics.

3.2   The Developers and Their Work

The present simulator allows for a single team working on the features. The team is composed of N_D. developers. The typical index for a developer is denoted by j. Each developer is characterized by a list of her skills, one for each activity, $s_{j,k}, k = 1, ...NA$. A skill is characterized by the following parameters:

- **minValue** $(min_{j,k})$: the minimum possible value of the skill in $k-th$ activity for $j - th$ developer, when her/his experience is zero.
- **maxValue** $(max_{j,k})$: the maximum possible value of the skill in $k - th$ activity for $j - th$ developer, when her/his experience is maximum.
- **experience** $(ex_{j,k})$: the number of days the $j - th$ developer has been working on feature development in $k - th$ activity.
- **maxExperience** $(maxEx_{j,k})$: the number of working days needed to reach the maximum experience of $j-th$ developer in $k-th$ activity, at which point the skill reaches its maximum value, and does not increase anymore.

The actual value, $v_{j,k}$, of skill $s_{j,k}$ for $k - th$ activity, where $j - th$ developer worked for $ex_{j,k}$ days is given by a linear interpolation, shown in eq. 3.

$$v_{j,k} = min_{j,k} + \frac{(max_{j,k} - min_{j,k})ex_{j,k}}{maxEx_{j,k}}, \ if \ ex_{j,k \leq maxEx_{j,k}} \tag{3}$$

$$max_{j,k} \ if \ ex_{j,k} > maxEx_{j,k}$$

Clearly, the use of another form of interpolation, such as for instance a logistic, would be easy. If we wish to simulate a system where no learning takes place, we can set $min_{j,k} = max_{j,k}$, with $maxEx_{j,k} > 0$. The value of $ex_{j,k}$ will in any case record the days $j - th$ developer has been working on $k - th$ activity. If the skill factor $s_{j,k}$ is equal to one (the default case), the time spent by the $j - th$ developer on a feature exactly matches the amount of effort dedicated to it. If $s_{j,k} > 1$, the developer is more clever than average, and her time spent working on the feature has a yield greater than the actual time. On the contrary, If $s_{j,k} < 1$, it will take a time longer that the actual effort to perform the work on the feature. Each developer works on a feature (in a specific activity) until the end of the day, or until the feature is completed. When the state of the system changes, for instance because a new feature is introduced, a feature is pulled to an activity, work on a feature ends, and in any case at the beginning of a new day, the system looks for idle developers, and tries to assign them to features available to be worked on in the activities they belong to. For each idle developer, the following steps are performed:

1. the activities s/he is most skilled in are searched in decreasing order of skill;
2. for each activity, the features waiting to be worked on are considered, in decreasing order of relevance;
3. the first feature in the list found, if any, is assigned to the developer; let it be feature $i - th$ in activity $k - th$; the time $t'_{i,k}$ to finish the feature is computed, taking into account the total estimated effort, yi,k, the work already

performed on the feature, $w_{i,k}$, the developer's skill in the activity, $s_{j,k}$, and a further penalty, p, applied if the developer was not already working on the feature the day before. The time to finish the feature is:

$$t'_{i,k} = p \frac{y_{i,k} w_{i,k}}{s_{j,k}} \qquad (4)$$

The penalty factor p is equal to one *(no penalty)* if the same developer, at the beginning of a day, works on the same feature s/he worked the day before. If the developer starts a new feature, or changes feature at the beginning of the day, it is assumed that s/he will have to devote extra time to understand how to work on the feature. In this case, the value of p is greater than one. Let us call T the current simulation time, and T_e the time marking the end of the working day.

1. If $T + t'_{i,k} > T_e$, the work on the feature is limited until the end of the day, so it is performed for a time $t_e = T_e - T$. The actual implementation effort considered,$w'_{i,k}$, is proportional to te, but also to the skill, and inversely proportional to the penalty factor p:

$$w'_{i,k} = \frac{t_e s_{j,k}}{p} \qquad (5)$$

The new work performed on the feature becomes:$w_{i,k}(T_e) = w_{i,k}(T) + w'_{i,k}$.

2. If $T + t'_{i,k} \leq T_e$, the work on the feature in k-th activity ends within the current day, the feature is moved to the *Done* state within the activity, and the developer is ready to start working on another feature.

If the skill of a developer in an activity is below a given threshold (set to 0.4 in the current simulator) s/he will never work in that activity.

3.3   The Events

The simulator is event-driven, meaning that the simulation proceeds by executings events, in order of their time. When an event is executed, the time of the simulation is set to the time of the event. The simulator holds an event queue, where events to be executed are stored sorted by time, and which the events are taken from to be executed. When an event is executed, it changes the state of the system, and can create new events, with times equal to, o greater than, the current time, inserting them into the event queue. The simulation ends when the event queue is empty, or if a maximum time is reached. The time is recorded in nominal working days, from the start of the simulation. It can be fractionary, denoting days partially spent. The simulation does not explicitly account for weekends, holidays, or overtime. A day can be considered to have 8 nominal working hours, or less if the time lost on average for organization tasks is accounted for. If we want to consider calendar days, it is always possible to convert from nominal working days to them. For instance, let us suppose that the starting day of the project is Monday, 25 October 2010, and that the current time is 7.5 days.

Since 30 and 31 October are a week-end, and November 1st is holiday, the 7th day after the start is November 3rd, and the 8th day is November 4th. So, day 7.5 happens in the middle of November 4th, say at noon if the working day starts at 8 a.m. and ends at 17 p.m., with a lunch interval between noon and 1 p.m. The relevant events of the simulation are the followings.

FeatureCreation: a new feature is created and inserted into the Backlog, and an event FeatureToPull is generated for the first activity, at the same time. This event refers only to features introduced after the start of the simulation, and not to the features initially included in the Backlog.

FeatureWorkEnded: the work of a developer on a feature, within a given activity, has ended, and the developer becomes idle. This may happen when the feature is actually finished, as regards the activity, or at the end of the working day. In the former case, the state of the feature is changed, and an event FeatureToPull is generated for the next activity, at the same time.

FeatureToPull: an activity is requested to pull a feature from the previous activity or from the Backlog if it is the first. If the activity is nil, it means that a feature in the state of *Finished* should be moved from the last activity to the *Released* state. If the activity has already reached its maximum number of features, or if there is no feature to pull in the previous activity, nothing happens. If there is a feature that can be pulled, it is pulled to the activity, and another event FeatureToPull is generated for the previous activity (if the activity is not the first), at the same time. All idle developers of the team are asked to find a feature ready to be worked. If a developer finds such a feature, the developer is assigned to the feature, the actual time taken to complete the work is computed (according to eq 4), and a FeatureWorkEnded event is generated and inserted into the event queue for the time when the work will end (at the end of the current day, or when the feature is finished).

The three events are enough to manage the whole simulation. The simulation is started by creating the starting features, putting them in the Backlog, generating as many FeatureToPull events (at $time = 0$) for the first activity as its maxFeatures value, and then generating as many FeatureCreation events for future times as required. The simulator is then asked to run, using the event queue created in this way. When the work on all features has been completed in all activities, no more feature can be pulled and no more work can start, so the event queue becomes empty, and the simulation ends.

3.4   The Object-Oriented Model

In Fig. 1 we present the UML class diagram of the OO model of the simulator, showing the classes of the system, and their relationships. The high-level classes of the model are the simulator itself, the KanbanSystem which includes the software project and the process the team of developers. Lower-level classes are Activity, Feature, Developer, Skill, and three kinds of Events. Utility classes used to record data for further analysis are WorkRecord, ActivityRecord and

FeatureChanged. In this class diagram there are the different actors of simulation, **who** works-*the developer*-**what** is developed-*the feature*- **when** the work is performed-*the events*-and finally **what** is performed- *the activities*. The simulator is implemented in Smalltalk language, a language very suited to event-driven simulation, and very flexible to accommodate any kind of changes and upgrades to the model.

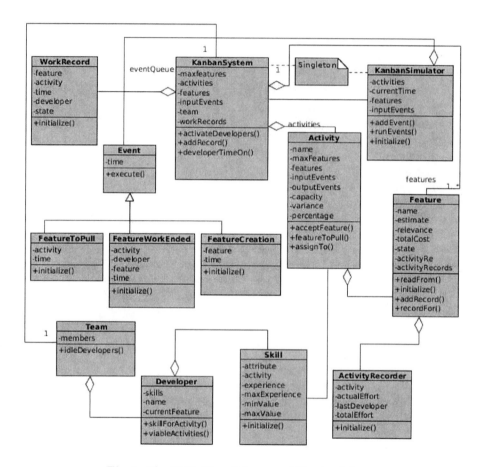

Fig. 1. The UML Class Diagram of the simulator

4   Results and Discussion

4.1   Preliminary Tests and Results

We performed some preliminary simulation to assess the overall model, and to highlight the differences between a limited-WIP and an unlimited process. The settings were those of a typical average software project, with an initial backlog of 100 features, and 40 features added during the development. The features' efforts are drawn from a Poisson distribution, with average equal to 5 man-days and standard deviation of 2.2 man-days. So, the total amount of man-days of the project is 700 (140 x 5). There are 4 activities, to be performed sequentially, shown in Table 1.

Table 1. The main features of the simulated activities

Activity	Limit	% of total effort	Skilled developers
1.Design	3	30%	3
2.Development	4	40%	5
3.Testing	3	20%	3
4.Deployment	2	10%	2

Note that the description of the activities is conventional. Any other description will yield the same results, provided that the limits (max. nr. of features) and percentage of total effort is the same. When a feature is pulled to an activity, the actual effort to complete it, $y_{i,k} = x_{i,k}\,r$, as described in Section 3.1, is computed. The lognormal distribution used has mean equal to 1 and standard deviation equal to 0.2-meaning that deviations of more than 20% from the theoretical effort are common. The team is composed of seven developers. Most of them are skilled in two activities, so the total number of skilled developers in 1 is greater than 7. For the sake of simplicity, all skills are set to one, and there is no skill improvement as the development proceeds. The penalty factor p of eq. 4 is set to 1.5. We performed the following simulation tests:

1. setting as described above;
2. settings as above, but with developers skilled in all activities;
3. settings as above, but with no feature limits in the activities (unlimited WIP).
4. unlimited WIP, with developers skilled in all activities.

The resulting Cumulative Flow Diagrams (CFD) of the four simulations are shown in Fig. 2. The times (horizontal axis) are in days of development. As you can see, the diagrams in the cases of limited and unlimited WIP look very different in the former case, there is an almost constant flow of features that are completed, while in the latter case the CFD is much more irregular. Another difference is between the case when developers are skilled just in one or two activities (see Table 1), and the case when developer can work in all four activities with the same proficiency (this situation is unlikely in the real world). In the former case, developers can work only to one or two activities, meaning that for instance at the beginning of the project the testing and deployment developers are idle, while designers are idle at the end of the project. This situation enforces some limits on the work that can be done, even when activities are not limited, and is reflected in Fig. 2.C, which show a CFD more structured than in the case of general-purpose developers. On the other hand, in this case the efficiency of the whole process is lower, and the time to complete all features is more than 20 longer than in the other cases. When developers work on every activity, and are thus never idle, the length of the project tends to be shorter.

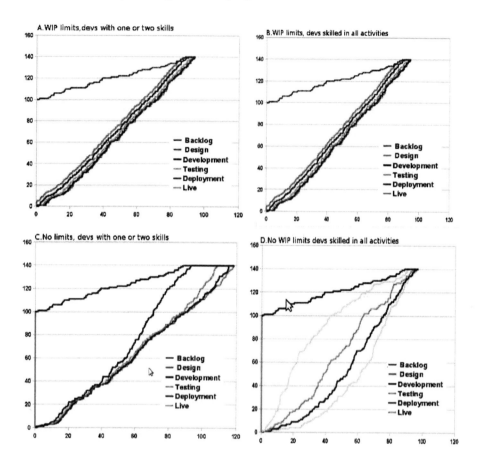

Fig. 2. CFD of four simulations, varying WIP limits and developers' skills

In general these simulations confirm the validity of the WIP-limited approach, and give insights on what really happens under different settings of the development.

4.2   Optimization of the Activity Limits

As said in the introduction, one of the uses of a process simulator is to optimize the parameters of the process. In the case of the Kanban process, the obvious parameters to optimize are the activity limits the maximum number of features admissible in each activity. To this purpose, we devised a paradigmatic setting of a typical project, and used the simulator to assess the optimum limits. The settings common to all optimizations are the followings:

1. There are 100 features to be completed. The effort needed for each feature is a random number drawn from a Poisson distribution with average of 5 days. features with zero effort are discarded. The features are the same for all optimizations.
2. There are 4 activities, as described in Table 1. The actual effort needed to complete an activity on a feature is not perturbed, so $y_{i,k} = x_{i,k}$.
3. The feature limits on the four activities are chosen between 1 and a maximum value which is 9, 12, 7 and 4 for activities 1, 2, 3 and 4, respectively. Let us denote M_k the limit for $k-th$ activity, thus $M_1 \in 1, 2, ..., 9$, $M_2 \in 1, 2, ..., 12$, and so on. An exhaustive search can be done by performing 3024 simulations, one for each possible combination of the four parameters.
4. The number of developers is 10. Developers may be skilled in just one activity, or in all 4 activities, depending on specific runs performed.
5. The penalty factor p is varied between 1 (*nopenalty*) and 3 (in the case of change of feature the time needed to complete it is 3 times longer).
6. The cost function to minimize, $f()$, is the sum of the time, t_c, needed to complete all 100 features, and the weighted sum of the limits:

$$f(M_1, M_2, M_3, M_4) = t_c + w \sum M_k$$

   where t_c is function of $M_1, .., M_4$, and the second term aims to minimize the limits themselves. The optimizations are performed for different values of w, typically 0 (no influence of limits), 0.2 (small influence), 1 or 2 (strong influence). Note that the order of magnitude of t_c is typically one hundred (days).
7. Time t_c is obtained averaging the project end time of 20 simulations, because tc varies randomly for each performed simulation. The average on 20 runs stabilizes it substantially.

We performed various optimizations, performing exhaustive searches after changing some parameters. Note that, in the case of more activities, wider search intervals, or more complex simulations, it would be easy to perform the optimization using minimization algorithms in place of the exhaustive search. To test the stability of the optimization, we computed the average, the standard deviation and other statistics of 20 different computation of the cost function (each obtained by averaging 20 simulation runs), for ten different values-randomly chosen-of the vector $M = (M1, M2, M3, M4)$, with a simulation referring to a penalty factor of 1.5, and to 10 developers with different skills. The weight w was set to 0.2. The standard deviation was always between 0.2% and 0.3% of the average, thus showing a substantial stability of the results. To demonstrate the feasibility and the power of the approach, we show an example of result in Fig. 2. It represents 3024 runs (exhaustive search), with penalty = 1 (no penalty) and 3 (high penalty to change feature). Cost function has $w = 1$. Developers can be with no specific skill (they can work on all 4 activities), or with just one skill. In the latter case 3 developers are able to work on activity 1, and 4, 2, and 1 developers are able to work on activities 2, 3 and 4, respectively. (The number of developers able to work in each activity is proportional to the activity's relative importance in the overall effort.)

The results are in ascending order of the cost function $f()$. The *jumps* represent limits able to delay the whole development, for instance a limit of 1 or 2 features in activity 2. The case with no skills is heavily penalized when *penalty* = 3, because developers can work in every activity, and are more prone to change the feature they work on in the next day, thus taking the penalty. If developers are constrained to work only on a single activity, this change is less likely (and even less likely when WIP is low). Table 2 shows the best 4 points (values of limits M_1, M_2, M_3, M_4) for the 4 cases optimized.

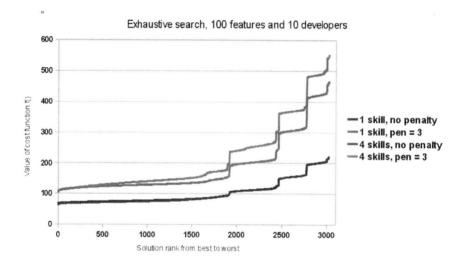

Fig. 3. Plot of the cost functions in ascending order for 4 exhaustive searches, with different values of the penalty and of the developers' skills

Table 2. The four best points found in the search, for the four cases considered

| Best points | no penalty | | penalty=3 | |
	1 skill	2 skill	3 skill	4 skill
1	3,6,4,1	4,5,3,2	3,4,3,1	3,5,3,2
2	3,5,4,1	4,6,3,2	3,5,3,1	3,6,3,2
3	3,6,3,2	5,5,3,2	3,5,2,2	3,7,3,2
4	4,5,4,1	5,6,3,2	3,4,4,1	4,4,3,2

5   Conclusions and Future Work

We presented a process simulation model developed for assessing the effectiveness of the WIP-limited approach, and to visualize the flow of work and the organization of work. The model has been designed and implemented using a full object-oriented approach, and is easily extensible to accommodate more detailed and realistic representations of the actual software development process. The simulation outputs can be elaborated, yielding all kinds of diagrams and statistical information to analyze every aspect of what actually happened during the simulation. We presented simulation results on WIP-limited and unlimited developments, varying the skills of the developers involved, showing substantial differences in the resulting CFDs. We also used the simulator to optimize, through exhaustive search, the WIP limits of the activities of the process. We analyzed the repeatability and robustness of the results, showing that the simulator can be very useful under this respect. Further studies are under work to extend the simulator toward more realistic settings. Among others, we are working on the following extensions: Non-instant availability of collaborators. Could be a specialist required to perform a task such as *"code security review"* or a business person, subject matter expert required to disambiguate the requirements. Modeling non-instant availability of collaborators with different delay parameters would be useful. Special cause variation work blocked due to external circumstances such as a test environment failure, lack of availability of a collaborator due to special cause reason (illness, vacation, business trip). Specialization of the workforce - for example, the design activity might be made up of various optional sub-activities, e.g. user interface design, database design, Web services design, etc. Some of these sub-activities may require a specialist, or one from a smaller pool of suitably talented people. We could model the mix of work items that require more or less specialization and model the number of sub-activities that have 1 or very few capable people, and simulate the effect. This modification would imply to explicitly model the decomposition of features in tasks. Management of high-priority features, and the effect of the team choosing to break the WIP limit from time-to-time. Explicit management of software product quality and bugs, with the need to rework at least partially some feature to fix its bugs.

References

1. Poppendieck, M., Poppendieck, T.: Lean software development: An agile toolkit. Addison Wesley, Boston (2003)
2. Womack, J.P., Jones, D.T., Roos, D.: The Machine That Changed the World: The Story of Lean Production. Harper Business, New York (1991)
3. Anderson D.J.: Kanban: Successful Evolutionary Change for Your Technology Business. Blue Hole Press (2010)
4. Kellner, M., Madachy, R.J., Raffo, M.: Software process simulation modeling: Why? What? How. Journal of Systems and Software 45, 91–105 (1999)
5. Zhang, H., Kitchenham, B., Pfahl, D.: Reflections on 10 years of software process simulation modeling: A systematic review. In: Wang, Q., Pfahl, D., Raffo, D.M. (eds.) ICSP 2008. LNCS, vol. 5007, pp. 345–356. Springer, Heidelberg (2008)
6. Martins, K., Lewandrowski, U.: Inventory safety stocks of Kanban control systems. Production Planning and Control 10, 520–529 (1999)

7. Huang, P.Y., Rees, L.P., Taylor, B.W.: A simulation analysis of the Japanese just-in-time technique (with kanbans) for a multiline, multistage production system. Decision Sciences 14, 326–344 (1983)

8. Hurrion, R.D.: An example of simulation optimisation using a neural network meta-model: finding the optimum number of kanbans in a manufacturing system. Journal of the Operational Research Society 48, 1105–1112 (1997)

9. Kchel, P., Nielnder, U.: Kanban Optimization by Simulation and Evolution. Production Planning & Control 13, 725–734 (2002)

10. Hao, Q., Shen, W.: Implementing a hybrid simulation model for a Kanban-based material handling system. Robotics and Computer-Integrated Manufacturing 24, 635–646 (2008)

11. Melis, M., Turnu, I., Cau, A., Concas, G.: Evaluating the Impact of Test-First Programming and Pair Programming through Software Process Simulation. Software Process Improvement and Practice 11, 345–360 (2006)

12. Melis, M., Turnu, I., Cau, A., Concas, G.: Modeling and simulation of open source development using an agile practice. Journal of Systems Architecture 52, 610–618 (2006)

13. Ladas, C.: Kanban simulation (December 2010),
http://www.leansoftwareengineering.com/2008/11/20/kanban/simulation/

14. Bowden, R.O., Hall, J.D.: Simulation optimization research and development. In: Proc. Winter Simulation Conference (WSC 1998), pp. 1693–1698 (1998)

15. Ohno T.: Just-In-Time for Today and Tomorrow. Productivity Press (1988)

16. Cockburn, A.: Crystal Clear: A Human-Powered Methodology for Small Teams. Addison Wesley, Reading (2004)

17. Ladas, C.: Scrumban. Modus Cooperandi Press, Seattle (2008)

18. Kniberg, H., Skarin, M.: Kanban and Scrum making the most of both, C4Media Inc. (2010)

A Feature Partitioning Method for Distributed Agile Release Planning

Ákos Szőke

Department of Measurement and Information Systems,
Budapest University of Technology and Economics, Budapest, Hungary
aszoke@mit.bme.hu,
http://www.mit.bme.hu/~aszoke/

Abstract. Agile software development represents a major approach that has gained increasing popularity in recent years. Economy forces agile organizations to overcome geographical distances to benefit from accessing a larger resource pool and to reduce development costs. However, agile and distributed development approaches differ significantly in their key tenets. While agile methods mainly rely on informal processes to facilitate coordination, distributed development typically relies on formal mechanisms. To address this situation, we present a distributed agile release planning approach to assist the release planning process of distributed agile development teams by identifying feature chunks that can be implemented co-located to minimize the communication needs between dispersed teams. The presented method demonstrates how this approach 1) necessitates less intensive communication and coordination, 2) can provide better utilization of resources, and 3) can produce higher quality feature distribution plans. Finally, the paper analyzes benefits and issues from the use of this approach.

Keywords: distributed development, agile release planning, partitioning.

1 Introduction

The ideas of agile software development [1] have gained acceptance in the mainstream software development community. Surveys pointed out that agile teams are often more successful than traditional ones [2, 3] – which explains its popularity. Several other studies demonstrated 60% increase in productivity, quality and improved stakeholder satisfaction [3, 4], 40% faster time-to-market and 60% and 40% reduction in pre- and post-release defect rates [4] comparing to the industry average.

The fifth State of Agile Development survey was conducted in 2010 [7]. The collected data includes information from 91 countries, from 4.770 participants – ranging from project managers, development managers, developers and senior managers. The survey revealed that most popular agile methods are Scrum [5](58%), XP [6](4%), and Scrum/XP Hybrid (17%). The 37% of the respondents worked in distributed agile environments – where the members of the teams are not physically co-located. Actually, the dispersion of team members ranges from being over adjacent buildings to being over different continents. The key advantages that Distributed Software Development (DSD) aspires to achieve are 1) lowering cost of labor (*cost reduction*), 2) increasing

A. Sillitti et al. (Eds.): XP 2011, LNBIP 77, pp. 27–42, 2011.

or decreasing work forces without employing or laying-off (*workforce scaling*), and 3) obtaining locally not available expertise (*talent application*) [8]. The special case of DSD is the Global Software Development (GSD) in which the team distribution extends national boundaries [9]. The GSD allows organizations to overcome geographical distances to benefit from accessing a larger resource pool and to reduce development costs [10].

The previously cited survey [7] points out that the first and the fourth most important agile techniques from the identified 22 ones are iteration and release planning respectively. Besides these facts, the survey also revealed the 13 most commonly cited greatest concerns listed by respondents about adopting agile within companies. The three out of the five most important ones are 1) the loss of management control (36%), 2) the lack of upfront planning (33%) and 3) the lack of predictability (27%). These considerations are closely connected with the present *informal* practice of agile planning. These critics underline the importance of providing a more established method for distributed agile planning, that lacks of solid theoretical basis currently. With our proposed method, our aim is to deal with these concerns. Therefore, we suggest a theoretically sound method to support distributed release planning. This method helps distributing the implementable features on the dispersed software development team by partitioning work into cohesive sets – so-called *feature chunks*. Feature chunk construction considers the 'cooperation need between dispersed teams' minimization objective, which includes demand of less intensive communication and coordination, and better resource utilization. We believe that the usage of the presented method may help to diminish the barriers (1-3) of agile adoption in distributed environments.

1.1 Challenges in Distributed Software Development

Several additional challenges may be observed in DSD comparing to the co-located situations [9, 11, 12]. Agile development usually relies on frequent informal interactions. However in DSD, the teams cannot see or speak in person which leads to *communication deficiency* (**C1**) due to the geographical separation [12]. Communication impedance also raises from time zone differences that also hinders the teams' communication. As a solution, DSD mandates that the development relies on formal documentation (such as specifications, designs) to mitigate impediments of communications between the teams.

Agile development is usually based on shared view of goals that are difficult to observe in separated locations – and it often induces *lack of trust* (**C2**) among dispersed teams [12]. To improve team cohesion in distributed software development, frequent personal communication is required.

Agile development usually mandates using people-oriented control, which is based on informal commitments. In these situations, the development is based on ongoing negotiation on the requirements between the developers and the customers. However, in distributed environments, it often leads to the *lack of control* (**C3**) [12]. Due to the lack of communication, the general DSD often relies on process-oriented development and upfront commitments to meet the customer expectations on every development location.

Addition to the previous challenges **C1-C3**, in [12] it was demonstrated that projects in distributed environments take about two and one-half times longer to complete – comparing to similar projects where the project team is co-located. The significant difference was explained by the communication and coordination issues rather than the size or complexity of the cross-site development [13]. As a consequence, distributed software development requires considerable effort from the team in order to be truly successful [14].

1.2   Related Work

Considering non-agile DSD, in [17] a method is offered to calculate the degree of relatedness of the work items at different sites using code change history. The calculated relatedness is used to distribute work in a way that minimizes the need for coordination across sites. In [18], experiences of a rapid production process are described using software components suited for distributed development in a large, geographically distributed situation. In this approach, each component can be owned by a particular site to promote independent work and to minimize coordination and communication needs.

Software outsourcing is an increasingly attractive business model for many large organizations. In [10] three outsourcing strategies are presented to maximize business value. In [16], good practices are presented that were observed in a very large (5.000 engineers) globally distributed development situation at Alcatel.

In comparison to the extensive research on agile software development in general, only few research dealt with DSD in the agile environment in specifically [11]. Experiences and practices of the adoption of Scrum [5], an agile management practice, by large companies such as Yahoo! or Microsoft is presented in [19] and in [20] respectively. In [14] experiences and proven practices to address challenges faced by geographically distributed agile teams are presented by the Microsoft's Patterns & Practices group. It pointed out that the decision makers must understand risk/reward trade-off needs before deciding to distribute software development, because it decreases the project's likelihood of success, increases the delivery time and quality, and reduces the team's performance. Besides cross-locations, differences in culture and language also results in low progress in globally distributed environments. To cope with these issues, in the literature, some strategies are proposed including the use of straddlers (technical or managerial liaisons) [10], bridgehead teams [15], or rotation of management [16].

Complementary agile release and iteration planning methods can be found in [25,26] and in [29]. Those methods fit well to the presented method.

1.3   Problem Statement and Analysis

As it was shown, DSD has its own unique set of challenges (**C1-3**) additional to the agile software development in itself. These challenges are emanated from inhibited communication because the teams are geographically separated from each other [12,13]. These obstacles of communication – especially informal communication – plays a critical role in the success of a distributed agile team, since they heavily rely on personal physical interactions [17].

The obstacles of informal communication seem a contradiction to the general ideas of agile methods [1], and they seem to preclude the use of agile methodologies [21, 2, 13, 12]. Communication and coordination problems result in reduced team productivity (**P1**), increased production interval (**P2**), increased communication cost (**P3**), and difficult process control across distributed teams (**P4**).

The desired reduction of informal communication deficiency effects can be accomplished by two general ways with minimizing communication among the dispersed teams. One of them is *increasing the formality of the interactions* with detailed documentation (i.e. specifications, designs) and conventions (i.e. coding standards, templates). In this way, theoretically, the lack of communication can be diminished. Although, this method contradicts to the ideas of agility – however, it is a well-tried approach to deal with geographical distances. The other method can be realized by *decreasing the need of interactions* between the teams. With this approach, the communication and synchronization needs are minimized, which is also a reasonable solution to the communication problem.

1.4 Objectives

Our contribution is inspired by David Parnas' and Melvin Conway's work. David Parnas recommends division of labor along with software modularity, and he defined software module as 'a responsibility assignment rather than a subprogram'. He emphasizes the idea of modular design that enables independent decisions about the internals of each module [22]. Additionally to Parnas, Melvin Conway recognized – which is known as *Conway's Law* – that the structure of software reflects the structure of the organization which designed it [30]. Conway explained this relation with that it is the necessary consequence of the communication needs between people as they are doing their work. Since these proposals appeared, researchers and practitioners have been arguing for that the system architecture plays a significant role in the coordination of development work.

Our proposed method intends to assist the release planning process of distributed agile development teams by minimizing communication and synchronization needs (**C1-3**) to minimize their negative effects (**P1-P4**). As a part of our solution – named *Feature Partitioning Method* (FPM) – we defined: 1) *Feature Architectural Similarity Analysis* (FASA): an analytic step to determine architectural similarities between features (deliverable functional and non-functional requirements) that can be exploited to identify features that are implemented in the similar sets of system modules (**S1**), and 2) *Feature Chunk Construction* (FCC): a feature partitioning step that rules the distribution of development work across sites considering minimization of communication and coordination needs among the dispersed teams (**S2**).

Structure of the Paper. The rest of the paper arranged as follows: Sec. 2 presents background information; Sec. 3 outlines the proposed method; Sec. 4 shows experiments; Sec. 5 discusses our solution and findings; and finally Sec. 6 concludes the paper.

2   Background

In this section, first, we introduce the agile development process at high-level and the different DSD strategies to provide the necessary background information.

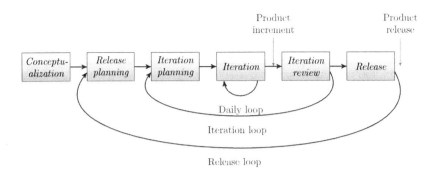

Fig. 1. Agile Development Cycles

2.1   Agile Software Development Process

From the project management point of view, agile software development process consists of the following phases: 1) *conceptualization* to define a vision, high-level ranked deliverables and project roadmap, 2) *release planning* to estimate deliverables and assign them into iterations, 3) *iteration planning* to break down selected deliverables into technical tasks that should be carried out by developers, 4) *iteration* to implement the technical tasks, to fix the defects and to discuss the daily progress, 5) *iteration review* to demonstrate product increments to stakeholders and conduct iteration retrospective for the next iteration, and finally 6) *release* to package and deploy software to customers [28, 23, 29] (Fig. 1).

To reduce the communication and coordination issues, our aim is to decrease the need of interactions between the distributed teams with identifying so-called *feature chunks*. These feature chunks can be treated logically roughly independently. Our proposed Feature Partitioning Method (FPM) intends to complement the release planning step in distributed agile environments by determining different sets of features that can be implemented roughly independently. Therefore, they can be realized with minimized communication needs among the sites.

2.2   Approaches to Distributed Development in Agile

In practice, generally two environmental variables determine the strategy of agile software development [5, 8, 11]. One of them is the *team cross-functionality*, which determines whether the agile team is acting as a group of people working toward the common goal on every site (i.e. cross functional), or the team is working toward a sub-goal on each site (i.e non-cross functional). The other variable is the *team distribution* which defines whether the team is located on the same, or on geographically different sites.

From these parameters, the following agile software development approaches are observed in practice 1) **Co-located**: the single agile team is co-located and cross-functional; 2) **Isolated**: agile teams are isolated across sites and not cross-functional; and 3) **Distributed**: agile teams are isolated across sites and cross-functional. Obviously, Co-located approach is out of our scope. Considering both Isolated and Distributed approaches, basically they require communication – especially informal, face-to-face communication – across sites to remove dependencies between work units. However, the communication intensities of these approaches are very different. In Isolated case, each team removes most dependencies locally (within the given site), while in Distributed case, the dependencies must be resolved across sites. Therefore, Distributed case is more difficult to implement due to delays in parties. Consequently, the former model is more often observed in practice [11, 8] and suggested by the Scrum Alliance [27].

Our proposed Feature Partitioning Method also follows the Isolated strategy since this approach aligns with our interaction minimization objective.

3 Feature Partitioning Method

In this section, we detail our previously outlined Feature Partitioning Method. First, we overview the method in the context, then we present its two parts: *Feature Architectural Similarity Analysis* (**S1**) (Sec. 3.1) and *Feature Chunk Construction* (**S2**) (Sec. 3.2).

3.1 Feature Architectural Similarity Analysis

The concept of architecture, design pattern and modularity are central in product development. Recent efforts strive for using design patterns and architectural styles, frequently in an informal way, to guarantee the quality of a design [31,32]. The two important characteristics of modularity are the *cohesiveness of modules* and the *coupling between modules*, which describe the interaction intensity between functional elements. Modules are identified in such a way that inter-module (between modules) interactions are relatively minimal (i.e. they are loosely coupled) while intra-module (within each module) interactions relatively high (i.e. they jointly serve a functionality, so they are cohesive) [33].

This underlines the importance of decomposition in distributed software development. Modularity enables development of different functional element groups (modules) in different sites independently, and integration ensures that the whole functionality can be delivered to the customer's site. As a consequence, objects of feature implementations (i.e. system modules) should be identified during release planning by the selected experienced members and stakeholders (typically managers, customer representatives and lead developers) of the distributed team in order to help partitioning features into feature chunks.

Module Relatedness of Features. In order to group features, we introduce the notion of *cohesiveness* between features from the standpoint of *architectural impact*. The higher the cohesiveness between features, the stronger the need to group those features together. The elements of application architecture can be defined as separated system modules (technical units) that often include user interface, application logic and data storage parts. To identify cohesiveness between features, we introduce a binary relation between features (FRs) and system modules (SMs), called ImplementedIn, to express the fact that a given FR is implemented in a given SM (i.e. directed, one-to-many relation). Please note, implementing cross-cutting features, e.g. performance or security, require the team to break down them into more specific ones such a way that each specific one can be related to a particular subset of modules. At this point, we have to stress the fact that our proposed FPM method is based upon two underlying assumptions: the architecture of the system (i.e. set of modules) is defined and the implementation of the identified features can be appointed to a subset of system modules.

Let define *module relatedness* of FRs as follows. Since every feature must be implemented in the system modules, every feature can be characterized by its `ImplementedIn` binary relation to these modules. As a consequence, characteristic variables of features are binary variables which express the fact that a given FR is implemented in a given SM or not. So it recommends using q number of binary variables (bits) on the ordinal scale expressing whether a given feature relates to the SM_h ($1 \leq h \leq q$). From now on, we call this variable as *Module Relatedness Variable (MRV)*, where the variable has q dimensions.

For example, the Fig. 2 shows some values of the previously defined MRV (in the cells '×' and '○' notations denote presence and absence of `ImplementedIn` relation). It can be read across an element's row to see its targeted module.

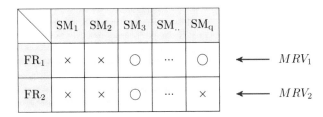

Fig. 2. Example Values on Module Relatedness Variable (MRV): each column denotes one dimension and every row shows an instance of the MRV

Feature Architectural Similarity Measure. Once the relations between features and system modules are determined and the features are characterized with module relatedness variables (MRVs), the next step is to define *feature architectural similarity* in terms of presence or absence of relations to SMs in each MRV. Let the following variables, which describes the congruence of characteristic variables of two MRVs, are defined:

$$p = \text{presence for both objects} \tag{1a}$$

$$q = \text{presence for the } i\text{th, absence for the } j\text{th object} \tag{1b}$$

$$r = \text{absence for the } i\text{th, presence for the } j\text{th object} \tag{1c}$$

$$s = \text{absence for both objects} \tag{1d}$$

For example, let $MRV_j = [\times, \times, \times, \bigcirc]$ and $MRV_{j'} = [\times, \bigcirc, \times, \bigcirc]$ are defined on FR_j and $FR_{j'}$ respectively. In this case, $p = 2, q = 1, r = 0$, and $s = 1$.

Generally, similarity (from now on denoted by $sim_{j,j'}$) is a quantity that reflects the strength of relationship between two objects (j and j'). It usually has a range of $[-1, 1]$ or normalized into $[0, 1]$. Contrary, a distance measures dissimilarity of two objects is denoted by $dist_{j,j'}$. The relationship between distance and similarity is given by $sim_{j,j'} = 1 - dist_{j,j'}$ for similarities that are bounded by 0 and 1. When similarity is 1 (i.e. exactly the same), the distance is 0 and when the similarity is 0 (i.e. totally different), the distance is 1. Often measuring distance is easier than measuring similarity [34]. However, once we can measure the distance, we can convert it to its appropriate similarity measure. Henceforth, we only focus on similarities for simplicity reasons.

Defining or selecting an appropriate similarity measure using the previous variables depends on the characteristics of the problem. Number of various measures defined in the literature in the last decades [34]. For example, Simple matching, i.e. $(p + s)/(p + q + r + s)$, is useful when both positive and negative values carry equal information (i.e. symmetry). Continuing the previous example, in Simple matching case, the similarity of FR_j and $FR_{j'}$ is equal to $sim = 3/4$.

Our goal is to group those features which are to be implemented in the similar set of system modules, i.e. they require similar architectural impact. Counting the non-existence relations in both objects has no meaningful contribution to the architectural similarity of features, so variable s should be left out from both the denominator and the numerator. As a consequence, to express the architectural similarity between FRs, we need to count the relations (p) to the same system modules and the number of relations between an FR and a SM (i.e. $p + q + r$), so we formulated the following measure:

$$\sim_{j,j'} = \frac{p}{p + q + r} \tag{2}$$

Thus, continuing the previous example, $\sim_{j,j'} = p/(p + q + r) = 2/3$. It is clear that, the range of both $\sim_{j,j'}$ and $(1 - \sim_{j,j'})$ (distance) are in $[0, 1]$. Thus, if we can measure architectural similarity/distance of features, then we can use this information to group them into *feature chunks* according to the values of the measurements.

3.2 Feature Chunk Construction

To support the parallel development, we propose a feature chunk construction step which aim is to break down the whole development work into cohesive feature chunks. In this case, connected blocks of features are partitioned into smaller blocks in such a way that the decomposition is carried out along the smallest similarities. This decomposition ensures that the communication demand and coordination complexity are reduced since the elements are grouped such a way that communications predominately occur within grouped FRs rather than between grouped FRs.

Feature Architectural Similarity Graph. The previously introduced similarity (2) can be used to compose a non-directed, edge-weighted graph that we call as Feature Architectural Similarity Graph (FASG). It can be constructed by representing features as vertices and relationships between features as edges where the edges are weighted with the strength of the architectural similarity ranging from $(0, 1]$ (cf. Sec. 3.1). FASGs can be interpreted as features with their *expected* communication intensities (weighed edges) between teams because they are implemented in the similar set of modules. At this point, we should lay emphasis on the difference between the notions of the feature architectural similarity (i.e. architecture impact) and the communication intensity between developers. Conway's law only states that there is a strong correlation between these two notions [30], but this correlation does not imply causation. In other words, there may be some feature implementations that do not necessitate communication between teams. Therefore, the presented FPM method considers a stricter approach: implementation of some features does not necessitate implementing them on the same site. However, during release planning it cannot be predicted without systematic and indepth analysis of the implementable features, system modules and their relations and this detailed up front analysis would contradict the ideas of agility.

Continuing the previous informal definition, let define the Feature Architectural Similarity Graph (FASG) more precisely as the following: The $G_{FS} \triangleq \langle W; \sim \rangle$ is a non-directed, edge weighted graph where

1. W: denote the set of deliverable features, where $j \in W$.
2. $\sim$: express the architectural similarity (see 2) between features ($\sim_{j,j'}: j, j' \in W$):

$$\sim_{j,j'} = \begin{cases} 1 & \text{if } \sim_{j,j'} > 0 \\ 0 & \text{otherwise (missing edge)} \end{cases} \tag{3a}$$

Therefore, if the $\sim_{j,j'} > 0$, then there is an edge between feature j and j' and the weight of edge is equal to the strength of $\sim_{j,j'}$ (cf. 2), otherwise the edge is missing.

To determine the proper feature decomposition, we apply a graph partitioning method on the FASG, which is a common technique in areas such as routing, and VLSI placement [36]. Partitioning G_{FS} into k partitions means that the goal is to find subsets $W_1, W_2, ..., W_k$ of features $j \in W$ such as that

1. $\bigcup_{i=1}^{k} W_i = W$ and $W_i \cap W_i' = \emptyset$ for $i \neq i'$ (subsets are disjoint set of features),
2. the sum of edge weights (similarities) that are crossing subsets is minimized.

A partial example of partitioning can be seen in Fig. 3. This figure shows the result of an FASG partitioning with parameter $k = 8$. In the presented FASG, the similarities of features are shown on the edges and the cost of partitioning is equal to the sum of cut edges (≈ 5.167).

3.3 Tool Support

To obtain a proof-of-concept of the presented FPM, we implemented a prototype in Matlab [37]. This prototype realizes the Kernighan-Lin (KL) method [38, 36] of graph partitioning. The previously presented Figure 3 was produced with it.

4 Experimentation

Simulations were carried out to evaluate our proposed Feature Partitioning Method. Using the extracted historical data as an input for our proposed method made it possible to compare the release planning result of the method with the historical result [39]. In this section, first we set research questions, then we present necessary background information, and finally we interpret our findings.

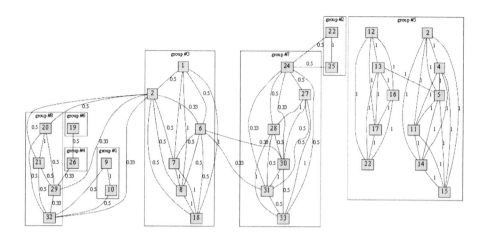

Fig. 3. FASG with 33 Elements in Partitioned Form

4.1 Research Questions

Our initial intends (**P1-3**) was to minimize the effects of informal communication deficiency in distributed agile environments. To validate our method the next questions were addressed: *How FPM can be compared with the intuitive one in terms of Q1) communication and coordination needs, Q2) resource workload, and Q3) feasibility?*

4.2 Context and Methodology

IRIS is an integrated client rating and client risk management system for credit institutions for analyzing the non-payment risk of clients and indicating potential clients so as to realize their future liabilities on the basis of their solvency and attitude [35]. The system is written in VB and C# (approx. 2 million SLOC, 41 modules), the applied methodology is a custom agile process.

The release planning process (Sec. 2.1) consisted of the following steps. First, the features were selected (expressed in User stories [24]) from the backlog – considering stakeholders' demands. Then every User story was estimated by two teams and assigned to these teams *intuitively*. The fix-membered teams worked in different locations, so they could not see or speak often in person that resulted from geographical separation. Communication was mostly based on video conferences, phone calls and emails; since all developers were Hungarians, there was no language, cultural or time zone barriers.

4.3 Data Collection

Five data sets (five releases: R_{1-5}) were selected to make a comparison between the algorithmic and the intuitive method. All releases had the same iteration length (80 working hours, i.e. 2 weeks), domain, customer, and development methodology, but they were characterized by different number of User stories (US – deliverable features), team capacities (TC – the amount of deliverable Story points [24] by the team in the releases), effective developer workforce (ED – available developers), and delivered User stories at the end of the releases (RUS – in Story point). (Please note, 1) two developers were participated in the project partly – one developer in each team; 2) the value of a Story point correlates with the required implementation effort of a User story.) Table 1 summarizes the *state variables* that were used to capture facts that were likely affecting the findings, where values between round brackets pointing out how these variables were divided between the sites of team 1 and 2 – respectively. These variables were collected from the IRIS's backlog.

4.4 Results and Analysis

To answer the questions of **Q1-3**, simulations were performed on the input data (summarized in Table 1) to compare the characteristics of the two approaches.

We constructed a *response variable* to test **Q1** (Sec. 4.1) – namely the *Communication and Coordination Intensity* between teams (CCI) in terms of the sum of cut edges in FASG – in order to set the historical (CCI^{hist}) cases against the algorithmic (CCI^{alg}) cases. As our aim is to promote independent work and to minimize the coordination and communication needs between teams, the less CCI value is treated better.

In Table 2, rows from R_1 to R_5 show that the historical cases had far greater CCI value than the algorithmic ones. This points out the fact that, due to the intuitive feature distribution, feature chunks were less efficiently separated (CCI^{hist}/CCI^{alg}) in the historical cases comparing to the algorithmic ones. Zero values in certain rows show that the algorithm found non-connected feature chunks, therefore, edge cutting was not performed. The $\sum$ CCI summarizes the differences between the historical and the algorithmic cases, and points out a remarkable difference of average communication and coordination intensities, which is ≈ 28 times less in the algorithmic cases. ($\nabla_{CCI} \triangleq CCI^{hist}/CCI^{alg} \approx 28$).

Considering the historical data (Table 1), the planned average velocity of User story development per person is $115/6 \approx 19.17$, and the planned team capacities are $TC_{T1} = 19.17 * 3.5 \approx 67.1$ and $TC_{T2} = 19.17 * 2.5 \approx 47.9$. To express the deviation of the historical planned team capacities ($TC_{T1,T2}$) from the historical actual team capacities ($RUS_{T1,T2}$) at team 1 and team 2 levels, we also constructed two additional *response variables* to test **Q2** – namely $\Delta_{T1} \triangleq |TC_{T1} - RUS_{T1}|$ and $\Delta_{T2} \triangleq |TC_{T2} - RUS_{T2}|$.

The historical Δ_{T1}^{hist} and Δ_{T2}^{hist} values are presented in Table 3. The columns RUS_{T1}^{alg} and RUS_{T2}^{alg} show the deliverable User stories at the end of the releases that were

Table 1. Historical requirements dispersion   **Table 2.** CCI between teams

	US	TC (TC_{T1}, TC_{T2})	ED (ED_{T1}, ED_{T2})	RUS_P (RUS_{T1}, RUS_{T2})		CCI^{hist}	CCI^{alg}	Efficiency (CCI^{hist}/CCI^{alg})
R_1	34	115 (67.1,47.9)	6 (3.5,2.5)	117.0 (70.0,47.0)	R_1	32.00	0.00	∞
R_2	25	115 (67.1,47.9)	6 (3.5,2.5)	85.5 (51.0,34.5)	R_2	30.00	2.67	11.24
R_3	27	115 (67.1,47.9)	6 (3.5,2.5)	137.5 (74.5,63.0)	R_3	21.83	0.00	∞
R_4	44	115 (67.1,47.9)	6 (3.5,2.5)	116.5 (60.5,56.0)	R_4	55.17	2.83	22.07
R_5	26	115 (67.1,47.9)	6 (3.5,2.5)	120.0 (73.0,47.0)	R_5	12.50	0.00	∞
$\sum$	156	575.00	30	576.5	$\sum$ CCI	151.50	5.50	27.55

proposed by the partitioning algorithm (partition numbers were $k = 2$). These values are significantly different from the historical values due to the optimal partitioning of the FRs (cp. Table 1). Based on the values of $RUS^{alg}_{T1,T2}$ and followed the similar granularity of historical resource allocation (resources were allocated to the teams as the multiple of 0.5), the proposed effective developer workforces ($ED^{alg}_{T1,T2}$ columns) also differ from the historical cases (cp. Table 1).

Table 3. Team capacity differences in the historical and the algorithmic cases

	Δ^{hist}_{T1}	Δ^{hist}_{T2}	RUS^{alg}_{T1}	ED^{alg}_{T1}	TC^{alg}_{T1}	Δ^{alg}_{T1}	RUS^{alg}_{T2}	ED^{alg}_{T2}	TC^{alg}_{T2}	Δ^{alg}_{T2}
R_1	2.92	0.92	108.0	5.5	105.4	2.58	9.0	0.5	9.6	0.58
R_2	16.08	13.42	23.5	1.0	19.2	4.33	62.0	3.0	57.5	4.50
R_3	7.42	15.08	82.5	4.0	76.7	5.83	55.0	3.0	57.5	2.50
R_4	6.58	8.08	98.0	5.0	95.8	2.17	18.5	1.0	19.2	0.67
R_5	5.92	0.92	78.0	4.0	76.7	1.33	42.0	2.0	38.3	3.67
$\sum$	38.92	38.42		19.5		16.25		9.5		11.92

Using the same average velocity of User story development per person as in the historical cases (i.e $115/6 \approx 19.17$) we could calculate the planned team capacities ($TC^{alg}_{T1,T2}$) and its deviation from the proposed capacities ($\Delta^{alg}_{T1} \triangleq |TC^{alg}_{T1} - RUS^{alg}_{T1}|$ and $\Delta^{alg}_{T2} \triangleq |TC^{alg}_{T2} - RUS^{alg}_{T2}|$). To set $\Delta^{alg}_{T1,T2}$ values against the $\Delta^{hist}_{T1,T2}$ values, we can conclude that the resource workload utilization can be considerably better (on average $\approx 64\%$) since the algorithm helped to allocate resources to teams according to their needs instead of allocating them uniformly ($\nabla_{Res} \triangleq ((\Delta^{hist}_{T1} + \Delta^{hist}_{T2}) - (\Delta^{alg}_{T1} + \Delta^{alg}_{T2})))/(\Delta^{hist}_{T1} + \Delta^{hist}_{T2})) = ((38.92 + 38.42) - (16.25 + 11.92))/(38.92 + 38.42) \approx 64\%$. As a consequence, the proposed method could provide lower implementation risk and more economical resource exploitation by decreasing resource over- and underload respectively. Moreover, the algorithm could support to plan resources better since the algorithmic cases required fewer resources by one developer considering all the releases (($\sum ED_{T1} + \sum ED_{T2}) - (\sum ED^{alg}_{T1} + \sum ED^{alg}_{T2}) = 30 - 29 = 1$).

Statistical analysis was also performed on the response variables. Besides the previously detailed average differences (∇_{CCI} and ∇_{Res}), the results of the analysis (Table 4) also underline the usefulness of the proposed method. The worst case decrease of CCI, that is defined as $\nabla^{wc}_{CCI} \triangleq Min(CCI^{hist})/Max(CCI^{alg}) \approx 4.5$, points out that the communication and coordination can be significantly reduced, and in the best case (theoretically) there are no communication and coordination needs between the teams during development ($\nabla^{bc}_{CCI} \triangleq Min(CCI^{alg})/Max(CCI^{hist}) = \infty$). Considering the Min and Max statistics of the $\Delta^{hist}_{T1,T2}$ and the $\Delta^{alg}_{T1,T2}$ variables, similar differences can be seen ($\nabla^{min}_{Res} \approx 37\%$ and $\nabla^{max}_{Res} \approx 64\%$ respectively) as in the average (c.f. ∇_{Res}).

From these, we can conclude that the proposed method 1) can break down the development work into cohesive feature chunks such a way that the dispersed teams are roughly working on the same set of modules, therefore communications predominately occur within grouped FRs rather than between grouped FRs; 2) necessitates less intensive communication and coordination needs (i.e. ∇^{bc}_{CCI}, ∇^{wc}_{CCI} and ∇_{CCI}) than the

Table 4. Comparison of Statistics

	Mean	Median	Min	Max	Std.dev.
CCI^{hist}	30.30	30.00	12.50	55.17	15.89
CCI^{alg}	1.10	0.00	0.00	2.83	1.51
$\Delta^{hist}_{T1,T2}$	7.73	7.00	0.92	16.08	5.55
$\Delta^{alg}_{T1,T2}$	2.82	2.54	0.58	5.83	1.74

intuitive ones (c.f. **Q1**); can provide better utilization of resources according to their needs instead of allocating them uniformly that can provide lower implementation risk and more economical resource exploitation (i.e. ∇^{min}_{Res}, ∇^{max}_{Res} and ∇_{Res}) by decreasing resource over- and underload respectively (c.f. **Q2**); 3) can provide higher quality feature distribution plans with the utilization of semi-automatic production of feature chunks, which makes it possible to re-partition the features any time within seconds in order to support what-if analysis or to adapt the plan to the continuously changing situations of agile environments (c.f. **Q3**).

5   Discussion and Future Work

The significant difference between co-located and distributed approaches is explained by the communication and coordination issues rather than the size or complexity of the cross-site development [13]. The communication and coordination problems result in **P1-4** (Sec. 1.3). In plan-driven situations, these communication and coordination issues (**C1-3**) are diminished with increasing the formality of the interactions using detailed documentations (i.e. specifications, design plans, project plans) and conventions (i.e. coding standards, templates). Although, this approach contradicts to the ideas of agility, and it seems to preclude the use of them [21, 2, 13, 12]. To reduce these issues in agile environments, our approach is to decrease the need of interactions between the teams with identifying so-called *feature chunks* that can be treated roughly independently.

As a solution, our proposed Feature Partitioning Method (FPM) (Sec. 3) was presented which extends agile release planning to distributed environments. The FPM consists of two successive steps namely *Feature Architectural Similarity Analysis* (FASA) (**S1**; Sec. 3.1) and *Feature Chunk Construction* (FCC) (**S2**; Sec. 3.2). First, in **S1**, we introduced a `ImplementedIn` relation between requirements (FRs) and system modules (SMs), and constructed a so-called *Module Relatedness Variable (MRV)* to indicate the fact that FRs are implemented in different set of SMs (Sec. 3.1). Then, we proposed an architectural similarity measure ($\sim_{j,j'}$; see 2) to characterize architectural similarity of features in terms of occurrence of relations between FRs and SMs. This measure is used to form *feature chunks* according to the values of the measurements.

Next, in **S2**, we constructed a so-called Feature Architectural Similarity Graph (FASG; Sec. 3.2) from the features and their architectural similarity relations. To support the parallel development, we introduced the feature chunk construction step which aim was to break down the whole development work into cohesive parts. To determine the proper decomposition of blocks we applied a graph partitioning method on the defined FASG. Actually, finding the optimal solution for the edge cutting minimization problem of graph partitioning for non-trivial cases is known to be NP-complete. A variety of algorithms were developed to solve this graph partitioning problem class [36]. The implemented algorithm is based on the Kernighan-Lin (KL) method [38, 36] – an $O(n^2 logn)$ algorithm – which is one of the earliest methods for graph partitioning, and more recent heuristics methods are often its variations. Although, there are more efficient global optimization algorithms to this problem class, we implemented KL method because of its relatively easy implementation and its acceptable results for practical applications. However, evaluation of other algorithms is recommended to provide a sophisticated insight (e.g. in terms of efficiency and quality of solutions) into the consequences of the usage of different algorithms.

The method is based upon two important underlying assumptions: the architecture of the system (i.e. set of modules) is defined and the implementation of the features can be appointed to a subset of system modules. In agile approaches, the architecture often evolves organically. Therefore, the cohesion and coupling between modules may decrease and increase respectively [6]. Therefore, the utility of the technique may be impaired over time, unless refactoring occurs. After refactoring, the ImplementedIn relations should also be maintained by the selected members of the distributed team (typically managers, customer representatives and lead developers) with the knowledge of the architecture, features and their relationships during release planning.

The presented method also assumes flexible team sizes that are derived from the partition sizes. This method gives an opportunity to adjust resource usages to the needs while the communication intensities are minimized. If the team sizes are fixed, then a complementary approach is needed. For example, the number of partitions should be increased and properly selected subsets of them should be allocated to each team. This extension can handle the additional constraint of the latter case. However, this case obviously worsens the effectiveness of the presented method considering the coordination and communication needs.

The method presumes that there are no dependencies (such as precedence or coupling – see [26]) between the deliverable items. However, in some situations, dependencies should be dealt with. Therefore, an extension of the method may be required. There are two additional characteristics of the method in which the presented approach may be superfluous. If there are too few numbers of system modules and features, then the partitioning can be made by human experts. Or, if the features have a very similar architectural impact, then the presented optimized approach cannot provide significant improvement in lowering the communication and coordination needs.

Considering the data sets, the evaluation showed that arranging development work (FRs) according to the identified feature chunks may significantly decrease the communication needs and coordination complexity of the distributed team. However, as our simulation carried out post mortem analysis, in-depth investigation of the method is recommended in different development situations (e.g more than two teams, larger team sizes, different module sizes). Complementary agile release and iteration planning methods can be found in [25, 26] and in [29] respectively. Those methods fit well to the presented method.

6 Conclusions

The obstacles of informal communication seem to preclude the use of agile methodologies in distributed environments. To address this situation, we presented a distributed agile release planning extension to assist the release planning process of distributed agile development teams by identifying feature chunks that can be implemented co-located to minimize the communication needs between the dispersed teams. The presented method is evaluated with simulations, which indicated that this approach 1) can necessitate less intensive communications and coordinations; 2) can provide better utilization of resources; and 3) can provide higher quality feature distribution plans by re-partition the features any time within seconds to support what-if analysis or to adapt the plans to the continuously changing situations of agile environments. We believe the results are even more impressive in more complex (more teams/features, etc.) situations.

References

1. Manifesto for agile software development, http://www.agilemanifesto.org
2. Dybå, T., Dingsøyr, T.: Empirical studies of agile software development: A systematic review. J. of Inf. & Softw. Tech. 50, 833–859 (2008)
3. Ambler, S.W.: Survey says: Agile works in practice. Dr. Dobb's Journal (March 2006), http://www.ddj.com/
4. Layman, L., et al.: Motivations and measurements in an agile case study. J. of Syst. Arch. 52, 654–667 (2006)
5. Schwaber, K., Beedle, M.: Agile Software Development with Scrum. Prentice Hall PTR, Englewood Cliffs (2001)
6. Beck, K., Andres, C.: Extreme Programming Explained: Embrace Change, 2nd edn. Addison-Wesley, Reading (2004)
7. VersionOne: 5th annual survey (2010), the state of agile development (December 2010), http://www.versionone.com/agilesurvey/
8. Sutherland, J., Schwaber, K.: The scrum papers: Nuts, bolts, and origins of an agile process (April 2007), http://old.crisp.se/scrum/books/
9. Layman, L., et al.: Essential communication practices for extreme programming in a global software development team. J. of Inf. & Softw. Tech. 48, 781–794 (2006)
10. Heeks, R., Krishna, S., Nicholsen, B., Sahay, S.: Synching or sinking: global software outsourcing relationships. IEEE Softw. 18, 54–60 (2001)
11. Marchenko, A., Abrahamsson, P.: Scrum in a multiproject environment: An ethnographically-inspired case study on the adoption challenges. In: AGILE 2008, pp. 15–26. IEEE Press, Los Alamitos (2008)
12. Ramesh, B., Cao, L., Mohan, K., Xu, P.: Can distributed software development be agile? Commun. ACM. 49, 41–46 (2006)
13. Herbsleb, J., Mockus, A.: An empirical study of speed and communication in globally distributed software development. IEEE Trans. Softw. Eng. 29, 481–494 (2003)
14. Miller, A.: Distributed agile development at microsoft patterns & practices. Technical report, Microsoft (2008)
15. Krishna, S., Sahay, S., Walsham, G.: Managing cross-cultural issues in global software outsourcing. Commun. ACM 47, 62–66 (2004)
16. Ebert, C., Neve, P.D.: Surviving global software development. IEEE Softw. 18, 62–69 (2001)
17. Mockus, A., Weiss, D.M.: Globalization by chunking: A quantitative approach. IEEE Softw. 18, 30–37 (2001)

18. Repenning, A., Ioannidou, A., Payton, M., Ye, W., Roschelle, J.: Using components for rapid distributed software development. IEEE Softw. 18, 38–45 (2001)
19. Cloke, G.: Get your agile freak on! agile adoption at yahoo! music. In: AGILE 2007, pp. 240–248. IEEE Press, Los Alamitos (2007)
20. Begel, A., Nagappan, N.: Usage and perceptions of agile software development in an industrial context: An exploratory study. In: ESEM 2007, pp. 255–264 (2007)
21. Abrahamsson, P., Salo, O., Ronkainen, J., Warsta, J.: Agile software development methods - review and analysis. Technical report, VTT Publications (2002)
22. Parnas, D.L.: On the criteria to be used in decomposing systems into modules. Commun. ACM. 15, 1053–1058 (1972)
23. Chow, T., Cao, D.-B.: A survey study of critical success factors in agile software projects. J. of Syst. and Softw. 81, 961–971 (2008)
24. Cohn, M.: Agile Estimating and Planning. Prentice Hall PTR, Englewood Cliffs (2005)
25. Szoke, A.: Bin-packing-based Planning of Agile Releases. In: Maciaszek, L.A., González-Pérez, C., Jablonski, S. (eds.) ENASE 2008/2009. CCIS, vol. 69, pp. 133–146. Springer, Heidelberg (2010)
26. Szoke, A.: Conceptual Scheduling Model and Optimized Release Scheduling for Agile Environments. J. of Inf. & Softw. Tech. (2011) (in press, accepted manuscript)
27. Scrum alliance homepage, http://www.scrumalliance.org/
28. Ngo-The, A., Ruhe, G.: Optimized resource allocation for software release planning. IEEE Trans. Softw. Eng. 35, 109–123 (2009)
29. Szoke, A.: Decision support for iteration scheduling in agile environments. In: Bomarius, F., Oivo, M., Jaring, P., Abrahamsson, P. (eds.) PROFES 2009. LNBIP, vol. 32, pp. 156–170. Springer, Heidelberg (2009)
30. Conway, M.E.: How Do Committees Invent? Datamation (1968)
31. Gamma, E., Helm, R., Johnson, R.E., Vlissides, J.: Design Patterns: Elements of Reusable Object-Oriented Software. Addison-Wesley, Reading (1995)
32. Buschmann, F., Henney, K., Schmidt, D.C.: Pattern-Oriented Software Architecture, vol. 4. Wiley, Chichester (2007)
33. Ulrich, K.T., Eppinger, S.D.: Product Design and Development, 3rd edn. McGraw-Hill, New York (2003)
34. Hennig, C., Hausdorf, B.: Design of dissimilarity measures: A new dissimilarity between species distribution areas. In: Data Science and Classification, pp. 29–37. Springer, Heidelberg (2006)
35. Multilogic Ltd. homepage, http://www.multilogic.hu
36. Fjallstrom, P.: Algorithms for graph partitioning: A survey. Technical report, EACIS (1998)
37. Mathworks Inc. homepage, http://www.mathworks.com/
38. Kernighan, B.W., Lin, S.: An efficient heuristic procedure for partitioning graphs. J. of The Bell Syst. Tech. 49, 291–307 (1970)
39. Kellner, M., Madachy, R., Raffo, D.: Software process simulation modeling: Why? what? how? J. of Syst. and Softw. 46, 91–105 (1999)

Collaboration in Pair Programming: Driving and Switching

Laura Plonka, Judith Segal, Helen Sharp, and Janet van der Linden

Centre for Research in Computing,
The Open University,
Milton Keynes, UK
http://crc.open.ac.uk/

Abstract. This paper reports on an empirical study about the mechanisms of the collaboration of drivers and navigators in Pair Programming (PP) sessions. Based on video recordings of professional software developers, we analysed the mechanisms of role switches and how developers split the task of driving. We found that developers do not evenly contribute to the task of driving and that they spend on average a third of the session without any computer interaction focusing mainly on communication. In addition, our results show that most pairs switch roles frequently and that the frequency and fluidity of switches indicate a high level of engagement on the part of both developers.

Keywords: Pair programming, empirical studies, collaboration.

1 Introduction

Pair Programming (PP) is a software development practice in which two programmers are working together on one computer, sharing mouse and keyboard [2, 17]. Over recent years, a wide range of studies [3, 13, 15, 16, 18] has investigated PP; most of those studies report positive results indicating benefits of PP. However, some studies are inconclusive and some studies even report contradictory results (see [10]). This accentuates the need for further studies. External factors have been identified that influence the effects of PP, e.g. task complexity [1] and personality [11], but there are still open questions regarding the effect of the developers' behaviour within PP sessions.

There are two roles in each pair: driver and navigator. The programmer who is typing is typically called the "driver" and the other one is called the "navigator". The programmers can switch these roles at any time. In this paper, we analyse some aspects of the role behaviour of driver and navigator such as the role distribution, the role switches and the mechanisms of switching based on PP sessions in industrial settings. The results provide new insights into the collaboration of the developers in terms of how developers split the task of "driving" and how and by whom switches are initiated.

A. Sillitti et al. (Eds.): XP 2011, LNBIP 77, pp. 43–59, 2011.

2   Related Work: The Roles of Driver and Navigator

Originally, the literature claimed that driver and navigator work on different levels of abstraction; the navigator acts and thinks on a strategic level [2, 8], is responsible for reviewing the driver's work [8, 12], and for "watching for defects, thinking of alternatives, looking up resources" [18] whereas the driver is responsible "for typing the code" [8] and for finding "the best way to implement this method right here" [2].

However, these role descriptions have been challenged by the results of recent studies [6, 7, 9] that show that driver and navigator do not think or act on different levels of abstraction. Freudenberg et al. [6, 9] conducted four one-week studies with experienced pair programmers in industrial settings. They showed firstly that a significant amount of talk is at an intermediate level of abstraction and secondly that driver and navigator tend to work on the same level of abstraction. The second result is also reported by Chong and Hurlbutt [7]. They stated that "aside from the task of typing" there was no division of labour between the driver and navigator. Furthermore, Freudenberg et al. reported [9] that driver and navigator switch roles regularly and with a fluid handover during a PP session and conclude that this implies that the navigator continually maintains a good understanding at different levels of abstraction. They suggest defining the roles of driver and navigator by "the additional physical and cognitive load of typing borne by the driver" rather than "by segmenting the problem space according to level of abstraction".

Another aspect of the roles of driver and navigator are the role switches. Based on the experience in one XP team , Dick and Zarnett [8] reported that developers did not switch roles and that this led to a drift of the navigator's attention. As a result, the pair did not develop a simple design. In addition, they observed a lack of communication between the driver and the navigator and reported that this resulted in substandard design. Vanhanen et al. [16] conducted a single case study in a large telecommunication company. They found that developers switched roles 2-3 times a day and reported that those switches typically took place after the lunch break or after a personal break of the driver. Additionally, they stated that developers who were already familiar with the task act as a driver and those who did not know the code felt that it was impossible to act as a driver. In contrast to Vanhanen et al., Rostaher and Hericko [14] found that developers switched roles on average 21 times in an average period of 358 min. Those results are based on self-reported data by professional developers; developers were asked to keep track of their switches using a software system. Additionally, they found that the frequency of changes correlated with programming experience and that more experienced pairs changed most often.

A more detailed analysis of the handover process for switching roles and the effects of switching and driving was conducted by Freudenberg et al. [5] and by Chong and Hurlbutt [7]. Freudenberg et al. observed 36 PP sessions (18 different pair constellations) all of which were audio taped and three of which were video recorded. All pairs worked on one computer using one mouse and one keyboard. For their study, they defined "driver" by saying that "the possession of the keyboard signalled who is in the driver role". They found that switches were mostly initiated by the driver; the keyboard was "offered and accepted" rather than being "taken without offering" [5]. Furthermore, they pointed out that mouse/keyboard were used both as input devices and as pointers to highlight the object of conversation on the screen. In addition, Freudenberg et al. [4] investigated developer collaboration; they found that PP is highly collaborative and that driver and navigator contribute almost equally to every subtask.

Chong and Hurlbutt [7] observed two different development teams. They sat behind the developers and took notes. Some of the sessions were audio-recorded. The data was analysed using a self-developed coding scheme. Chong and Hurlbutt analysed the keyboard and mouse switching and the effect of controlling the keyboard. They found that pairs who work on a shared machine and use dual mice/keyboards switch more frequently than pairs with a single mouse/keyboard; developers using dual mice/keyboards did not drive at the same time but the navigator jumped in during pauses or periods of hesitation. According to Chong and Hurlbutt, the switches occurred when "it was easier for a programmer to execute an action himself" when a developer "was more practiced in a particular subtask", or when one developer was called away during the session. Additionally, it seemed that sometimes developers were just eager to type. As an effect of switching, Chong and Hurlbutt stated that frequent switches helped the developers to "maintain a high level of mutual awareness of each other's action". In contrast, where developer pairs used a single mouse and a single keyboard, "switching required more coordination and an explicit physical relocation of the keyboard", the developer with control over the keyboard in the beginning "generally retained control for the whole session" and "maintaining active engagement in the task appeared more effortful". Additionally, they found that being driver affects the power in decision-making.

These studies provide insight into the effects of switching and driving, which indicate that the number of switches and the driving distribution affect PP and should be investigated in more detail. However, none of the studies above focuses on driving times or how driving times are distributed among the developers, and most analysis about switches is based on contemporaneous notes and audio-recordings rather than video recordings (except for three sessions in [5]). Since the switches include non verbal interactions such as shifting the keyboard and those switches can happen very frequently [5, 7], we analyse switches based on video recordings. This allows us to replay important episodes and to analyse switches in more detail. Furthermore, video recordings allow us to measure the driving times of the developers.

3   Study Methodology

This paper is based on four one-week studies in four different companies. During our studies, the developers worked on their day-to-day tasks in their usual working environment. In this section, the study background, data gathering and analysis are described.

Fig. 1. On the left: Screenshot of a fully synchronized video of a PP session: This shows the developers' screen (Eclipse IDE) and, bottom right, the video recording of the developers. On the right: Recording setup in one of the companies. The setup was installed in the usual working environment of the developers.

3.1   Data Gathering

Audio and video recordings were taken of the PP sessions. Using these recordings the driving times of each developer, the non–driving times (episodes in which neither developer is driving), and the switching behaviour were analysed, along with the communication of the developers.

The recordings of the session consist of the following three data sources:

- Audio recordings of the verbal communication between the participants,
- a video of the programmers capturing who is driver and who is navigator,
- and a full-resolution screen recording capturing all computer activities.

All three data sources are fully synchronized and stored in a single video file so that all information is available at once (see figure 1). The PP sessions were recorded in the developers' day-to-day work environment and while solving day-to-day tasks. Our recording setup was installed at one computer in each participating company (see figure 1). The location of this computer was chosen by the company. In one company the recording equipment was at a computer located in an extra room, in the three other companies it was in the development team office. Although the developer pairs had to work physically on this computer for the recordings they were able to work virtually at one of the developers' machines using a remote desktop setup.

3.2   Data Background

We recorded 21 PP session in four different companies. All companies work in different industries and all used agile approaches in the teams we observed. Two of the companies had just introduced PP and used Scrum, the other two had used PP for more than one year and used an adapted agile approach. In all four companies, PP was encouraged by the team leaders but the team leaders did not assign pairs or tasks. Instead the developers decided when to use PP and in which pair constellation. The forming of the pairs was done during their daily meeting or spontaneously during the day.

Table 1. Overview: Number of recordings and developers' backgrounds

Industry	# of recorded sessions	# of participating developers	# of different pair constellations	av programming experience (in years)	av PP experience (in years)
Geographic information systems	6	8	6	7.9	6.5
Transport and logistics	7	8	6	9.7	1
Email marketing	4	6	4	7.1	2.9
CRM systems estate	4	7	4	6.8	1.6

Table 2. Coding scheme for analysing non–driving and driving times

Coding scheme driving and non–driving times	
Code	**Description**
D1.isDriving, D2.isDriving (D1: Developer 1, D2: Developer 2) (driving time)	Driving is coded when a developer is using the mouse or the keyboard. Having a hand on the mouse or keyboard without using it is not coded as driving.
BothDriving (driving time)	BothDriving is coded when both developers have their hands on mouse and keyboard, the keyboard/mouse is in use but it is not apparent who is using it.
NoOneIsDriving (Non–driving time)	NoOneIsDriving is coded if none of the developers are driving, e.g. when they are discussing something.

Participation in the study was voluntary for all developers; in total 20 different pair constellations with 31 developers were recorded, with some developers being recorded more than once. 17 pairs used one mouse/keyboard and four pairs used dual keyboards and mice (the developers decided this). A PP session lasted between one and a half hours to three and a half hours; in total we video taped about 37 hours of PP sessions. Table 1 provides an overview of the recordings.

3.3 Analysis Process

The video data was coded based on a self-developed coding scheme and subsequently the occurrence of some of the codes was counted, for example, to investigate the frequency of switches; or the length of time of a code was recorded, for example to measure driver distribution among the developers.

Definition of the term of driving
In the context of this study, we define "driving" as being in control over mouse/keyboard and using one or both of them as an input device (this can include

browsing, writing code, executing programs, etc.). This means that it is not considered as driving when developers only have their hand on mouse/keyboard. This definition evolved during the analysis based on the observation that some developers tend to place their hand on the keyboard or mouse although they are not typing; for example, when they are engaged in a discussion with their partner.

We will refer to the developer who is driving as the driver and to the other as the navigator. The developers keep those role names (even when the driver stops typing) until they switch roles. For this paper navigator is defined as "not being the driver" without implying any kind of behaviour in the role of the navigator.

Table 3. Coding scheme for analysing switches: Who initiates the switches?

Coding scheme switches: Who initiates switches?		
Code	**Description**	**Examples**
Driver-Initiated	A switch is initiated by the driver if the driver offers the keyboard/mouse to the navigator. This can happen – by passing the keyboard (physically), – by offering the keyboard/mouse verbally to the navigator, – or by a combination of both. Additionally, a switch is driver initiated if the driver states that he does not know how to continue and pushes the keyboard away from himself (even if he does not pass it to the navigator).	1.Example: Driver: *"Now it's your turn. I think it makes sense (if you drive now)."* Navigator: *"Yes, it's my turn now because we want to do the java debugging."* 2.Example: Driver: *"I do not know how."* Driver takes his hands from the keyboard Navigator: *"Ok."* Navigator takes the keyboard
Navigator-Initiated	A switch initiated by the navigator if – the navigator asks for the keyboard/mouse (verbally), – or the navigator just takes the keyboard/mouse (physically).	1.Example: Navigator: *"May I?"* 2.Example: Navigator: *"It's too complicated to dictate, let me do it."*
Undefined	A switch is initiated by "undefined" if right before the switch both developers had their hand on the keyboard and mouse at the same time (one developer is using the mouse and the other one the keyboard).	-
D1Initiated, D2Initiated	For each switch it was coded which developer initiated the switch.	-

Definition of the term of switching

We define switches as a change of driver. This means a switch occurs whenever a navigator becomes a driver. Developers can switch roles without any driving breaks or developers can switch after a driving break; for example, one developer is driving, then the developers start a discussion and after this discussion the other developer becomes the driver. However, it is not a switch if the same developer continues driving after the discussion.

Coding scheme for analysing driving and non–driving times

The driving and non–driving times are coded in the videos and afterwards quantitatively analysed to investigate the percentage of driving and non–driving times of the PP session. Certain events and episodes during the session can greatly influence the percentage of the non–driving times and the driving times of each developer. Those events include stand up meetings that might take place during the recordings (this would increase the non–driving time), breaks of both developers or the absence of one developer (the other developer might continue driving during this time, so it might affect the driving distributions among the developers). To reduce bias, episodes in which one or both of the developers were absent during the session were cut out and not included in the calculation of driving and non–driving times. Table 2 describes the "driving" codes.

Coding scheme for analysing switching behaviour

A switch is a change of driver. A switch can be initiated verbally or physically by the navigator or the driver. For analysing the switches we developed a coding scheme that focuses on who is initiating a switch (by role (driver or navigator) and by developer) and how a switch is initiated. Table 3 provides an overview of the codes that were used to identify who initiated the switches. Table 4 presents the coding scheme to investigate how developers switch roles.

Fig. 2. Example: Switch physically initiated by the driver
Context: In this phase of the session, the developers switch roles according to small subtasks. In this example, the developer on the left just finished a simple subtask and passes the keyboard without any comment -just a smile on his face- to his partner. His partner says: *"Ah, you take the easy road again!"* and takes the keyboard. The developer on the left starts laughing.

4   Results

In this section, we firstly describe the results of the driving and non–driving times and then the role switches. The implications of our results will be discussed in section 5.

4.1   Driving and Non–driving Times

For each PP session, the length of driving times and non–driving times were analysed. We found that PP sessions consist on average of 33.3% of non–driving times and 66.7% of driving times (the sum of the driving times of both developers).

Fig. 3. Example: Switch physically initiated by navigator
This example shows how the navigator (on the left) initiates a switch although the mouse is still being used by the driver. The navigator positions his hand (left hand) on the mouse without asking and the driver takes his hand away. The developer on the left passes the mouse from his left to his right hand and starts driving.

Break of driving or non–driving time?

The driving and non–driving times were coded in the videos; sequences were coded as driving when a developer was typing or using the mouse and as soon as they stopped typing or stopped using the mouse the sequence was coded as non–driving. This means our coding does not distinguish between a short driving break (the driver stops typing just for a second and then starts again) and non–driving times. We decided to investigate how those short driving breaks would affect the non–driving times. We found that the percentage of non–driving times would decrease by 2.4% percent if we would consider breaks up to 3 seconds not as non–driving times and by 4.1% for breaks up to 5 seconds. This shows that those small breaks do not highly affect the percentage of non–driving times.

4.2   Non–driving Times

Given that the proportion of non–driving times was relatively high, we decided to investigate the non–driving times in detail. Figure 4 provides a graphical representation (box plot) of the non–driving times. This figure shows that in half of the sessions the percentage of the non–driving times lies between 27.8% and 36.8% with a median of 31.2% and it shows four outliers in the data set; one session has a very low amount and three sessions have a very high amount of non–driving times (up to 54.5% of the session). The fact that developers spend on average a third of the session without any computer interaction led us to investigate the reasons for these non–driving times.

Reasons for non–driving times

Based on the video analysis, we found five reasons for non–driving times.

- **Waiting times**

  There are times that developers have to wait for the computer to be responsive again, for example when compiling code, running tests or starting applications. Additionally, developers sometimes face technical problems, for example, problems with version control systems or problems with the IDE that make it unresponsive for a while.

Table 4. Coding scheme for analysing switches: How are switches initiated?

Coding scheme switches: How are switches initiated?		
Code	**Description**	**Examples**
physically-Initiated	A switch is initiated physically when • the driver passes the keyboard to the navigator. • the navigator takes the keyboard without asking although it wasn't offered by the driver.	For example, see figures 3 and 2.
verballyIni-tiated	A switch is initiated verbally when • the navigator asks the driver to switch, • the driver verbally offers the keyboard/mouse to the navigator or asks the navigator to switch.	1.Example: Driver: *"It's about the coupon system. So it's your turn now."* 2.Example: Driver: *"Do you want to do it?"*
verballyAnd-PhysicallyIni-tiated	A switch is initiated verbally and physically when • the driver asks the navigator to switch and is passing the keyboard at the same time, • the driver states that s/he does not know how to continue and pushes the keyboard away, • when the navigator asks to switch and takes the keyboard while asking without waiting for any response of the driver.	Example: Navigator: *"May I suggest something?"* Navigator is taking the keyboard while saying that.
Conflict	A conflict occurs if after a non–driving time, both developers try to drive at the same time.	-
Reject	Reject is coded when a developer attempts to switch but the partner refuses to switch.	Example: Driver: *"Do you want to continue?"* Nav: *"I think you know it better. I'm, hm, we reached the limit of my knowledge."* Driver continues driving.

- **Discussions/Explanations**

  Most pairs seem to have a continuous flow of communication during the whole session. However, there are episodes during the session in which the developers concentrate exclusively on discussions and explanations. While focusing on the explanations, it seemed that the non–driving times were sometimes interrupted by very short sequences of driving times in which developers use mouse and cursor as a pointer to highlight certain lines on the screen to support their explanations. This means they explain, point, and explain again.

- **Use of external representations**
  Some developers seem to prefer to discuss the structure of the code/design and their solution strategies on paper. Hence, the developers use a sheet of paper to draw, explain and discuss their ideas without using the computer.
- **Searching for advice from a third party**
  Pair programmers can use each other as an information resource. Nevertheless, there are situations in which the expertise of the two developers is not enough to make a decision, or situations in which a developer pair cannot solve the problem. In those cases developers can involve other developers or the team leader in their discussion in order to find a solution and progress with the task. During those times both developers usually stop typing and concentrate on the conversation.
- **Interruptions**
  Pair programmers get interrupted by other developers or even by co-workers from different departments. While in some cases one developer deals with the interruption and the other one continues the work, in other cases both developers stop working in order to deal with the interruption. This leads to non–driving times for the pair.

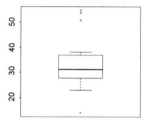 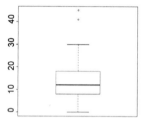

Fig. 4. Box plot: Percent of non–driving times per session from 21 PP sessions

Fig. 5. Box plot: Average number of switches per hour for all 21 sessions

The proportion for each reason hasn't yet been analysed in detail, but based on our observation of waiting times, discussion and explanation and the use of external representations seem to be the major reasons for the non–driving times. The pairs of the three outlier sessions with a very high amount of non–driving time faced serious technical problems or had difficulties finding an approach to solve the task or were working on a very complex problem which led to the use of external representations and discussions. The low amount of non–driving times in one outlier session can be explained by the fact that one developer was familiar with the task and knew a strategy how to solve the task already.

4.3 Driving Times: Driver Distribution among the Developers

In this section, the analysis focuses on the driver distribution among the developers to investigate if the driver distribution is balanced among the developers.

Therefore, we analysed the percentage of driving time for each developer with respect to the total driving time of each session (so non–driving times are not included). We say the driver distribution is balanced if the driving times of each developer is between 40% and 60%. We found that the driver distribution is balanced in 7 out of 21 sessions whereas the distribution is extremely unbalanced in four sessions.

4.4 Role Switches

We coded the role switches according to the coding scheme presented in table 3 and table 4. In total, we analysed 512 role switches in the 21 sessions. The codes "Reject" and "Conflict" hardly occurred (on average less then once per hour) and hence, we will not focus on them in detail.

How often do pair programmers switch roles?

As a result of our analysis, we found that developers switch roles on average 15.67 times per hour with a standard deviation of 12.19. Due to this high standard deviation, the number of average role switches will be presented as a box plot. Figure 5 shows that in half of the sessions the number of switches lies between 8 and 18 with a median of 12 switches per hour. Additionally, it shows two outliers with more than 40 switches per hour.

Are switches initiated evenly by both developers?

Based on the results of the driving times, we found that in two thirds of the cases one developer dominates the driving. We investigated whether the switches are initiated by both developers or whether one developer dominates the initiation of switches. In 16 sessions, the initiation of switches is balanced among the developers (each developer initiates 40 to 60 percent of the switches). In four sessions, one developer dominates the initiation of switches and in one session the developers do not switch at all. This shows that even though the driver distribution is mostly dominated by one developer, the switches are in most cases evenly initiated by both developers.

Correlation between driver distribution and number of switches

We analysed the correlation between the number of switches and the driving distribution among the developers. The pairs who had a balanced driver distribution switched roles on average 16 times per hour with a standard deviation of 10.12. The pairs with an unbalanced driver distribution had on average 16.46 role switches per hour with a standard deviation of 13.73. This indicates that the number of switches does not correlate with the driver distribution among the developers. The driver distribution can be independent of the number of switches because developers can switch just to show or to point at something on the screen and then switch back. Figure 6 visualizes this pattern of switches.

Which role initiates switches?

Additionally, we investigated the role of the switch initiator. Switches are initiated by the navigator in 82% of the cases and in 14% by the driver. In the remaining 4%, the initiation could not be clearly assigned (see figure 7).

Fig. 6. This figure illustrates that the driver distribution can be independent of the number of switches. In this example, developer 2 is driving only for a short period of time and developer 1 is driving for longer periods. Even though this pair might switch on a regular basis, their driver distribution is not necessarily balanced.

What are the mechanisms for switching roles?

Developers can initiate switches by asking or offering the keyboard/mouse verbally or they can just pass or take it. We analysed which mechanisms they use to switch roles. We found that developers initiate switches physically without any verbal cues in 81% of all switches. However, before they take the mouse or keyboard there are usually non verbal cues as for example leaning forward or placing their hands next to the mouse or the keyboard before they actually take it. In 11% of the switches the developers initiated a switch verbally and in 8% developers combined verbal and non verbal cues to initiate a switch (see figure 8).

Fig. 7. Which role initiates switches?   **Fig. 8.** How are the switches initiated?

5   Discussion

5.1   Discussion of the Results

Here we discuss our results presented above, which we summarize as:

1. A PP session consists of on average 33.3% non–driving times.
2. Developers do not split the driving times evenly; instead in two thirds of the cases one developer dominates the driving.
3. Developers switch roles on average 15.67 times per hour.
4. In most of the sessions both developers (not roles) initiate switches evenly.
5. Most of the switches (81%) are physically initiated.
6. 82% of the switches are initiated by the navigator.
7. The codes "reject" and "conflict" hardly occurred (on average less than once per hour).

These results lead us to the following conclusions:

Communication intensive non–driving times

Our first result shows that developers spend on average a third of a PP session without any computer interactions. We found five reasons for these times:

(a) waiting time, (b) explanation/discussions, (c) the use of external representations, and to a lesser degree (d) searching for advice from a third party, and (e) interruptions. Waiting times (a) and interruptions (e) are not initiated by the developers. We haven't analysed waiting times in detail, but we assume that developers continue their usual communication during those times. In the cases (b)-(d), the non–driving times are initiated by the developers and lead to communication intensive activities which are focused on the current task. Searching for advice requires communication with a third party, whereas explanation/discussions and the use of external representations lead to intra pair communication. During these times developers stop their computer interaction in order to focus exclusively on communication.

The relatively high amount of non–driving times and the communication intensive activities which take place during these times emphasize the role of communication among the developers in PP sessions.

Unbalanced driving distribution and drivers don't mind driving

We found (result 2) that in most cases developers do not split the driving times evenly: usually one developer dominates the driving so developers do not contribute evenly to the task in terms of driving. However, the driver doesn't seem to initiate switches often (result 7: only 14% of the switches are initiated by the driver) in order to balance the driving distribution among the developers. This indicates that an unbalanced distribution does not seem to be an issue for the dominating driver and that the driver does not perceive typing as additional workload.

Freudenberg et al. [9] suggest that the task of driving is an "additional physical and cognitive load" for the driver. Our results challenge the suggestion that the driver perceives driving as a "load" as we did not find any indicator for that.

Simple and intuitive handover process

Result 5 shows that 81% of the switches are physically initiated without any verbal communication (only with non verbal cues). The physically initiated switches indicate that switching roles is a very fluid and effortless process that does not require a complicated handover mechanism. This is also supported by the fact (result 7) that we hardly found any "rejects" or "conflicts" in the sessions.

The finding about the simple and intuitive handover process supports the results by Freudenberg et al. [9] that switching is a very fluid process. However, the fact that switches are mostly initiated by the navigator (result 6) contradicts the results reported by Freudenberg et al. [5] who reported that most of the switches (switch of the keyboard) were initiated by the driver.

Driver and navigator focus on the same subtask

Most of the switches (82%) are initiated by the navigator (result 6). Even in these cases, the process of switching is very effortless and does not require any kind of extra explanation from the driver. For example, the driver does not explain the next steps before handing the keyboard and mouse over to his partner. This indicates that the navigator was actively involved and understood the work of the driver as this is a precondition to take over control so effortlessly.

This is consistent with the findings from Freudenberg et al. [6, 9] and Chong [7] who stated that driver and navigator work on the same level of abstraction and switch between these levels as a pair.

Switches as an indicator for engagement
We found that pairs switch on average 15.67 times per hour (result 3) and that in most PP sessions switches are initiated by both developers (result 4). So, both developers use the mechanism of switching regularly. A high frequency of switching could indicate a good engagement of both developers because initiating a switch and continuing to drive (even for a short period of time) requires an understanding of the current activity. Hence, frequent switches might be an indicator for both developers being actively involved during the whole PP session. However, the reverse (few switches means little engagement) can't be concluded based on our data.

Interestingly, the driving distribution can't be used as an indicator for engagement; even a balanced driving distribution does not mean that both developers are actively involved during the session, for example, one developer is driving the first half of the session the other one the second half, but they may not be engaged while their partner is driving.

The finding that switches could be an indicator for engagement is consistent with Chong and Hurlbutt's finding [7] that frequent switches help to maintain mutual awareness of each other's action. Additionally, Chong and Hurlbutt [7] and Dick and Zarnet [8] stated that a lack of switching has a negative effect such as a drift of the navigator's attention and that "maintaining active engagement appeared more effortful". However, the frequency of switching in our study is higher than in the studies conducted by Dick and Zarnet [8] and Vanhanen et al. [16] who reported that pairs switched not at all or 2-3 times a day, respectively.

Some of our results and conclusions contradict results from existing literature, for example, the frequency of switches. This might be due to a different data gathering and analysis process. Our study focuses mainly on the switching and driving behaviour of the developers, therefore we gathered very detailed data using video recordings of the PP sessions and analysed the data by coding these videos in a way that the results can be quantified as well. Most of the other studies [6–9, 14] used observational data, audio recordings or self-reported data. Those data sources capture less detailed data about the switching and driving behaviour. However, the main focus of those studies was different and the data served their purpose. Additionally, some of these studies might have used a different definition of switching and driving and some papers do not define these terms. These differences in the studies could lead to different results.

5.2   Limitations of the Study

Our results are based on PP sessions from four different companies. Although these companies work in different industries, generalisability might be limited by the small number of companies and the fact that all companies were based in Germany. Participation in the study was voluntary, hence, it is possible that developers with a positive attitude towards PP or who are confident about their PP skills are more likely to take part. Nevertheless, our participants had a range of programming and PP experience. Finally, the possible effect of being video taped should be taken into account before generalising the results.

6   Future work

This study provides new findings about driving and switching behaviours of pair programmers. We have shown how developers split the driving time, how they spend the non–driving times, and how and how often they switch roles. However, not all developer pairs have a similar amount of non–driving times, a similar driving distribution, or the same frequency of switches. This raises the questions of how developers decide who is driving and why developers initiate switches. In addition, we found that the non–driving times are communication intensive and argued that the frequency of switches could be an indicator of the engagement of the developers. We plan to investigate the effect of non–driving times, the driving distribution and the switches on the engagement and collaboration of the developers further. In our next study, for which we have already gathered different kinds of data, we will address the following questions:

1. How does the amount of non–driving time affect communication in PP? Are non–driving times more communication-intensive than driving times?
2. What factors (for example, PP experience, hardware setting) influence the driving distribution? Does the driving distribution affect the collaboration of the developers?
3. Why do developers switch roles? How does the frequency of switches affect the collaboration of the developers?

The answers to these questions will provide us with a rich picture about the roles of driver and navigator.

7   Summary

This paper presents new insights into switching and driving behaviours of developers and the amount of non–driving times together with an analysis of the reasons for those times based on a detailed video analysis of industrial developers. We provide a new perspective on the collaboration of the developers: we have shown that developers do not evenly contribute to the task of driving, that the driving distribution cannot be used as an indicator for the engagement of the developers, but that a high frequency of switches might indicate that both developers are actively engaged throughout the PP session. Additionally, we found that independent of the driving times, most pairs switch roles frequently and in a very fluid way. The role switches are mostly physically initiated by the navigator without any complicated handover process or additional explanation by the driver. This simple handover process indicates that both developers know the current activity. The fact that most of the switches are not initiated by the driver suggests that the driver does not perceive the task of driving as an additional workload as suggested in the literature.

Moreover, we found that developers spend on average one third of the session without any computer interactions and that these non–driving times are communication intensive. The relatively high amount of non–driving time emphasizes the crucial role of communication in PP. Our future work includes investigating the effects of the switching and driving behaviour on the communication between the developers and additionally identifying which factors, for example, the PP experience of the developers or the hardware setting (dual mice/keyboard vs. single mouse/keyboard) influence those behaviours.

Acknowledgements

The authors would like to thank the participating companies.

References

[1] Arisholm, E., Gallis, H., Dyba, T., Sjoberg, D.I.K.: Evaluating pair programming with respect to system complexity and programmer expertise. IEEE Trans. Softw. Eng. 33, 65–86 (2007)

[2] Beck, K.: Extreme Programming Explained: Embrace Change. Addison-Wesley Professional, Reading (1999)

[3] Begel, A., Nagappan, N.: Pair programming: what's in it for me? In: ESEM 2008: Proceedings of the Second ACM-IEEE International Symposium on Empirical Software Engineering and Measurement, pp. 120–128. ACM, New York (2008)

[4] Bryant, S., Romero, P., du Boulay, B.: The collaborative nature of pair programming. In: Abrahamsson, P., Marchesi, M., Succi, G. (eds.) XP 2006. LNCS, vol. 4044, pp. 53–64. Springer, Heidelberg (2006)

[5] Bryant, S., Romero, P., du Boulay, B.: Pair programming and the re-appropriation of individual tools for collaborative programming. In: Proceedings of the 2005 International ACM SIGGROUP Conference on Supporting Group Work, pp. 332–333. ACM, New York (2005)

[6] Bryant, S., Romero, P., du Boulay, B.: Pair programming and the mysterious role of the navigator. International Journal of Human Computer Studies 66(7), 519–529 (2008)

[7] Chong, J., Hurlbutt, T.: The social dynamics of pair programming. In: Proceedings of ICSE 2007, pp. 354–363 (2007)

[8] Dick, A.J., Zarnett, B.: Paired programming and personality traits. In: Proceedings of XP 2002 (2002)

[9] Freudenberg, S., Romero, P., du Boulay, B.: "talking the talk": Is intermediate-level conversation the key to the pair programming success story? In: AGILE 2007, pp. 84–91 (2007)

[10] Hannay, J.E., Dybå, T., Arisholm, E., Sjøberg, D.I.K.: The effectiveness of pair programming: A meta-analysis. Information and Software Technology 51(7), 1110–1122 (2009)

[11] Hannay, J.E., Arisholm, E., Engvik, H., Sjoberg, D.I.K.: Effects of personality on pair programming. IEEE Transactions on Software Engineering 36, 61–80 (2010)

[12] Jensen, R.: A pair programming experience. The Journal of Defensive Software Engineering, 22–24 (2003)
[13] Layman, L., Williams, L., Cunningham, L.: Exploring extreme programming in context: an industrial case study. In: Agile Development Conference, pp. 32–41 (2004)
[14] Rostaher, M., Hericko, M.: Tracking test first pair programming-an experiment. LNCS, pp. 174–184. Springer, Heidelberg (2002)
[15] Vanhanen, J., Lassenius, C.: Perceived effects of pair programming in an industrial context. In: 33rd EUROMICRO Conference on Software Engineering and Advanced Applications, pp. 211–218 (2007)
[16] Vanhanen, J., Korpi, H.: Experiences of using pair programming in an agile project. In: HICSS 2007: Proceedings of the 40th Annual Hawaii International Conference on System Sciences, p. 274b. IEEE Computer Society, Los Alamitos (2007)
[17] Williams, L., Kessler, R.: Pair programming illuminated. Addison-Wesley Longman Publishing Co., Inc., Boston (2002)
[18] Williams, L., Kessler, R.R., Cunningham, W., Jeffries, R.: Strengthening the case for pair programming. IEEE Software 17(4), 19–25 (2000)

Using Silent Grouping to Size User Stories

Ken Power

Cisco Systems, Inc., Galway, Ireland
ken.power@gmail.com

Abstract. User stories are used to describe the functionality delivered in a product or system. Planning Poker is a common technique for sizing user stories, however it has challenges. It can be time consuming and teams can get bogged down in unnecessary discussion. This paper describes a technique called Silent Grouping that can be used to compliment Planning Poker, explaining how to apply it so that large sets of user stories can be sized in minutes. Experiences of seven Scrum teams from Cisco's Unified Communications Business Unit are used as examples. The paper shows how to apply the technique with co-located teams, and includes an example of how it was used with distributed teams. Silent Grouping has several advantages. It is fast, which in turn leads to significant time and cost savings. It also has more subtle benefits. This paper discusses the techniques, challenges, cost savings and benefits of Silent Grouping.

Keywords: User story, planning poker, silent grouping, planning, sizing, points, release planning, estimation.

1 Introduction

Mike Cohn writes that a user story *"describes functionality that will be valuable to either a user or purchaser of a system or software"* [1]. Many agile teams use user stories to describe the functionality they are building [2]. User stories are a common practice in Scrum [2, 3]. Kent Beck describes Stories as one of the primary practices in Extreme Programming, describing them as *"units of customer-visible functionality"* [4].

User stories are generally sized using Relative Estimation – a means of considering the overall magnitude of a user story and then comparing it with other user stories [5]. Using relative estimation, a point value is assigned to each user story to indicate its overall magnitude. The point value can be used to compare user stories to each other to understand how 'big' they are. For example two user stories each with a point size of 8 should be similar in size. A user story with a point value of 2 should be twice as big as a user story with a point value of 1. Mike Cohn's book "Agile Estimating and Planning" is a good source for a more detailed descriptions and examples of relative estimation [5]. Steve McConnell discusses story points under the chapter on Proxy Based Estimates [7].

Planning Poker is a widely-used technique for sizing user stories [5]. It is a technique based on Delphi estimation that helps the team to size user stories using

A. Sillitti et al. (Eds.): XP 2011, LNBIP 77, pp. 60–72, 2011.

point values [5]. This paper does not argue against using Planning Poker. Planning Poker is a valuable and useful tool. One objective of this paper is to show that teams can benefit from using both Planning Poker and Silent Grouping.

A downside of Planning Poker is that it can take a long time. There are different factors that can contribute to Planning Poker taking more time than necessary. For example, the facilitator may not always be able to prevent the team from getting into too much discussion, or might even have difficulty judging when the team has had 'enough' discussion on an individual user story.

Jean Tabaka describes a technique called Silent Grouping, which is part of a set of techniques used to help teams process large amounts of information [6]. The technique in [6] is described in the context of conducting a retrospective, but it is equally applicable to grouping user stories. This paper considers the application of a specific variant of Silent Grouping to the problem of processing a large amount of information in the form of a set of user stories that need to be sized. In this context the groups represent user story point sizes, e.g., there is a group each for '1', '2', '3', '5', '8', etc. Participants place the set of user stories in one of these groups. All user stories of a similar size end up grouped together. See Section 3 of this paper for more details.

The scope of this paper is the Silent Grouping technique, and not any of the activities that take place before or after Silent Grouping.

1.1 Structure of Paper

Section 2 presents the research methodology used. Section 3 describes the Silent Grouping technique in detail. There are detailed steps described for running the technique as an exercise. Some variations are also discussed. Section 4 presents an analysis of the data obtained from four workshops. The structure of each of the teams is described, and there is some discussion of how the technique works with co-located and distributed teams. The role of product owners is also discussed, as is the use of Planning Poker with Silent Grouping. Section 5 discusses the results in terms of release planning, time savings, cost savings, and some other aspects. Finally, Section 6 presents conclusions, summarizing some of the key benefits and applications of the Silent Grouping technique.

2 Methodology

This paper discusses experiences with seven different Scrum Teams and four products from Cisco's Unified Communications Business Unit. This research was conducted through a number of planning and sizing workshops with these teams during 2010. The teams were located at different sites in the USA and Ireland. The researcher was physically present with each team and facilitated, observed and video recorded the planning and sizing sessions.

The Teams

As noted, there are seven Scrum Teams and four products used in this study. The products are coded as P1, U1, F1 and C1. The teams all work on products that provide real time voice, video and messaging functionality. The team behind P1 is one of four cross-functional feature teams that each contributed to Desktop Application 1. The other teams for Desktop Application 1 did not use Silent Grouping for this release, and so are not discussed in this paper. The two Scrum teams behind F1 develop a voice and video communications engine that is used in multiple products. The team behind U1 develops a component library that is used in multiple products. Table 1 shows the products, the number of teams, and the number of people. It also provides a brief description of the type of product and the dependencies.

Table 1. Data Describing the Products and Teams

Product	Number of Agile Teams	Number of People	Location	Type of Product	Dependencies
P1	1 of 4 Cross Functional Feature Teams	12	Galway	Existing Desktop Client; New features to support Security Services	New features developed in Server product; 3rd Party Security Server
U1	1 Scrum Team	9	Galway	API Library	Communications Components developed by in-company teams
F1	2 Scrum Teams	18	San Jose, North Carolina	Communications Engine for Voice and Video	3rd Party software libraries; in-company libraries
C1	3 Scrum Teams	16	Galway	Desktop Client	F1; several in-company libraries

The workshops took place between June and December 2010. Table 2 shows the exact dates of each workshop.

Table 2. Silent Grouping Workshop Dates

Product	Workshop Date
P1	17-Jun-2010, 21-Jul-2010
U1	20-Aug-2010
F1	01-Oct-2010
C1	01-Dec-2010

Note that the team for P1 had two workshops. The reason for this is that their management was on holidays during the first workshop. The managers did not have confidence in Relative Sizing and user story points, as they had not used these before. The team was asked to perform a deeper analysis of each user story, including task level breakdown and estimation for each user story in the release. They repeated the sizing exercise in July using Silent Grouping. Interestingly, the resulting release plan and user story sizing was largely the same. There were some minor variances due to new user stories being added and larger user stories getting decomposed in the interim period. Although it took time, this helped to increase the confidence of the team and management in relative sizing. For the purposes of this paper, the data used for team P1 is from the second workshop on July 21st 2010.

Release Planning and User Stories

Each of the teams studied needed to plan for a full release. The length of the release in all cases was approximately 3 months. That means they needed to identify and size as many as possible of the main user stories for that 3-month period. The data in Table 3 summarizes the quantity of user stories for each product.

Table 3. Number of User Stories per Product

Product	Total Number of User Stories
P1	80
F1	102
U1	46
C1	150
Total	**378**

3   The Silent Grouping Technique

As with the technique described in [6], the team should have completed the exercise of gathering the user stories as a prerequisite to the Silent Grouping exercise. The Silent Grouping technique has four main parts, as summarized in Table 4. This section discusses each of these parts in detail.

Table 4. The Goals of Each Part of Silent Grouping

Part	Goals
Preparation	Lay the ground rules; set expectations
Round 1: Individual Placement	Quickly get an initial size estimate for all of the user stories
Round 2: Group Placement	Give everyone an opportunity to (silently) provide input to all user stories
Discussion and Reflection	Resolve any disputes; reflect on experience; gain consensus before moving on

3.1   Preparation

The facilitator prepares the board. This can be a whiteboard, corkboard, flip chart paper taped to the wall, or other means. The board should look like Figure 1 before the team begins. The columns represent the groups referred to in the name of the technique.

The team needs to decide on a scale to use for user story point sizes. All teams in this study use the Fibonacci sequence from 1 to 34 for user story point sizes. The user stories should be placed somewhere visible and easily accessible so a smooth flow can be established. Pinning or sticking them to an adjacent wall space or laying them out on a table works well.

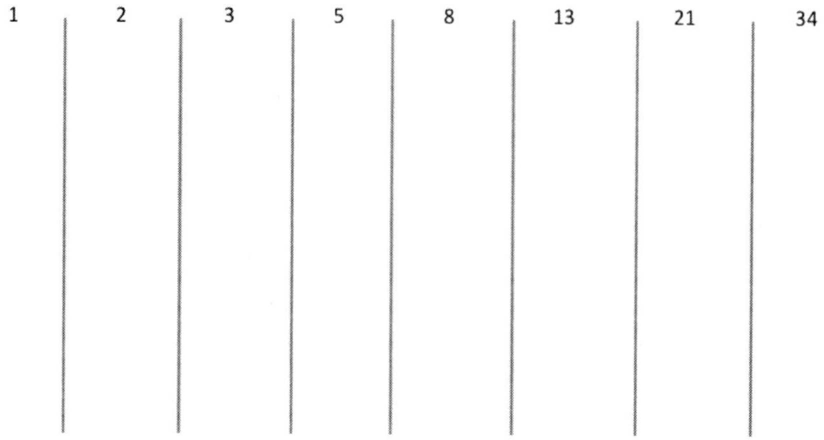

Fig. 1. Blank Sizing Wall with Columns per Point Size

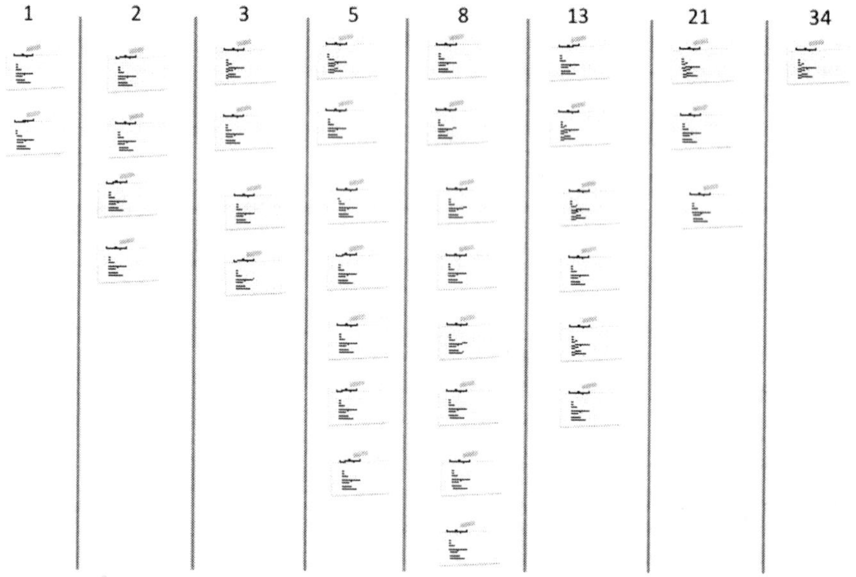

Fig. 2. Sizing Wall with User Stories After Silent Grouping

Tell the team what to expect and how to execute the technique. Lay the ground rules. Reinforce the point that silence is important. The desired outcome is a set of user stories that is sized using relative sizing. The wall from Figure 1 should look like Figure 2 after the team has finished the exercise, where all of the user stories have been placed in the appropriate column (or group) that indicates the size of the user story in points.

3.1.1 Parking Lot
It is useful to set up a Parking Lot ahead of starting the exercise. This can be simply a sheet of flip chart paper stuck to the wall, with the title 'Parking Lot' written across the top. This is where the facilitator will place any disputed user stories so they can be dealt with after the Silent Grouping exercise.

3.2 Round 1: Individual Placement

Team members take turns, one at a time, to place one user story on the board. The goal in this round is to get all the user stories on the board, and hence get an initial size estimate for all user stories. It is useful for the team to form a line rather than stepping back to ad-hoc locations after sizing. This helps prevent the possibility of someone missing a turn. If there is furniture in the middle of the room then a useful technique is to have the team move in circles around the furniture, and 'get back in line' when they have taken their turn.

3.3 Round 2: Group Placement

The team stands around the board. At this point all user stories are on the board. Team members take turns stepping forward and moving one user story at a time. The goal in this round is to get to consensus on the size of all the user stories.

There can be contention in this round. A user story can get moved repeatedly, e.g., one team member can move a user story, e.g., from a 5 to an 8, and another team member can move it back to a 5. The team has been instructed to consider why the user story might have been moved. Very often, this act of observation and conscious consideration is enough to resolve the disagreement, and the parties will agree on a size without any verbal discussion.

On rare occasions two or more people can move a user story back and forth between two (or more) columns, and nobody is prepared to compromise. This is generally a signal that more discussion is required for this specific user story. When the facilitator observes this interaction they silently remove the user story form the board and place it in the Parking Lot that they prepared earlier. In practice this tends to occur relatively rarely. Later sections quantify how often this occurred for the seven teams under discussion in this paper.

Risks to watch out for in this round include people not participating. This can take a number of forms. They can stand back and just observe, and not size anything after Round 1. They can become disengaged and not observe the proceedings at all. Both of these can be signs of underlying issues. This is where the skill and experience of the facilitator is important, first in recognizing the symptoms, and then dealing with it.

3.4 Discussion and Reflection

The facilitator facilitates a short discussion between the team to gauge the level of confidence in the sizes. The Fist of Five is a good technique to use here [6]. It quickly gives a sense for how confident the team is in the sizing that they just performed.

3.5 Variations

3.5.1 Have Just One Round
A common variation is to have just one round where anyone can move any user story. I have found that there can be a tendency to focus too early on the few user stories where there is disagreement, and consequently it takes longer to get all the user stories on the board. Hence, I prefer and recommend to use a Round 1 with the explicit goal of getting all the user stories sized quickly.

3.5.2 Allow a Little Talking
I have seen cases where limited talking was allowed during the Silent Grouping session. Although it goes against the very name of the technique, it can be beneficial. It is common for some whispering to occur, particularly during Round 2 if two or more people disagree on the size of a user story. A quick and quietly whispered conversation can often resolve the disagreement and clear up any misunderstandings. However, it is a slippery slope. The facilitator needs to be aware of the effects of this and the example it sets for the rest of the team. It requires careful balance and awareness of the different forces at play in the room.

4 Analysis

The data in Table 5 shows the basic data from the four workshops.

Table 5. Basic Data From the Four Silent Grouping Workshops

Product	Total Number of User Stories	Total Number Sized using Planning Poker	Time using Planning Poker (minutes)	Total Number sized Using Silent Sizing	Time Using Silent Sizing - Round 1 (minutes)	Time Using Silent Sizing - Round 2 (minutes)	Total Time Using Silent Sizing (minutes)	Average Time Per User Story Planning Poker (minutes)	Average Time Per User Story using Silent Sizing (minutes)	% Stories Sized Using Planning Poker	% Stories Sized Using Silent Sizing
P1	80	10	370	70	8	7	15	37	0.2	12.5	87.5
F1	102	20	720	82	15	20	35	36	0.4	19.6	80.4
U1	46	4	180	42	7.5	5	12.5	45	0.3	8.7	91.3
C1	150	0	0	150	8	9	17	N/A	0.1	0.0	100.0
Totals	378	34	1270	344	38.5	41	79.5	N/A	0.2	9.0	91.0

Some photographs of the walls containing the sized user stories can be seen later in Figure 6. The data is further analyzed and interpreted in the remainder of this section.

4.1 Team Location

4.1.1 Co-located Teams
The Scrum Teams for products P1, U1, and C1 were all co-located so the entire Scrum Team was present for the Silent Grouping workshops.

4.1.2 Distributed Teams

Product F1 has two Scrum Teams. One is located entirely in San Jose. The second is located primarily in North Carolina, with some team members dispersed and working from other locations. The Silent Grouping workshop was held at the San Jose campus. Remote team members joined via video and audio conferencing. At the time of the workshop the teams had not split areas of functionality between the two teams, so the entire team was involved in the backlog sizing. The team in San Jose conducted the Silent Grouping exercise while the remote teams observed. The room was set up to allow remote participants to see and hear in detail what was happening during the session. A Program Manager in the room in San Jose acted as proxy for the remote team members and they communicated using Instant Messaging. The San Jose ScrumMaster reviewed the outcome in detail with the remote team members afterwards. This subsequent review with remote participants took about 20 minutes. Though not ideal, these were the compromises made in this specific case to compensate for having distributed teams.

The team used a number of different technologies to facilitate involvement of the remote team members. The photographs in Figure 3 show the main room in which the workshop was conducted. In the top photo the San Jose team are sizing the user stories on the wall while there are two large screens showing other team members at other sites observing. The room has microphones coming form the ceiling and on the desks, so that discussions can be shared from anywhere in the room. The high definition video camera in the lower photo shows remote participants what is happening in real time. It is powerful enough that it can be zoomed in to show the detail written on the cards.

4.2 The Role of Product Owners during Silent Grouping

Product Owners are not allowed to size user stories. They are allowed to observe the Silent Grouping exercise, and should be available to answer questions and provide input as needed before and after the session. During one of the sessions a particular Product Owner did not agree with the sizes the team were giving to a subset of user stories relating to a particular feature. He wanted to interject and question the team. Product Owners must resist the urge to contradict the team's sizing or interrupt the flow of the Silent Grouping session with questions or comments.

4.3 Using Planning Poker and Silent Grouping

Figure 4 shows the amount of user stories sized using Silent Grouping and with Planning Poker. All teams used Silent Grouping for at least 80% or more of their user stories. The teams for C1 used Silent Grouping for 100% of their user stories.

4.4 Average Time Required to Size User Stories

As can be seen from Figure 5 the average time to size a user story using Silent Grouping can be significantly faster than using Planning Poker. One of the ScrumMasters noted afterwards that it would have taken them many days to size the user stories without Silent Grouping. Another Product Owner acknowledged that the time they

Fig. 3. Including Remote Participants

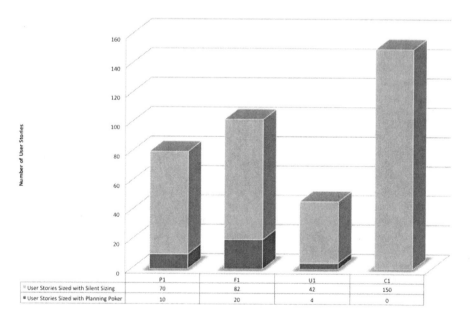

	P1	F1	U1	C1
User Stories Sized with Silent Sizing	70	82	42	150
User Stories Sized with Planning Poker	10	20	4	0

Fig. 4. Quantity of User Stories sized using Planning Poker and Silent Grouping

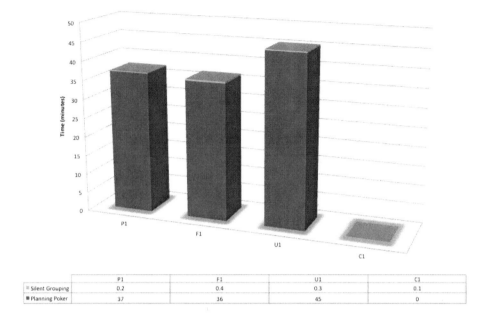

Fig. 5. Average Time to Size User Stories using Planning Poker and Silent Grouping

had spent using Planning Poker was valuable and had brought out a lot of needed discussion, but that it had reached the point where the time was critical and the team needed to show a tentative plan. Silent Grouping allowed them to do in minutes what would otherwise have taken many days spread out over a number of weeks.

4.5 User Stories Moved to Parking Lot

In two of the four workshops it was necessary to move user stories to the Parking Lot after a (silent) dispute arose over the sizes. Even in these cases the number of user stories moved was relatively small, accounting for only 5% and 4.3% respectively of the overall set of user stories.

Table 6. User Stories moved to Parking Lot during Silent Grouping

Product	Total Number of User Stories	Number of Stories moved to Parking Lot	% of User Stories moved to Parking Lot
P1	80	4	5.0
F1	102	0	0.0
U1	46	2	4.3
C1	150	0	0.0
Total	**378**	**6**	**1.6**

The disagreement in size derived from misunderstandings or lack of sufficient detail on the work required to deliver the user story. These user stories were sized later in the same workshop using Planning Poker.

5   Discussion

5.1   Release Planning

All of the teams in this study were required by organization policy to create detailed release plans for a three-month period. Among other things, these release plans need to show the amount of Sprints, the duration of the Sprint, the overall release theme, and the theme for each sprint. In addition, and of particular relevance to this study, the teams also needed to show the user stories they planned to deliver in each Sprint over that three month period. There was an acceptance that plans will change, but they still need to provide that vision of what the product will deliver. Silent Grouping proved to be a very effective technique for sizing the backlog of user stories and helping the team to efficiently and effectively prepare release plans.

5.2   Time Savings

From measuring the average time taken to size a subset of the user stories using Planning Poker, we can infer the approximate time it would have taken to size the entire set of user stories using Planning Poker. From this we can extrapolate the estimated time saved using Silent Grouping. The data for the four workshops is shown in Table 7.

Table 7. Estimated Time Savings using Silent Grouping

Product	Time Using Silent Sizing - Round 1 (minutes)	Time Using Silent Sizing - Round 2 (minutes)	Total Time Using Silent Sizing (minutes)	Average Time Per User Story Planning Poker (minutes)	Average Time Per User Story using Silent Sizing (minutes)	Estimated Time if Planning Poker were used for all (minutes)	Estimated Time Saving using Silent Sizing (minutes)	Estimated Time if Planning Poker were used for all (hours)	Estimated Time Saving using Silent Sizing (hours)	Total Estamated Person-Hour Savings (Hours)	Total Estamated Person-Day Savings (Days)
P1	8	7	15	37	0.2	2960.0	2575.0	49.3	42.9	515.0	68.7
F1	15	20	35	36	0.4	3672.0	2917.0	61.2	48.6	437.6	58.3
U1	7.5	5	12.5	45	0.3	2070.0	1877.5	34.5	31.3	563.3	75.1
C1	8	9	17	N/A	0.1	4425.0	4408.0	73.8	73.5	1175.5	156.7
Totals	38.5	41	79.5	N/A	0.2	13127.0	11777.5	218.8	196.3	2691.3	358.8

The three Scrum teams for product C1 did not use Planning Poker, so the table above uses an average of the times for the other Scrum teams to provide an illustrative example.

5.3   Cost Savings

It is difficult to quantify the real cost savings of using Silent Grouping, but it can be inferred that because there is significant time saved, there is also a cost saving. By taking the projected time saving in person hours, and applying a nominal hourly cost of $50 per person, we can calculate a hypothetical cost savings gained by using Silent Grouping.

Table 8. Hypothetical Cost Savings using Silent Grouping

Product	Total Number of User Stories	Total Number Sized using Planning Poker	Time using Planning Poker (minutes)	Total Number sized Using Silent Sizing	Estimated Time Saving using Silent Sizing (hours)	Hypothetical Cost Savings ($)
P1	80	10	370	70	42.9	USD 25,750.00
F1	102	20	720	82	48.6	USD 21,877.50
U1	46	4	180	42	31.3	USD 28,162.50
C1	150	0	0	150	73.5	USD 58,773.33
Totals	378	34	1270	344	196.3	USD 134,563.33

Even if the actual figures were only 1/10th of the hypothetical figures calculated in Table 8, that is still a significant saving.

5.4   User Story Sizes Make a 'V' Shape

A number of participants across several of the workshops made an interesting observation that the shape of the user stories, when they are in their respective columns, form a 'V' shape. This implies that the majority of user stories fall in the mid range of size estimates. This can be seen from pictures of walls, as shown in Figure 6.

Fig. 6. Triangular Shape of Sized User Stories

No further study was done on this point, but it is an interesting observation.

5.5 Silence Helps Everyone Be Heard

Planning Poker helps make sure that everyone has an input to the sizing of a user story. However there is still a risk that more extroverted personalities can dominate the surrounding discussions. Grouping user stories in silence prevents the discussion from being dominated by more assertive personalities. Several people noted that they found the silence a very positive aspect. They found they could safely think and express their opinions on user story size without fear of rebuttal.

5.6 Its Fun

Many people commented that it was a fun technique. Actually getting up and moving around and physically moving cards or notes on the wall made people feel more connected to the sizing. The video recordings of the Silent Grouping sessions attest to this. Laughter can be heard and seen in all of the recordings.

6 Conclusions

Relative Sizing is a powerful technique for sizing user stories using 'user story points'. Planning Poker is a useful, fun and effective method of sizing user stories using relative sizing. A significant advantage of Planning Poker is the group discussion that occurs. Everyone on the team gets an opportunity to understand the user story details. A downside with Planning Poker is that it can take a long time. Some factors that lead to it taking a long time can include a tendency for teams to get stuck in protracted discussion. Using Planning Poker at the start of user story sizing, and then applying Silent Grouping for the majority of the backlog is an effective way of using the both techniques together.

References

1. Cohn, M.: User stories applied: for agile software development. Addison-Wesley, Boston (2004)
2. Cohn, M.: Succeeding with agile: software development using Scrum. Addison-Wesley, Upper Saddle River (2010)
3. Schwaber, K., Beedle, M.: Agile software development with Scrum. Prentice Hall, Upper Saddle River (2002)
4. Beck, K., Andres, C.: Extreme programming explained: embrace change. Addison-Wesley, Boston (2005)
5. Cohn, M.: Agile estimating and planning. Prentice Hall PTR, London: Pearson Education [distributor], Upper Saddle River(2005)
6. Tabaka, J.: Collaboration explained: facilitation skills for software project leaders. Addison-Wesley, Upper Saddle River (2006)
7. McConnell, S.: Software estimation: demystifying the black art. Microsoft Press, Redmond (2006)

Supporting Self-organizing Agile Teams
What's Senior Management Got to Do with It?

Rashina Hoda, James Noble, and Stuart Marshall

Victoria University of Wellington,
New Zealand
{rashina,kjx,stuart}@ecs.vuw.ac.nz
http://www.ecs.vuw.ac.nz

Abstract. Self-organizing Agile teams need a supportive environment to emerge and flourish. Through a Grounded Theory study of 58 Agile practitioners across 23 different software organizations in New Zealand and India, we found that senior management support is a critical environmental factor influencing self-organizing Agile teams. We describe the influence of senior management, and show how their support can create and sustain a supportive environment for self-organizing Agile teams.

Keywords: Agile Software Development, Self-Organizing Teams, Senior Management, Organizational Culture, Grounded Theory.

1 Introduction

The importance of senior management support in the adoption and use of Agile methods has been widely acknowlegded [5, 10, 14, 15, 22, 34]. Senior management has been found to influence organizational culture, which in turn influences the adoption of Agile methods in an organization [43, 46]. There is, however, little empirical evidence across multiple organizations, cultures, and countries to show how exactly senior managemment influences and supports self-organizing Agile teams in practice. Our research establishes senior management support as a critical environmental factor influencing self-organizing Agile teams and explains how senior management influences and supports such teams.

In this paper, we present the results of a Grounded Theory study involving 58 Agile practitioners from 23 different software development organizations in New Zealand and India conducted over a period of 4 years. Our study revealed that senior management support is a critical environmental factor influencing self-organizing Agile teams. We describe how senior management within organizations influences self-organizing Agile teams and how their support can enable self-organization in Agile teams. The rest of the paper is structured as follows: section 2 presents a brief background on self-organizing Agile teams and the role of senior management. Section 3 describes our research method. Section 4 presents the results of the study that describe the influence of senior management on self-organizing Agile teams. Section 5 discusses our findings in light of related work. Section 6 describes limitations of our study, followed by the conclusion in section 6.

A. Sillitti et al. (Eds.): XP 2011, LNBIP 77, pp. 73–87, 2011.

2   Background

Self-organizing teams are at the heart of Agile software development [10, 12, 24, 32, 39, 41]. Self-organizing teams are considered the source of the best architecture, requirements, and design [24]. Self-organization is one of the principles behind the Agile Manifesto and has been identified as one of the critical success factors of Agile projects [4, 10, 24]. While Scrum specifically mentions self-organizing Agile teams, the concept of *"empowered"* teams has only recently been added to XP [48].

Agile teams are meant to be democratic teams—where all members are considered peers at the same level, without a strict hierarchy. Team members are empowered with collective decision making and cross-functional skills, which increases their ability to self-organize [34]. Self-organizing Agile teams are described as teams composed of *"individuals [that] manage their own workload, shift work among themselves based on need and best fit, and participate in team decision making"* [23]. Self-organizing teams must have a common focus, mutual trust, respect, and the ability to organize repeatedly to meet new challenges [12]. Sutherland, a co-creator of Scrum, explains that self-organizing teams consist of *"members with diverse backgrounds"* who are *"given a free hand"* by the top management [44].

Self-organizing Agile teams are not leaderless, uncontrolled teams [12, 45]. Leadership in self-organizing teams is meant to be light-touch and adaptive, providing feedback and subtle direction [3, 4, 9, 45]. Management in Agile teams is meant to be more facilitative and co-ordinating [34]. Leaders of Agile teams are responsible for setting direction, aligning people, obtaining resources, and motivating the teams [3].

Cockburn et al. point out that while the success of any process is largely dependent on the people, the ability of the people to achieve their goals is dependent on the level of support they receive from users, customers, and management [12]. They argue that Agile organizations practice *"leadership-collaboration"* instead of command and control style management, and that management in Agile organizations trust their teams to deliver to their best potential. They suggest that Agile teams function best in an organizational culture that supports people and collaborations.

In keeping with the Grounded Theory research method, related literature on the role of senior management is discussed in light of the results towards the end of the paper.

3   Research Method

Grounded Theory (GT) is the systematic generation of theory from data analyzed by a rigorous research method [17, 19]. GT was developed by sociologists Glaser and Strauss [20]. We chose GT as our research method for several reasons. Firstly, Agile methods focus on people and interactions and GT, used as a qualitative research method, allows us to study social interactions and behaviour. Secondly, GT is most suited to areas of research which have not been explored in great detail before, and the research literature on Agile team-customer relationships is scarce [21]. Finally, GT is being increasingly used to study Agile teams [11, 13, 31, 47]. Following Glaser's guidelines, we started out with a general area of interest — Agile project management — rather than beginning with a specific research problem [13].

3.1 Data Collection

We interviewed 58 Agile practitioners from 23 different software development organizations over 3 years from New Zealand and India. Figure 3 shows the participants and project details. In order to respect their confidentiality, we refer to the participants by numbers P1 to P58. All the teams were using Agile methods, primarily combinations of Scrum and eXtreme Programming (XP) — two of the most popular Agile methods today [5,36,40]. The teams practiced Agile practices such as iterative development, daily stand-ups, release and iteration planning, test driven-development (TDD), continuous integration and others. Participants' organizations offered products and services such as web-based applications, front and back-office applications, and local and off-shored software development services. Table 1 shows the participants and projects details.

The level of Agile experience varied across the different teams. While some teams had under a year of experience, others had been practicing Agile for over 5 years. The Indian teams were mostly catering to off-shored customers in Europe and USA, while

Table 1. Participants and Projects (P#: Participant Number, Position: Agile Coach (AC), Agile Trainer (AT), Developer (Dev), Customer Rep (Cust Rep), Business Analyst (BA), Senior Management (SM); *Organizational Size: XS < 50, S < 500, M < 5000, L < 50,000, XL > 100,000 employees)

P#	Positions	Method	Org. Size*	Location	Domain	Team Size	Project (months)	Iteration (weeks)
P1-P9	Dev x 3, BA, AC x 2, AT, Tester, Cust. Rep.	Scrum	M	NZ	Health	7	9	2
P10	AC	Scrum & XP	L	NZ	Social Services	4 to 10	3 to 12	2
P11-P18	Dev x 6, AC, SM	Scrum & XP	S	NZ	Environment	4 to 6	12	1
P19	SM	Scrum & XP	S	NZ	E-commerce	4	2	4
P20	AC	Scrum & XP	XL	NZ	Telecom & Transportation	6 to 15	12	4
P21	Cust. Rep.	Scrum	XS	NZ	Entertainment	6 to 8	9	4
P22	AC	Scrum & XP	S	NZ	Government Education	4 to 9	4	2
P23	AC	Scrum & XP	XS	NZ	Software Development	8	12	1
P24-P25	Dev x 2	Scrum	XS	NZ	Software Development	8 to 10	8	2
P26	AC	Scrum & XP	S	NZ	Farming	8	12	2
P27-P35	Dev x 4, AC, Tester, Sales Manager, SM x 2	Scrum & XP	S	India	Agile Software Development & Consultancy	5	6	2
P36-P39	AC x 4	Scrum & XP	M	India	Software Development	7 to 8	3 to 6	2
P40	SM	Scrum & XP	S	India	CRM and Finance	7 to 8	ongoing	3
P41	Designer	Scrum & XP	S	India	Web-based Services	5	1	2
P42	AC	Scrum & XP	L	India	Telecom	8 to 15	3	4
P43	AT	Scrum & XP	XS	India	Agile Training	7	8	2 to 4
P44-P45	Dev x 2	Scrum & XP	XS	India	Software Development	4	1	1
P46-P53	Dev, BA x 2, AT, AC, KS, HR, SM	Scrum & XP	M	India	Agile Software Products & Consultancy	15	12	1
P54	AC	Scrum & XP	M	India	Financial Services	8 to 11	36	2
P55	AC	RUP	XS	Canada	Telecom	10 to 15	10 to 15	2 to 4
P56	SM	Scrum	M	USA	Oil and Energy	5 to 8	12	2
P57	Cust. Rep.	Scrum & XP	M	USA	CRM and Cloud Computing	variable	variable	2 to 4
P58	AC	Scrum & XP	XS	USA	Health	variable	variable	2 to 4

most of the NZ teams were catering to in-house customers, some of whom were located in separate cities. We include more details of the context in sections below as necessary.

We collected data by conducting face-to-face, semi-structured interviews with Agile practitioners using open-ended questions. The interviews were approximately an hour long and focused on the participants' experiences of working with Agile methods, in particular the challenges faced in Agile projects and the strategies used to overcome them. We also observed several Agile practices such as daily stand-up meetings (co-located and distributed), release planning, iteration planning, and demonstrations. In order to get a rounded perspective, we interviewed practitioners in various roles: Developers, Agile Coach (Scrum Master or XP Coach), Agile Trainer, Customer, Business Analyst, Tester, and Senior Management. Senior Management was typically made up of chief executive officers, vice presidents, departmental heads, and senior managers. Data collection and analysis were iterative so that the constant comparison of data helped guide future interviews, and the analysis of interviews and observations fed back into the emerging results.

3.2 Data Analysis

We used open coding to analyze the interview transcripts in detail [16, 17]. We began by collating key points from each interview transcript. Then we assigned a *code*—a phrase that summaries the key point in 2 or 3 words—to each key point [16]. The codes arising out of each interview were constantly compared against the codes from the same interview, and those from other interviews and observations. This is GT's *constant comparison method* [18, 20] which was used again to group these codes to produce a higher level of abstraction, called *concepts* in GT.

The constant comparison method was repeated on the concepts to produce another level of abstraction called a *category*. As a result of this analysis, the concepts *Organizational Culture, Negotiating Contracts, Financial Sponsorship*, and *Resource Management* gave rise to the category *Senior Management Support*.

We analyzed the observations and compared them to the concepts derived from the interviews. We found our observations did not contradict but rather supported the data provided in interviews, thereby strengthening the interview data. The use of *memoing*—theorizing write-up of ideas about codes and their relationships—was vital in recording the relationships between codes [17]. The conceptual *sorting* of memos was done to derive an outline of the emergent theory, showing relationships between concepts.

3.3 Generating a Theory

The final step of GT is generating a theory, also known as *theoretical coding*. Theoretical coding involves conceptualizing how the categories (and their properties) relate to each other as a hypotheses to be integrated into a theory [17]. Following Glaser's recommendation, we employed theoretical coding at the later stages of analysis [18], rather than a coding paradigm from the beginning as advocated by Strauss [42].

Our research has led to a grounded theory of self-organizing Agile teams [28,30]. The theory of self-organizing Agile teams explains how software development teams take on one or more informal, implicit, transient, and spontaneous *roles* and perform balanced *practices* while facing critical environmental *factors*. These roles include *Mentor, Coordinator, Translator, Champion, Promoter*, and *Terminator* [28]. The practices involve balancing freedom and responsibility, cross-functionality and specialization, and continuous learning and iteration pressure [27]. The factors are senior management support and level of customer involvement [25,26,29]. Different aspects of the theory including roles, practices, and level of customer involvement as an environmental factor has been described elsewhere [25, 26, 27, 28, 29].

In the following sections, we describe senior management support—a critical environmental factor influencing self-organizing Agile teams. We have selected quotations drawn from our interviews that shed particular light on the concepts. Due to space reasons we cannot describe *all* the underlying key points, codes, and concepts from our interviews and observation that further ground the discussion.

4   Senior Management Influence and Support

A majority of the participants described how self-organizing Agile teams are greatly influenced by the senior management at their own organizations [28].

> "*..the organizations I see getting the most benefit from Scrum, from Agile, are organizations where senior management really gets it! Where senior management has been has been through training...Senior management took the time to read, learn about Agile. The least successful Agile adoptions are ones where senior management has no interest in Agile, they have no interest in what Agile is.*" — P43, Scrum Trainer, India

Senior management influences organizational culture, the types of contracts governing projects, financial sponsorhip, and resource management. A senior management that does not support self-organizing Agile teams causes several challenges for the team in each of these areas.

4.1   Organizational Culture

Organizational culture has been defined as "*a standard set of basic suppositions invented, discovered or developed by the group when learning to face problems of external adaptation and internal integration*" [38]. Organizational culture has a strong influence on the ability of an Agile team to be self-organizing.

Traditional software development teams typically adopt strictly hierarchical organization structures. Self-organizing Agile teams on the other hand, require organization structures that are informal in practice, where the boundaries of hierarchy do not prohibit free flow of information and feedback. In an informal organizational structure, the senior management is directly accessible by all employees (maintaining an 'open-doors' policy), and accepts feedback—both positive and negative.

Agile organizations, where all the teams operate using Agile software development, are characterized by informal organizational structures. Informality in organizational structure promotes openness. Openness was one of the most common traits mentioned by participants that made the organizational culture condusive for Agile teams. In such organizations, team members are free to voice opinions, raise concerns, seek management support in resolving their concerns, make collaborative decisions, and adapt to changes in their environment. This freedom provided by senior management is crucial for the team to achieve and sustain autonomy [28].

> *"don't expect that you're going to be in any other traditional hierarchical company...no matter if its 4 years or three years [of experience], they [team] can walk up to [CEO's name] and say 'this what you did, is bullshit' (laughs) and [CEO's name] will say 'oh, ok fine, let's discuss what happened'. So people have that freedom to voice their opinion very clearly. At the same time people will [give] feedback to you."* — P52, Human Resource Manager, India

Starting with an informal structure has a cascading effect. Informality in the organizational structure leads to openness marked by free-flow of communication and feedback, which in turn leads to an organizational culture of trust. An organizational culture where teams trust their senior management to support them, and when senior management trusts the teams to perform and display responsibility, makes fertile grounds for self-organization to emerge.

> *"one of the big things that's made a difference there, is they already had an* **environment of trust**. *There was no fear in the organisation. You often see a level of fearfulness in very bureaucratic organisations, people are not prepared to give people—to give bad news, you know, the automatic punishment for being the bearer of bad news. I didn't see any of that at [company name], the level of confidence, the level of trust between management and the people on the ground was quite high already. So I think the ground was fertile for Agile...And that was because of the management attitude and the supportive nature of the managers."* — P26, Agile Coach, New Zealand

In contrast, an organization with a strict hierarchical structure is not condusive to self-organizing Agile teams. A common example is that of a government sector organization, with a strict hierarchical structure. The software development teams in such organizations form one of the lowest levels of hierarchy, topped by middle management, and then senior management. Such hierarchical structure is often coupled with heavy-weight processes requiring substantial documentaion, long change management processes, and slow software delivery and deployment processes. Such a culture retricts both team's ability to practice light-weight Agile methods, and their ability to self-organize.

A strict hierarchical structure also has a cascading effect. The hierarchy in such an organization enforces a lack of openness marked by restricted and indirect lines of communication and feedback, which in turn leads to an environment of fear. Teams are afraid of voicing opinions, raising concerns, making collaborative decisions, and adapting to changes in their environment:

> *"...government business drivers are not 'time to market' or producing anything useful...the documentation is definitely more important than actual working software. They are not impressed at all by demos and working software—they almost didn't care! 'Why don't they have a big upfront design document?' It*

basically took me ages to basically force them to accept vertical slicing of that. I think its a fear of giving up control. Control doesn't exist, but they are afraid to give it up ... I was the PM on that project, they are still working on it, I went away screaming!" — P23, Agile Coach, NZ

On the other hand, some government sector organizations find that their culture, while seemingly different, can be receptive to changes brought on by Agile methods.

"It's interesting because it's [Agile] probably a much better fit [to our culture] than you might think. On one hand [in] our organization...part of the culture is that people do tend to work in isolation...But because it's very scientifically oriented there's quite an openness to sharing ideas and information as well...once they [in-house customers] were exposed to the Agile development group and they were sitting in the room with them and the whiteboard and things, they became very open and very communicative. They would have never have volunteered that or expected that, but once they had people around them that were used to operating that way they were very open to that. So it fit quite well is what I'm saying, it fit pretty well." — P18, Senior Management, NZ

Senior management support, in terms of providing freedom and establishing an organizational culture of trust, is therefore extremely important for self-organizing Agile to establish and flourish. A senior management that supports self-organizing Agile teams will (a) maintain an informal structure, (b) provide freedom for teams to provide feedback, and (c) create an organizational culture of trust.

4.2 Negotiating Contracts

Self-organizing Agile teams are influenced by the type of contracts that govern their projects. Senior management—either directly in smaller organizations, or through their sales department in larger organizations—is responsible for negotiating contracts with customers. A customer can demand a fixed-bid contract where the cost, time, and scope of the project are fixed up-front. If senior management accepts the customer's demand for a fixed-bid contract, it has far-reaching consequences for the self-organizing Agile team. Teams find that *"fixed price doesn't work well with Agile"* because *"Agile talks about embracing change [and] can't do fixed price projects with changes coming in"* (P42, P27).

The process of fixing the cost, time, and scope of the project in a fixed-bid contract involves estimating the project. Senior management that does not support self-organizing Agile teams, fixes the cost, time, and scope based estimates provided by managers, rather than the teams. As a result the team is placed under pressure to deliver to often unrealistic estimates. The negative consequences of a fixed-bid contract in an Agile project are captured in the following comment by an Agile trainer and coach who worked several with Indian organizations:

"The whole premise of the fixed-bid contract is that requirements will be fixed. The nature of software development is that requirements are inherently unstable and so when you are entering into contract negotiation, you are dealing with the recognition that the requirements will be unstable...Biggest source

of dysfunction is not actually from the customer—the greater source of dys-function comes from within the organization where the contract—fixed bid contract—is negotiated by the sales team, it is negotiated for the smallest amount of money possible. And so the team from day one is under pressure to over-commit and under-deliver and that I see again and again and again!"
— P43, Agile Trainer, India

In contrast, senior management that is aware of the negative consequences of fixed-bid contracts on the teams better supports self-organizing Agile teams for example, they provide customers with options such as offering an iteration on a trial basis, swapping features, the flexibility to buy more iterations or terminate the contract with an itera-tion's notice. For example, an Indian senior manager encouraged customers to buy a few iterations, instead of signing one contract for a large project:

"Most of the time...[we] sell a certain number of iterations." — P34, Senior Management, India

By allowing the customers to use Agile development on a trial basis, Agile practitioners are able to build confidence among customers and provide them with risk coverage. Once the customers have tried a few iterations, then they are offered the option to buy more iterations or features as needed:

"One thing we [development firm] used to do and worked very well—we used to tell the customers you don't have any risks...in case of Agile we enter into a contract with the client—OK we'll show you working software every fifteen days, you'll have the option of ending the project within one sprint's notice. Maximum they can lose is one sprint. Advantage we show to client they don't have to make up their entire mind. . . [they] can include changes in sprints -they see it as a huge benefit to them." — P27, Developer, India

Some Agile practitioners allow the customers to swap features. The project is delivered at the same time and price as initially specified in the contract, but the customer can remove product features that they no longer require and replace them with new ones (requiring approximately equivalent effort) that are of more business value to them:

". . . customer after seeing demo after fourth iteration realizes the features built, say the thirteenth feature, is not required and he needs something else. . . he can swap the two." — P27, Developer, India

By providing the customers with the option to quit the project in the worst case scenario, their financial risks are covered. If the customers are unhappy with the results, they could always quit the project.

If a customer is still insistent on a fixed-bid contract, senior management can support a self-organizing Agile team by inviting the team to estimate their projects. Based on the rate of development per iteration—the team velocity—the team can estimate the time required for developing a particular set of requirements in a given domain. Then some amount of extra time could be added to the estimated time as a buffer. The contract is then drawn on this estimated time (including buffer) for a fixed price and scope.

"Agile will not ask you in how much time will you [need to] complete the project...but [the customer will]. Sometimes you've got to map internal Agile practices to customer practices....Actually it comes from a lot of experience on Agile. When you know that okay this is generally the velocity of the team that the team is able to do within the given domain, the given complexity and then you make some rough estimates, including some buffer. [Customer says] 'okay I want these features, tell me the time'. so then we'll make prediction based on Agile data that this is the team size, this is the velocity, we assume the team won't change then the Agile burndown chart will say let's say 2 weeks so we'll say okay another 2 days of buffer, so 2 weeks ands 2 days, something like that." — P28, Developer, India

A small amount of buffer time was important to allow the customer the possibility of introducing changes in requirements along the way, while giving the development team time to respond to those changes. Buffering was a practical strategy of working with a fixed-bid contract while using Agile methods.

Finally, senior management in Agile organizations are very careful about negotiating contracts that are *"Agile-friendly"*. They frequently have a specialized sales team that understand Agile methods and the consequences of the contract on the self-organizing Agile teams.

"In the sales room, even the way we work is Agile. We have two groups, one for marketing, one for sales. We have stages for each teams—we use kind of post-its and put them up. So even our sales is Agile." — P33, Sales Manager, India

Senior management that supports self-organizing Agile teams will (a) try to convince customers to try flexible contract options, (b) engage the team in providing estimates for the fixed-bid contract, along with adding a contingency buffer, or (c) negotiate *"Agile friendly"* contracts.

4.3   Financial Sponsorship

Self-organizing Agile teams need financial sponsorship from their senior management in the form Agile training and an infrastructure that's supportive of self-organizing practices. The team needs senior management support in order to benefit from the presence of a *Mentor* in the form of an Agile Coach [28]. The Agile Coach is often a contracting consultant, hired specifically to train a new team on Agile principles, values, and practices. In other cases, an existing project manager in the organization may take up the *Mentor* role. The senior management provides financial support by either hiring contracting Agile Coaches or sponsoring these managers, and occasionally other team members, to receive Agile training (e.g. a Scrum Master Certification).

Financial support is also required in the form of infrastructure support, such as setting up an open-plan workplace and tools for electronic communication and collaboration with distant customers. A supportive senior management champions the cause of self-organizing Agile teams and provides financial support for such an infrastructure.

"In most organizations I'd say skype would be blocked. They [senior management in non-Agile organizations] say we do chat or call their friends abroad and waste time but here in [this organization], skype is there on every machine because the management knows that it is an important communication tool...So yeah definitely the change in the mindset of the organization has to be there. For example, they [senior management] have provided LCD TVs within the rooms and there are a lot of skype meeting rooms which have LCD TVs, camera, and you have skype installed. If I stand up, you actually go through those moves and you can see the customer and they can see us, so like that. Again there is that initiative from the senior management because they might as well say that 'okay do it on your own machine or we cannot provide LCD TVs for every team!' So that drive has to come from them definitely." — P29, Developer, India

"...level of sponsorship means...the senior manager...say 'This is the methodology we are adopting. I expect you to change your practices and techniques to support that, and here's some money to do so...here's some time, here's some resources." — P7, Agile Coach, NZ

Senior management that supports self-organizing Agile teams is willing to make such financial investments as (a) hiring a *Mentor* for new teams or providing existing Project Managers with Agile training and (b) providing the infrastructure necessary for effective functioning of the self-organizing Agile teams.

4.4   Human Resource Management

An important role of senior management is the way they manage human resources. For self-organizing Agile teams, dedicated teams are highly desired. When team members are allocated to multiple projects, it has a negative influence on the teams' ability to perform and self-organize. One of the main characteristics of self-organizing Agile teams is high levels of cohesion and collaboration within the team. The team's ability to self-organize is dependent on understanding each others' strengths and weaknesses and forming a team culture of openness and respect. It takes time for a team to learn about each other and self-organize based on members' individual abilities.

"What I think affected our project...[the developer] was working on another project, he didn't have enough time, so he didn't have the space to chat with anybody, to discuss ideas with anybody, to work with anybody, so he was really just on his own, and I think that really impacted a lot of the work he did in the last few months ... When you're working in a team like this [Agile team] and you've got to work quite closely, the individuals in the team matter." — P21, Customer Rep, NZ

If the members are split across multiple projects, it affects their ability to perform group programming that enables self-organization. Senior management that does not realize the implications of their resource management can have a negative influence on the team:

"[explaining how resource management works]...resource-assignment, right...If I am VP (vice president)...for me, resource is a pure mathematical figure. 0.25 is

2 hours. if I divide, make the equation work, I'll be happy! Ground reality is different. People can't work 0.25! One side as a VP I want to get business, I have to do equations: 0.5 from here, 0.5 from here etc and make it 3...pure mathematics...not feasible in ground reality...People have to be mature enough...[its] just a matter of understanding the ground reality: if they [senior management] are a developer how would they react to the situation?" — P39, Agile Coach, India

On the other hand, supportive senior management values their teams and respects their human side as much, if not more, than their technical skills:

"...I personally feel it's one of those companies where does a lot for the people. They [senior management] definitely understand people, values, and you know, they understand their emotions...so we do respect people and you know if they [team] have any concerns or worries we [company] will try to understand it." — P52, Human Resource Manager, India

Resource management in terms of the hiring process and removal of individuals from teams is also influenced by senior management. In Agile organizations where senior management supports self-organizing Agile teams, their Human Resources departments are set up specifically to hire people that are likely to fit into Agile teams.

Sometimes, team members need to be removed from an Agile team because of their inability to fit into the culture. One of the team members typically takes on a *Terminator* role and seeks senior management support in removing such individuals [28].

Senior management supports self-organizing Agile teams through managing resources by (a) providing dedicated resources to projects, (b) hiring individuals to fit into an Agile culture, and (c) removing individuals who threaten self-organizing teams with the help of a *Terminator*.

5   Discussion and Related Work

Senior management influences the organizational structure and culture in an organization [34]. The importance of senior management support in the form of a condusive organizational culture has been widely acknowledged [5,22,14,15,34,10,43,46]. Agile methods challenge conventional management ideas, and require changes in organization structure, culture, and management practices in traditional software development organizations [15,34]. Changing mindsets and cultures, however, is no trivial task [8].

Beck highlights the influence of organizational culture on the use of Agile methods and argues that an environment of isolation, timidity, and secrecy will cause challenges [6]. Our research supports the claim that an environment of openness, communication, and trust is imperative for self-organizing Agile teams. The influence of senior management in creating and maintaining such an environment is extremely important.

A study of the influence of organizational culture on Agile method use found correlations between certain aspects of organizational culture and the use of Agile practices [43]. In particular, the study found that organizations that value collaboration, feedback, learning, and empowerment of people are better suited to support Agile methods. Our findings support these claims, as well as the conclusion that hierarchically structured organizations are not well suited to Agile methods. Management in Agile teams is meant to be facilitative and collaborative [34,43]. Empowerment and collective decision making in Agile teams are seen to increase their ability to self-organize [34]. Similarly, our research shows that these aspects of organizational culture have a strong influence on the self-organizing ability of Agile teams.

Tolfo and Wazlawick studied the influence of organizational culture on the adoption of XP [46]. Their study concludes that while XP generally assumes the existence of a condusive environment for XP teams, such an organizational culture is not always present in software organizations. In particular, the level of autonomy an organization provides to its members was found to be an important ingredient of a condusive organizational culture. Our findings supports this claim and link senior management support to self-organizing teams.

Most studies that have explored the influence of senior management support and organizational culture have focussed on XP teams [37,46]. Studies exploring the influence of organizational culture on Scrum teams, however, are limited. In a Scrum-based study, Moe et al. found that the management did not provide an environment conducive to self-organization that led to reduced external autonomy [33]. Our research found that self-organizing Agile teams (practicing Scrum or combinations of Scrum and XP) require a condusive organizational culture marked by freedom, openness, trust, and an informal organizational structure. In contrast, an organization with a hierarchical organizational structure and an environment of restricted, formal, and indirect communication restricts the teams' ability to self-organize.

In a paper on introducing lean principles with Agile practices in a Fortune 500 company, Parnell-Klabo described various difficulties in securing a buy-in for a pilot project [35]. Some of these included obtaining facility space for collocation, gaining executive support, and influencing the change curve.

Several attributes of Agile methods are well aligned with senior management's business drivers discussed in this chapter. For example, fast delivery and rapid response to changes in business and technology are key attributes of Agile methods [1, 5, 7, 24]. It would appear then that convincing senior management to support self-organizing Agile teams would be an easy task. However, this is not always the case. Organizations don't change for the sake of change, they change when they see benefit from it.

A single case-study of adopting XP at a diverse, multidisciplinary web-development environment at IBM highlights the existence of skepticism amongst senior management regarding Agile nomenclature [22]. For example, the use of the XP term "*planning game*" was not well received by senior executives who preferred more formal-sounding terms like "*planning process*". Our participants shared experiences of facing skepticism when trying to secure senior management support. Our findings suggest that convincing senior management not only requires that a team member takes on the role of a *Champion*, but also that they understand senior management's business drivers [28]. These business drivers include applicability of Agile methods to project context, time-to-market, customer demands, and process improvement. In other words, senior management does not undertake drastic changes in their organizations without a strong incentive. Understanding the business drivers particular to different organizations and their senior management is critical for a *Champion* advocating the introduction and continued support for self-organizing Agile teams.

Most of the above studies have explored the influence of management support on the adoption and use of Agile methods. Our findings show the influence of senior management support on self-organizing Agile teams in particular, and highlight strategies used by teams to secure such support, in an effort to achieve and sustain self-organization.

6   Limitations

Since the codes, concepts, and category emerged directly from the data, which in turn was collected directly from real world, the results are grounded in the context of the data [2]. We do not claim the results to be universally applicable: rather, they accurately characterize the context studied [2]. Our choice of research destinations and participants were limited in some ways by our access to them.

7   Conclusion

We conducted a Grounded Theory study, involving 58 Agile practitioners from 23 different software development organizations in New Zealand and India, over a period of 4 years. The results establish senior management support as a critical environmental factor influencing self-organizing Agile teams.

In this paper, we have described the importance of senior management in supporting self-organizing Agile teams. Senior management influences self-organizing teams through organizational culture, negotiating contracts, financial sponsorship, and resource management. Senior management supports self-organizing Agile teams by creating and maintaining an open and informal organizational culture, negotiating "*Agile-friendly*" contracts, providing financial sponsorship, and managing human resources in a way that supports self-organization. In contrast, senior management that does not manage these factors effectively causes challenges for a self-organizing teams at best and disables self-organization in Agile teams at worst. Future studies could explore other ways in which senior management may influence and support self-organizing Agile teams in other cultures.

Acknowledgments.   Our thanks to all the participants. This research is supported by a BuildIT PhD scholarship (NZ), an Agile Alliance academic grant (USA).

References

1. Abrahamsson, P., Warsta, J., Siponen, M.T., Ronkainen, J.: New directions on agile methods: a comparative analysis. In: Proceedings of 25th International Conference on Software Engineering, pp. 244–254 (2003)
2. Adolph, S., Hall, W., Kruchten, P.: A methodological leg to stand on: lessons learned using grounded theory to study software development. In: CASCON 2008, pp. 166–178. ACM, New York (2008)
3. Anderson, L., Alleman, G.B., Beck, K., Blotner, J., Cunningham, W., Poppendieck, M., Wirfs-Brock, R.: Agile management - an oxymoron?: who needs managers anyway? In: OOPSLA 2003, pp. 275–277. ACM, New York (2003)

4. Augustine, S.: Managing Agile Projects. Prentice Hall PTR, Upper Saddle River (2005)
5. Beck, K.: Extreme Programming Explained: Embrace Change, 1st edn. Addison-Wesley Professional, Reading (1999)
6. Beck, K., Andres, C.: Extreme Programming Explained: Embrace Change, 2nd edn. Addison-Wesley Professional, Reading (2004)
7. Boehm, B.: Get ready for agile methods, with care. Computer 35(1), 64–69 (2002)
8. Boehm, B.W., Turner, R.: Rebalancing your organization's agility and discipline. In: XP/Agile Universe, pp. 1–8 (2003)
9. Chau, T., Maurer, F.: Knowledge sharing in agile software teams. In: Lenski, W. (ed.) Logic Versus Approximation. LNCS, vol. 3075, pp. 173–183. Springer, Heidelberg (2004)
10. Chow, T., Cao, D.: A survey study of critical success factors in agile software projects. J. Syst. Softw. 81(6), 961–971 (2008)
11. Cockburn, A.: People and Methodologies in Software Development. PhD thesis, University of Oslo, Norway (2003)
12. Cockburn, A., Highsmith, J.: Agile software development: The people factor. Computer 34(11), 131–133 (2001)
13. Coleman, G., O'Connor, R.: Using grounded theory to understand software process improvement: A study of Irish software product companies. Inf. Softw. Technol. 49(6), 654–667 (2007)
14. Coram, M., Bohner, S.: The impact of agile methods on software project management, pp. 363–370 (2005)
15. Dybå, T., Dingsoyr, T.: Empirical studies of Agile software development: A systematic review. Inf. Softw. Technol. 50(9-10), 833–859 (2008)
16. Georgieva, S., Allan, G.: Best practices in project management through a grounded theory lens. Electronic Journal of Business Research Methods (2008)
17. Glaser, B.: Theoretical Sensitivity: Advances in the Methodology of Grounded Theory. Sociology Press, Mill Valley (1978)
18. Glaser, B.: Basics of Grounded Theory Analysis: Emergence vs Forcing. Sociology Press, Mill Valley (1992)
19. Glaser, B.: The Grounded Theory Perspective III: Theoretical Coding. Sociology Press, Mill Valley (2005)
20. Glaser, B., Strauss, A.L.: The Discovery of Grounded Theory. Aldine, Chicago (1967)
21. Grisham, P.S., Perry, D.E.: Customer relationships and extreme programming. In: HSSE 2005: Proceedings of the 2005 Workshop on Human and Social Factors of Software Engineering, pp. 1–6. ACM, New York (2005)
22. Grossman, F., Bergin, J., Leip, D., Merritt, S., Gotel, O.: One XP experience: introducing agile (XP) software development into a culture that is willing but not ready. In: CASCON 2004: Proceedings of the 2004 Conference of the Centre for Advanced Studies on Collaborative Research, pp. 242–254. IBM Press (2004)
23. Highsmith, J.: Agile Project Management: Creating Innovative Products. Addison-Weasley, USA (2004)
24. Highsmith, J., Fowler, M.: The Agile Manifesto. Software Development Magazine 9(8), 29–30 (2001)
25. Hoda, R., Noble, J., Marshall, S.: Negotiating Contracts for Agile Projects: A Practical Perspective. In: Abrahamsson, P., Marchesi, M., Maurer, F. (eds.) XP 2009. LNBIP, vol. 31, pp. 186–191. Springer, Heidelberg (2009)
26. Hoda, R., Noble, J., Marshall, S.: Agile Undercover: When Customers Don't Collaborate. In: Sillitti, A., Martin, A., Wang, X., Whitworth, E. (eds.) XP 2010. LNBIP, vol. 48, pp. 73–87. Springer, Heidelberg (2010)

27. Hoda, R., Noble, J., Marshall, S.: Balancing Acts: Walking the Agile Tightrope. In: Co-operative and Human Aspects of Software Engineering workshop at ICSE 2010, South Africa. ACM, New York (2010)

28. Hoda, R., Noble, J., Marshall, S.: Organizing Self-Organizing Teams. In: ICSE 2010: Proceedings of the 32nd ACM/IEEE International Conference on Software Engineering, South Africa, pp. 285–294. ACM, New York (2010)

29. Hoda, R., Noble, J., Marshall, S.: Impact of Inadequate Customer Involvement on Self-Organizing Agile Teams. Journal of Information and Software Technology (2010) (in press)

30. Hoda, R.: Self-Organizing Agile Teams: A Grounded Theory. PhD thesis, Victoria University of Wellington, Wellington, New Zealand (2010) (submitted)

31. Martin, A., Biddle, R., Noble, J.: The XP customer role: A grounded theory. In: AGILE 2009, Chicago. IEEE Computer Society, Los Alamitos (2009)

32. Martin, R.: Agile Software Development: principles, patterns, and practices. Pearson Education, NJ (2002)

33. Moe, N.B., Dingsoyr, T., Dybå, T.: Understanding self-organizing teams in agile software development. In: ASWEC 2008, Washington, pp. 76–85. IEEE, Los Alamitos (2008)

34. Nerur, S., et al.: Challenges of migrating to Agile methodologies. Commun. ACM 48(5), 72–78 (2005)

35. Parnell-Klabo, E.: Introducing Lean principles with Agile practices at a Fortune 500 company. In: AGILE 2006: Proceedings of the Conference on AGILE 2006, Washington, DC, USA, pp. 232–242. IEEE Computer Society, Los Alamitos (2006)

36. Pikkarainen, M., Haikara, J., Salo, O., Abrahamsson, P., Still, J.: The impact of agile practices on communication in software development. Empirical Softw. Engg. 13(3), 303–337 (2008)

37. Robinson, H., Sharp, H.: Organisational culture and XP: three case studies. In: Agile Development Conference/Australasian Database Conference, pp. 49–58 (2005)

38. Schein, E.H.: Organizational Culture and Leadership, 1st edn. Jossey-Bass Publishers, San Franciso (1985)

39. Schwaber, K.: Scrum guide. Scrum Alliance Resources,
http://www.scrum.org/storage/scrumguides/Scrum%20Guide.pdf
(last accessed on November 9, 2010)

40. Schwaber, K., Beedle, M.: Agile Software Development with SCRUM. Prentice-Hall, Englewood Cliffs (2002)

41. Sharp, H., Robinson, H.: An ethnographic study of XP practice. Empirical Softw. Engg. 9(4), 353–375 (2004)

42. Strauss, A., Corbin, J.: Basics of qualitative research: grounded theory procedures and techniques. Sage Publications, Newbury Park (1990)

43. Strode, D.E., Huff, S.L., Tretiakov, A.: The Impact of Organizational Culture on Agile Method Use. In: Proceedings of the 42nd Hawaii International Conference on System Sciences, Washington, DC, USA, pp. 1–9. IEEE Computer Society, Los Alamitos (2009)

44. Sutherland, J.: Roots of Scrum: Takeuchi and Self-Organizing Teams. World Wide Web electronic publication, http://jeffsutherland.com (last accessed on March 31, 2010)

45. Takeuchi, H., Nonaka, I.: The new new product development game. Hardvard Business Review 64(1), 137–146 (1986)

46. Tolfo, C., Wazlawick, R.S.: The influence of organizational culture on the adoption of extreme programming. Journal of Systems and Software 81(11), 1955–1967 (2008)

47. Whitworth, E., Biddle, R.: The social nature of Agile teams. In: Agile 2007, USA, pp. 26–36. IEEE Computer Society, Los Alamitos (2007)

48. XP: Extreme programming: A gentle introduction. World Wide Web electronic publication, http://www.extremeprogramming.org/ (last accessed on October 23, 2010)

From Manufacture to Software Development: A Comparative Review

Eduardo T. Katayama and Alfredo Goldman

Department of Computer Science, University of São Paulo
Rua do Matão, 1010
Zip 05508-090 - São Paulo - SP - Brazil
{eduardo,alfredo}@ime.usp.br

Abstract. Agile Software Development methods have caught the attention of software engineers and researchers worldwide, but scientific research on the subject still remains quite scarce. The aim of this study is to organize and facilitate future works on Agile methods derived from manufacturing industry. This comparative review is performed from the standpoint of using Abrahamsson et al.'s analytical perspectives: project management support, life-cycle coverage, type of practical guidance, adaptability in actual use, type of research objectives and existence of empirical evidence. Our results show that Agile methods derived from manufacturing industry cover various phases of the life-cycle and that most fail to provide adequate project management support. To describe the status of research on Agile methods derived from manufacturing, we conducted a literature search in the ISI Web of Science. After ten years of application empirical evidence remains quite limited.

Keywords: lean software development, theory of constraints, comparative review, agile software development.

1 Introduction

This paper describes and extends the results of a comparative review published in the recent book *Agile Software Development: Current Research and Future Directions* [1], about the performance of Agile methods from the standpoint of six different analytical perspectives. In this paper, we conducted a study on how manufacturing principles and techniques (which were not present in the original study) perform from several standpoints. As in [1], we used the following features as the analytical perspectives: project management support, life-cycle coverage, type of practical guidance, adaptability in actual use, type of research objectives and existence of empirical evidence.

The need for this kind of study comes from circustances where researchers and practitioners are not aware of all the existing approaches or their suitability for changing real-life software development situations. As for researchers, the lack of systematic knowledge hinder the ability to establish a reliable and cumulative research tradition [2].

A. Sillitti et al. (Eds.): XP 2011, LNBIP 77, pp. 88–101, 2011.
© Springer-Verlag Berlin Heidelberg 2011

We focused the study on extending the paper "Agile Software Development Methods: A Comparative Review" [1], organizing and analyzing the software methods derived from manufacturing industry that claim to be aligned with the agile principles [34,3]. Based on the results of the analysis, practitioners may be in a better position to understand the various properties of each method, and hence to choose the most appropriate method in a more informed and systematic way.

The analytic framework from Abrahamsson et al. [1] (see Table 1) is used to scrutinize and guide the review of the existing Agile methods.

Table 1. Abrahamsson et al.'s perspectives for the analysis, further references can be found at the original paper [1]

Perspective	Description
Project management support	Does the method support project management activities?
Software development life-cycle	Which stages of the software development life-cycle does the method cover?
Availability of concrete guidance for application	Does the method mainly rely on abstract principles or does it provide concrete guidance: abstract principles vs. concrete guidance?
Adaptability in actual use	Is the method argued to fit per se in all Agile development situations: universally predefined vs. situation appropriate?
Research objective	What is the method developer's research objective: critical, interpretative, means-end oriented?
Empirical evidence	Does the method have empirical support for its claims?

The remaining of the paper is organized as follows: the next section presents a short overview of the existing Agile methods derived from manufacturing industry. The third section presents a short description of the analytical perspectives from Abrahamsson et al. [1] and the rationale for them. The fourth section presents a comparative analysis of the referred methods. Finally, the fifth section concludes this study, recapitulating the key findings.

2 An Overview of Agile Methods Derived from Manufacturing Industry

Agile Software Development is an umbrella term for several software development methods that were developed from the 1990s. These methods share a common philosophy, which values and principles were described in the Manifesto for Agile Software Development [8].

There was a connection between Lean Manufacturing and Agile Software Development. From the beginning, many developers of the various Agile methods were influenced by the ideas of Lean Manufacturing [17]. Lean Manufacturing and Agile software methods have a very similar philosophy. Both place a lot of stress on adaptive planning and people-focused approach.

In the last few years, more ideas have appeared in the Agile world with a clear manufacturing heritage. The application of Lean Manufacturing principles to product development is described in Managing the Design Factory [36]. The Poppendiecks have applied Lean Manufacturing principles to software development [34, 35]. Goldratt wrote about bottleneck stations in manufacturing [19] and then, widened the discussion to constraints in general (Theory of Constraints) [21]. David Anderson applied the Theory of Constraints and queue size to software projects [4]. Cockburn have written about strategies for dealing with bottlenecks that have reached their capacities [10].

2.1 Lean Software Development

Lean Software Development is the application of Lean Thinking to the software development process. Organizations that are truly Lean[1] have a strong competitive advantage because they respond very rapidly and in a highly disciplined manner to market demand, rather than trying to predict the future.

There are seven principles of Lean Software Development, based on Lean Thinking [35]:

- *Eliminate Waste*: anything that does not add value from the customer perspective is waste. The three biggest wastes in software development are: building the wrong thing; failing to learn and thrashing, practices that interfere with the smooth flow of value;
- *Build Quality in*: minimizes the need for inspection by building quality into the product. Inspection should be used as an information-gathering device, not as a way of assuring quality or blaming workers [15];
- *Create Knowledge*: most software is not a predictable problem [27]. In [45], Ziv et al. states that uncertainty is inherent and inevitable in software development processes and products. Development is "creating a recipe" while production is "following the recipe" [34];
- *Defer Commitment*: avoids premature decisions and generates greater value. Deferring commitment means making decisions on time when enough information has been gathered to make a better informed decision. In [41], Thimbleby notice that premature design commitment is a design failure mode that restricts learning, exacerbates the impacts of defects, limits the usefulness of the product and increases the cost of changing;
- *Deliver Fast*: companies that compete for speed often have a significant advantage over theirs competitors, because they use fewer resources, deliver superior quality, have more certainty, and are more attuned to their customers needs [40];
- *Respect People*: thinking people provides the most sustainable competitive advantage. Treating employees with genuine respect means empowering the workers [37] and making everybody as a part of the team [44], engaging

---

[1] We will use the term "Lean" to refer to Lean in software development.

thinking people at every level of the organization. In [44], Bodek describes the benefit of this approach, as "Instead of waiting for management to change my job, I am now empowered to change it myself. I am empowered to do creative things at work";

– *Optimize the Whole*: Lean Thinking suggests that optimizing individual parts almost always leads to a sub-optimized overall system. A Lean organization optimizes the whole value stream, from the time it receives an order to address a customer need until software is deployed and the need is addressed.

2.2 Theory of Constraints

Goldratt's Theory of Constraints has been examined among Agile developers [11, 7, 35, 3]. Two important threads from Goldratt's writing are:

The Theory of Constraints (TOC). The Theory of Constraints [19,18] shares with other theories of organizational change the assumption that the whole organization is focused on overall throughput, not on micro-optimization [7]. The theory is based on the idea that every complex system usually have one aspect of that system that limits its ability to achieve its goal or optimal functioning. To achieve any significant improvement of the system, the constraint must be identified and resolved.

The TOC processes aim to identify the constraints and to restructure the rest of the organization around them, through the use of the Five Focusing Steps [18]:

1. Identify the constraint (the resource or policy that prevents the organization from obtaining more of the goal);
2. Decide how to exploit the constraint (get the maximum capacity out of the constrained process);
3. Subordinate all other processes to the above decision (align the whole system or organization to support the decision made above);
4. Elevate the constraint (make other major changes needed to break the constraint);
5. If, after all these steps, the constraint has moved, return to Step 1. Do not let inertia become the constraint.

According to Cockburn [11], it is not so much the simple statement of the TOC that is interesting, but all the special solutions being catalogued for different situations. As an example, he cites a case study of applying the Theory of Constraints to software development from David Anderson [6].

Critical Chain Project Management (CCPM). Critical Chain Project Management is an extension of TOC designed specifically for project environments. Goldratt claims that the traditional method of generating task time estimatives is the primary reason for increased expense of projects and their inability to finish on time.

In [20], Goldratt claims that the commonly accepted principle is to add safety to generate a task time length that will guarantee that the step gets completed. He asserts that estimatives for a task are based on individuals providing values that they feel will have 80-90% of chance to complete the step. These estimatives are further padded by managers creating an excessive safety time. However, even if things go well, the safety time will be wasted by multitasking, student syndrome [20] and parkinson's law [33].

Goldratt approach recommends that estimatives should be acknowledged as estimatives (instead of a truth) and the safety margin attached to individual estimates should be removed from the activities and accumulated in a project buffer. With this approach, individual activities will be completed much faster, and the project buffer can be spread across all activities to absorb variation.

According to Poppendieck [35], in order for Critical Chain to work, everyone must abandon the expectation that activities should be delivered within the estimated timeframe. If the team members are penalized for exceeding the time estimated, then they will double the estimates before turning it in, removing any benefit that the buffer planning method might have offered [11].

One problem with Critical Chain for software development lies in the assumption that all of the activities needed to complete development should be known in advance and that dependencies among them are understood [35]. As we have seen in Section 2.1, these assumptions are inappropriate for most software development. This does not mean that Critical Chain does not work, only that it is easy to misuse.

In the book *Agile Estimating and Planning* [12], Cohn explains in details how to use Critical Chain to do agile planning for projects that are planned far in advance with superficial understanding of requirements. Others practitioners [3, 5, 30] have been using this method as a complement to other software methods such as *Feature Driven Development* and *Incremental Development*.

3   Abrahamsson et al.'s Analytical Perspectives for the Analysis

In this section, we present a short description of the six analytical perspectives (see Table 1) proposed from Abrahamsson et al.

Methods should be efficient (as opposed to time and resource consuming) [26]. Efficiency requires the existence of *project management* activities to enable an appropriate organization and execution of software development tasks.

A *software development life-cycle* is a sequence of processes that an organization employs to conceive, design, and commercialize a software product [9, 14]. The software development life-cycle perspective is needed to observe which phases of the software development process are covered by the Agile methods under attention.

Software development methods are often used for other purposes than originally intended by theirs authors [31]. Boehm [9] concludes that the lack of concrete guidance has caused many software projects to fail. Thus, in order to evaluate how well the methods can be used for the purposes that they have been designed for, a perspective provided by the *availability of concrete guidance for application* is needed.

The perspective of *adaptability in actual use* stems from the works of Kumar and Welke [26], Malouin and Laundry [29], and Truex et al. [42]. This perspective is used for exploring how well Agile methods recognize that one ready-made solution does not fit all Agile Software Development situations, and if guidance is given on how to adapt an Agile method in different situations.

The analysis of the Agile methods in relation to their *research objective* is used for highlighting the goals of method developers while *empirical support* is needed for finding out what kind of empirical evidence the Agile methods are grounded upon.

4 Comparative Review of the Agile Methods Derived from Manufacturing Industry

In this section, we compare the existing Agile methods derived from manufacturing industry. The task of comparing any methodology with another is difficult and the result is often based upon the subjective judgement of the authors [39]. Informal comparison indicates a lack of systematic framework to guide the analysis. Quasi-formal comparison attempts to overcome the subjective limitations of the informal comparison technique by offering different strategies for composing the baseline for comparison, i.e. the analytical framework [1]. While many analytical tools have been proposed and used to carry out the quasi-formal comparison [32, 28, 24, 25]. The six analytical perspectives proposed from Abrahamsson et al [1] were seen as relevant and complementary to the research purposes of this paper. The conclusions reached in this paper were drawn from literatures studies.

Figure 1 presents the evaluation for the first three perspectives. Each method is divided into three bars. The uppermost bar indicates the provided support for project management. The middle bar indicates how well the software production process is described (pertaining to software development life-cycle analysis). The length of the bar shows which phases of software development are supported by each Agile method. Finally, the lowest bar shows if a method mainly relies on abstract principles or if it provides concrete guidance.

In general, gray color in a block indicates that the method covers the perspective analyzed while white indicates lack of support.

4.1 Project Management

Agile software development methods greatly differ from the way they cover project management. Currently, only Agile modeling and Pragmatic Programmer do not address the managerial perspective at all.

Lean Software Development provides a management philosophy together with a set of principles and practical tools that help the enterprise to maximize the

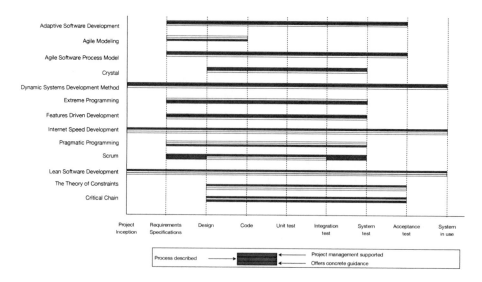

Fig. 1. Comparing project management, life-cycle, and concrete guidance support. This figure extends the material in Abrahamsson et al.'s paper [1] by adding three software development methods (Lean Software Development, The Theory of Constraints and Critical Chain).

customer value and avoid waste. The Theory of Constraints is an overall management philosophy that is geared to help organizations achieve their goals continually [18,43]. Although Lean Software Development and Theory of Constraints are not explicit about planning and managing projects, the principles can be used to provide guidance for those who are attempting to manage software development more effectively.

Critical Chain is an extension of TOC designed specifically for project environments, Goldratt considers product development to be a project. CCPM is a method from planning and managing projects that places the main emphasis on the resources required to execute project tasks, keeping the resources equally loaded while preserving them flexible in their start times to switch between tasks and task chains quickly, to keep the whole project on schedule [20].

4.2   Software Development Life-Cycle

In Figure 1, the overall length of the bar demonstrates which software development life-cycle phases are supported by the different Agile methods. Figure 1 shows that Agile methods are focused on different aspects of the software development life-cycle.

Lean Software Development is an approach that addresses all phases of the software development life-cycle. Critical Chain is used to address the tasks associated with a project, so it can cover the phases from design to acceptance tests. The Theory of Constraints have been used for different aspects in software development covering the phases from design to acceptance test [20].

4.3   Availability of Concrete Guidance for Application

The lowest bar in Figure 1 indicates whether the method relies on concrete guidance (gray color) or on abstract principles (white color).

In Lean Software Development, a set of thinking tools is provided to help identifying problem areas and discovering possible solutions. Each principle also includes a "try this" showing steps to start applying Lean at work immediately. However, since these are principles, the organizations should develop their own practices in order to add value. A concrete guidance on how this should be done is not provided, although some practices are recommended. In [34], Poppendieck & Poppendieck state that Lean Software Development "should be used to translate the seven Lean principles into agile practices that will work in your organization. Many books and articles describe alternate agile practices and techniques in some details".

The Theory of Constraints places emphasis on abstract principles over concrete guidance. Organizations should develop their practices themselves, however, concrete guidance on how this should be done is not provided. Critical Chain is a set of processes and practices for project management well-defined, offering concrete guidelines on how to manage the resources [13]. In a webcast series, Goldratt explain all the steps for implementing Critical Chain [22].

4.4   Adaptability in Actual Use

The majority of Agile software methods allow adaptability in actual use, but refrain from offering guidance on how to perform the adaptation. In Lean Software Development [35], Poppendieck & Poppendieck state that practices must take context into account, so the practices should be tailored to individual software development domains. A set of practices tools is given, enabling to select design solutions, methods, and organizational structures based on fitness for a purpose. This approach allows situation appropriate modifications. For example, regarding Lean Software Development Poppendieck & Poppendieck suggests that the principles "are not cookbook recipes for software development, but guideposts for devising appropriate practices for your environment". This implies that Lean Software Development supports appropriateness, however there are some lack of guidance on how to perform tailoring and adaptation during the development.

The Theory of Constraints allows adaptability in actual use. However, there are a lack of guidance on how to perform tailoring and adaption during the development. Although some tools help the adaptation, a study conducted by Sirias [38] shows that when a heterogeneous group was posed with the same problem and the same tools, they come up with different solutions.

Critical Chain explicitly provides criteria on how to implement the methodology for a project. In the Critical Chain Project Management (CCPM) Webcast [22], a detailed roadmap is presented helping to create a specific strategy and tactics for achieving the goal [22]. Thus, the adjustment is made by choosing a set of "universal solutions" that fits the environment.

4.5   Primary Research Objectives

The principal research objective of Agile software methods developers is means-end oriented. Their primary goal is to provide technical solutions for the practitioners in the field.

The research objective of Lean Software Development is both means-end oriented and emancipatory. This means-end oriented research objective can be observed in a simple statement by Poppendieck & Poppendieck [35]: "our objective is to help organizations get started down the path toward more effective software development". Lean Software Development also makes an attempt to show why the Agile practices work and how Lean ideas should be adapted to development organization.

The research objective by Goldratt [19, 20] is both means-end oriented and interpretative. The Theory of Constraints and Critical Chain are geared to help organizations achieve their goal continually, with a set of pragmatic methods based on the experience of applying the TOC concepts on projects. Goldratt reveals his interpretative research objective when trying to identify the constraint and restructure the rest of the organization around it, through the use of the thinking tools [23].

4.6   Empirical Evidence

The development of Agile Software Development approaches is not based on systematic research [16]. The only meta-analysis performed up-to-date in the area is done by Dybå and Dingsøyr, in which the authors perform a systematic review of empirical studies in Agile Software Development. They conclude that the field is still nascent and the quality of the research falls evidently short [16].

To describe the status of empirical research on Lean Software Development and Theory of Constraints, we conducted a literature search in the ISI Web of Science[2]. We found 70 scientific publications regarding Lean Software Development and Theory of Constraints, published between 1997 and 2010.

During the literature review stage, we noticed that most of the citations to it were unrelated to the topic on which our research was focused. Since the number of publications were high, we needed to identify the more relevant and concentrate our review on them. This motivated us to classify the references according to their purpose. A given publication was not considered if it satisfied any one of the following criteria:

- The link to the work was broken;
- The work corresponds to the title of a panel, workshop or a tutorial;
- The work is not related to software development.

---

[2] Search conducted on 22 November 2010, using the terms "lean AND software AND development" and "theory AND of AND constraints AND software AND development" as topics for subject areas computer science: software engineering, theory and methods and information systems. Document types proceeding paper, review or article. Databases: SCI-EXPANDED, SSCI, A&HCI, CPCI-S, CPCI-SSH.

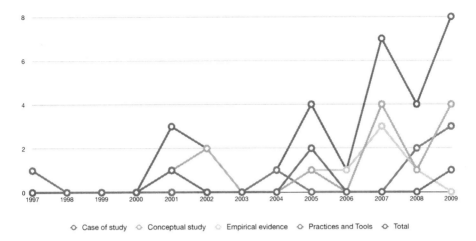

Fig. 2. Publications on Theory of Constraints and Lean Software Development

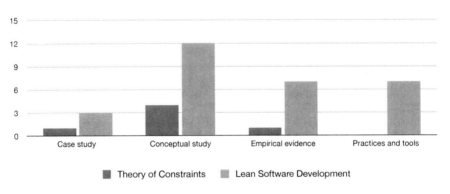

Fig. 3. Publications on Theory of Constraints and Lean Software Development in 2010. Note that all publications from 2010 have not been indexed at the time of the search.

Each publication was assigned to one of the following categories:

- *Case study*: an empirical inquiry that investigates a phenomenon within its real-life context;
- *Empirical evidence*: a direct observation or experience to describe or explain phenomena;
- *Tools and practices*: a study that investigate tools and practices;
- *Concept study*: a subjective study, depending on the observer, that includes producing ideas and taking into account the pros and cons of implementing it.

As all publications from 2010 have not been indexed at the time of the search, we decided to split the trend in publications for case study, empirical evidence, tools and practices, conceptual study and the total in two figures. Figure 2 illustrates the trend in publications between 1997 and 2009. Figure 3 shows the

Table 2. Total number of publications per categories

	Case study	Conceptual study	Empirical evidence	Practices and Tools
Lean Software Development	3	12	5	6
Theory of Constraints	1	4	0	0

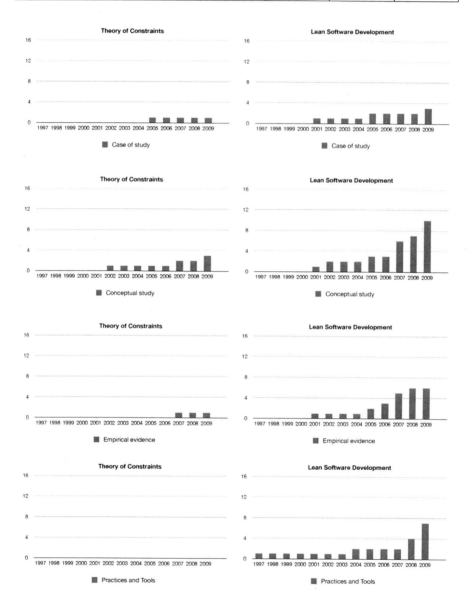

Fig. 4. Cumulative sum charts of publications on agile methods derived from manufacturing industry

number of publications per categories in 2010. There seems to be a growth in the number of publications in total. Table 2 shows the total number of publications for each category. Figure 4 shows a graphical representation of Table 2.

Experiences from the usage of Lean Software Development and Theory of Constraints can be identified mostly in commercial settings. Although these studies and reports provide necessary insight into the possibilities and restrictions of Lean Software Development and Theory of Constraints, concrete data is more difficult to find. The existing empirical studies are mostly focused on Lean Software Development.

The results of analysis confirm the initial conjecture. The existing empirical studies from Agile Software engineering derived from manufacturing are still scarce.

5   Conclusion

The principles and methods of Agile Software Development derived from manufacturing industry have given rise to a substantial amount of debate and academic works. However, academic research on the subject still remains with short supply. The existing works in this field have come mainly from practitioners. The aim of this study has been to provide a systematic approach of the Agile methods derived from manufacturing industry. The existing methods were reviewed from Abrahamsson et al.'s perspective to determine the current situation.

Above all, it was found that the Agile methods derived from manufacturing industry (without emphasizing the process through which software development proceeds) cover various phases of the software life-cycle. The majority of them do not present adequate support for project management, and only Critical Chain offered concrete guidance to support its solutions or adaptations in different development situations. While the method developer's research objective has been predominantly means-end oriented (technical), related empirical evidence to date is very limited.

References

1. Abrahamsson, P., Oza, N., Siponen, M.: Agile Software Development Methods: A Comparative Review. In: Agile Software Development: Current Research and Future Directions, 1st edn., pp. 31–58. Springer, Heidelberg (2010)
2. Abrahamsson, P., Warsta, J., Siponen, T., Ronkainen, J.: New directions on agile methods: a comparative analysis. In: Proceedings of the 25th International Conference on Software Engineering, pp. 244–254. IEEE Computer Society, Los Alamitos (2003)
3. Anderson, D.: Agile Management for Software Engineering: Applying the Theory of Constraints for Business Results. Prentice Hall, Englewood Cliffs (2003)
4. Anderson, D.: Managing lean software development with cumulative flow diagrams. In: BorCon 2004, white paper (2004), http://conferences.embarcadero.com/jp/article/32096

5. Anderson, D.: Scheduling ui design with critical chain project management (2004), http://www.agilemanagement.net/Articles/Papers/Scheduling_UI_Design_v1_5.pdf
6. Anderson, D., Dumitriu, D.: From worst to best in 9 months - implementing drum-buffer-rope in microsoft's it department. In: Proceedings of the TOCICO Conference, TOCICO 2005, Barcelona (2005)
7. Beck, K., Andres, C.: Extreme Programming Explained: Embrace Change, 2nd edn. Addison-Wesley Professional, Reading (2004)
8. Beck, K., Beedle, M., van Bennekum, A., Cockburn, A., Cunningham, W., Fowler, M., Grenning, J., Highsmith, J., Hunt, A., Jeffries, R., Kern, J., Marick, B., Martin, R., Mallor, S., Schwaber, K., Sutherland, J.: The Agile Manifesto. Technical report, The Agile Alliance (2001), http://www.agilemanifesto.org
9. Boehm, B.: A spiral model of software development and enhancement. SIGSOFT Softw. Eng. Notes 11, 14–24 (1986)
10. Cockburn, A.: Two case studies motivating efficiency as a "spendable" quantity. In: ICAM 2005 International Conference on Agility (2005)
11. Cockburn, A.: Agile Software Development: The Cooperative Game. Addison-Wesley Professional, Reading (2006)
12. Cohn, M.: Agile Estimating and Planning. Prentice Hall PTR, Englewood Cliffs (2005)
13. Cox III, J., Schleier, J.: Theory of Constraints Handbook. McGraw-Hill Professional, New York (2010)
14. Cugola, G., Ghezzi, C.: Software processes: a retrospective and a path to the future. Software Process Improvement and Practice 4, 101–123 (1998)
15. Deming, W.E.: Out of the Crisis. The MIT Press, Cambridge (2000)
16. Dybå, T., Dingsøyrr, T.: Empirical studies of agile software development: A systematic review. In: Information and Software Technology (2008)
17. Fowler, M.: Agileversuslean (2008), http://martinfowler.com/bliki/AgileVersusLean.html
18. Goldratt, E.: Theory of Constraints, Illustrated edn. North River Press (1990)
19. Goldratt, E.: The Goal, Illustrated edn. North River Press (1992)
20. Goldratt, E.: Critical Chain, Illustrated edn. North River Press (1997)
21. Goldratt, E.: What is This Thing Called the Theory of Constraints. North River Press (1999)
22. Goldratt, E.: Critical chain project management (ccpm) webcast (2008)
23. Goldratt, E.: Standing on the shoulders of giants. Goldratt Consulting White Paper (2008)
24. Hirscheim, R.: Information systems epistemology: An historical perspective. In: Research Methods in Information Systems. Elsevier Science Publisher, Amsterdam
25. Iivari, J., Hirschheim, R.: Analyzing information systems development a comparison and analysis of eight is development approaches. Information Systems (1996)
26. Kumar, K., Welke, J.: Methodology Engineering: a proposal for situation-specific methodology construction, pp. 257–269. John Wiley & Sons, Inc., Chichester (1992)
27. Larman, C.: Agile and Iterative Development: A Manager's Guide. Addison-Wesley Professional, Reading (2003)
28. Lyytinen, K.: A taxonomic perspective of information systems development: theoretical constructs and recommendations. John Wiley & Sons, Inc., Chichester (1987)
29. Malouin, J., Landry, M.: The miracle of universal methods in systems design. Journal of Applied System Analysis 10, 47–62 (1983)

30. Miranda, E.: Combining critical chain planning and incremental development in software project (2004), `http://www.featuredrivendevelopment.com/files/PmiCriticalIncremental.pdf`
31. Nandhakumar, J., Avision, J.: The fiction of methodology development: a filed study of information system development. Information Technology & People 12(2), 176–191 (1999)
32. Olle, T., Sol, H., Verrijn-Stuart, A.: Information systems design methodologies: A comparative review. North-Holland, Amsterdam (1982)
33. Parkinson, C.N.: Parkinson's Law. Buccaneer Books (1993)
34. Poppendieck, M., Poppendieck, T.: Lean Software Development: An Agile Toolkit. Addison-Wesley Professional, Reading (2003)
35. Poppendieck, M., Poppendieck, T.: Implementing Lean Software Development: From Concept to Cash. Addison-Wesley Professional, Reading (2006)
36. Reinertsen, D.: Managing the Design Factory: A Product Developers Tool Kit. Simon & Schuster Ltd., New York (1998)
37. Simons, R.: Designing high-performance jobs. Harvard Business Review (2005)
38. Sirias, D.: Writing mis mini-cases to enhance cooperative learning: A theory of constraints approach. Journal of Information Systems Education (2002)
39. Song, X., Osterweil, L.J.: Comparing design methodologies through process modeling. In: 1st International Conference on Software Process. IEEE Computer Society, Los Alamitos (1991)
40. Spear, S.: Chasing the Rabbit: How Market Leaders Outdistance the Competition and How Great Companies Can Catch Up and Win, 1st edn. McGraw-Hill, New York (2008)
41. Thimbleby, H.: Delaying commitment. IEEE Computer Society Press 5, 78–86 (1988)
42. Truex, D.P., Baskerville, R., Travis, J.: A methodological systems development: The deferred meaning of systems development methods. In: Accounting, Management and Information Technology (2001)
43. Watson, K.J., Blackstone, J.H., Gardiner, S.C.: The evolution of a management philosophy: The theory of constraints. Journal of Operations Management 25, 387–402 (2007)
44. Zak, A.: Respect for people (2008), `http://leanconnections.com/lean-management-articles/respect-for-people`
45. Ziv, H., Richardson, D.J., Klösch, R.: The uncertainty principle in software engineering (1996), `http://www.ics.uci.edu/~ziv/papers/icse97.ps`

Effective Communication in Distributed Agile Software Development Teams

Siva Dorairaj, James Noble, and Petra Malik

School of Engineering and Computer Science,
Victoria University of Wellington,
Wellington, New Zealand
{siva.dorairaj,james.noble,petra.malik}@ecs.vuw.ac.nz

Abstract. Agile methods prefer team members to be collocated to promote effective communication between team members. Effective communication is crucial for distributed Agile software development where team members are scattered across different geographic locations, and often across several time zones. We are conducting in a Grounded Theory study that explores distributed Agile software development from the perspective of Agile practitioners. We present the causes of communication challenges, and the strategies adopted by our participants to overcome communication challenges in distributed Agile teams.

Keywords: Agile Methods, Grounded Theory, Distributed Software Development, Communication.

1   Introduction

Effective communication is important for software development teams to facilitate knowledge transfer rapidly between team members, to allow team members to understand the requirements from clients, and to help team members perform development activities efficiently [1, 2]. Realising the benefits of effective communication, Agile methods prefer team members to be collocated to promote effective communication through frequent interactions between team members. [3]. Moreover, one of the 12 principles behind the Agile Manifesto asserts that face-to-face conversation is the most efficient and effective method of conveying information to and within a development team [4]. Several studies, however, indicate that communication is the main challenge for distributed software development where team members are scattered across different geographic locations, and often across several time zones [1, 5, 6, 7, 8].

In this paper we present the findings of an ongoing Grounded Theory study that explores distributed Agile software development from the perspective of Agile practitioners. This study involved 18 Agile practitioners from 10 different software companies in the USA and India. We analyse the causes of communication challenges, and present the practical strategies adopted by

A. Sillitti et al. (Eds.): XP 2011, LNBIP 77, pp. 102–116, 2011.

Agile practitioners to overcome the communication challenges in distributed Agile software development.

The rest of the paper is structured as follows: section 2 describes the research method, data collection and data analysis; sections 3 describes the context of the study; sections 4 and 5 present the results of the study; section 6 describes several related work; section 7 describes limitations of our study, followed by conclusion in section 8.

2   Research Method

Grounded Theory (GT) is an inductive research method originally developed by Barney G. Glaser and Anslem L. Strauss [9]. The Grounded Theory Institute [10] defines GT as *"the systematic generation of theory from systematic research"*. GT emphasises the generation of a *grounded theory* regarding an area of interest. The term *"grounded theory"* refers to a theory that is developed inductively from a corpus of data. GT researchers gather data, particularly qualitative data from interviews and observations, and systematically discover a theory derived directly from the data.

We chose GT as our research method for several reasons. Firstly, GT is suitable to be used in areas that are under-explored or where a new perspective might be beneficial [11], and the literature on distributed Agile software development is scarce [5, 12]. Secondly, GT allows researchers to study social interactions and behaviour of people in the context of solving problems [9], and Agile methods focus on people and their interactions in the teams. Thirdly, GT is increasingly being used successfully to study the social nature of Agile teams [13, 14, 15]. GT allows a theory to emerge from systematic analysis of qualitative data from practitioners of Agile software development.

A GT research project begins with a general area of interest, and not with specific research questions, because defining research questions leads to a preconceived conceptual description [16]. This does not mean that there is no specific problem for the research, but rather the problem and its concerns will emerge in the initial stages of data analysis. [16, 17]. Using Glaser's approach, we started out our research with a general area of interest — distributed Agile software development. As we progressed through data collection and data analysis, several concerns have emerged. We investigated further on several concerns, and reported our findings [18, 19]. Further progress in data analysis gave rise to the research questions: "What are the causes of communication challenges in distributed Agile teams?", and "What are the strategies adopted by Agile practitioners to overcome communication challenges faced by the distributed teams?". We continued data collection by focusing on our research questions. Grounded Theory gives us the capability to answer these questions. In order to maintain consistency in the application of Grounded Theory, all data was collected and analysed personally by the primary researcher.

2.1   Data Collection

Our data collection technique was interviewing the Agile practitioners. We wanted to acquire our participant's experience in regard to distributed Agile software development. Initially, we emailed the Agile practitioners informing them about our research and gain their consent for an interview. We then scheduled the interviews for an hour at a mutually agreed location. We conducted face-to-face, one-on-one interviews with our participants using open-ended questions. Face-to-face interviews provided us with the opportunity not only to gather verbal information but also to observe the body language of the participants during the conversations. The interviews were voice-recorded with the consent from the participants. Although Glaser [16] advises against recording interviews, we find it convenient to maintain a record of interviews, and to analyse the data at ease.

We had prepared an interview guide with a set of guiding questions. We commenced the interview by asking the participants about their experience, and their roles and responsibilities in the distributed Agile projects. We asked the participants to highlight the challenges they faced in distributed Agile projects, and the strategies adopted by their team to manage their projects effectively. We phrased our questions cautiously so that the issues in distributed Agile software development would emerge from the participants rather than from our own agenda. The ongoing analysis during the interview reveals participant's concerns. We gradually focused our attention on these concerns rather than our prepared questions.

2.2   Data Analysis

Data collection and data analysis occurs simultaneously in a GT study. We avoided collecting all the data during a specific data collection phase, and then analysing them in a subsequent data analysis phase. Rather, we analysed interviews during and after each interview. The key concerns that emerged from the ongoing data analysis enabled adjustments to the inquiry by including these concerns in subsequent interviews. The developing theory guided the future interviews, and the choice of future participants. Voice recording the interviews helped us to concentrate on the conversation and conduct continuous analysis during the interview.

We transcribed each interview and reviewed the transcripts line-by-line to explore the meaning in the data by searching for similarities and differences. We collated key points from the data and assigned a *code*, a summary phrase, to each key point. This is the *coding* [9] process that involves categorisation, interpretation and analysis of the data. As we identified codes, we constantly compared each code with the codes from the same interview, and those from other interviews. This is called the *constant comparison method* [20]. The codes that related to a common theme were grouped together to produce a second level of abstractions called a *concept*. As we continuously compare the codes, many fresh concepts emerge. These concepts were analysed using constant comparison to produce a third level of abstractions called a *category*.

As a result of the analysis, the concepts *Time Zone Factor, Lack of Communication Tools, Language Barriers,* and *Lack of Teamwork* gave rise to the category *Lack of Effective Communication.*

Another set of concepts uncovered from the analysis were *Reducing Time Zone Factor, Leveraging Communication Tools and Techniques, Addressing Language Barriers, Developing Trusted Relationships, Increasing Effective Formal Communication,* and *Increasing Effective Informal Communication.* From these concepts, the category *Increasing Effective Communication* had emerged.

2.3   The Emergence of Theory

The ongoing study requires the data collection and data analysis to be continued until *theoretical saturation* [9] is attained – that is when no more new concepts or categories emerge from the data. We will continuously write-up memos on the ideas about the codes, concepts and categories, and their inter-relationships with one another. Glaser [16] describes that this *theoretical memoing* is the "core stage" of a Grounded Theory study. The collection of the theoretical memos developed during the data analysis helps to generate the theory. *Sorting* the theoretical memos is an "essential step" carried out to help formulate the theory [21]. These sorted memos are then weaved together to explicate the research phenomenon. This explication is called a *grounded theory* — a theory that is truly grounded in the data. The grounded theory generated from the sorted memos richly explicates the research phenomenon, and exhibits a strong connections between the concepts and categories [21, 17].

3   Context

We interviewed 18 Agile practitioners from 10 different software organisations in the USA and India to which we had access. All the participants we interviewed have adopted Agile methods, primarily Scrum and XP, in their distributed software development projects. All the participants have at least 4 years of experience in distributed Agile software development projects. Moreover, all the participants have experience in collocated Agile projects prior to their involvement in the distributed Agile projects. In order to acquire a comprehensive understanding of the concerns in distributed Agile software development, we had interviewed participants from a range of different roles within the distributed Agile projects. In particular, we interviewed Scrum Masters, Agile Coaches, Developers, Application Testers, and Business Analysts.

Table 1 shows the summary of the distributed Agile projects investigated in our study. The project distribution varied from 2 to 3 countries, the project durations varied from 6 to 24 months, and the team size varied from 8 to 22 people on different projects. Due to privacy and ethical consideration, we will only identify the distributed Agile software development projects using the codes C1 to C14, and our participants using the codes P1 to P18.

Table 1. Summary of Distributed Agile Projects. (Agile Role: Developer(Dev), Agile Coach(AC), Scrum Master (SM), Application Tester (AT), Business Analyst(BA)).

Project (code)	Participant (code)	Agile Role	Project Distribution	Agile Method	Team Size	Project Duration (months)
C1	P1	Dev	USA-India	Scrum	8 to 10	10
C2	P2	AC	USA-India	Scrum & XP	12 to 14	12
C3	P3	SM	USA-Western Europe-India	Scrum	10	8
C4	P4	AC	USA-China	Scrum & XP	10	8
C5	P5	AC	USA-India	Scrum & XP	8	12
C6	P6	Dev	USA-UK	Scrum & XP	20 to 22	8
C7	P7	AC	USA-Argentina-India	Scrum	18	6
C8	P8	Dev	USA-Australia-India	Scrum & XP	9 to 10	8
C9	P9	Dev	Brazil-Western Europe	Scrum & Lean	14	24
C10	P10	SM	USA-Argentina-India	Scrum	10 to 12	8
C11	P11	SM	USA-Middle East-India	Scrum & XP	13	10
C12	P12	Dev	USA-India	Scrum & XP	12	18
C12	P13	Dev	USA-India	Scrum & XP	12	18
C12	P14	Dev	USA-India	Scrum & XP	12	18
C13	P15	AT	USA-India	Scrum & XP	16	18
C13	P16	SM	USA-India	Scrum & XP	16	18
C13	P17	Dev	USA-India	Scrum & XP	16	18
C14	P18	BA	UK-India	Scrum & XP	8	12

4   Causes of Lack of Effective Communication

In this section, we describe the causes of the communication challenges in distributed Agile software development derived from the concepts *Time Zone, Lack of Communication Tools, Language Barriers*, and *Lack of Teamwork* that gave rise to the category *Lack of Effective Communication*. We present selected quotations drawn from our interviews that lead us to the emergence of the category *Lack of Effective Communication*.

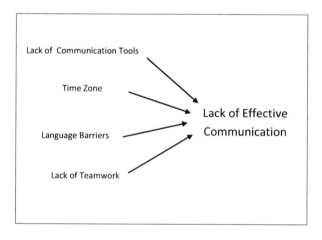

Fig. 1. Emergence of category *Lack of Effective Communication*

Figure 1 shows the concepts that gave rise to the category *Lack of Effective Communication.*

4.1   Time Zone

Due to difference in time zones, communication between the globally distributed development team members is difficult:

> *"We are in central time zone; we were off by 12 hours. We were holding up our daily calls."* —P1, Developer.

> *"The time difference between west coast [of the USA and India] is 12.5 hours. Communication among [distributed] team members can be so difficult."* —P16, Scrum Master.

Time zone differences provides minimum communication opportunity to distributed team members:

> *"They are doing the calls in the morning when the India folks are at home. Those India QC folks are going to have only 45 minutes communication with the USA folks onshore."* —P1, Developer.

Scheduling group meetings outside normal working hours can be difficult during certain time of the year:

> *"In the winter it was very hard to have meetings outside office hours because of shorter time [overlaps]."* —P9, Developer.

Time zone difficulties are common is many distributed Agile projects because the client companies are frequently located in developed countries (e.g the USA, or the UK), and the offshore teams are located in developing countries (e.g. India, or Latin America).

4.2   Lack of Communication Tools

Distributed Agile projects may suffer if the distributed teams do not have suitable communication tools:

> *"And this [distributed] project failed because we did not have the right tools in place. We did not have any video conference. We should have used more video or voice instead of written communication."* —P9, Developer.

Appropriate communication tools are important to help the team communicate effectively:

> *"It is much harder [to communicate] in a group meeting using the phone. So [the team] should use Web based conferencing."* —P6, Developer.

Ideally, teams should have access to different communication tools and use them as necessary.

4.3   Language Barriers

Agile practitioners whose native language is not English often face language barriers when communicating in English with team members:

> "*Meetings were [conducted] in English, [but] English was not the main language for everyone.*" —P7, Agile Coach.

> "*[There] were four developers, [and] only one had a good [command of] English.*" —P9, Developer.

Language barriers can exist even among the Agile practitioners who have good command of English:

> "*When [the Indian team members] speak English, they would try to speak faster than what is comfortable for them because their understanding is that Americans talk fast and they too talk fast.*"—P1, Developer.

Language barriers can limit communication in the team:

> "*The meeting was longer [than usual], and because of that [language barrier], they did not talk much. Some people took a long time to think the idea and express [it] properly in English.*" —P7, Agile Coach.

Language barriers are common in many distributed Agile projects because a particular language (often English) is used to communicate between distributed Agile teams although part of the team are not native speakers of that language.

4.4   Lack of Teamwork

All team members should ideally communicate with all other team members, and not just with several selected people in a team:

> "*Our only communication that time was with the software architect, and that was not enough. We did not have direct communication with the rest of the team.*" —P9, Developer.

Overall communication is affected when some team members do not wish to contribute to the team's effort to communicate to each other:

> "*Most people would be like "Leave me alone! I do not want to be known." That was a big challenge for us because our [distributed] team needed visibility, [and] we needed everyone to communicate in the team.*" —P8, Developer.

> "*In the current project, the Indian folks haven't even been engaged on the [phone] calls.*" —P1, Developer.

All the team members should understand the importance of teamwork in a distributed software development, and contribute to the entire team's effort to promote effective communication.

5   Strategies for Increasing Effective Communication

In this section, we describe the strategies adopted by our participants to overcome the challenges faced by distributed Agile teams. These strategies are derived from the concepts *Reducing Time Zone, Leveraging Communication Tools and Techniques, Addressing Language Barriers, Developing Trusted Relationships, Increasing Effective Formal Communication*, and *Increasing Effective Informal Communication that gave rise to the category Increasing Effective Communication. We present selected quotations drawn from our interviews that had lead us to the emergence of the category Increasing Effective Communication.*

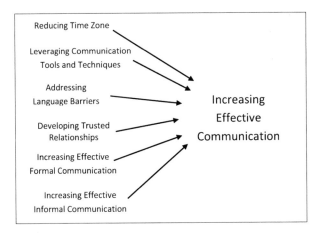

Fig. 2. Emergence of category *Increasing Effective Communication*

Figure 2 shows the concepts that gave rise to the category *Increasing Effective Communication*.

5.1   Reducing Time Zone

Our participants realise that team members should be ideally distributed between countries that have smaller time difference to minimise communication difficulty:

> *"The best way is to have the whole team in the same time zone instead of splitting these teams across different time zones. The time zone is painful!"* —P5, Agile Coach.

> *"It is always better that [the teams] are closer together, in terms of physical distance and also in time difference. It would be ideal to work with people from the same time zone."* —P4, Agile Coach.

Agile methods prefer teams to be collocated. If the Agile teams are distributed, the time zone should be ideally reduced to minimise communication difficulties.

5.2   Leveraging Communication Tools and Techniques

Our practitioners realise that face-to-face communication is the best way to communicate effectively. Distributed teams should be ideally provided with video, voice or text communication options to address the communication challenges faced in distributed software development:

> *"Face-to-face communication is still the best! Team members [need to] leverage tools to the best extend to increase the communication. Teams that are across geographical boundaries use tools like instant messaging, email, video conferencing, web-based backlog management tools."* —P5, Agile Coach.

In a distributed team, face-to-face meetings are expensive and difficult to schedule. Video-conferencing is often used as an alternative technique to capture the visual aspect of communication, such as body language, allowing the team to communicate effectively:

> *"When we started using video conferencing, we found the visual aspect in communication is so important that we encourage teams to, at least once or twice a month, have video conferencing."* —P1, Developer.

The distributed team should be ideally ready to use different tools and techniques at the spur of the moment. Writing or drawing on a board and combining video communication can increase communication for distributed teams:

> *"When we start to get into intense discussion, we often go into Skype. As I am talking, I will be writing and drawing [on the board]. They can hear it and read at the same time. You get the web-cam to point to the whiteboard and say, "Look, this is what I mean!" "* —P3, Scrum Master.

Our participants (P1, P2, P3, P4, P5, P6, P9) explain that leveraging communication tools and techniques promoted effective communication in their distributed teams.

5.3   Addressing Language Barriers

Agile practitioners can address the language barriers by consciously speaking in a manner that promotes clear communication:

> *"We tell [the Indian team] to speak slowly and deliberately. Their English is much better and communication got much better."* —P1, Developer.

> *"When we are having an audio conference, and if someone's accent is different, we may not be able to understand everything. So, we try to talk slower than usual."* —P14, Developer.

Prior to a scheduled meeting, the onsite and offshore team members should casually discuss about the matters that will be brought up in the meeting. This will give them the opportunity to express themselves clearly, and team members can understand each other well during the meeting:

"Before we have the daily Scrum meetings, the offshore team sends an email answering basic Scrum questions - what did I do yesterday, what am I going to do today, what are my problems and impediments - so that they can have it in writing [before the meeting]." —P3, Scrum Master.

Our participants (P1, P3, P7, P9, P14) realise that the concerns arising from language barriers must be addresed as early as possible to improve effective communication and to build good relationships in the distributed teams.

5.4   Developing Trusted Relationships

Our participants describe that developing team relationships is important to communicate effectively with the team members in distributed software development:

"The key to that [effective communication] was good [team] relationships. It is [about] building [team] relationships and rapport with the people before you get distributed to different countries. You have to learn to make friends with people that you are working with." —P11, Scrum Master.

When team members have developed trusted relationships, it is much easier for the team to communicate with each other:

"By having enough trust, you know [that] you are not going to offend somebody in some manner while having discussions." —P1, Developer.

Trusted relationship helps the distributed team members to interact with people in the teams:

"If you do not know someone, you blame him, but if you know him, you try to understand what he does. Knowing the people [in the team] helps me to talk to people, [and] interact with people." —P9, Developer.

Trust provides a significant bond in team relationships. Our participants find that the distributed team members interact and communicate frequently once the trusted relationships have been developed.

5.5   Increasing Effective Formal Communication

Formal communication includes official meetings during inceptions, formal weekly meetings and daily standups, and specification documents from clients. The customer and development team should ideally meet face-to-face during an inception phase to discuss the project goals, and gain commitment from the team to produce value to the project:

"One really ideal time [to communicate] is during inception. It is very critical to have the whole team there [at inception] because that is where the shared understanding of the entire project is established. That is so critical to the success of the project. An inception is useful for the product owner to crystallise their idea in front of the team, in collaboration with the team." —P2, Agile Coach.

Due to budget constraints, sometimes only the key stakeholders attend the inception meeting to discuss the significant business and requirements risks which must be addressed before the project kickoff. The outcome of the meeting should be clearly explained to the rest of the team.

> "*When we had the inception, we met up with the client and talked about the goal of the project, and their vision, [and] what is the scope. When I came back, I helped to rap up the team, and give knowledge about the analysis of the inception.*" —P11, Scrum Master.

Daily stand-up meetings between distributed team members are important because these meetings help the team to respond quickly to the changes in the project:

> "*I have seen so many dysfunctional stand-up meetings and the reason is always that there are people in the stand up meeting sharing information that is not meaningful for others. So the important thing is that the information is valuable for everyone on that daily meetings. They have to be aware [that] information is important.*" —P4, Agile Coach.

Team members should realise that it is possible to get quick responses from the stakeholders during stand-up meetings. Team members should prepare to communicate effectively during the stand-up meetings:

> "*During the stand-up, all the client party will be there, and that will be the best time for me [to ask questions]. They may discuss among themselves and respond. I'll prepare the most important question to ask in stand-ups. I feel this is more effective than emails.*" —P15, Application Tester.

> "*People [in the team] can communicate with each other at any point of time either through phone or video. We would have two daily stand-ups because it helps people to talk.*" —P8, Developer.

Our participants (P1, P2, P4, P8, P11, P15) feel that team members should communicate effectively during all scheduled meetings.

5.6   Increasing Effective Informal Communication

Informal communication includes face-to-face conversation, casual communication through video-conferencing or telephone, written communication through email, online chat and short message service (SMS) which are not formally scheduled by the teams. Informal communication can increase knowledge transfer between people in the distributed teams and build trust.

Our participant realise that effective informal communication helps to develop a strong team:

> "*... the first 15 minutes [of video conferencing] was open time and you could talk about anything you want. And, that is when we started seeing a very strong team building and that became probably the strongest thing we did as far as building team.*" —P1, Developer.

Casual conversations amongst team members helps to increase understanding of their software development project:

> *"Teams that are motivated to make it [distributed software development] work, can use all the means of communication. They often casually talk on phone to know things better."* —P6, Developer.

Informal communication does not occur frequently when team members are distributed mainly due to time zone difference and language barriers. Team that deliberately create the opportunity to communicate casually are able to develop strong teams.

6   Related Work

Paasivaara and Lassenius [12] discuss potential challenges in adopting Agile methods in globally distributed software development. The researchers recognise that the application of Agile methods to globally distributed software development poses severe communication challenges. In our study, we found that distributed Agile teams were facing communication challenges due to lack of communication tools, time zone, language barriers, and lack of team work.

Vax and Michaud [22] describe the potential challenges in distributed software development such as the inability to meet face-to-face on daily basis, language and cultural barriers, and lack of trust. The researchers explain that adopting Agile methods to distributed projects can be challenging but by constructing the right team with the right skills and expertise, and effectively leveraging tools and techniques, the teams can acquire tremendous benefits in terms of scalability, productivity, cost management, risk reduction and improved software quality. The researchers address the challenges derived from distributed teams by building trust, developing effective communication plan, sharing electronic workspace, reducing time zones and conducting frequent retrospective.

Young and Terashima [23] recognise that having distributed Agile teams present many challenges that slowed down software development processes. The researchers describe the strategies adopted by distributed Agile teams to overcome time zones problems and cultures differences. In order to deliver successful software releases, the distributed teams deliberately made conscious efforts to improve communication, built strong working relationships amongst the distributed team members, and ensured that the software architecture was suitable for all teams. In our study, we found that our participants overcome communication challenges by reducing time zones, leveraging communication tools and techniques, addressing language barriers, developing trusted relationships, and increasing formal and informal communication in distributed Agile teams.

Korkala and Abrahamsson [5] recognise that distributed software development is increasingly becoming important for software companies. The researchers explain that distributed software development is already burdened with several challenges, and Agile methods bring further challenges in the form of their reliance on informal communication and volatile requirements. The researchers describe that the high volatile requirements in Agile software development are managed through effective communication. In our study, we found that increasing effective communication helps to resolve communication challenges in distributed Agile teams.

7 Limitation

An inherent limitation of doing Grounded Theory study is that the findings are grounded in the specific contexts explored in the research. These contexts were dictated by our choice of research destination which was limited to 10 software development projects the USA and India. We do not claim that our findings are generally applicable to all distributed Agile software development projects, but rather our findings accurately characterize the contexts studied [24].

8 Conclusion

Our research explored distributed Agile software development from the perspective of the Agile practitioners. We interviewed 18 Agile practitioners from 10 different software organisations in the USA and India. The results of our Grounded Theory study reveal that distributed Agile teams face communication challenges caused by the time zone, lack of communication tools, language barriers, and lack of teamwork. The participants adopted several practical strategies to overcome communication challenges in distributed Agile software development by reducing time zone, leveraging communication tools and techniques, addressing language barriers, developing trusted relationships, increasing formal communication, and increasing informal communication. Participants found the strategies to be largely useful and effective in their own contexts. Future studies could explore the viability of these strategies in different contexts such as with distributed teams from other countries and cultures.

Acknowledgments. Thanks are due to all Agile practitioners who participated in this research. This research is supported by Universiti Tenaga Nasional (Malaysia) PhD scholarship.

References

1. Herbsleb, J.D., Mockus, A.: An empirical study of speed and communication in globally distributed software development. IEEE Transactions on Software Engineering 29(6), 481–494 (2003)
2. Pikkarainen, M., Haikara, J., Salo, O., Abrahamsson, P., Still, J.: The impact of Agile practices on communication in software development. Empirical Software Engineering 13, 303–337 (2008)
3. Cockburn, A.: Agile Software Development. Addison-Wesley, Indianapolis (2002)

4. Beck, K., Beedle, M., van Bennekum, A., Cockburn, A., Cunningham, W., Fowler, M., Grenning, J., Highsmith, J., Hunt, A., Jeffries, R., Kern, J., Marick, B., Martin, R.C., Mellor, S., Schwaber, K., Sutherland, J., Thomas, D.: Manifesto for Agile Software Development, http://www.agilemanifesto.org/principles.html (last accessed on February 16, 2011)
5. Korkala, M., Abrahamsson, P.: Communication in distributed Agile development: A case study. In: 33rd EUROMICRO Conference on Software Engineering and Advanced Applications, pp. 203–210 (2007)
6. Korkala, M., Pikkarainen, M., Conboy, K.: Distributed agile development: A case study of customer communication challenges. In: Abrahamsson, P., Marchesi, M., Maurer, F. (eds.) XP 2009. LNBIP, vol. 31, pp. 161–167. Springer, Heidelberg (2009)
7. Mockus, A., Herbsleb, J.D.: Challenges of global software development. In: Proceedings of the Seventh International Software Metrics Symposium, pp. 182–184 (2001)
8. Prikladnicki, R., Audy, J.L.N., Damian, D., de Oliveira, T.C.: Distributed software development: Practices and challenges in different business strategies of offshoring and onshoring. In: International Conference on Global Software Engineering, pp. 262–274 (2007)
9. Glaser, B.G., Strauss, A.L.: The Discovery of Grounded Theory: Strategies for Qualitative Research. Sociology Press, Aldine (1967)
10. Phine, J.: Grounded Theory Institute. The Grounded Theory methodology of Barney G. Glaser, http://www.groundedtheory.com (last accessed on February 16, 2011)
11. Schreiber, R.S., Stern, P.N.: Using Grounded Theory in Nursing. Springer Publishing, Broadway (2001)
12. Paasivaara, M., Lassenius, C.: Could global software development benefit from Agile methods? In: Proceedings of the IEEE International Conference on Global Software Engineering, pp. 109–113. IEEE Computer Society, Washington, DC (2006)
13. Hoda, R., Noble, J., Marshall, S.: Balancing acts: Walking the Agile tightrope. In: Proceedings of the 2010 ICSE Workshop on Cooperative and Human Aspects of Software Engineering, pp. 5–12. ACM, New York (2010)
14. Martin, A., Biddle, R., Noble, J.: The XP customer team: A grounded theory. In: Proceedings of the AGILE, pp. 57–64 (2009)
15. Whitworth, E., Biddle, R.: The social nature of Agile teams. In: Proceedings of the AGILE, pp. 26–36. IEEE Computer Society, Washington, DC (2007)
16. Glaser, B.: Doing Grounded Theory: Issues and Discussions. Sociology Press, Mill Valley (1998)
17. Glaser, B.: Basics of Grounded Theory Analysis: Emergence vs Forcing. Sociology Press, Mill Valley (1992)
18. Dorairaj, S., Noble, J., Malik, P.: Understanding the importance of trust in distributed agile projects: A practical perspective. In: Sillitti, A., Martin, A., Wang, X., Whitworth, E. (eds.) XP 2010. LNBIP, vol. 48, pp. 172–177. Springer, Heidelberg (2010)
19. Dorairaj, S., Noble, J., Malik, P.: Bridging cultural differences: A grounded theory perspective. In: Proceedings of the 4th India Software Engineering Conference, Thiruvananthapuram, Kerala, India (2011) (to be published)
20. Glaser, B.G.: The constant comparative method of qualitative analysis. Social Problems 12(4), 436–445 (1965)

21. Glaser, B.: Theoritical Sensitivity: Advances in Methodology of Grounded Theory. Sociology Press, Mill Valley (1978)
22. Vax, M., Michaud, S.: Distributed Agile: Growing a practice together. In: Proceedings of the AGILE, pp. 310–314. IEEE Computer Society, Los Alamitos (2008)
23. Young, C., Terashima, H.: How did we adapt Agile processes to our distributed development? In: Proceedings of the AGILE, pp. 304–309. IEEE Computer Society, Los Alamitos (2008)
24. Adolph, S., Hall, W., Kruchten, P.: A methodological leg to stand on: Lessons learned using grounded theory to study software development. In: Proceedings of the 2008 Conference of the Center for Advanced Studies on Collaborative Research, pp. 166–178. ACM, New York (2008)

Simulating Kanban and Scrum vs. Waterfall with System Dynamics

Luisanna Cocco, Katiuscia Mannaro, Giulio Concas, and Michele Marchesi

University of Cagliari, DIEE - Dipartimento di Ingegneria Elettrica ed Elettronica,
Piazza D'Armi, 09123 Cagliari, Italy
{luisanna.cocco,mannaro,concas,michele}@diee.unica.it

Abstract. Nowadays, Scrum is the most used Agile Methodology, while the Lean-Kanban approach is perhaps the fastest growing AM. On the other hand, traditional, waterfall-like approaches are still very used in real-life software projects, due to the ease of up-front planning and budgeting, that however are seldom matched upon project completion. In our opinion, more effort is needed to study and model the inner structure and behavior of these approaches, highlighting positive and negative feedback loops that are strategic to understand their features, and to decide on their adoption. In this paper we analyze the dynamic behavior of the adoption of Kanban and Scrum, versus a traditional software development process such as the Waterfall approach. We use a system dynamics model, based on the relationships between system variables, to assess the relative benefits of the studied approaches. The model is simulated using a commercial tool. The proposed model visualizes the relationships among these software development processes, and can be used to study their relative advantages and disadvantages.

Keywords: System Dynamics, Modeling, Simulation, Waterfall, Scrum, Kanban.

1 Introduction

Scrum and Lean-Kanban have been proposed as two possible different solutions to quickly respond to changing customer requirements, without compromising the quality of the code. Scrum is presently the most used Agile Methodology (AM) [1], while the Lean-Kanban approach is perhaps the fastest growing AM. On the other hand, traditional, waterfall-like approaches are still very used in real-life software projects, due to the ease of up-front planning and budgeting, and consequently of managing the contracts with the customer. However, it is well known that up-front planning is almost never met during actual carrying out of the project. The overall goal of this paper is to build and simulate a software development process model in order to highlight similarities and differences between Scrum and Lean-Kanban, and to compare them with a predictive Waterfall process.

The model is built by using an analysis of feedback loops among the components of the processes, such as requirements, iterations, releases and so on,

A. Sillitti et al. (Eds.): XP 2011, LNBIP 77, pp. 117–131, 2011.

and through workflows and delays, to control their dynamics. We simulated the models using a commercial tool available on the market: Vensim[1]. Software processes simulation can be useful under various aspects: it can help to improve current processes, or to enforce motivation for changes [2].

In order to compare these processes, we start with a paradigmatic project with fixed requirements, expressed as a given number of features to be incrementally implemented. To our knowledge, this is the first time that Scrum and Kanban AMs are studied by using systems dynamics models.

The remainder of the paper is organized as follows: in Section 2 we present a brief description of some key software concepts of the three software development approaches: Waterfall, Scrum and Lean-Kanban. Section 3 gives an overview of the software process simulation techniques and provides an introduction of the simulation model used in this study and developed in section 5. Section 4 presents related researches, while section 5 describes the details of the simulation model. Subsection 5.2 shows the analysis of data obtained from the simulation of the three models described in Section 5. Section 6 summarizes the conclusions of our research, and ends the study with recommendations for future works.

2   An Overview of Waterfall, Lean-Kanban and Scrum Processes

In this section we take a look at the considered software development approaches, to identify their relative strengths and weaknesses.

The Waterfall model was introduced by Royce in 1970. It is a traditional "heavyweight" software development methodology in which all process phases (planning, design, development, testing and deployment) are performed in a sequential series of steps. Each phase starts only when the previous one has ended. It is possible to step back to the previous phase, but it is not possible to go back in the process, for instance in order to accomodate a substantial change of requirements. This methodology requires to define a stable set of requirements only during the phase of requirements definition, and feedbacks to previous stages are not easily introduced.

In response to this kind of rigid, hard to follow methodology, Agile Methodologies, so named in 2001 in the Agile Manifesto [3], have been introduced. Among them, Scrum and Lean-Kanban are Agile process tools [4] based on incremental development. They both use pull scheduling and emphasize on delivering releasable software often.

The original term Scrum comes from a study by Takeuchi and Nonaka [5] that was published at 1986 in the Harvard Business Review. In 1993 Jeff Sutherland developed the Scrum process at Easel Corporation, by using their study and their analogy as the name of the process as a whole. Finally, Ken Schwaber [6], [7] formalized the process for the worldwide software industry in the first published paper on Scrum at OOPSLA 1995. Scrum [8] is a simple agile framework, adaptabile also to contexts different from software development [9]. Scrum has

---

[1] http:www.vensim.com

three roles (Product Owner, Scrum Master, Team), three ceremonies (Sprint Planning, Sprint Review, and Daily Scrum Meeting), and three artifacts (Product Backlog, Sprint Backlog, and Burndown Chart). Adopting Scrum implies to use timeboxed iterations and to break the work into a list of smaller deliverables, ordered according to a priority given by the Product Owner. Changes to requirements are not accepted during the iteration, but are welcomed otherwise. Scrum projects are organized with the help of daily Scrums: 15 minutes update meetings, and monthly Sprints, or iterations, that are designed to keep the project flowing quickly. Generally, at the end of every iteration the team releases working code, and a retrospective meeting is held also to look for ways to improve the process for the next iteration.

Lean software development is a translation of Lean manufacturing [10] to the software development domain. The Lean approach emphasizes improving the flow of value given to the customer, eliminating waste (Muda), and consider the whole project, avoiding local optimizations.

Kanban is a Japanese term that translated literally means visual (Kan) and card or board (ban). Adopting Kanban means to break the work into work items, to write their description on cards, and to put the cards on a Kanban board, so that the flow of work is made visible to all members of the team, and the Work in Process (WIP) limits are made explicit on the board. The Kanban board provides a high visibility to the software process, because it shows the assignment of work to developers, communicates priorities and highlights bottlenecks. One of the key goals of Lean-Kanban approach is to minimize WIP, so that only what is needed is developed, there is a constant flow of released work items to the customer, and developers focus only to deliver a few items at a time. So, the process is optimized and lead time can be reduced.

In a nutshell, Scrum and Lean-Kanban approaches are both agile processes aiming to quickly adapt the process by using feedbacks loops. In Lean-Kanban the feedback loops are shorter, and work does not flow through time-boxed iterations, but flows continuously and smoothly. Kanban is less prescriptive than Scrum and it is able to release anytime, while Scrum will release new features only at the end of the iterations. Moreover, in Scrum it is not possible to change the requirements in the middle of the sprint.

3   Software Process Simulation

Simulation is a research methodology that allows to estimate the behavior of a system under some conditions, and can be applied in different research fields. In the simulation domain there are three main techniques: system dynamics, agent-based simulation and discrete event simulation.

In [11], Kellner, Madachy and Raffo discussed the "why, what and how" of software process simulation. We agree with them that there are several advantages of simulating models of software processes. Simulation models can be used for planning, control and operational management, process improvement and technology adoption, training and learning.

The System Dynamics approach (SD) to modeling and simulation, introduced by Jay W. Forrester [12] of the Massachusetts Institute of Technology during the mid-1950s, is suitable to analyze and model non-linear and complex systems containing dynamic variables that change over time. It uses information feedback systems to model and understand the structure of the system under study. The system structure is described trough a diagram whose variables are grouped into stocks (or levels), flows (or rate) and auxiliary variables and/or constant, while links connect the information flows. The stock variables represent values increasing or decreasing through time and depend on their previous values. The second type of variable (flows variables) is linked directly to stocks, determining their change. Finally, auxiliary variable describe the system. In SD the analysis is carried out by identifying cause-effect relationships inside the system. Positive and negative feedback loops are represented by a causal loop diagram.

Agent-based modeling (ABM) allows the study of complex systems, for simulating systems of autonomous and interacting agents. We can artificially reproduce relevant portions of the real world through the introduction of heterogeneous, autonomous and interacting agents. In this way, it is possible to study the effects of different settings at the aggregate level.

Discrete event simulation (DES) allows the simulation of dynamic systems and describes how the system states change upon the occurrence of certain events. These events describe process steps and can be programmed before the simulation, or generated during the simulation. DES allows to accurately model the activities, roles and artifact of a software process. DES models, however, may not be able to represent feedback loops accurately [13].

In conclusion, SD allows to capture accurately the effects of feedback and to represent clearly the relationships between dynamic variables, unlike the discrete event simulation that instead allows to accurately represent sequential activities, and entities or attributes.

4   Related Works

System dynamics modeling has been used in similar research, where there are multiple and interacting software processes, time delays, and other nonlinear effects such as communication level, amount of overtime and workload, schedule pressure, budget pressure, rate of requirement change, and so on.

In the field of the Agile Methodologies many system dynamics models were introduced. The main goals of these researches aim to better understand the agile process and to evaluate its effectiveness. Most of the performed research was made on Extreme Programming (XP), or generic AMs. Other processes such as Scrum, however, are almost absent. For example, Chichacly in [14] investigated when AMs may work by using a System Dynamics Modeling and comparing AMs with a traditional waterfall process. In [15] the author explored whether agile project management has a unique structure or will fit within the generic conceptually formed system dynamic project management structures. An analysis of factors that impact on productivity during agile web development and maintenance phases was conducted by Xiaoying Kong et al. [16]. Another analysis published in [17] gives both theoretical insights into the dynamics of agile software development, and practical suggestions for managing these projects.

In [18] Brooks' Law and the effects of Pair Programming are presented by modeling the process through the system dynamics, and the advantages of this approach are shown.

Misic et al in [19] present a system dynamics model of two key practices of Extreme Programming: pair programming and pair switching, and task switching. A comparison between XP and a traditional approach is carried out and the conditions under which one approach appears to give better results than the other are outlined.

Also in [20] a model of XP software development process has been developed by using the system dynamics simulation techniques. The authors validated the process model with a typical XP project and studied the effects of XP by changing the adoption levels of XP practices.

In another paper, Wernick et al. [21] investigated the impact of pair programming on the long term evolution of software systems by using system dynamics to build simulation models which predict the trend in system growth, with and without pair programming.

5 Model Structure

Our model uses a simplified version both of the Waterfall process and of the Scrum and Lean-Kanban approach, so that its structure is easier to understand and to model. The Waterfall process has been selected because it represents the most opposite methodology to agile processes, and Scrum and Lean-Kanban have been selected because there are not enough scientific empirical studies about them. The objectives of the study are to identify relationships and mechanisms within a software project, so the model is focused on the tendencies of the simulation results and not on specific, quantitative aspects.

According to SD modeling, our model is represented in terms of stocks, and flows in an out of them. The first step has been to identify what are the flows in the main process, which in our case are the project requirements. The auxiliary variables control the "valves" acting on the alternative outflows of each stage.

Based on what normally happens, we made the assumption that a project is developed by a small team – let us suppose 10 developers. The software development process is conceptualized as transforming a initial stock of requirements that need to be developed (Original Work to Do) to a stock of developed requirements (Live). The initial stock of requirements, and the team size, is the same for all simulated processes. A requirement is defined as a set of functionalities to implement. The size of the project for the three processes is estimated as 210 requirements (features in Scrum and Lean-Kanban) to develop that have unit weight and equal size.

We have implemented the three processes with a different subdivision of the work:

- **Scrum:** the work has been split into a set of Sprint backlogs, each including a random number (in the range 15-21) of features selected from a Gaussian distribution. These backlogs are developed during short fixed-length iterations of 2 weeks;
- **Lean-Kanban:** the work has been split in a set of iterations. For each iteration, a random number of 6 - 10 features have been selected from a Gaussian distribution;
- **Waterfall:** the work is not split, but all the features to develop are placed in "Selected Requirements", with a stock of requirements to do that we assume to be 210 for the entire project.

In order to simplify the model, all phases of planning, design, coding, testing and similar have been merged into just one development phase, represented by the *requirements development rate* valve. In Scrum and Waterfall processes, the planning phase has been taken into account by introducing some delays equal to the time spent to planning.

The *requirements development rate* is the speed at which requirements flow to "Fraction Work Done". This rate is determined by the team's productivity, by the number of developers and by the error rate and it is defined by the following equation:

requirements development rate = *IF THEN ELSE (switch=1, IF THEN ELSE (Selected Requirements > 0.05:AND:Selected Requirements ≥ productivity ×n° developers,(productivity ×n° developers) × (1-error in Kanban), IF THEN ELSE (Selected Requirements >0.05:AND:Selected Requirements < productivity ×n° developers,Selected Requirements × (1-error in Kanban), Selected Requirements)),IF THEN ELSE(Selected Requirements > 0.05:AND: Selected Requirements ≥ productivity ×n° developers, (productivity ×n° developers) × (1-error in sprint Scrum or in Waterfall), IF THEN ELSE (Selected Requirements > 0.05:AND: Selected Requirements < productivity ×n° developers, Selected Requirements × (1-error in sprint Scrum or in Waterfall), Selected Requirements)))*

We set an average productivity of 0.025 requirements per hour (the number of requirements developed in one hour) because we assume that a developer is able to implement a requirement in about 5 days. Moreover, the fewer errors there are in the process, the sooner the project will be finished.

As mentioned before, the requirements for each approach are developed in the "requirements development rate" valve. In our model, for each iteration, only a fraction of the requirements referred to by the "Selected Requirements" variable is completed because a fraction of the work is done incorrectly due to three types of error: *effect of uncertain customer requirements, problem in the software design, bug introduced during the development.*

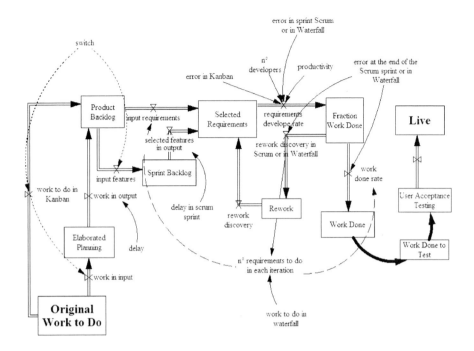

Fig. 1. Simplified version of the structure of the proposed model

As requirements are implemented, they flow into the "User Acceptance Testing" variable, representing the feedback given by the customer. This phase introduces another delay in the process, with a different weight according to the simulated software process. In general terms user acceptance testing is considered to be an essential step before the system is eventually accepted by the end user. If the acceptance test is successfully passed, then the requirements are accepted and are considered completed (the accepted requirements flow into the "Live" level). Otherwise, a rework must be performed, which includes a delay due to the correction.

A simplified version of the model structure with stocks and flows is shown in Fig. 1.

In Table 1 we report the initial parameters we used. Note that the model data have been gathered through a series of interviews with software development professionals in various organizations, and through a review of the literature.

5.1   Consequences of Errors and Delays on Software Development

In our model, the length of the iteration is affected by three main effects: delays, errors and rework on software already developed. These effects influence project outcomes and determine the system development speed. In our model, an important role is assigned to the delays. Fig. 3 shows a simplified view of the model.

Table 1. Initial Parameters of the proposed model

	Waterfall	Scrum	Lean-Kanban
n^o features in Scrum	-	Integer[Random Normal (15 , 21)]	-
n^o selected features in Kanban	-	-	Integer[Random Normal (6 , 10)]
Scrum delay	-	2 hours	-
Waterfall delay	120 hours	-	-
Delay for meeting of sprint planning	-	Integer[Random Normal (4 , 8)]	-
Delay for retrospective meeting	1 hours	-	-
Bug introduced during the development	Random Normal (0.0071, 0.0095)	Random Normal (0.0071, 0.0095)	Random Normal (0.0071, 0.0095)
Problem in the software design	0	Random Normal [0.001, 0.0014]	Random Normal (0.001, 0.0014)
Effect of uncertain customer requirements	0	Random Normal (0.0047, 0.0071)	Random Normal (0.0047, 0.0071)

Our simulator has been designed with the goal to highlight the main differences among the Waterfall, Scrum and Lean-Kanban approaches. Waterfall is very prescriptive and assumes specific sequential phases: each phase must be clearly ended before the next may start. All phases must be completed before you can start the process again. Moreover, if requirements change during project development, the waterfall model requires the completion of a full cycle before they can be revisited. The planning phase in our Waterfall model implies a delay equal to *waterfall delay*. The other phases have been modeled in *requirements development rate*.

Scrum and Lean-Kanban are agile and lean processes, which are less prescriptive than Waterfall. Moreover, Scrum is more prescriptive than Lean-Kanban. In particular, Scrum prescribes roles such as the role of the Product Owner – a single person with a final authority representing the customer's interest in backlog prioritization and requirements questions. Moreover, a Sprint Planning Meeting and a Sprint Retrospective Meeting are prescribed, respectively to plan the iteration and at the end of every sprint. The sprint review meeting aims to discuss what went well and what to improve in the next sprint. In our model, these meetings and the activity of the Product Owner are modeled through the following variables: *delay for Sprint Planning Meeting, delay for Retrospective Meeting* and *Scrum delay*.

As regards the effects of errors and of rework, Fig. 2 shows the causal loop effect on the error rate. We identify a reinforcing feedback loop (positive feedback) where cause and effect can be circular and an effect strengthens its own cause, or where sometimes a cause has multiple opposing effects. For

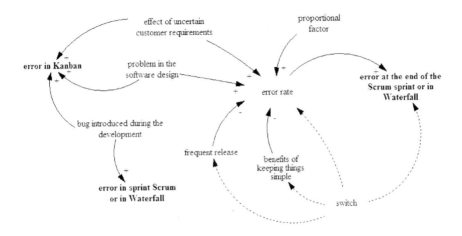

Fig. 2. Causal loop diagram of error rate

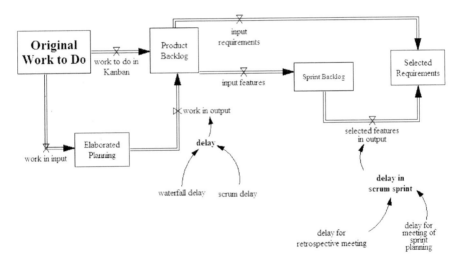

Fig. 3. Delays in the proposed System Dynamic model

example, in the our case, the *effect of uncertain customer requirements* reinforces *error rate* and at the same time *benefits of keeping things simple* decreases *error rate.*

As mentioned before, a fraction of the work is considered to be done incorrectly due to three types of error: *effect of uncertain customer requirements, problem in the software design, bug introduced during the development.* In Lean-Kanban process, these three errors are discovered and corrected in the *requirements development rate* valve, instead in Scrum and in Waterfall only the *bug introduced*

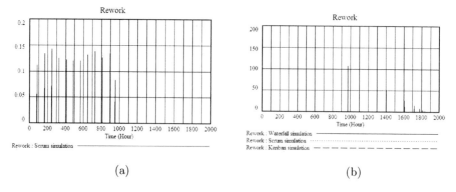

Fig. 4. (a) Rework in Scrum approach – (b) Rework in Waterfall

during the development error passes through in the *rework discovery in Scrum or Waterfall* valve characterized by the following equation:

rework discovery in Scrum or in Waterfall = *IF THEN ELSE(switch= 0:OR:switch=2,IF THEN ELSE(Selected Requirements < 0.05, Fraction work done × (error at the end of the Scrum sprint or in Waterfall), 0),0)*

The other two errors can be discovered only at the end of the iteration.

In the Waterfall model, the error rate at the end of the iteration increases because the releases are not frequent and the work size in an iteration is more heavyweight than in Scrum and Kanban, so according to [22] " *an error introduced during the requirements phase, but not discovered until maintenance, can be as much as 100 times more than that of fixing the error during the early development phases*", the variable (*effect of uncertain customer requirements* and the variable *problem in the software design*) are proportional to the *proportional factor* variable.

In Fig. 4 the time trends of the rework in Scrum and in the Waterfall approach at the end of the iteration are reported, respectively.

5.2   Results

We mentioned that Lean-Kanban approach does not prescribe roles and meetings, and the number of requirements to implement at any given time is very small. So also our proposed Lean-Kanban model limits the work in progress and minimizes the lead time. In Fig. 5 and in Fig. 6 we can observe that very many requirements are implemented in a Waterfall iteration. The number of selected requirements in Lean-Kanban and in Scrum is much smaller than in Waterfall model, while in Kanban this number is smaller than in Scrum. In fact, "Selected Requirements" variable is equal to "Original Work" after a time interval equal to the *Waterfall delay*. This variable highlights the speed with which the requirements flow from "Selected Requirements" level to "Fraction Work Done" level.

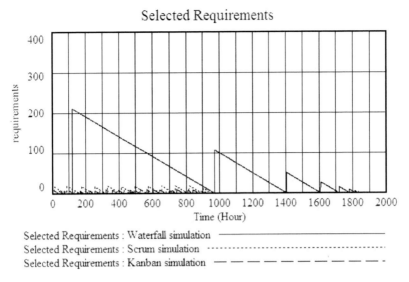

Fig. 5. Selected Requirements in the three approaches

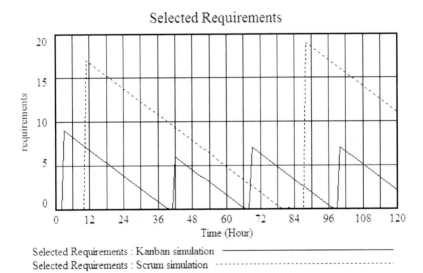

Fig. 6. Selected Requirements in Scrum and Lean-Kanban

For each approach we report the time trend of "Selected Requirements" that is characterized by a waveform that is repeated periodically during the simulation. The waveform's period coincides with the length of each iteration, and we can observe that the initial amplitude of the waveform in Waterfall approach is larger than in Scrum and Lean-Kanban approach.

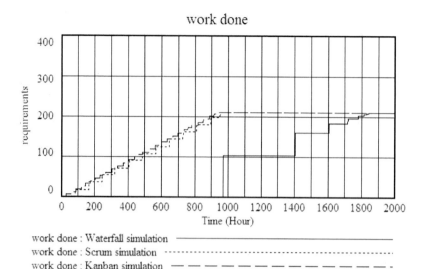

work done : Waterfall simulation ———————————————
work done : Scrum simulation ·······································
work done : Kanban simulation — — — — — — — — — — — — — — — —·

Fig. 7. Work Done

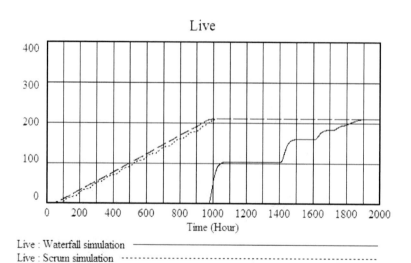

Live : Waterfall simulation ———————————————
Live : Scrum simulation ·······································
Live : Kanban simulation — — — — — — — — — — — — — — — —

Fig. 8. Live

Moreover as can be seen in Figure 4 (a) in the Scrum approach the amount of rework at the end of the iteration is lower than the amount of rework in Waterfall approach (see Fig.4 (b)). In agreement with this is the fact that in Scrum approach the rework is calculated with a smaller number of requirements with respect to the amount of requirements in Waterfall approach. In fact if in the proposed model the rework is calculated with "n^o Requirements to Do in each Iteration" equivalent to the "Number of Features in Scrum" in Scrum approach (as mentioned in Scrum the number of requirements can vary between 15 and 21), instead in the Waterfall process the "Original Work to Do" is not broken into iterations, and so the rework at the end of the iteration is calculated with a number of requirements equivalent to "n^o requirements to do in each iteration" which coincides with "work to do in Waterfall" equal to "Original Work to Do" and then to 210 requirements.

We think that the outputs obtained by our model are sensible if compared to real world data. Fig. 7 and Fig. 8 show a simulation fitting the behavior of a real project. In Fig. 7 we show the time trend of the work done during the tree approaches before the software goes "Live" and the acceptance testing has been carried out, while in Fig. 8 after the customer requirements has been validated.

The proposed model and the analysis of the data suggest that Lean-Kanban approach is more efficient than the other two approaches, thanks to a software development mechanism that allows frequent releases and the division of the work in very small time chunks.

6   Conclusions

We developed a simplified system dynamics model for describing the behavior of three different approaches to the software development under similar starting conditions. We compared by means of simulation techniques a heavy and pre-scriptive approach, Waterfall, with two agile and less prescriptive process tools, Scrum and Lean-Kanban.

In order to avoid a too complex model, all the variables influencing the processes were not included in our simulation, so our study has been carried out under some limiting assumptions that could threaten its validity. But this is a first model and it can be considered as a valid starting point for further studies. We described some strengths and weaknesses of three software process methods by modeling their environment with a continuous-time simulation tool. Although Lean-Kanban is well known in software development processes, it has not yet investigated in depth in research works. In our model, the Kanban workflow was managed through an effective control mechanism to limit the work in progress and minimize the lead time. One of the advantages of this approach is that the work is better controlled, so that the effects of errors are kept limited. On the contrary, in the Waterfall case often projects may fail to complete due to the difficulty to correct errors, including errors in requirements.

The resulting behavior of the simulation model presented is quite realistic, and its behavior is the same also by changing the project size. However, this is a first model that needs to be further elaborated and validated, for example by adding new variables or new relationships among factors. This will be the subject of our future work, which will also include studies to empirically validate the simulation results using data from real projects.

References

1. VersionOne: State of Agile Survey (2009), Available on the web:
   `http://www.versionone.com/pdf/2009_State_of_Agile_Development_Survey_Results.pdf` (access Date: November 2010)
2. Andersson, C., Karlsson, L., Nedstam, J., Höst, M., Nilsson, B.I.: Understanding Software Processes through System Dynamics Simulation: A Case Study. In: Ninth Annual IEEE International Conference and Workshop on the Engineering of Computer-Based Systems, ECBS, p. 0041 (2002)
3. `http://agilemanifesto.org/`
4. Kniberg, H., Skarin, M.: Kanban and Scrum making the most of both. Managing Editor: Diana Plesa. Enterprise software development series. InfoQ. USA (2010) ISBN 978-0-557-13832-6
5. Takeuchi, H., Nonaka, I.: The New New Product Development Game. Harvard Business Review (January-February 1986)
6. Ken, S.: Scrum Development Process, White Paper (1997)
7. Ken, S.: Agile Project Management with Scrum. Microsoft Press, Redmond (2004)
8. Scrum Alliance, `http://www.scrumalliance.org`
9. Marchesi, M., Mannaro, K., Uras, S., Locci, M.: Distributed Scrum in Research Project Management. In: Concas, G., Damiani, E., Scotto, M., Succi, G. (eds.) XP 2007. LNCS, vol. 4536, pp. 240–244. Springer, Heidelberg (2007)
10. Womack, J.P., Jones, D.T., Roos, D.: The Machine That Changed the World: The Story of Lean Production. Harper Perennial (November 1991)
11. Kellner, M.I., Madachy, R.J., Raffo, D.M.: Software process simulation modeling: Why? What, How? Journal of Systems and Software 46, 91–105 (1999)
12. Forrester, J.W.: Industrial dynamics. MIT Press, Cambridge (1961)
13. Martin, R.H., Raffo, D.M.: A Model of the Software Development Process Using Both Continuous and Discret Models. International Journal of Software Process Improvement and Practice 5(2-3), 147–157 (2000)
14. Karim, C.: Modeling Agile Development: When is it Effective? In: Proceedings of the 2007 System Dynamics Conference. Boston, MA (2007) (print)
15. Tignor, W.W.: Agile Project Management. In: International Conference of the System Dynamics Society, Albuquerque, NM 2009 (July 26-30, 2009)
16. Xiaoying, K., Li, L., David, L.: Modelling an Agile Web Maintenance Process (2005)
17. van Oorschot, K.E., Sengputa, K., van Wassenhove, L.N.: Dynamics of Agile Software Development. In: Proceedings of the 27th International Conference of the System Dynamics Society, Albuquerque, New, Mexico, USA, July 26-30 (2009)
18. Wu, M., Yan, H.: Simulation in Software Engineering with System Dynamics: A Case Study. Journal of Software 4(10), 1127–1135 (2009)
19. Misic, V.B., Gevaert, H., Rennie, M.: Extreme dynamics: towards a system dynamics model of the extreme programming software development process. In: 5th International Workshop on Software Process Simulation and Modeling (ProSim 2004), W11L Workshop - 26th International Conference on Software Engineering (2004/911), Edingburgh, Scotland, UK, May 24-25. IEE Seminar Digest, vol. 2004(911), pp. 237–242 (2004) ISBN: 0 86341 426 5

20. Yong, Y., Zhou, B.: Evaluating Extreme Programming Effect through System Dynamics Modeling. In: Proceedings 2009 International Conference on Computational Intelligence and Software Engineering (CiSE 2009), Wuhan, China, pp. 1–4 (2009)
21. Wernick, P., Hall, T.: The impact of using pair programming on system evolution a simulation-based study. In: Proceedings of 20th IEEE International Conference on Software Maintenance, pp. 422–426 (2004)
22. Conte, S.D., Dunsmore, H.E., Shen, V.Y.: Software Engineering Metrics and Models. Benjamin/Cummings, New York (1986)

Factors Affecting Effectiveness of Agile Usage – Insights from the BBC Worldwide Case Study

Mali Senapathi[1], Peter Middleton[2], and Gareth Evans[3]

[1] Auckland University of Technology, New Zealand
mali.senapathi@aut.ac.nz
[2] Queen's University Belfast, Northern Ireland
p.middleton@qub.ac.uk
[3] Assurity Consulting Limited, New Zealand
gareth.evans@assurity.co.nz

Abstract. The past decade has seen significant changes in systems development with many organizations adopting agile methodologies as a viable methodology for developing systems. An increasing number of research studies reveal the growing popularity and acceptance of agile methodologies. While most academic research has focused on adoption and adaptation of agile methods, there is very limited understanding of their post-adoption usage and incorporation within organizations. What factors explain the effective usage of agile methodologies? A synthesis of past research in Systems Development Methodologies, Information Systems implementation, Diffusion of Innovations, and Agile Methodologies was conducted to develop a research model that identifies the main factors pertinent to the propagation and effective usage of agile methodologies in organizations. The model is tested by applying it to the usage of Kanban for Software Engineering practices at BBC Worldwide, London. Insights gained from the case study are discussed.

Keywords: Agile usage, effectiveness of agile usage, Kanban.

1 Introduction

Agile methodologies (AM) emerged as a popular alternative to address the problems inherent in established methods to systems development [1]. AM have gained widespread acceptance in both the academic and industrial contexts with an increasing number of studies reporting their high adoption and success rates [2, 3] over the past decade. However, most academic research has mainly focused on the adoption and adaptation of agile methods [4]. Moreover, they offer a very broad range of experiences without providing a unified view of current practice [2], which suggest that there is an imprecise understanding of their use and practice in organizations beyond the adoption phase. This discrepancy may be explained in a number of ways. One explanation is that most organizations that have adopted agile methods are still trialling on a project by project basis, and their routinized use and spread throughout the organization is yet to happen. Moreover, researchers have highlighted the lack of quality and decreasing reliability in the findings of agile

A. Sillitti et al. (Eds.): XP 2011, LNBIP 77, pp. 132–145, 2011.

empirical studies in the literature [2]. More research is therefore needed into understanding the actual practice of AM in organisations.

According to [5], diffusion of innovations is a six-staged process comprising initiation, adoption, adaptation, acceptance, use, and incorporation. While studies on the initial phases (initiation, adoption, adaptation) provide insights into the early phases of diffusion of an innovation, studies that focus on the later stages of diffusion provide valuable insights into how an innovation can be effectively propagated within the organization. Therefore, the factors which drive an Information Systems (IS) innovation varies across different implementation phases [6]. Moreover, since AM denote a radical departure from traditional systems development approaches, they bring with them a host of new challenges which encompass various social, technical and organizational aspects [7-9]. With a change in the primary approach to systems development it is expected that there will be substantial changes in the systems development process, which in turn will have an impact on the various factors that will affect agile adoption and use during the different implementation phases. We need to be able to identify these set of factors that might influence its continued and effective usage in organizations. Therefore the key research questions guiding this study are: How can agile usage effectiveness be measured? What are the factors that affect agile usage effectiveness?

Most studies that report higher adoption rates and success of agile methods do not define, much less measure 'effectiveness' of the usage of agile practices or identify the factors that affect effectiveness. The answers to these questions lie in research to evaluate the post-adoption use of agile methods. This implies that there is an increasing need for a better understanding beyond the adoption stage as many organizations have completed adoption and agile methods have started to become well-established processes of these organizations [1]. A better understanding of the various factors that affect successful incorporation of agile methods is believed to provide valuable insights from at least three perspectives: a) provide new theoretical insights into the factors affecting the effectiveness of agile usage, b) improve our understanding of post adoption use, processes and impact of agile methodologies, and c) contribute to industrial practice by providing insights into how agile methods can be effectively used in organizations.

Given that the usage of agile methodologies is a versatile concept, the current study draws from well-established theories such as diffusion of innovations and IS implementation research which have been extensively used throughout the IS literature to explain the constructs relating to the adoption and implementation of new IS innovations. The next section summarizes this literature and presents a conceptual framework based on innovation, sociological, technological, team and organisational factors influencing the effective usage of agile methodologies in organisations. We then outline the research design used in the study before presenting the results and analysis of the case study. The final part concludes with some implications for research and practice.

2   Theoretical Background and the Research Framework

The definition adopted for usage in the present study is similar to that proposed by [10] who suggests that acceptance is preceded by, and based on, usage of the innovation beyond the pilot project stage, i.e., Usage -> Acceptance -> Incorporation, where usage is specified using two measures: *horizontal usage* - concerned with the use of the innovation across the organization, and *vertical usage* - concerned with the depth of usage. Applying these definitions' to the context of agile methodologies, *Horizontal Usage* is defined as the overall use of agile practices across the organization– for example, percentage of projects and developers/analysts using agile practices, and *Vertical Usage* is defined as the maximum intensity of their use, i.e., depth of use of specific agile values, practices, and policies.

In software development, terms such as 'agile' or 'agile methodology' commonly refers to one of the major agile methods such as extreme programming (XP), feature-driven development, crystal method, Scrum, and dynamic systems development method - each of which prescribes a set of core practices, values and principles. However, in practice, most organizations do not strictly follow or adhere to any one particular agile method, but use a tailored approach by combining a number of good agile practices from different agile methods that best suits their contextual requirements, *"if you dumped all these good practices out onto a table, you'd have quite a buffet of very good practices with which to tailor your own process. And that's exactly what most organizations do"* [11]. Therefore, in the current study, agile usage does not refer to one particular agile method such as Scrum but rather to the continued usage of agile practices, where practices might include combination of practices from XP and Scrum, or implementing the core properties of a kanban system while continuing to use some XP and Scrum practices.

Table 1. Factors expected to relate to agile usage and agile usage effectiveness

Theoretical factors		Agile Usage	Agile Usage Effectiveness
Agile innovation	Relative advantage	Horizontal usage	• Quality of developed system and development process • Productivity of development process • Customer satisfaction
	Compatibility		
Sociological	Experience		
	Knowledge/expertise		
Technological	Agile practices		
	Tool support		
Team	Team management	Vertical usage	
	Methodology champion		
Organizational	Management support		

Based on a synthesis of past research in diffusion of innovations, IS implementation, and agile implementation literature, five groups of factors potentially affecting Agile Usage were identified: (1) Agile innovation factors (*relative advantage, compatibility*) mainly adopted from the innovation diffusion literature, (2) Sociological factors (*experience level, Knowledge/expertise (domain expertise, language expertise, etc.,*) adopted from eXtreme Programming (XP) evaluation framework [12], (3) Technological factors (*agile practices, tool support (project management/use of automation tools)* adopted from XP evaluation framework [12], (4) Team factors (team management, methodology champion) adopted from XP literature, and (5) Organizational factors (*top management support*) adopted from the IS implementation literature. Table 1 summarizes the different perspectives examined under each of the implementation factors in terms of their relationship to the degree of agile usage and its effectiveness.

The resulting conceptual framework is depicted in Figure 1.

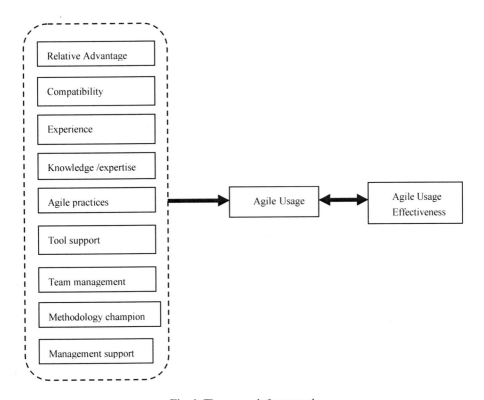

Fig. 1. The research framework

We now briefly discuss the theoretical rationale for the consideration of these factors and their influence on agile usage and its effectiveness.

Innovation factors
Relative advantage: *the degree to which the innovation is perceived better than its precursor* [13]. There is sufficient empirical evidence to suggest that relative advantage is a significant factor in predicting the usage of Systems Development Methodologies [14, 15]. In the context of agile methods, relative advantage would refer to the degree to which the chosen agile practices are found to better meet the contextual needs of the project and provide specific benefits such as increased productivity, improved quality, reduced time and costs, and higher customer satisfaction in comparison to its precursor practices.

Compatibility: *the degree to which the innovation is perceived as being consistent with the existing values, needs, and past experiences of adopters* [13]. Since the adoption of agile methods represents a major shift in the paradigm of systems development [16], it entails major alterations to work practices, investment in tools that support and facilitate rapid iterative development, versioning/configuration management, JUnits, refactoring and other agile techniques [9]. In terms of post-implementation stages, compatibility is described as the fit between an innovation and a particular context [10], which implies that the chosen agile practices must match its context in order to be effective and successfully infused in the organization. For example, [4] found that the use of multiple languages such as Java, C++, and Motif, in a large legacy project caused serious challenges to the adoption of XP practices such as code ownership, refactoring, and automated testing.

Sociological factors
Though organizations play a significant role in adopting contemporary innovations such as agile methods/practices, their acceptance and continued usage beyond the adoption stage really depends on the actual users/teams who use the practices to develop software [17, 18]. Some of the specific individual sociological factors that impact usage include attitude, experience, technical knowledge and expertise [19].

Experience: People with the right attitude and experience will embrace the newer practices easily and faster, and high level of team experience is said to contribute to increased productivity [12].

Knowledge/Expertise: Users and teams with high levels of technical expertise in terms of programming languages, different application domains, and other related software development technical practices, may not be subject to the learning curve associated with an unfamiliar domain, or with learning an unfamiliar programming language [12].

Technological factors
Agile practices: There is often a substantial difference between the textbook 'vanilla' version and the actual "method-in-action" used in practice as most prescribed practices are tailored to meet the contextual needs of software development [20, 21]. For example, [20] found that different XP practices reached different levels of assimilation at different periods of usage, and practices that addressed specific needs of the adopting team reached deeper assimilation levels.

Tool support: While the significance of tool support in the adoption of software process innovations in general has been recognized [22], their importance in facilitating the acceptance of agile practices in terms of providing support in adhering to specific XP practices such as refactoring, continuous integration, and test-driven development is also documented [4].

Team factors
Given the increasingly important role of teams in agile software development, team characteristics and practices that facilitate the use of agile methods are more likely to affect their effective use.

Team Management: team practices that empower the team to be more autonomous and key decision-makers in deciding project scope, schedule, and choice of tasks, tools, practices etc., are deemed critical in facilitating the acceptance and continued usage of agile practices [4].

Methodology Champion: Any innovative idea or practice without a champion is not likely to succeed [23]. In the context of AM, methodology champions play the significant role of change agents in encouraging and facilitating the on-going usage of agile practices [24], which include responsibilities such as mentoring, and ensuring that agile practices are strictly followed and adhered to by team members [4].

Organizational factors
Top Management support: Top Management support refers to ongoing, continual support and encouragement of the top management executives in the adoption and implementation of innovations [25], and is one of the main organizational factors that is consistently reported to facilitate systems development methodology implementation [15]. Lack of management support and interest has been found to be one of the biggest obstacles in implementing systems development methodologies [26] and successful diffusion of agile methods/practices [3].

3 Research Design

A case study methodology was employed in this study because it enables investigation of a contemporary phenomenon within its natural setting [27], and is especially appropriate for newer topic areas such as post-adoption use or assimilation of agile practices, where theory and research are still in their early formative stages [28, 29].

The data collected mainly involved interviews with the members of the Digital Hub (Digi-Hub) development team that was involved with the implementation of Kanban at BBC Worldwide, London in 2009. BBC Worldwide is the main commercial arm and a wholly owned subsidiary of the British Broadcasting Corporation [30]. Its mission is to create, acquire, develop and exploit media content and brands around the world in order to maximise the value of the BBC's assets for the benefit of the UK licence payer. The Digi-Hub team was made up of 9 staff: Project Manager, Business Analyst, Software Architect, Tester, Lead Developer, 3 Developers and a Support Developer. It was working on a mix of developing new software and software maintenance. The technology used was C#, .NET, MS SQL Server, and legacy Connected Service Framework (CSF) code.

In a separate study, [31] examined how the lean ideas behind the Toyota Production System could be applied to software project management. Based on a detailed investigation of the Digi-Hub development team over a 12 month period, the study found that lead time to deliver software improved by 37%, consistency of delivery rose by 47% and defects reported by customers fell 24%. In summary, their study concluded that the performance of the software development team improved by adopting a lean approach.

The current study is part of a bigger research initiative which involves a multiple-case study design and a quantitative survey. And, since the case of BBC Worldwide provided specific evidence of improvements in quality, productivity, it was deemed an appropriate case for testing the theoretical framework developed in the current study. In fact, it was an appropriate example of a critical case which met the conditions for testing a well-formulated theory (i.e., the proposed research model), the outcomes of which might result in confirming, challenging, or extending the theory [27]. Therefore, the main goal of the current study is to test the research model in an attempt to identify additional predictor constructs or variables that might influence agile usage, or avoid inadvertent exclusion of variables in the proposed model. The study analyses the significance of each of the factors on the effectiveness of the usage of agile practices at the team level.

Agile Usage: Usage is a key measure of successful implementation of a Systems Development Methodology in organizations. Since the current study is more interested in how extensively and deeply agile practices are used after adoption rather than its adoption per se, the interpretation of [10] was used to measure usage using the following two measures:

1) Horizontal usage - percentage of projects and developers/analysts using agile practices

2) Vertical usage - extent of use – i.e., maximum intensity of their use, i.e., depth of use of specific agile values, practices, and policies

Agile Usage Effectiveness: Agile effectiveness as a factor affecting agile usage will be measured using three variables: two of these are associated with the successful usage of systems development methodologies and have been identified as the core criteria for assessing post-implementation effectiveness [15, 32]. They are: 1) productivity improvements in the development process, and 2) improved quality of the delivered system. In addition, a third construct, customer satisfaction, which is recognized as a key measure of agile effectiveness in the agile literature [33, 34] was used to measure agile effectiveness.

4 Data Analysis and Findings

Innovation factors
Relative advantage: At BBC Worldwide, the Digi-Hub team was delivering enterprise messaging systems, which was very complex, poorly architected with very large and complex legacy code base. The team was initially using Scrum as a methodology when it realized that Scrum's time-boxed iterations were difficult to adhere to in practice, because a piece of work would become a lot bigger once started and the team was not able to visualize many things that they were doing at the same time, and there was reprioritization by the business all the time. The specific advantages of using Kanban in comparison with its precursor method/practices such as Scrum were i) limiting the work in progress, i.e., stopping context-switching and getting efficiency out of visualizing the process and gaining an understanding of the whole process, ii) reducing batch size, i.e., by reducing the size of units of work going through the pipeline overheads are reduced including changes in requirements and iii) 'granularity of visualisation', " .. *in Scrum you don't get the granularity of visualisation, Kanban*

is very granular, and what really happens is once you start visualising your work, the whole team gets a collective understanding of how they build software" (Developer, Digi-Hub team).

Compatibility: There were not any major compatibility issues as the team had been using many Scrum and XP technical practices for almost more than 9 months before Kanban was introduced. The team very soon recognised that Kanban was a good fit that matched the contextual requirements of the project requirements and the team.

Sociological factors

Experience: Team members had high levels of experience and technical competence in software development. Though they were familiar with XP and Scrum practices, no one had used Kanban before. But most team members had the attitude and the willingness to learn and change, and were self-motivated.

Knowledge/Expertise: The team was not familiar with the business domain, but had high levels of technical knowledge and expertise, for example programming languages, Microsoft Stack, Webservices, user interfaces. The rationale was that it is much easier for people with high levels of technical expertise to pick up a new business domain. According to one of the developers, *"if you have technical expertise you can usually understand new business domains quickly"*.

Technological factors

Agile practices: Though they were a Scrum team which used two-weekly sprint time-boxed iterations, retrospectives, planning meetings etc., when they moved to Kanban they incorporated Kanban properties without making major changes to some of the existing XP/Scrum practices that were working well, for example, daily meetings, refactoring, test-driven development. Therefore deeper and intensive use of agile practices with an emphasis on optimizing the existing process eventually led to a mature implementation of Kanban *"we visualised our workflow, limited WIP, we used models, collected data to manage and measure of flow,...i.e, we had all the five properties from David Anderson's book, and we had some of the emergent properties as well"* (Developer, Digi-Hub team).

Tool support: A number of technical tools such as Cucumber for automated testing, TeamCity for continous integration were used, and a lot of data was collected from the Kanban board which in conjunction with other internal systems for logging hours etc., were fed into the project management practices.

Team factors

Team Management: Kanban was implemented at BBC Worldwide during 2008-2009 which were early days for Kanban with not much literature, but the team worked together by learning from each other and ensured that the strengths and expertise of different members were well reflected in the choice of their tasks and decisions (for example, some members of the team were very strong on test driven development) and had a common understanding of what the team thought good practices were. The team enjoyed a lot of autonomy in terms of being able to make decisions relating to breaking quite a high level problem into smaller chunks, choice of relevant tools, etc.

Methodology Champion: The role of the methodology champion was not to strictly enforce the technical practices on the team (the team by itself adhered to practices), but rather act as a mentor who facilitated the effective use of kanban practices, and guided the team in the right direction whenever there were major problems or issues.

Organizational factors

Top Management support: The governance structure when the team moved to Kanban in 2008 was:

Business Board (Strategy & Budget)
Project Board (Detail & authorise specific work)
Product Owner (reconcile Business & Customer wants)
Users requesting work (Sign off work completed)
End users (200 – 300 people)

The team received very strong support from the Project Board, Product Owner, and IT management, and also in terms of knowledgeable colleagues, and benefited from hearing to world renowned speakers such as Martin Fowler, Craig Larman, David Anderson, etc., come and talk at BBC Worldwide. However, support at the business board level was not as strong due to a lack of understanding of the changes in methodologies and technical practices.

4.1 Agile Usage and Effectiveness

4.1.1 Agile Usage

Horizontal usage of agile practices at BBC Worldwide increased consistently after the implementation of Kanban. Before Kanban was introduced almost half (50%) of the projects were using Scrum, and when Kanban was implemented the usage eventually increased to almost 80%. Kanban usage continued to spread widely as other teams (i.e., other than Digi-Hub) also started implementing Kanban. Use of Kanban spread into the BBC from BBC Worldwide, the spread being referred to as *Kanban flu*. The number of analysts/developers etc working on Kanban projects also increased steadily in almost exactly the same proportion as the number of projects described above. In particular vertical usage was found to play a significant role in determining the effectiveness of usage which is best reflected in words of a developer on the team, *"the depth of adoption maps to an exponential curve of success – I think if you just do a couple of practices you are not going to get much benefit. If you do a lot of them and they are deeply engrained you are likely to be more successful"*

4.1.2 Agile Usage Effectiveness

Usage effectiveness was analyzed using three main factors: improved quality of the development process, improved productivity during the development process, and customer Satisfaction. Specific improvements were recorded based on the data collected between October 2008 and October 2009 (refer to [31] for a detailed investigation and more specific discussion of the results and findings).

Quality: The quality of the development process improved which was measured by the number of live defects (live defects are the bugs reported by customers during a week plus the bugs still open). The numbers of live defects reported by customers fell by 24%, i.e., bugs were being fixed more quickly and the mean numbers of bugs open each week also slightly declined.

Productivity: Three important measures were used to measure improvements in productivity: i) lead time: the total elapsed time from when a customer requests software to when the finished software is released to the customer. It tracks how quickly and reliably software is delivered to customers. Lead time to deliver software improved by 37%, and consistency of delivery rose by 47% ii) development time: this measure gives insight into the efficiency of development. Development time is recorded in working days - variation in delivery times reduced by 78% from 30.5 to 6.8, and the mean time to develop fewer and smaller software features declined by 73% from 9.2 to 2.5 working days. iii) Release Frequency (RF) is defined as the number of items released to customers per month - RF increased by a factor of 8 from 2 in November 2007 to 16 in October 2009.

Customer Satisfaction: The team was customer focused and responsive to customer needs, and was able to respond to the needs of the business by delivering new functionality faster and with more predictability. It was believed that a lot of the team's behaviour was driven by focusing on customer needs and satisfaction, *" that's driving a lot of your behaviour as well- so if you are focusing on what the customer receives, then a lot of these practices will start to make more sense – breaking work into smaller units means more frequent feedback from customers which is reflected back into requirements of unstarted work"*

4.1.3 Summary of Findings

In summary, data analysis from the interviews confirmed that all the factors, i.e., (1) Agile innovation factors (*relative advantage, compatibility*) (2) Sociological factors (*experience level, Knowledge/expertise*) (3) Technological factors (*agile practices, tool support*) (4) Team factors (team management, methodology champion and (5) Organizational factors (*top management support*) played a significant role in affecting effective usage of agile practices. Both horizontal and vertical usage increased significantly and specific improvements in effectiveness measures were recorded.

Agile innovation factors appeared to be influential in the company's acceptance and continued use of agile practices. The team's high levels of experience, technical knowledge and competence, and working in a collaborative, autonomous and self-organizing team style affected the successful usage of agile practices. The emphasis on deeply adopting all the core properties/practices of Kanban where the change was driven by attempting to optimise the existing process without making major changes to existing workflow, job titles, roles and responsibilities, etc., also played a critical role [35]. The methodology champion's role in actively and vigorously promoting his vision for introducing Kanban and using a variety of influence processes to experiment with and implement the various practices had a significant impact on the overall success of the change process. And given that the methodology champion who acted as the key driver for the entire initiative has left the team, the question for BBC Worldwide is, "will the initiative survive?" Top management support will be crucial to sustain the efforts of such initiatives with a focus on continuous improvement as one developer rightly pointed out, " *it is about making the system that people work in more productive as opposed to the people working in the system. That's really the key difference- a lot of managers focus on people, whereas continuous improvement is always more effective when you focus on the system..*"

In addition, another factor, *budget and schedule constraint* was identified to affect the effective use of agile practices. The team felt that sufficient budget was needed to take on technical debt, practices to change the system such as budget to support appropriate testing environments, automate deployment, etc., This has been confirmed in another study on the acceptance of XP practices [4] which found that projects with relatively less restriction on budget and delivery schedule afforded a lot of flexibility to the team and enabled a deeper adoption of XP practices compared to teams that had strict schedule and budgetary constraints. This will be further verified in the forthcoming case studies before incorporating it into the final framework.

5   Conclusions

Given the obvious limitations of any case study approach including issues relating to generalization of findings, the study does not allow any definite conclusions. Replication of the study in different contexts should provide a cross-case comparison and analysis of the results and add to the generalizability of the findings. In this study, our aim was to develop a theoretical model in order to gain a better understanding of the factors that facilitate effective usage of agile practices. The main goal of the study was to test the research model, and therefore the case of BBC Worldwide which had been using agile practices continually for almost more than two years with specific evidence of improvements in quality, productivity, was deemed an appropriate case for testing the theoretical framework developed in the current study. Though the findings from this study confirm that the various factors identified in the framework play a significant role in affecting the increased and continued use of agile practices, it should be noted that these factors represent general factors conducive to agile usage. However, usage effectiveness or success in certain organizations may be influenced by specific factors or measures not identified in the model.

However, it should be emphasized that this study reports research-in-progress, i.e. only part of a larger flexible design research project which involves multiple case studies and a quantitative survey. Further case studies are planned which will be used to refine the factors identified in the research model. Extant literature on agile research will then be used to design the survey instrument by identifying potential indicators to measure each factor of the model. A world wide survey targeting all agile practitioners will be conducted to finalize the model. The goal of the survey would be to empirically validate the factors and the relationships proposed in the agile usage model and their importance for the overall effective usage of agile practices.

6   Implications of the Study

The findings from this study provide important implications for both the research and practitioner communities.

From a research perspective, the current study draws upon related streams of literature to synthesize the various factors that relate to the effectiveness of agile usage. It focused on identifying factors that may explain agile usage during the later stages of adoption, i.e., the post-adoption stage of usage. The emphasis is on how extensively and deeply the innovation is used after adoption, rather than its adoption per se. In the context of software process innovations, this notion is generally referred to as the innovation's degree of assimilation into the organization [36, 37]. Agile research that focuses on post-adoption and later stages of the assimilation, i.e., usage and routinization of agile practices is emerging. While [24] studied the assimilation of XP/Scrum practices using three case studies, [4] focused on the acceptance of XP practices across different teams within the same organization. [24] highlight the need to include agile methods other than XP, and the need for a more quantitative approach to determine the levels of ISD usage across the ISD community with more generalisable results. These studies provide some insights into the post-adoption use of specific agile methods/practices such as XP or Scrum. However, there is very limited empirical research that have studied the actual use of agile practices using appropriate theoretical concepts or frameworks [24]. Moreover, the relationship between agile usage and agile effectiveness i.e., usage as a factor affecting effectiveness, has been omitted from this important stream of research. The current study can be seen as a first step in addressing this important gap in the agile extant literature which has developed a theoretical framework by identifying a set of factors that might affect the continued usage of agile practices, where 'usage' refers to the use of agile practices ranging from the use of specific methods/practices such as XP or Scrum to the use of combination of properties/practices from different methods such as XP, Scrum, waterfall, etc.

For the practitioner community, the study has identified i) the important factors that might play a significant role in affecting usage, i.e., both the vertical (intensity of use) and horizontal (spread of use) usage of agile practices, and ii) the effect of usage on effectiveness, i.e., the bi-directional relationship between usage and its effectiveness (improvements in quality, productivity, and customer satisfaction), i.e. the more extensive and deeper the usage the more effective will be its use, and increased effectiveness of agile usage will in turn have an impact on the increased usage of agile practices in the organization. In practice, the results can guide IS managers seeking to propagate the continued use of agile practices for systems development. In general, it is important that managers monitor and evaluate the innovation factors such as relative advantage which will help not only to sustain the effective usage of agile practices but will also enable recognition of any need for change. Since higher levels of technical knowledge and competence, experience, and the willingness to learn and change at the team level are key factors that affect the effective use of agile practices, managers should cultivate such expertise among their staff through effective coaching, training, and technical support programs. Adequate technical support is necessary to overcome resistance and compatibility issues, and impart necessary skills to the development teams. Methodology champions should ensure deeper adoption of all the core agile properties/practices in order to reap the real benefits of effective agile implementation. Top management support will be crucial to sustain the efforts of such initiatives so that the whole organization can evolve to be agile.

References

1. Abrahamsson, P., Conboy, K., Wang, X.: Lots done, more to do: the current state of agile systems development research. European Journal of Information Systems 18, 281–284 (2009)
2. Dyba, T., Dingsoyr, T.: Empirical studies of agile software development: A systematic review. Information and Software Technology 50 (2008)
3. Vijayasarathy, L.R., Turk, D.: Agile Software Development: A survey of early adopters. Journal of Information Technology Management 19(2) (2008)
4. Mangalaraj, G., Mahapatra, R., Nerur, S.: Acceptance of software process innovations - the case of extreme programmin. Empirical Software Engineering 18, 344–354 (2009)
5. Kwon, T.H., Zmud, R.W.: Unifying the fragmented models of information systems implementation. In: Critical Issues in Information Systems Research, pp. 227–251. John Wiley & Sons, Inc., Chichester (1987)
6. Karahanna, E.: Symbolic Adoption of Information Technology. In: Proceedings of Decision Sciences International Conference, Athens, Greece (1999)
7. Boehm, B.: Get Ready for Agile Methods, with Care. IEEE Computer 35(1), 64–69 (2002)
8. Highsmith, J., Cockburn, A.: Agile Software Development: The Business of Innovation. Computer, 120–122 (September 2001)
9. Nerur, S., Mahapatra, R.: Challenges of Migrating to Agile Methodologies. Communications of the ACM 48(5), 73–78 (2005)
10. McChesney, I.R., Glass, D.: Post-implementation management of CASE methodology. European Journal of Information Systems 2(3), 201–209 (1993)
11. Patton, J.: Kanban Development Oversimplified (2009), http://www.agileproductdesign.com/blog/2009/kanban_over_simplified.html [November 27, 2010]
12. Williams, L., Layman, L., Krebs, W.: Extreme Programming Evaluation Framework for Object-Oriented Languages Version 1.4, in NCSU Technical Report (2004)
13. Rogers, E.M.: Diffusion of Innovations, 5th edn. Free Press, New York (2003)
14. Hardgrave, B.C., Davis, F.D., Riemenschneider, C.K.: Investigating Determinants of Software Developers' Intentions to Follow Methodologies. Journal of Management Information Systems 20(1), 123–151 (2003)
15. Huisman, M., Iivari, J.: The Individual Deployment of Systems Development Methodologies. In: Pidduck, A.B., Mylopoulos, J., Woo, C.C., Ozsu, M.T. (eds.) CAiSE 2002. LNCS, vol. 2348, pp. 134–150. Springer, Heidelberg (2002)
16. Rajlich, V.: Changing the paradigm of software engineering. Communications of the ACM 49(8), 67–70 (2006)
17. Hardgrave, B.C., Johnson, R.: Toward an information systems development acceptance model: the case of object-oriented systems development. IEEE Transactions on Engineering Management 50(3), 322–336 (2003)
18. Khalifa, M., Verner, J.: Drivers for Software Development Usage. IEEE Transactions on Engineering Management 47(3), 360–369 (2000)
19. Agarwal, R., Prasad, J.: A Field Study of the Adoption of Software Process Innovations by Information Systems Professionals. IEEE Transactions on Engineering Management 47(3), 295–308 (2000)
20. Pikkarainen, M., Wang, X., Kieran, C.: Agile Practices in Use from an Innovation Assimilation Perspective: A Multiple Case Study. In: Twenty Eighth International Conference on Information Systems, Montreal (2007)

21. Fitzgerald, B.: The use of systems development methodolgies in practice: a field study. Information Systems Journal 7, 201–212 (1997)
22. Green, G.C., Hevner, A.R., Webb Collins, R.: The impacts of quality and productivity perceptions on the use of software process improvement innovations. Information and Software Technology 47(8), 543–553 (2005)
23. Van de Ven, A.H.: Central Problems in the Management of Innovation. Management Science 32(5), 590–607 (1986)
24. Pikkarainen, M., Wang, X., Conboy, K.: Agile Practices in Use from an Innovation Assimilation Perspective: A Multiple Case Study. In: Twenty Eighth International Conference on Information Systems, Montreal (2007)
25. Sultan, F., Chan, L.: The adoption of new technology: the case of object-oriented computing in software companies. IEEE Transactions on Engineering Management 47(1), 106–206 (2000)
26. Roberts, T.L., et al.: Factors that impact implementing a SDM. IEEE Transactions on Software Engineering 24(8), 640–649 (1998)
27. Yin, R.K.: Case Study Research: Design and Methods. Sage Publications, CA (1994)
28. Benbasat, I., Goldstein, D.K., Mead, M.: The Case Research Strategy in Studies of Information Systems. MIS Quarterly 11(3), 369–386 (1987)
29. Eisenhardt, K.M.: Building Theories from Case Study Research. The Academy of Management Review 14(4), 532–550 (1989)
30. BBCWorldwide (2010), http://www.bbcworldwide.com/about-us.aspx
31. Middleton, P., Joyce, D.: Lean Software Development: BBC Worldwide Case Study. In: Lean Software and Systems Conference, Atlanta (2010)
32. Iivari, J.: Why are CASE tools not used? Communications of the ACM 39(10), 94–103 (1996)
33. Cockburn, A., Highsmith, J.: Agile Software Development: The People Factor. Software Management (2001)
34. Misra, S.C., Kumar, V., Kumar, U.: Identifying some important success factors in adopting agile software development practices. The Journal of Systems and Software 82, 1869–1890 (2009)
35. Anderson, D.: Kanban, Successful Evolutionary Change For Your Technology Business (2010)
36. Fichman, R.G., Kemerer, C.F.: The Assimilation of Software Process Innovations: An Organizational Learning Perspective. Management Science 43(10), 1345–1363 (1997)
37. Gallivan, M.J.: Organizational Adoption and Assimilation of Comlex Technological Innovations: Development of a New Framework. The DATABASE for Advances in Information Systems 32(3), 51–80 (2001)

Challenges to Teamwork: A Multiple Case Study of Two Agile Teams

Viktoria Gulliksen Stray[1], Nils Brede Moe[2], and Torgeir Dingsøyr[2]

[1] University of Oslo, Gaustadalléen 23,
0373 Oslo, Norway
stray@ifi.uio.no
[2] SINTEF, SP Andersens veg 15 B,
7465 Trondheim, Norway
{nils.b.moe,torgeird}@sintef.no

Abstract. Agile software development has become the standard in many companies. While there are reports of major improvements with agile development over traditional development, many teams still strive to work effectively as a team. A multiple case study in two companies discovered challenges related to communication, learning and selecting the tasks according to the priority list. For example, the fact that the developers were not actively involved in the planning process, resulted in weak team orientation; even though the teams had identified and discussed recurring problems, they found it difficult to improve their teamwork practices; and because customers and support communicated tasks directly to the developers and developers chose tasks according to interest and expertise, following the priority list became difficult. We provide practical suggestions for teamwork in agile software development that intend to overcome these problems and strengthen team orientation and team learning in order to achieve effective agile teams.

Keywords: Teamwork, Team orientation, Team communication, Team learning, Agile methods, Agile Software development, Scrum, Kanban.

1 Introduction

Teamwork is important in software engineering and is a particular focus in agile development. Teamwork has been extensively studied in a number of fields, but little of this knowledge has been applied in the context of software development. One of the reasons may be that the general knowledge needs to be tailored to software development to become useful. Hence, there is a need for additional studies on teamwork in this specific area.

Agile methods such as Extreme Programming (XP) and Scrum direct software development in small, self-managing teams. While there are reports of major improvement with agile development methods over traditional development methods [1], effective teamwork is still a challenge. In a number of studies in small and large Scrum teams in various consulting and product development settings in companies of variable size through the last five years, we have observed three recurring challenges [2-4]:

A. Sillitti et al. (Eds.): XP 2011, LNBIP 77, pp. 146–161, 2011.
© Springer-Verlag Berlin Heidelberg 2011

Solving the wrong tasks: Team members often work on tasks that have low priority or are not even prioritized. Many developers also choose only tasks within a given component, type of module or type of technology due to interest or felt ownership independently of priority. These practices are not consistent with the focus in most agile methods on delivering the highest prioritized functionality to the customer.

Lack of communication: Sometimes critical decisions are taken by the project management without involving the team. This happens despite the strong emphasis on communication and shared decision-making in agile development methods. On the other hand, many team members approach only the team leader in the daily meeting and not the whole team. Moreover, we have observed team-members who did not pay attention when important issues were raised, and even a few who fell asleep in planning meetings.

Unreleased potential of learning: Agile development methods suggest several ways of giving feedback and create opportunities for analyzing experience. However, we have observed that many teams spend little time reflecting on how to improve how they work, and they do not discuss obvious problems. Some of the teams that carry out regular retrospective meetings struggle to convert their analysis into changes in action. Among those who try to remedy identified problems actively, several give up after seeing little change.

In this paper, we discuss and explain these three challenges further. We investigate the following research question: *Why do many software teams find it hard to adhere to the task priority list, communicate well, and release the potential of learning?* The remainder of the paper is organized as follows. Section 2 describes recent research on teamwork in other fields, as well as in agile software development. Section 3 presents the research design chosen for this study. Section 4 reports the results from two case studies. Section 5 discusses these results in relation to general teamwork theory. Section 6 concludes, including giving suggestions for theory and practice.

2   Teamwork

One of the main characteristics of agile methods is that software development should be organized in small, self-managed teams [5]. The focus on teamwork as a research area within software development is relatively recent, but teamwork has been subject of research in several other disciplines for many years, from small group research to work life research to management science [6-11]. Activities found to be important for successful teamwork are as follows: responding constructively to views expressed by others, giving others the benefit of the doubt, providing support to others, and recognizing the interests and achievements of others. These activities have been demonstrated to be important because they promote individual performance, which boosts team performance, which in turn boosts organization performance [10].

Exploiting the potential advantages of setting up work teams, such as increased productivity, innovation, and employee satisfaction, requires a successful implementation in a given organizational context. Teams themselves can influence the internal organization of teams, but team performance depends not only on the competence of the team itself in managing and executing its work; it also depends on the organizational context provided by management [6].

Which processes and components that comprise teamwork and how teamwork contributes to team effectiveness and team performance have been the focus of a number of studies [12-16]. Salas et al. [15] identify 136 models and frameworks in a literature review and discusses a representative sample of 11 of them in more detail.

Moe et al. [17] suggest five elements from team effectiveness models that are particularly challenging in agile software development. Here, we have chosen to focus on two of them: *team orientation* [18, 19] and *team learning* [18, 20], which are both critical for self-managing teams and explain challenges observed in two teams studied. For a deeper understanding of teamwork, it is necessary to understand the different processes of a team. Marks et al. have developed a recurring phase model of team processes [16] which we have used. In the next sections we describe the two elements team orientation and team learning, and then present the framework for team processes.

2.1 Team Orientation

Team orientation refers to the team tasks and the attitudes that team members have towards one another. It reflects an acceptance of team norms, the level of group cohesiveness, and the importance of team membership, e.g. assigning high priority to team goals and participating willingly in all relevant aspects of the team [21].

High team orientation is claimed to improve the overall team performance in self-managing teams, makes team members coordinate more, and also to improve individual effort [22]. A high team orientation implies that the teams have shared goals, and work together to achieve these goals. Team members take alternative solutions provided by other team members into account, and appraise that input to determine what is most correct. Another indicator of high team orientation is increased task involvement, information sharing, strategizing, and participatory goal setting. If team members do not show interest in other person's tasks, or do not ask for input and suggestions to alternative solutions, that is a sign of low team orientation.

2.2 Team Learning

Learning is important in all software teams. Also, for agile teams to stay self-managed a capacity for double-loop learning that allows operating norms and rules to change is required [18]. Double-loop learning is distinguished from single-loop learning in that it concerns the underlying values. If an agile team repeatedly changes practices without solving their problems, this is a sign that they have not understood the underlying causes of their problem, and is practicing single-looped learning. Lynn [23] argues that learning has a direct impact on cycle time and product success, and has identified two factors that are central for learning; capturing knowledge, and a change in behavior based on the captured knowledge. Practices that must be in place for this to happen are among others; recording and reviewing information, have goal clarity, goal stability and vision support. Establishing shared mental models is a factor related to learning. Salas et al. [15] describe behavioral markers such as anticipating and predicting other team member's needs. In addition, that the team is able to identify changes in the team or task and implicitly adjust strategies as needed.

2.3 Team Processes

For understanding team processes in this study we use the taxonomy developed by Marks et al. [16] through their extensive literature review. The taxonomy includes three categories: *transition phase processes*, *action phase processes*, and *interpersonal processes*. Transition phases are periods of time when team members focus on processes such as mission analysis, evaluation, establishing shared vision, planning, goal specification, and formulating strategies. Planning meetings in agile software development are transition phase processes. During action phases, team members conduct activities leading directly to goal accomplishment. In this phase the team concentrate on task accomplishments, monitoring progress, coordinating team members, as well as monitoring and backing up their fellow team members. Solving tasks will alternate between transition phase processes and action phase processes. The interpersonal processes includes conflict management, motivation and confidence building, and happens throughout transition and action phases.

3 Research Design and Method

We have studied two teams as the basis for the findings presented in the next section. In this embedded multiple case study [24], we report on two concepts, *team orientation*, and *team learning* through description of episodes from the two cases.

Table 1. Characteristics of the two teams in this study, North and South

Project	North	South
Product	Geographical information system	Content management system
Agile Method	Scrum	Scrum/Kanban
Years using agile methods	2	10
Team size	4	10

We chose two teams as cases from companies operating in different domains with varying years of experience using agile methods, see Table 1. Both teams used agile development practices to improve their ability to deliver iteratively and on time, increase software quality, and to improve teamwork and team communication.

The project in Company North started in February 2007 and was supposed to be delivered by January 2008, but was not finished by February 2008 when our data collection ended.

The project we observed in Company South started in April 2000. Scrum was used from the beginning. The client of the project was a Fortune 500 industrial company and the main product of the project was a custom-made web-based content management system (CMS). We observed the team from March 2010 to October 2010.

We have collected data from observations, semi-structured interviews and documents. To understand how *team orientation* was developed and maintained in the projects, we observed activities where the team interacted with each other and with the surroundings: daily work and meetings (daily stand-up, planning, review, and retrospective). For understanding *team learning* the daily meetings and retrospectives were important. The interviews and studying project documents also provided us with vital information for understanding the two factors. An overview of the data collected can be seen in Table 2. The observations lasted from 10 minutes to a full day. The interviews lasted from 20 to 60 minutes and were audio-recorded and transcribed.

Table 2. Overview of the data collected for the study

Source	Company North	Company South
Observations	Daily stand-up meetings (19), sprint planning meetings (4), sprint reviews (6), retrospective meetings (1) and other meetings (42), as well as observation of coding, testing and informal communication. The 72 observations were documented in field notes, which also included pictures.	Daily stand-up meetings (15), retrospective meetings (2), other meetings (31), and observation of coding, testing and informal communication. The 48 observations were documented in field notes, which also included pictures.
Interviews	Developers (3), scrum-master (1), product owner (1). The 5 interviews were transcribed.	Developers (6), Project leaders (2, one technical and one functional). The 8 interviews were transcribed.
Documents	Product backlogs, sprint backlogs, burn down charts, index cards and recorded data from Team System.	Presentations and reports.

We took field notes and pictures as well as collected iteration and project plans, meeting minutes, progress charts, and index cards used on project walls. We integrated all our notes to produce a detailed record of each session.

On the basis of this broad material, we used meta-ethnographic methods to analyze and synthesize data from the transcribed interviews, dialogues, and field notes. The transcribed interviews were imported into a tool for analyzing qualitative data, NVivo. We categorized interesting expressions using the teamwork concepts described in Section 2. After the analysis we presented the findings in feedback meetings with the companies.

4 Case Analysis

In this section we present the two projects and report characteristic episodes, which show aspects of team orientation and team learning. The projects were perceived as successful by the customers, team members and management, but they still had some challenges. One might think that the North project experienced challenges because they only had been using agile methodology for two years, but we observed similar difficulties in the South project even though they had used agile methods for ten years.

4.1 North Project

The goal of the North project was to redevelop a software package used internally to handle reports from customers. Initially the project consisted of two developers (one junior developer recently hired and working 100% on the project, and an experienced developer working 50-100% on the project), a scrum-master, a product owner, and a project manager. The scrum-master also did some development. In addition he had the role as department head, which meant he had many other obligations. The project manager was cooperating with the product owner to define the features, in addition to being responsible for the budget and communicating with the top management. The product owner and the project manager were situated in another city. Two months after start-up, a third experienced programmer joined the team. He was working 50-100% on the project.

4.1.1 Team Orientation

To achieve team orientation the team goals and vision need to be established among all team members. The one in charge for this in the North project was the product owner. However he was situated in another city and the team had to communicate with him using phone and e-mail. In the beginning they communicated on a daily basis, but the project owner was working on multiple projects and was often not available. Sometimes the team got stuck because they could not get immediate feedback from him and then discussions ended without conclusions since they were lacking vital information. During the last phase of the project one developer said while writing code: *"We need to talk to the Product-owner, but he is on a vacation. I guess he do not really care too much, and this affects us as well."*

The scrum-master was the head of department, and he often got tied up in other tasks. He frequently left in the middle of a workshop or meeting to answer an important phone call. When this happened the discussions and processes in the meeting were put on hold until he got back. It seemed like the scrum master gave priority to other tasks, and this affected the team members as well.

The team meetings usually worked well and included everyone, however the planning meetings where the product owner and project manager participated often failed when it came to building team orientation. In one meeting we observed that the two developers, who usually participated actively in other meetings, were mostly quiet. We also noticed that the discussions focused on issues relevant to the product owner, project manager and scrum-master. The meeting did not have a clear agenda, and the topics discussed often excluded the developers. At the last part of the meeting, there was not enough time available for planning the upcoming sprint in detail, which was the primary goal of the meeting. This affected the developer's chance of really committing to the team goals and plans, which is necessary for achieving team orientation.

Not only the meetings were important for building team orientation. The scrum-master and the team early identified what they called project concerns. A project concern [25] is a functional aspect that is considered to be of such importance that it should be treated separately and be specifically visible through the project. The team defined the concerns to be performance and reliability. The concerns were supposed to make it easier for the team to prioritize, decide and lead when working on the architecture and implementation. We observed several times that this helped the team identify and dealing with conflicting features and when prioritizing. This obviously strengthened the team orientation.

The project showed good progress in the first phase, however soon the situation changed. One reason was that the developers worked less than planned on the project. In this company, developers worked on several projects at the same time, and also needed to solve support requests on products they had worked on earlier. The effect of this was that developers were frequently interrupted, the project lost resources and developers had to work not only on their running projects. In a standup–meeting, the scrum-master asked: *"Will you work on the project this week?"* Developer 1: *"Yes, probably today or tomorrow."* Developer 2: *"I will most likely work on the project today."* In the following stand-up we observed that developer 2 had not done anything because of several emerging issues in other projects

When talking about the effect of this, one developer said: *"When you during a sprint realized that you would not finish, you did not care if you were 70% or 90% done. It didn't matter. These tasks were just moved to the next sprint, but then we also needed to add several other tasks to show progress... We classified tasks as finished before they were complete ... Each sprint starts with doing things that we have said were done, and then you know you will not finish the sprint. Since we knew we could not finish, we did not care if we didn't complete all the tasks during a sprint. Some tasks were moved 4 sprints before they were even started."*

An unrealistic plan made the team members prioritize individual goals over team goals. As a consequence when picking tasks, a developer picked the one he was most interested in solving, not the one with the highest priority. Subsequently this affected team orientation.

4.1.2 Team Learning

In one retrospective the problem of adding too many features, loosing resources, and not doing proper testing was discussed, and the team agreed that next time they would start on the right level and schedule enough time for testing. Our data indicate that this situation did not change much. The team did not manage to transform their experience into action, there was no real team learning. The project introduced "The wall" in this phase to get a better overview of the project status. Every task was then visible on the wall, and categorized into "not started", "in progress" and "finished". "The wall" made it visible to everyone that they were working on a lot of tasks in parallel, however they did not change the process.

One month before the final deadline, it became apparent to everyone that the team was delivering too slowly and could not meet the deadline. The scrum-master said: *"We found a solution to the problem. We agreed on postponing the deadline, keeping the functionality, and then isolate the team."* The scrum-master decided that the team was not even allowed to receive phone calls, while in isolation. This was broadcasted generally in the company. The scrum-master now collocated with the team to help protecting them. The team also agreed on working overtime.

Isolation of the team was not 100% effective, especially when the scrum-master was absent. One developer said: *"The isolation works how it should do, but we end up in a dilemma. Like today, it's crazy in the other project, where the customers are starting to use the system this week. And I'm the only one who can fix problems. Then I just need to help if they are having problems. I do not like to decide which project*

Fig. 1. The team with "The wall", giving an overview of project status

will not meet its deadlines, because that is what it is all about. But now the scrum-master has decided what to prioritize. However I feel I need to do it anyway; during the day or before I go home. There is no time allocated to this kind of support, and there are several people expecting me to solve the problems."

The isolation was most effective when the scrum-master was in the area, but the developers also felt it easier to say *"No, I'm busy"* when asked about something. The scrum-master also commented: *"I can see that the team is working harder and more focused. Earlier, they seemed relaxed the first week of the sprint. Now they are relaxing the first day, but then they start to feel the pressure. But I do not know how long we can do this, how long the effect will last."*

4.2 South Project

The project in South had two teams, one worked on maintenance and new development of the CMS-system, while the other worked with SharePoint development. The project had two project leaders, one functional and one technical. The product owner in the project was located in another country. The CMS team has been the focus of this study. This team consisted of nine developers and one technical project leader who also had the role as the team leader. Most of the developers were working 80-90% of their time on this project. Some of the developers had been on the project since the start. Before we started our study this project switched from Scrum-based development, which is time-boxed, to flow-based development, in their case Kanban. We were told that the motivation for doing this was the need for handling frequent changes to the plan, like interruptions from the customers and solving bugs.

4.2.1 Team Orientation

Team orientation requires that the team members know what the project plans and goals are. However, most of the team members in the South project did not know the project plans, nor did they have a clear understanding of the project long-term goals and vision. One developer said: *"I don't know how the release goals are defined. We get them in an e-mail from the project leader. The decisions on what to solve are not taken by the people who will work on it, but in collaboration between the project leaders and the product owner. We almost don't know what to do until we see the task on the board"*. The fact that the product owner was located in another country, made it hard for the team members to communicate with him directly. One developer said: *"Often, if I want to say something I write an e-mail to the project leader in English, and then he takes it further to the product owner"*.

At the time we observed the South project they ran the project using a flow-based development process, Kanban, but they still conducted daily standup-meetings, which is a scrum practice. These daily meetings were held every morning at 9 o'clock by the interactive white board located in the middle of the office space, and lasted from 2 to 15 minutes. The daily meetings were seen as important for exchange of information and the intention was to make sure the developers communicated about their work at the start of their day. Even if this meeting was experienced as the most important meeting during the day people often came late. We were also told that some people disliked these meetings and we saw people acting uncomfortable and being silent. One person complained it was too early in the morning. The interviews also revealed that some team members did not pay attention to what others were saying. They found the meeting of low interest because the issues discussed were not seen as relevant to their own work. This was a bit surprising since the meeting only discussed what was going on in the project. This was a clear indication of low team orientation.

The team had an interactive white board where everyone could see all tasks in prioritized order given by the product owner. This white board showed all the change requests and bugs for the next release and made the status of the project visible for everyone. The team members were supposed to pick the task with the highest priority. However, we experienced that team members often chose tasks according to their interest and area of expertise. The team members often felt it was obvious who should do what, and they seldom broke this pattern. This made them even more specialized and the amount of redundancy was very low. One project manager said: *"We are very sensitive to the specialist competence. Today one of the developers has five tasks on the board. I asked him if there are any of them anyone else can solve, but there weren't. So we clearly have trouble transferring knowledge. But the project is so big that everyone cannot know everything."*

We also observed that some tasks did not get picked, even when it had the highest priority. The result was that the team leader had to delegate those tasks. The specialization resulted in own goals becoming more important than team goals. However we also observed that the team members often helped each other when one got a problem he or she could not solve.

A daily challenge was the pressure of working on tasks not on the board. Accordingly, tasks not prioritized by the product owner or by the team. These tasks were often related to operation issues, customer requests and support. The team members found it difficult to say no to the customer. One developer said: *"It often happens that the client goes directly to a developer and says: ``We have to do something about this now!" But I guess that is OK since it obviously must be a high priority task. The problem is that often the result of this is that we have to go past the limit we have set for maximum number of tasks we are supposed to have in progress."*

Performing many tasks not agreed on by the team is an indication of problems with the team orientation.

4.2.2 Team Learning

The daily meeting was seen as the most important forum for information flow in the project. The meeting was not working as intended, which was confirmed through the interviews. Several interviewees complained that they did not get enough information about what was going on in the project. Some felt that only a few people, often the people that had been on the project for the longest time, got a full overview of the project. One developer said: *"The information flow has been poor since the start of the project ten years ago. We should have done something about it."*

In the project the team had a positive attitude towards learning and appreciated the retrospective meetings, which were the primary means for discussing problems. Problems were identified, however they had difficulties solving them, for instance improving the daily meeting. They never found an approach that satisfied all team members. They had tried several ways; one of them was to focus on each individual in the team. They forced everyone to talk, by passing a ball around. A person was then supposed to talk when he or she got the ball. Unfortunately, not all team members followed what the team had agreed on doing, and started throwing the ball around to be funny. The team then stopped using the ball. They then tried to make the meeting go faster by only focusing on the obstacles slowing or stopping their progress. However if the team members said "no" when asked if they had any problems, the team leader said "back to work" and the meeting was over after about 2 minutes. When this happened there was almost no exchange of information. The third way of running the meeting was that the team lead pointed to specific tasks at the board asking for status. We observed that not all team members were satisfied with this way either, but this was the method in use when our data collection ended.

Because of the request from people outside the team, measures were taken to protect the team members. This did not work out as intended. One project leader said: *"We have tried to isolate people by making them pair program. We thought that maybe we could remove noise by having people sit together to produce on a task. It is much more difficult to reply to e-mails and answering the phone when you sit together with someone. We believed in this, but it was very hard to establish. There was no culture for doing it. I think you have to push really hard for it to work, maybe so much that it gets uncomfortable. People slide back to their usual patterns."*

While the team focused on solving their challenges, they forgot to pay attention to what was actually working well. One effect was the team stopped doing their regular learning workshop. In the interviews, almost everyone claimed that they missed this workshop.

Kanban focuses on limiting the amount of work in progress and visualizing work on the board. The team was satisfied with trying to keep the "work in progress" at a low level because they felt that when they managed to do this it made them more effective. We were also told that the product owner appreciated this way of coordinating work, since he now could constantly reprioritize and add tasks, instead of having to come up with a list of items for the next iteration every other week.

Fig. 2. A daily meeting, focusing on specific tasks

5 Discussion

We have described teamwork in projects North and South with two and ten years of agile experience, Table 3 summarizes the key findings. Even though we report on their problems, we want to emphasize that the projects were perceived as successful by the customers, team members and management. Still there are several possibilities to improve the team performance. In the following, we discuss the two cases in light of our research question. Then we give some suggestions for practice.

Table 3. Summary of key observations

	Observations	North	South
Team orientation	People running in and out of meetings	X	
	Product owner giving priority to other tasks and projects	X	
	Meetings without a clear agenda	X	
	Topics discussed exclude developers in meetings	X	
	Scrum master delegating tasks directly to developers	X	X
	Unrealistic product backlog and sprint plans	X	
	Missing understanding of project plans and goals	X	X
	Product owner in another location	X	X
	Team members not paying attention in the daily meeting	X	X
	Picking tasks according to own priorities	X	X
	Working on unplanned tasks	X	X
Team learning	Not managing to transform lessons learned into action	X	X
	Isolation of team members to avoid interruptions	X	X
	Not paying attention to what is working well		X
	Project status information altered to show progress	X	

5.1 Three Problems

Our research question is *"why do many software teams find it hard to follow the task priority list, experience lack of communication, and in releasing the potential of learning?"*. These three problems were manifested in both cases:

Following the task priority list was a challenge in both projects for several reasons. Specialization of team members in South, and unrealistic plans in the North project, was an important reason why the team did not always work on the tasks with the highest priority. When a team-member finished a task he picked a new one related to his own priorities. The specialization led to little involvement in other people's tasks. In both projects, they did not pay enough attention to the "truck factor", meaning that if one the developers gets hit by a truck, other team members should be able to pick up on the work of any developer. This resulted in little knowledge sharing and lack of redundant knowledge in the team.

Both in North and South, there were tasks that were communicated directly to developers, which obstructed the progress of the team on the common goals. These tasks were either directly from the customer in the current project, or support requests from previous projects. In addition, there was little commitment to an overall plan, which is an obstacle for achieving team orientation.

The teams were not sufficiently able to give everyone in the team insight in and ownership to plans and goals. Most developers in South expressed they knew little about the overall plan, and in North, we observed planning meetings as a discussion between the product owner, scrum-master and project manager, with little involvement by the developers. In North the project constantly had to fight for resources, which lowered team members motivation.

Fully agile teams are supposed to have a flat team structure with peers. In North a small core of the teams, product owner and scrum-master, covered up issues rather than make them more transparent and empower others to participate. The project status information was altered to show management more progress than they really had. In South the scrum master had to delegate tasks directly to developers. This violates the flat structure of agile teams.

Lack of communication was shown in the daily meetings in South. Team members seemed to dislike the daily meetings, and people were not paying attention to what others presented as it was seen as irrelevant to them, also people were not present from the beginning of these meetings. In North, project meetings were frequently disturbed because key persons went in and out. Further, communication with the product owner in both projects was cumbersome, as this person was not collocated with the team and was primarily reached by email.

The unreleased potential of learning was shown through some of the problems the teams experienced. In North, the team was aware that they lost resources and that plans were unrealistic, but they did not do much to solve the problems until the very last phase of the project when they started isolation. The fact that support work was not a part of the official assignment of resources in North, although sprint burn down charts visualized that resources drifted away, shows problems with team learning. In South, they were aware of problems with the daily meetings, tried several practices to solve it, but these did not satisfactorily improve the situation. Also, in South, some practices that were working well gradually fell out of use.

5.2 Suggestions for Practice

This section will give some suggestions for practice on the basis of our observations, structured according to transition phase processes, action phase processes and interpersonal processes [16], as described in Section 2:

Transition phase processes:
Mechanisms to facilitate team orientation and team learning were missing in the planning meetings in North, resulting in few common goals and a lack of shared mental models. The meeting culture in North made involvement by the whole group difficult, and limited access to the product owner made the transition phases cumbersome. We observed that if the plans were perceived as unrealistic by the team members, their motivation for actually finishing all the tasks in the sprint decreased because they knew they couldn't make it. In South, the team did not have to deal with unrealistic product backlogs and sprint plans because they used Kanban and therefore did not have to commit to a plan or spend time on planning in detail. Instead, they solved tasks that were constantly prioritized by the product owner. This made the project more flexible and less dependent on the product owner attending meetings at specific times. However, a consequential challenge was that the team members did not have a clear understanding of the vision and long-term goals of the project. This leads to the following suggestions for practice in the transition phase:

- Allocate enough time, resources and facilitation in this phase in order to establish team orientation and make grounds for team learning.
- Consider moving to more flow-based development if the sprint plan is often unrealistic.

Action phase processes:
In North, the productivity increased when they isolated the team. Moreover, both the teams in South and North had developed a culture of helping each other and had established an open dialogue. The policy in South was to not have more than 14 "work in progress" tasks, but we observed that they often struggled to keep below this number.

In both North and South they had the challenge that team members chose tasks according to their interest and expertise instead of following the priority list. However in South this behaviour was more visible because of the visual white board. Also low redundancy became visible on the board when the team exceeded the "work in progress" limit and at the same time one person had too many tasks, and no one was able to help that team member.

This leads to the following suggestions for practice in the action phase:

- Protect the team from external tasks during the action phases.
- Consider ways of limiting "work in progress".
- Create a culture for collaboration when solving tasks and problems.
- The use of visual boards such as an interactive whiteboard makes low team orientation visible, and improves shared mental models.
- Find ways to increase the amount of redundancy in the team.

Interpersonal processes:
Some conflicts were not dealt with in the teams, like customers getting priority by talking to developers directly, or when team members did not follow team decisions. In hectic periods, forums for discussing interpersonal issues, like daily meetings and retrospective meetings were abandoned. In South, the team was good at giving both negative and positive feedback to each other when testing and reviewing the code of each other. In North, most of the feedback to developers was on code not working correctly. This leads to the following suggestions for practice for interpersonal processes:

- Provide forums for conflict resolution. Discuss deviations between agreed processes and practice, and adjust accordingly.
- Encourage team members to give feedback to each other, especially positive feedback.

6 Conclusion

This study investigated teamwork, in particular team orientation and team learning, in two software development teams that used agile methods. We identified many challenges related to team orientation, such as a lack of understanding of project plans and goals, and trouble with running the daily meeting in a satisfactory way. We also observed in both projects that team members chose tasks according to their area of interest and expertise instead of following the priority list, which made the redundancy low because the developers had little competence to solve tasks outside their specific area. To overcome this problem, the team leader had to delegate tasks not chosen by anyone. This meant that one of the principles of self organizing teams was violated. Two challenges related to team learning were the problem of transforming experience into action and lack of paying attention to what was working well.

Some of the challenges we observed were related to the choice of the specific agile method. Successful sprint planning meetings in Scrum depends very much on the product owner. In North, the product owner and managers frequently discussed topics that were irrelevant to the sprint planning in these meetings, which resulted in plans that the developers found unrealistic. This had a negative effect on their team orientation. With Kanban development in South, the team did not have to spend time on planning in detail but could solve tasks that were constantly prioritized and added by the product owner. This made the project more flexible and less dependent on the product owner to attend meetings at specific times. However, a challenge resulting from this was that the team members had no clear understanding of the vision and long-term goals of the project.

Based on our observations we provide some suggestions for practice. For example, if the sprint plans are unrealistic and change frequently during the sprint, one should consider moving from time-boxed development to flow-based development. If team orientation is low, consider using visual boards such as an interactive white board to improve shared mental models.

In the future we would like to see more studies of software engineering practice making use of existing teamwork literature. In particular, one should investigate team leadership, self-managing teams, shared leadership and mechanisms for team learning and increase of team motivation. These are areas that may have a profound impact on the effectiveness and efficiency of software engineering.

Acknowledgments. This work was supported by the Research Council of Norway through grant 193236/I40.

References

1. Dybå, T., Dingsøyr, T.: Empirical Studies of Agile Software Development: A Systematic Review. Information and Software Technology 50, 833–859 (2008)
2. Moe, N.B., Dingsøyr, T., Dybå, T.: A teamwork model for understanding an agile team: A case study of a Scrum project. Information and Software Technology 52, 480–491 (2010)
3. Moe, N.B., Dingsoyr, T., Dybå, T.: Overcoming Barriers to Self-Management in Software Teams. IEEE Software 26(6), 20–26 (2009)
4. Moe, N.B., Dingsøyr, T., Dybå, T.: Understanding Self-organizing Teams in Agile Software Development. In: 19th Australian Conference on Software Engineering. IEEE Computer Society, Perth (2008)
5. Good, J., Romero, P.: Collaborative and social aspects of software development. International Journal of Human-Computer Studies 66(7), 481–483 (2008)
6. Guzzo, R.A., Dickson, M.W.: Teams in organizations: Recent research on performance and effectiveness. Annual Review of Psychology 47, 307–338 (1996)
7. Cohen, S.G., Bailey, D.E.: What makes teams work: Group effectiveness research from the shop floor to the executive suite. Journal of Management 23(3), 239–290 (1997)
8. Sapsed, J., et al.: Teamworking and knowledge management: a review of converging themes. International Journal of Management Reviews 4(1), 71–85 (2002)
9. Mathieu, J., et al.: Team Effectiveness 1997-2007: A Review of Recent Advancements and a Glimpse Into the Future. Journal of Management (34), 410–476 (2008)
10. Katzenbach, J., Smith, D.: The discipline of teams. Harvard Business Review 71, 111 (1993)
11. Sandberg, Å.: Enriching production: perspectives on Volvo's Uddevalla plant as an alternative to lean production. MPRA Paper (1995)
12. Langfred, C.W.: The paradox of self-management: Individual and group autonomy in work groups. Journal of Organizational Behavior 21(5), 563–585 (2000)
13. Burke, C.S., et al.: What type of leadership behaviors are functional in teams? A meta-analysis. Leadership Quarterly 17(3), 288–307 (2006)
14. Hoegl, M., Gemuenden, H.G.: Teamwork Quality and the Success of Innovative Projects: A Theoretical Concept and Empirical Evidence. Organization Science 12(4), 435–449 (2001)
15. Salas, E., et al.: Fostering Team Effectiveness in Organizations: Toward an Integrative Theoretical Framework. In: 52nd Nebraska Symposium on Motivation, Lincoln, NE (2007)
16. Marks, M.A., Mathieu, J.E., Zaccaro, S.J.: A temporally based framework and taxonomy of team processes. Academy of Management Review 26(3), 356–376 (2001)

17. Moe, N.B., Dingsøyr, T., Røyrvik, E.A.: Putting Agile Teamwork to the Test – An Preliminary Instrument for Empirically Assessing and Improving Agile Software Development. In: Abrahamsson, P., Marchesi, M., Maurer, F. (eds.) XP 2009. LNBIP, vol. 31, pp. 114–123. Springer, Heidelberg (2009)
18. Morgan, G.: Images of Organizations, p. 504. SAGE publications, Thousand Oaks (2006)
19. Nonaka, I., Takeuchi, H.: The knowledge-creating company: how Japanese companies create the dynamics of innovation, vol. XII, p. 284s. Oxford University Press, New York (1995)
20. Nerur, S., Balijepally, V.: Theoretical reflections on agile development methodologies. Communications of the ACM 50(3), 83 (2007)
21. Dickinson, T.L., McIntyre, R.M.: A conceptual framework of teamwork measurement. In: Brannick, M.T., Salas, E., Prince, C. (eds.) Team Performance Assessment and Measurement: Theory, Methods, and Applications, pp. 19–43. Psychology Press, NJ (1997)
22. Salas, E., Sims, D.E., Burke, C.S.: Is there a "big five" in teamwork? Small Group Research 36(5), 555–599 (2005)
23. Lynn, G., Skov, R., Abel, K.: Practices that support team learning and their impact on speed to market and new product success (1999)
24. Yin, R.K.: Case study research: design and methods, vol. xiv, p. 219s. Sage, Thousand Oaks (2009)
25. Walderhaug, S., et al.: MAFIIA – an Architectural Description Framework: Experience from the Health Care Domain. In: Konstantas, D., et al. (eds.) Interoperability of Enterprise Software and Applications, pp. 43–54. Springer, Geneva (2005)

TaskBoard - Using XP to Implement Problem-Based Learning in an Introductory Programming Course*

Halley Wesley A.S. Gondim, Ana Paula L. Ambrósio, and Fábio M. Costa

Institute of Informatics – Federal University of Goias (UFG)
Campus II - Samambaia - Caixa Postal 131 - CEP 74001-970
Goiania - GO - Brasil
{halley,apaula,fmc}@inf.ufg.br
http://www.inf.ufg.br

Abstract. Introductory courses on Algorithms and Computer Programming typically present high failure rates. The lack of motivation and the difficulty encountered by some students are among the factors that lead to poor achievement. This paper presents a new teaching methodology for CS1, integrating PBL with the flexibility of Extreme Programming, creating a more collaborative, challenging and dynamic learning experience. The method also contributes to raise the quality of code and to enhance students' abilities by using best practices from Software Engineering. In order to implement the method we developed an application called TaskBoard, which assists groups of students in the process of XP-based problem solving, facilitating the development, management and persistence of the solutions and related artifacts.

Keywords: Computer Education, Introduction to Programming, Problem-Based Learning, Extreme Programming.

1 Introduction

The introductory course on algorithms and computer programming (CS1) represents a challenge for Computer Science undergraduate programs. It is considered one of the seven great challenges in the teaching of Computing [17]. The proposal of new methods for teaching this course has been the subject of extensive debate among academics [2,3,6] and has resulted in curriculum recommendations by the ACM and the IEEE Computer Society.

Problems with this course have been pointed out as responsible for the high failure and drop out rates in Computer Science programs [14]. This raises even greater worries when we consider that enrollment in Computer Science majors have been decreasing worldwide [9]. Enhancing this course has thus become vital.

When freshmen students first enter the course, most of them face difficulties due to lack of logic and algorithmic reasoning, and ignorance of language syntax

---

* This work was partly supported by the HP Technology for Teaching Higher Education Grant 2007.

A. Sillitti et al. (Eds.): XP 2011, LNBIP 77, pp. 162–175, 2011.

details. Many students are led to believe that programming is an overly difficult task and face extra obstacles when beginning to learn software development [20]. Among the main difficulties students face are: the development of strategies to divide larger problems into smaller ones; the understanding of programming mechanics (flow control structures, variable assignment and declarations); and the application of programming techniques to different situations and problems [7,16,20].

Different approaches to teaching computer programming have been proposed as attempts to solve these issues. At the Institute of Informatics, UFG, we have adopted a new methodology based on the combination of PBL with tablet PCs and visual programming languages [1]. The use of PBL in disciplines as diverse as computing and medicine has become common and among its benefits we can name increased content retention and motivation both for students and instructors. In addition, it has been demonstrated that PBL helps to develop logic reasoning and the fundamental abilities of collaborative work and research [21].

Another common practice used to facilitate the learning of computer programming is related to agile development methodologies. Keefe [13] describes a study on the use of XP practices in an introductory programming course as a mean to add value to current pedagogical approaches, highlighting the benefits of the use of such practices for the students.

In this paper we present a new teaching methodology for the Computer Programming I course, integrating PBL with the flexibility of extreme programming to create a learning environment that is more collaborative, challenging and dynamic, also helping to raise code quality and the ability to analyze problems. Closely linked to the methodology, we present TaskBoard, a distributed application that assists in the use of the methodology by providing functionality to collaboratively develop and manage the solutions to problems, as well as to persist the artifacts that are generated during the process.

The paper is organized as follows. Section 2 describes the PBL method used at our institution. Section 3 briefly describes principles of extreme programming, while Section 4 discusses the adaptation of PBL with the use of XP. Section 5 presents the tool we developed to support the methodology, while Section 6 presents the results of an experiment carried out to validate the approach. Section 7 discusses related work and Section 8 concludes the paper and points to future work.

2 Problem-Based Learning and Adaptations for CS1

Problem-based learning (PBL) is well-known as an instructional method that promotes knowledge retention by students, at the same time that it helps to develop abilities for collaborative work and other desirable professional attitudes [19]. Fundamentally, the method is characterized by the use of real-world problems, leveraging group knowledge and encouraging students to develop critical reasoning and problem-solving abilities, at the same time as they master the essential concepts of the subject area. According to the principles of PBL, the knowledge constructed while seeking to identify and solve problems, as well as the abilities developed during the process, are as relevant as the problem solution itself [4].

The definition of typical PBL lectures takes into account the themes that students should master after each class. Each theme is presented to students in the form of a problem, which is meant to be worked on by tutorial groups that have eight to ten students. Among the students in a tutorial group, one is chosen as the coordinator and another one as the secretary, noting that these roles rotate from session to session. During the first group meeting for a given problem, the problem is first discussed, encouraging the proposal of hypotheses and solutions. Learning objectives are then identified, pointing to topics for individual study (which is performed outside of classroom hours). In the next session, the group meets again to discuss, synthesize and apply the newly acquired knowledge about the problem. The cycle for a problem varies in length, but is typically a week or two.

The definition of PBL presented above is commonly advocated by the early adopters in disciplines such as medical studies. It has even been adopted, with very little adaptations, to teach Computer Programming [18]. In our context, however, we felt that the original approach is too orthodox, leading to a lack of flexibility and not taking into account important limitations and the learning style that is more typical of our students. Considering this, in the first semester of 2008 we started a series of experiments to adapt the PBL method to the teaching and learning needs of our CS1 course. The main motivation was the low level of achievement by students and the high drop out rates, not to mention a generalized lack of student motivation.

We developed a variation of PBL based on an adaptation of the seven-step method proposed in [18]. Our method is illustrated in Figure 1 and consists of four steps. As explained above, a problem in PBL is motivated by one or more target concepts that students must learn (e.g., variables and assignment). During the first session the problem is introduced, together with a list of the concepts it contains, and students have time to discuss it within the group. The main results produced by students in this session is a description of the main aspects of the problem and a brief description of previous knowledge that will help solve it. Students also produce a brief explanation showing where the target concept(s) will be applied in the solution. This session is followed by extra-class activities, mainly self-study of the target concept(s). This study is instrumented both with a list of reference materials and a list of small programming exercises that involve aspects of the target concept(s). In the next session, the groups meet again to produce a solution to the problem, based on the application of the knowledge they gathered during the self-study step. Normally, the solution presented by a group is a combination of attempts made by each student during the self-study step and is not very sophisticated. However, it is still a complete application of the target concept(s). In order to complement learning and show further applications and implications of the target concept(s), a third session consists in a more traditional lecture, where the concepts are reviewed, showing

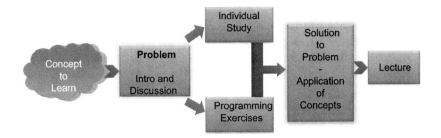

Fig. 1. Adaptation of the PBL method

its different nuances (some of them may not have been covered in the students' solution to the problem), and examples of their use are shown. The typical cycle for a problem thus takes three classroom meetings (sessions). In addition, depending on the problem, a fourth meeting is used to solve small exercises to further consolidate learning, and an individual assignment is given to students to enhance the solution previously presented for the problem.

Because we don't have enough resources to run separate tutorial groups, the meetings take place in a lab with four round tables, each one serving as the meeting place for a different group of five students. During the meetings there is one tablet PC for each student, which they use both for note taking (normally using digital ink) and for programming. The meetings are assisted by an instructor and an assistant instructor (the latter is typically a student who has taken the same course on a previous semester). The instructors play the role of consultants, helping to steer the work in the groups and responding to students' questions.

In terms of programming tools, we first used visual programming environments, namely Alice [8] and Scratch [15], for the first few weeks of the course as a means to introduce the basic computer programming concepts. It turned out, however, that students got distracted by the visual appeal of such systems and spent most of the time trying to perfect the visual appearance of the output (typically 3-D or 2-D animations). This motivated us to adopt a less visual approach, but still one that allowed for the graphical representation of program structures. As a result, from the second semester of 2009, we began using SICAS [11], a flowchart-based programming environment for beginners, where students design and implement algorithms in the form of structured flowcharts. The tool has all the programming constructs of structured programming languages and allows for the live execution of flowcharts, as well as code generation in Java, C and pseudo-code.

After the first few weeks using the beginners programming environment, we switch to using the C language. The overall idea is that students can begin mastering the fundamental concepts of algorithms without needing to worry with syntax. In this way, only when students are comfortable with algorithms and program logic, we introduce a full programming language.

Further details about our method and its evaluation can be found in [1].

3   Extreme Programming

XP is an agile software development methodology introduced in the late 90's [5], which, together with other so called agile methodologies became widely used practice in the software industry. Contrary to classic methodologies, XP emphasizes coding and the people involved [5]. It applies to small and medium sized projects, with vague, imprecise or constantly changing requirements. To this end, it adopts the strategy of constantly monitoring progress and carrying out several small adjustments during the development process.

The practices associated with XP were first introduced in a higher education environment in 1999 [22]. Since then, XP has become widely used as a methodology to teach software development [13]. In addition, some of its practices have been adopted as tools to teach Computer Programming at different levels [10].

In our case, we adopted XP as a mean to structure the use of problem-based learning. We identified a strong relationship between some of the XP practices and the steps of the PBL method. Indeed, the practices of XP can be used as concrete vehicles to carry out each of the steps in the PBL method, with the added benefit that students get familiar with a widely used development methodology. We note, however, that we adapted the practices of XP to our context and the specific needs of our teaching/learning environment. This is in agreement with the idea that the adoption of XP does not mean strictly following each of its practices, but instead adapting them to the particular context [5]. In the next section we outline our approach, showing how we adapted XP to work within the context of our PBL teaching environment.

4   Adaptation of PBL with the Principles of XP

The idea of integrating PBL with the principles of XP, together with the use of flowcharts and digital ink, originated from our experience with the use of new technologies and methodologies to teach computer programming. Observing the process of constructing solutions in the PBL method, we noted the need for a process that, besides organizing development could also introduce some elementary software engineering practices. As a result, we created an environment in which students could apply the practices of XP while learning to program, leading to better coding and raising awareness with respect to the need to adopt good software engineering practices in their projects.

Comparing PBL with XP, we noted that most steps of PBL are compatible with the practices of XP, which makes the adaptation more natural. Aiming to have more agility in the development of problem solutions, we introduced some XP practices that had no immediate counterpart in PBL, mainly: the elaboration of test cases, break down in subproblems, pair programming, simple design and refactoring. The introduction of these practices contributes to raise the code quality and team involvement.

In order to enhance the learning environment, we also adopt the use of flowcharts and digital ink. Flowcharts are useful to improve students' understanding of small programming problems, being an appropriate tool for beginners. The use of flowcharts place the focus on the algorithm (instead of programming syntax), helping students visualize the solution in a more natural way. Digital ink, in turn is a valuable tool for note taking during the several steps of the problem solving process, enabling students to more naturally express their thoughts and insights when working towards the solution.

The use of XP thus enabled us to better adapt the several steps of the PBL method for the teaching of computer programming. The proposed adaptation of PBL is outlined in what follows.

- **Problem title** – In this first step, students are given the problem statement, which has to be carefully read and discussed within the group, aiming to find an appropriate title for the problem. This title will be the name of the XP project.
- **Brainstorming** – This step is devoted to open discussion of the problem, leading to ideas and hypotheses for its solution. This step is further divided into: aspects of the problem, requirements analysis, and problem subdivision into increments. During this step, students must fully understand the context of the problem statement and what is required for its solution. Based on the group discussion, possible solutions are suggested and the different aspects of the problem are associated to the constructs of the programming language in use. Students must also identify the inputs and outputs for the problem, as well as enumerate previous knowledge that will be helpful for the solution, together with the aspects of the problem for which they need further knowledge. This latter part constitutes the learning objectives and serves as the basis for the self-study step which follows.
- **Self-study** – In this step students use the hypotheses and learning objectives formulated during the previous step as the basis for research on the topic. The goal is to understand the concepts that are necessary for the solution so that each student can productively contribute to the group's efforts during the next step.
- **Problem solution** – This step, which may last one or more meetings depending on the size of the problem, begins with a group-based discussion aiming to collect and refine the solution elements brought in by each student. This is followed by a break down of the problem in tasks, which are expressed as cards. Following the XP methodology, at the beginning of each meeting, the group discusses the cards that should be implemented or further subdivided. In addition, before starting the implementation of a card, the group must elaborate appropriate test cases. The goal is to achieve a better understanding of the task before starting to implement it, enabling a reduction in the amount of coding mistakes. Together with the test cases, students must also produce a sketch of each activity/card. This sketch is produced in the form of a flowchart drawn using digital ink, which is a very agile and flexible form of representing visual information. When students

are confident they master the card's content, they start coding using pair programming. Currently, a third party IDE is used for this purpose, but future versions of the environment will integrate a standard IDE. The use of pair programming in this step enables constant revision of the code, which, together with the previously defined test cases, contribute to raise the quality of programs. In addition, the ownership of the code is not restricted to the group members that started the coding corresponding to a card. This means that other pairs in the same group can get hold of the code in order to test (using the test cases), complete, refactor and fix bugs. When the coding that corresponds to all cards is finished, students start the integration phase, putting the several pieces of code together in order to produce a complete solution to the problem.

5   TaskBoard

The TaskBoard tool was developed with the goal of supporting the solution of programming problems using the PBL + XP methodology presented above. It provides support for each of the steps presented in Section 4 and enables the use of flowcharts and digital ink in a distributed, interactive and collaborative environment. The tool also provides for the persistence and sharing of all the artifacts produced by students during the process of problem solving. The tool is illustrated in Figure 2, which shows the main screen with the links for accessing each of the steps described in Section 4.

Following the methodology, each group of students first performs the problem analysis, identifying the several aspects of the problem, the problem is discussed, input and output, previous knowledge and learning objectives. In the step that follows self-study, students get together to divide the problem into subproblems, proposing a solution to each subproblem using flowcharts and code and validating the solution using the specified input/output and test cases. Each member of a

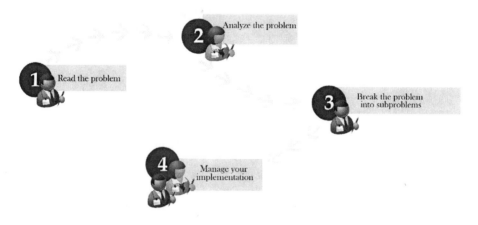

Fig. 2. Main screen of the TaskBoard tool

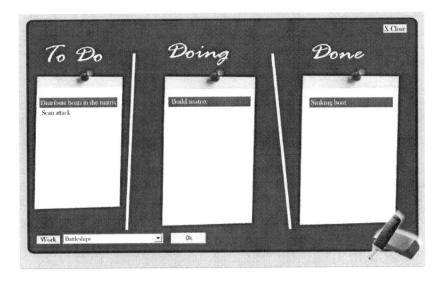

Fig. 3. The task board: showing the state of the cards

group, as well as the instructor, can follow the evolution of the problem using the task board, a part of the tool that shows the state of each task (not initiated, in progress, and completed), as illustrated in Figure 3.

The requirements for the TaskBoard tool were elicited as the result of a study that applied the methodology in a group of forty students. The functional requirements directly correspond to the steps of the methodology (see Section 4) and include functions for the creation and visualization of: student and group records; problem specifications; task cards; and problem analysis sketches. It also includes functions for maintenance of the task board. The non-functional requirements in turn are the following: access control to the artifacts produced by students, so that one group cannot access the artifacts produced by another group; concurrency control, so that the integrity of an artifact is not compromised by simultaneous accesses by the students; and log generation and visualization.

Using the tool, each group has its own task board, which is viewable and accessible (read and write) by all group members. The instructor in turn has access to the task boards of all groups. In this way, the instructor can monitor progress and check the aspects of a problem (given by the corresponding cards) where students are having most difficulty. This provides valuable input to prepare the lecture that follows the solution of each problem.

The architecture of the TaskBoard tool follows the client-server model, where the clients are desktop applications that enable access (read and write) to content (the artifacts used in problem solving) maintained on a server. The server in turn implements the business logic dictated by the above mentioned requirements. Actual storage of the artifacts produced by the students is carried out using the MySQL database management system. The tool itself (both client and server sides) was developed in C#, using the Microsoft .NET framework 4.0, together with Windows Form Application and Windows Presentation Foundation (the latter for the support for digital ink).

6 Evaluation

To validate and evaluate the methodology and its accompanying tool, we performed a real-classroom experiment in the Programming I course at UFG at the end of the first semester of 2010. A total of 40 students participated in the experiment, divided into two classes of 20 students each. Each class was further divided into 4 groups of 5 students. The experiment took three weeks (six meetings), including an introductory lesson on the principles of XP and the use of the TaskBoard tool. The development of the project (associated with the problem) by the students took four meetings, during which each group analyzed the problem and implemented a solution. The sixth meeting consisted of a review lecture about the concepts introduced in the problem. We note that this group of students were already used to working on problems using our original PBL method (described in Section 2), which may have influenced their perception of the new methodology.

The work of the mentor/teacher was mainly to verify students followed the PBL steps and used the Taskboard tools, helping with doubts and guiding the students, not letting them go astray. Only one tutor was designated to help all students. Special attention was given to the storage of the steps in the tool.

The evaluation was based on a three-part questionnaire. The first part had 18 multiple choice questions about the methodology and the second was specific to the TaskBoard tool (7 questions). The third part was composed of an open-ended question about the methodology and the tool. The multiple choice questions were organized according to the Likert scale, with 5 gradings (the end result for each question was obtained by the sum of the positive grades, ignoring the neutral grade). The results, along with the questions, are presented and discussed below, also considering the observation of student's attitudes in the classroom.

Classroom observation showed that the majority of students did not like the tool at first, mainly because it was perceived to be restrictive in terms of the sequence of steps and in terms of the ability to use existing code found on the Web. With TaskBoard, students were induced to follow a process step-by-step, documenting each stage, with each step subject to evaluation by the instructor. Furthermore, the use of PBL + XP introduced new ideas and checkpoints in the process, such as pair programming, refactoring and test cases, which added to the typical routine students were used to.

Observing the questionnaire results and the attitudes of students in the classroom, we concluded that the requirement to follow a well-defined process prevents students from going straight to coding, which favors the initial analysis of the problem, thus to a better understanding of it. The subdivision of the problem enables reduction of scope and abstraction, making it easier to analyze inputs and outputs, as well as the test cases and other aspects of the problem. However

Table 1. Survey questionnaire and percentage of positive answers

Questions	Positive Answers
01) Has the use of PBL + XP enhanced your understanding of the problem	45%
02) Did the subdivision of the problem in smaller problems help understand the overall problem	66%
03) Was it easy to break the problem into subproblems	21%
04) The design of test cases facilitated the understanding/solution of the problem and its validation	45%
05) Did your group use refactoring	17%
06) Was it easy to define the test cases	21%
07) Was it easy to define examples of input and output	55%
08) Did the group use pair programming in an effective way	17%
09) Did pair programming facilitate the implementation of the solution	31%
10) Did pair programming reduce the number of program errors	52%
11) Do you consider that working with shared code and analysis artifacts is a good practice	48%
12) Was it easy to integrate the cards to produce a complete solution	37%
13) Did the use of test cases reduced the occurrence of program erros	38%
14) Did the use of the PBL+xp methodology enable the group to solve the problem in less time	24%
15) Did the methodology enable the group to better structure the treatment to the problem	51%
16) Did the use of flowcharts help to build the solution	55%
17) Did the methodology help with group work	48%
18) Based on the methodology, did you feel that it provided motivation to work with the problem	44%
About Taskboard Tools	
19) Did the taskboard tool help to apply the methodology	38%
20) Did the taskboard tool help structure the problem solution	48%
21) Does the Taskboard tool have a user-friendly and easy to use interface	41%
22) Is the use of the TaskBoard tool intuitive considering the sequence of steps to solve the problem	28%
23) Does the TaskBoard tool provide good support for the documentation of the solution process	55%
24) Should the TaskBoard tool be always used for problem solving in this course	27% always
25) Did the use of digital ink make more productive the annotation and sketching of the solution	55%

this is not an easy task, and students faced some difficulty breaking the problems into subproblems during the early stages of problem solving. The subproblems became more visible only after they had worked for a while on the solution. In general, though, the end result in this aspect was considered satisfactory as most solutions were adequately structured as a collection of functions. Likewise, they also faced difficulty in the integration process, where they needed to put the solutions to subproblems together to make the final solution to the problem.

Regarding the use of test cases, students understood the need to not only code the solution, but also to ensure that the program works correctly. Importantly, they developed this awareness during the analysis of the problem, which resulted in less errors with respect to program logic. In addition, according to students' comments in the classroom, the tests "helped to understand the problem better". It should be noted that the definition of test cases was introduced with XP, and was not originally used in PBL. This was also the case with input and output definition. Even though they were not comfortable with their definition at first, we observed that as students progressed in the experiment, they became more comfortable with the technique. The specification of inputs and outputs is related to the subdivision of the problem into subproblems, as its usually easier to see the interface of smaller functional units. Conversely, the specification of inputs and outputs helped validate the subproblems and, later, to integrate them to form the complete solution.

Pair programming in turn was not effectively used by all groups. This was expected since it was their first contact with this practice. Nevertheless, all groups tried it to some extent and the groups that effectively used the practice generally liked the experience, being able to see how it positively affected their solutions. Those that used pair programming were able to see the benefits of working in pairs to implement the cards, especially regarding the exchange of knowledge and the identification of missing parts or parts that needed enhancements.

The use of shared code had the desired effect that students with difficulties could more easily catch up with what others were doing. This also contributed to circumvent the problem of group members that don't like to share information or are too shy to ask questions. One of the major concerns of students was the way problem solving steps were documented. Before the experiment, they used to document their solutions in a free form, using digital ink and the Windows Journal application. This documentation, however, was disconnected from the actual solution artifacts and were not shared among the students in a group. Using TaskBoard, not only do students document all the steps, but this documentation is visible to all students in the group, as well as to the instructor. And since the server is accessible via the Internet, access to the documentation can be made anywhere at any time. Never the less, when asked about the use of Taskboard, only 27% of students said it should always be used, while 45% said it should be used only at times, and 7% said it should never be used. We attributed the low acceptance of the tool to the shock of practices, especially the requirement to develop solutions from scratch (instead of reusing code found on the Web), which was a natural consequence of the use of the tool.

However, the overall evaluation of the tool was positive. Most believed the integration of the two methodologies to be beneficial.

– "There's not too much to criticize about the combination of these two methodologies; it helps more that hinders the programmer; nothing to complain."

- "The PBL + XP methodology is helpful in the process of software development. It divides the work and organizes the necessary tasks to complete the program."
- "In general, the methodology is good, mainly due to team work, which is widely used when programming almost all software we use."
- "It is very dynamic and pair programming facilitates learning."
- "The employed methodology was very useful. This same method should be used in the following semesters; I believe this will enhance learning."

Furthermore, the evaluation also served to evaluate the adopted PBL approach, reflected in the tool. It verified that the students like using digital ink as a natural and flexible way to express one's reasoning, both for note taking and diagram drawing. They like flowcharts and think it helps in reasoning about the solution. They also complained about the role of the instructor, something they have always complained about in PBL:

- "A more active participation of the instructor in teaching the specificities of the language is needed. If the instructor teaches about the syntax and semantics of the language constructs, the student has more time to dedicate to program logic and does not need to spend too much time seeking information about the particularities of the language."

Suggestions to improve the tool include:

- "The integration of a compiler would make TaskBoard a more interesting tool."
- "I would like to see a set of class notes where students can have immediate reference to the topics dealt with during the classes."

7   Related Work

With the possibility of adapting XP, many opportunities arise for the proposal of teaching methodologies for computer programming courses. According to [13], the use of agile development methodologies to create small programs in introductory programming courses can bring many benefits to students.

Greca [12] used six practices of XP (pair programming, simple design, refactoring, test-driven development, coding patterns and collective ownership of code) in the context of a C programming course. Another approach for the use of XP practices in a computer programming course can be found in [13], which applied pair programming, followed by the practice of analysis and tests. Based on practical examples that were expanded with time, the authors introduced the practices of simple design and refactoring, showing visible benefits for the students.

8   Conclusion

This paper presents the PBL + XP methodology and describes the TaskBoard tool, which supports the implementation of the methodology in introductory

Computer Programming courses. The tool encourages students to follow a problem-solving process that is structured around the principles of problem-based learning and uses concepts and practices drawn from a well-known agile software development methodology. This provides a unified framework for students to work on a problem, from the analysis of the problem statement to its solution. It also facilitates the management of team work and helps ensure the quality of the solutions. We performed a pilot study to evaluate the tool and associated methodology in the Computer Programming I course. The results are encouraging and point to further improvements to make the methodology and tool more productive and interesting for the students. As the next steps in the research, we plan to make adjustments to the methodology, removing elements that were considered too advanced for beginner programmers, notably the practices of refactoring. The practice of pair programming, though not entirely embraced by students, was considered extremely valid and should be encouraged in our forthcoming trials. In addition, we plan to introduce the methodology and tool at an earlier stage in the course, so that students can get familiar with it before starting to deal with more complex programs. In this way, we hope that most of the drawbacks pointed out in the evaluation will be diminished, further leveraging the proposed methodology. Finally, we plan to enhance the TaskBoard tool and make it widely available for use in the community.

References

1. Ambrósio, A.P.L., Costa, F.M.: Evaluating the impact of pbl and tablet pcs in an algorithms and computer programming course. In: Proceedings of the 41st ACM Technical Symposium on Computer Science Education, SIGCSE 2010, pp. 495–499. ACM, New York (2010)
2. Astrachan, O., Bruce, K., Koffman, E., Kölling, M., Reges, S.: Resolved: objects early has failed. In: Proceedings of the 36th SIGCSE Technical Symposium on Computer Science Education, pp. 451–452. ACM, New York (2005)
3. Bailie, F., Courtney, M., Murray, K., Schiaffino, R., Tuohy, S.: Objects first-does it work? Journal of Computing Sciences in Colleges 19(2), 303–305 (2003)
4. Barrows, H.S.: Problem-based learning in medicine and beyond: A brief overview. New Directions for Teaching and Learning, 3–12 (1996)
5. Beck, K., Andres, C.: Extreme programming explained: embrace change. Addison-Wesley Professional, Reading (2004)
6. Bruce, K.B.: Controversy on how to teach CS 1: a discussion on the SIGCSE-members mailing list. ACM SIGCSE Bulletin 37(2), 111–117 (2005)
7. Carbone, A., Hurst, J., Mitchell, I., Gunstone, D.: Characteristics of programming exercises that lead to poor learning tendencies: Part II. In: Proceedings of the 6th Annual Conference on Innovation and Technology in Computer Science Education, pp. 93–96. ACM, New York (2001)
8. Dann, W.P., Cooper, S., Pausch, R.: Learning to Program with Alice. Prentice-Hall, Inc., Upper Saddle River (2006)
9. Denning, P.J.: The field of programmers myth. Communications of the ACM 47(7), 20 (2004)

10. George, B., Williams, L.: An initial investigation of test driven development in industry. In: Proceedings of the 2003 ACM Symposium on Applied Computing, pp. 1135–1139. ACM, New York (2003)
11. Gomes, A., Mendes, A.: SICAS: Interactive system for algorithm development and simulation. In: Computers and Education in an Interconnected Society, vol. 1, pp. 159–166. Kluwer Academic Publ., Dordrecht (2001)
12. Greca, A., Jovanovic, V., Harris, J.K.: Enhancing learning success in the introductory programming course. In: Frontiers in Education Conference. STIPES, vol. 1, pp. 4–15 (2003)
13. Keefe, K., Sheard, J., Dick, M.: Adopting XP practices for teaching object oriented programming. In: Proceedings of the 8th Austalian Conference on Computing Education, vol. 52, p. 100. Australian Computer Society, Inc. (2006)
14. Kumar, A.N.: The effect of closed labs in computer science I: an assessment. Journal of Computing Sciences in Colleges 18(5), 48 (2003)
15. Maloney, J., Resnick, M., Rusk, N., Silverman, B., Eastmond, E.: The scratch programming language and environment. Trans. Comput. Educ. 10, 16:1–16:15 (2010)
16. McCracken, M., Almstrum, V., Diaz, D., Guzdial, M., Hagan, D., Kolikant, Y.B.D., Laxer, C., Thomas, L., Utting, I., Wilusz, T.: A multi-national, multi-institutional study of assessment of programming skills of first-year CS students. ACM SIGCSE Bulletin 33(4), 180 (2001)
17. Mcgettrick, A., Boyle, R., Ibbett, R., Lloyd, J., Lovegrove, G., Mander, K.: Grand challenges in computing: Education–A summary. The Computer Journal 48(1), 42 (2005)
18. Nuutila, E., Torma, S., Kinnunen, P., Malmi, L.: Learning Programming with the PBL Method-Experiences on PBL Cases and Tutoring. In: Bennedsen, J., Caspersen, M.E., Kölling, M. (eds.) Reflections on the Teaching of Programming. LNCS, vol. 4821, pp. 47–67. Springer, Heidelberg (2008)
19. Ribeiro, L.R.C., Mizukami, M.G.: An experiment with PBL in higher education as appraised by the teacher and students. Interface-Comunicação, Saúde, Educação 9, 357–368 (2005)
20. Thomas, L., Ratcliffe, M., Woodbury, J., Jarman, E.: Learning styles and performance in the introductory programming sequence. In: Proceedings of the 33rd SIGCSE Technical Symposium on Computer Science Education, pp. 33–37. ACM, New York (2002)
21. Vignochi, C.M., Benetti, C.S., Machado, C.L.B., Manfroi, W.C.: Considerações Sobre Aprendizagem Baseada em Problemas na Educação em Saúde. Revista HCPA 29(1) (2009)
22. Williams, L.: But, Isn't That Cheating? In: Frontiers in Education Conference. Citeseer, vol. 2, pp. 12–26 (1999)

Using Function Points in Agile Projects

Célio Santana[1,2], Fabiana Leoneo[2], Alexandre Vasconcelos[2], and Cristine Gusmão[3]

[1] Universidade Federal de Rural de Pernambuco, Unidade Acadêmica de Garanhuns, Av.
Av. Bom Pastor S/N Garanhuns/PE, Pernambuco, Brazil CEP CEP 55.296-901
[2] Universidade Federal de Pernambuco, Centro de Informática, Prof. Luiz Freire Avenue
S/N, 50740-540 Recife, Pernambuco, Brazil
[3] Universidade Federal de Pernambuco, Centro de Telesaúde, Hospital das Clínicas,
2° andar, Av. Prof. Moraes Rego S/N, Recife, Pernambuco, Brazil CEP 50.670-420
{casj,fls2,amlv}@cin.ufpe.br,
cristine.gusmao@nutes.ufpe.br

Abstract. Agile development has become increasingly common in the organizational software development environment. This paper examines whether function points would be compatible with story points on agile projects. Specifically, it addresses the question of whether function points are a relevant measure of velocity. Although any unit of measure can be used, this paper contrasts theoretical concepts about Story Points (SP) and function points (FP) as units for measuring size. It was also realized a statistical correlation between FP and SP using 2191 stories and 18 iterations in a Brazilian public agency. The conclusion drawn from this study was that function points, in that particular case, could be related with the initial value of the Story Points found after the planning poker.

Keywords: Function Point, Function Point Analysis, Story Points.

1 Introduction

The software industry is almost 60 years old, which makes it a fairly maturity industry. One would think that after six decades the software industry would have well established methods for measuring productivity and quality, and would also have collected a large volume of accurate benchmark data of thousand of measured projects. However, this is not quite the case [1].

Initially, to measure productivity and quality was used one unit called lines of code (LOC). At the time, circa 1950, that metric was fairly effective, once that coding took about 50% of the effort to build an application [1].

Between 1957 and 1967 the situation changed dramatically. Low level assembly languages started to be replaced by more powerful procedural languages such as COBOL and FORTRAM. Applications sizes grew from 1.000 lines of code past to 100.000 lines of code, raising problems when using LOC metrics [1].

These economics problems were what caused IBM to assign Allan Albretch to develop a useful metric that was independent of code volumes, and which could both

A. Sillitti et al. (Eds.): XP 2011, LNBIP 77, pp. 176–191, 2011.

economic productivity and quality without distortion. In 1979, Allan Albrecht was the first to publicate a method for functionally sizing software called function point analysis (FPA) [2].

The use of FPA, as a measure of the functional size of software, has grown since the mid 70's from a few interested organizations to an impressive list of organizations worldwide. The successful adoption of FPA was ratified with the creation of the ISO/IEC 14143:2007 [3].

In 2001 was presented the Agile Manifesto that proposed new values and principles based in responding to changes quickly and light documentation. This vision seems antagonist than that proposed by traditional engineering [4].

Schuh [5] defines agile development as a counter movement to 30 years of increasingly heavy-handed processes, meant to refashion computer programming into software engineering, rendering it as manageable and predictable as any other engineering discipline.

Mnkandla [4] states that the agile movement could mark the emergence of a new engineering discipline, that has shifted the values of the software development process from the mechanistic (i.e., driven by process and rules of science) to the organic (i.e., driven by softer issues of people and their interactions). Boehm [5] view believes in agile methodologies as a challenge to the mainstream software development community that presents a counter-culture movement, which addresses change from a radically different perspective.

To an agile team, a plan is one view of the future, but many alternatives are possible. As a team gains knowledge and experience, it will count into the plan [6]. A measurement system which supports this kind of experience is considered "special" and some metrics used in this context are Story Points (SP) and Ideal Days [1].

Jones [1] states that one of the agile weaknesses is the widespread failure to measure projects using standards metrics, such as function points. Based in this statement an ad-hoc search were conducted in the following sources: ACM Digital Library [1], CiteSeerX[2], IEEE Xplorer[3], Scopus[4] and SpringerLink[5].

Just one source was published, and presented relevant work showing scientific evidence about the function point analysis and story points running in agile software development environments. The work was published by Fuqua [7] who conducted a study by using function points in agile projects and tried to correlate with story points in those projects.

Other relevant work about this subject, not found in the ad-hoc search, was presented by Jones [1] in a book, where he states that according to its empirical basis[6], it is noted that two function points is equal to one story point on average. But it is worth noting that this measure is an average of its empirical database.

---

[1] http://portal.acm.org/
[2] http://citeseer.ist.psu.edu/
[3] http://ieeexplore.ieee.org/
[4] http://www.scopus.com/
[5] http://www.springerlink.com/
[6] www.isbsg.org

In this light, this paper presents conceptual differences between function points and story points. The goal of this paper is to present the theoretical relationship between story points and function points as well as providing empirical data from a real life case study where one project was measured using these two approaches.

After this introductory section, the section 2 explores function points analysis. The section 3 presents the concept of story points. Section 4 shows the size measurement concept which are related with FPA and SP. The section 5 shows theoretical differences between both techniques. Section 6 presents the case studied in a Brazilian public agency. And section 7 shows the summary, related works and threats of validity of the work.

2   Function Point Analysis

Once there was growth in the use of function points, there has been wider application and use of the measure. Since happened its formation in 1986, the International Function Point Users Group (IFPUG) has continuously enhanced the original Albrecht method for functionally sizing software.

This International Standard is the latest release in the continually improvement IFPUG method. This aims to promote the consistent interpretation of functional size measurement in conformance with ISO/IEC 14143-1:2007. The IFPUG functional size measurement method is known as function point analysis and its units of functional size are called Function Points. The IFPUG version of Function Points is published in The Counting Practices Manual in its actual version 4.3 [8].

IFPUG's method for function point analysis is an ISO standard and must be conformant to ISO/IEC 14143-1:2007. The method can measure "functional size" not addressing "non-functional size". This does not mean that the nonfunctional size cannot, or should not, be measured. Instead it, must be clearly stated as a separate measure [8]. The process diagram of IFPUG FPA counting is shown in Figure 1.

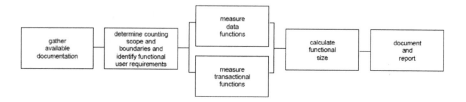

Fig. 1. FPA Procedure Diagram [8]

The first stage in the function point counting procedure is to gather the available documentation. To support a functional size measurement, it shall describe the functionality delivered by the software or the functionality that is impacted by the software project that is being measured.

Suitable documentation may include requirements, data/object models, class diagrams, data flow diagrams, use cases, procedural descriptions, report layouts, screen layouts, user manuals and other software development artifacts. If sufficient documentation is not available, it is important to access experts who are able to provide additional information to address any gaps in the documentation. The ideal requirements are called perfect requirements by the FPA practitioners.

The next stage is responsible for counting scope which defines the set of Functional User Requirements to be included in the function point count. Also in this stage it is necessary determine the boundary which is a conceptual interface between the software under construction and its users.

Identifying the functional requirements is related with the concept of elementary process which is the smallest unit of activity that is meaningful to the user. To identify each elementary process, the following activities shall be performed:

- Is meaningful to the user;
- Constitutes a complete transaction;
- Is self-contained;
- Leaves the business of the application being counted in a consistent state,

Following these rules it is necessary to identify all unique elementary processes.

After that, it is necessary to measure data functions, which represents functionality provided to the user to meet internal and external data storage requirements. A data function is either an internal logical file or an external interface file.

An internal logical file (ILF) is a user recognizable group of logically related data or control information maintained within the boundary of the application being measured.

An external interface file (EIF) is a user recognizable group of logically related data or control information, which is referenced by the application being measured, but which is maintained within the boundary of another application.

In parallel, could be performed the measuring of transactional functions. A transactional function is an elementary process that provides functionality to the user for processing data. A transactional function is an external input, external output, or external inquiry.

An external input (EI) is an elementary process that processes data or control information sent from outside the boundary. The primary intent of an EI is to maintain one or more ILFs and/or to alter the behavior of the system.

An external output (EO) is an elementary process that sends data or control information outside the application's boundary and includes additional processing beyond that of an external inquiry. The primary intent of an external output is to present information to a user through processing logic other than or in addition to the retrieval of data or control information. The processing logic must contain at least one mathematical formula or calculation, create derived data, maintain one or more ILFs, and/or alter the behavior of the system.

An external inquiry (EQ) is an elementary process that sends data or control information outside the boundary. The primary intent of an external inquiry is to present information to a user through the retrieval of data or control information. The processing logic contains no mathematical formula or calculation, and creates no derived data. No ILF is maintained during the processing, nor is the behavior of the system altered.

On systems which present perfect requirements, different measurements performed by different people must have the same final result. Imperfect requirements lead the measurement performer to take assumptions about that requirement, and this kind of assumption could lead different results in counting the same sample of requirements. Because of this property, is considered that FPA is an objective method for measuring software.

3 Story Points

Story points are a unit of measure for expressing the overall size of a user story, feature, or other piece of work. When we estimate with story points we assign a point value to each item. The raw value we assign is unimportant. What matters are the relative values [6].

The number of story points associated with a story represents the overall size of the story. There is no set formula for defining the size of a story. Rather, a story point estimate is an amalgamation of the amount of effort involved in developing the feature, the complexity of developing it, the risk inherent in it, and so on [6].

There are two common ways to get started. The first approach is to select a story that you expect to be one of the smallest stories you will work with, and say that story is estimated at 1 story point. The second approach is to select a story that seems somewhat medium-sized and give it a number somewhere in the middle of the range you expect to use. A story that is assigned a two should be twice as much as a story that is assigned a one [6].

Story estimates need to be owned collectively by the team. A story comprises multiple tasks and a task estimate is owned by the individual who will perform the task. Story estimates, however, are owned by the team for two reasons: First, since the team do not know yet who will work on the story, the ownership of the story cannot be more precisely assigned than to the team collectively. Second, estimates derived by the team, rather than a single individual, are probably more useful [9].

At the end of an iteration the team counts the number of story points they completed. Then they use that as a forecast of how many story points they'll complete in upcoming iterations of the same length. The term velocity refers to the number of story points a team completes, or expects to complete, in an iteration [9].

4 Size Measurement

A software measurement is a quantifiable dimension, attribute, or amount of any aspect of a software program, product, or process. It is the raw data which are associated with various elements of the software process and product. A typical set of metrics might include [10]:

- Quality.
- Size. (target of the study)
- Complexity.
- Effort
- Productivity,
- Cost.
- Schedule.
- Rework.

Two ways for measuring software size were catalogued in 1992 [11]. The first consider the physical source lines and logical source statements. Counts of physical lines described size in terms of the physical length of the code as it appears when printed for people to read.

The other way counts of logical statements, on the other hand, attempt to characterize size in terms of the number of software instructions, irrespective of their relationship to the physical formats in which they appear.

Both function points and story points measure the size of the software and are based on the count of logical expressions.

Function points address functional size [8] while story points represent the business value of one user story [6].

In Fact, Agile teams separate estimates of size from estimates of duration [9] while function points are complemented by other methods when it comes to effort and cost estimate such as COCOMO II [12].

5   Function Points X Story Points

Although FP and SP estimate the size of the software to be delivered, some particularities make measures applied by both techniques to the same product have different sizes, variations and deviant behavior at the end of the measurement. Some of the strongest of these particularities are detailed in the following subsections.

5.1   Team Expertise X Standardized Methods

A nice feature of story points is that each team defines them as they see fit. One team may decide to define a story point as an ideal day of work and another team may define a story point as a measure of the complexity of the story [9].

In the last statement, Cohn suggests that the story points can vary from several teams based in their experience to assess the effort, complexity and risk associated with certain stories.

Any assumptions made in function points are considered a counting interpretation. A specification bringing perfect requirements, where no assumptions are made, must present the same final result. Any assumptions regarding primary intent must be documented for helps in next counting. Thus function point leaves no space for using expertise.

For Example, considering function point a small function for including one email address in a virtual schedule may be the same "size" of a function with perform a complex integral calculus with receive one equation as parameter and return the string with the result. The same example in story points should present very different results and these results could be different among different teams.

In the other hand, considering function points, store one formulary containing fifteen fields may be different for including one containing sixteen, while in story points this kind of difference is rare.

So this aspect is seen in a different way in both techniques.

5.2 Functional Size X Product Size

According to ISO 9126 [13] non-functional requirements are that specifies criteria which can be used to judge the operation of a system, rather than specific behaviors. This should be contrasted with functional requirements that define specific behavior or functions.

Considering the IFPUG definition, functional size is the size of the software derived by quantifying the Functional User Requirements we should assume that non-functional requirements are not covered in function points [8].

The IFPUG Framework for Functional Sizing [14] defines some kind of "sizes" presented in the software development such as functional size, technical size and quality size which are related to:

- **Functional User Requirements:** a sub-set of the user requirements. The Functional User Requirements represent the user practices and procedures that the software must perform to fulfill the users' needs. They exclude Quality Requirements and any Technical Requirements
- **Quality Requirements:** any requirements relating to software quality as defined in ISO 9126:1991
- **Technical Requirements:** requirements related to the technology and environment, for the development, maintenance, support and execution of the software.

The combination of the functional size, technical size and quality size represents de *Product Size*. But, this concept is not detailed by the IFPUG.

Considering the statement that story point estimate is an amalgamation of the amount of effort involved in developing the feature, the complexity of developing it, and the risk inherent in building it [6], it look like the story point is concerned in define a product size since the agile team considers any kind of risk and complexity to determine the size of the story, and this assumptions are related to Quality and Technical requirements.

Nowadays, IFPUG is building a metric called Software Non-Functional Assessment Process (SNAP). The SNAP Project Team expects to develop a project assessment method that will use series of questions grouped by category to measure the impact of non-functional requirements on the development and delivery (size) of the software product. The resulting size will be the size of the non-functional requirements, just as the functional size is the size of the functional requirements [15].

In a simple way, we still cannot consider the theoretical concept that SNAP size + FP Size = SP Size because the agile method considers the environment of the project and not just the product.

For example, in function points a bookstore which have no requirements for security, available, performance and its access are made in a local machine, will have the same FP size of this same bookstore considering the same restrictions of the amazon.com. In story points, the amazon.com will be much larger than its offline, unsecure, slow and unstable version.

5.3 Small Pieces X Whole Product

In the Agile Manifesto[7] were defined 12 principles, which one of them states: "Deliver working software frequently, from a couple of weeks to a couple of months, with preference to the shorter timescale". This statement reinforces the adoption of interactive life cycle, largely adopted in agile projects.

This continuous delivery in small "timeboxes" reduces the total of points delivered in iteration. Sometimes one big story, called epic, must be disaggregated for fit in one cycle. In fact, split stories are not a simple task in agile projects.

There are number of times when it may be necessary to split a user story into multiple smaller parts [6]. First, a user story should be split when it is too large to fit within a single iteration. Sometimes a user story won't fit in iteration because it is bigger than a full iteration.

Alternatively, a story may be small enough to fit within iteration but it won't fit within the iteration being planned because there isn't enough room left. The team may feel they will have time to develop a portion of a story in the iteration, but not the entire story.

Second, it can be useful to split a large user story (an epic) if a more accurate estimate is necessary.

But the question about splitting stories is raised from another Cohn's statement [9]: When a story, possibly an epic, is disaggregated into its constituent stories, the sum of the estimates for the individual stories does not need to equal the estimate of the initial story or epic. Similarly, a story may be disaggregated into constituent tasks. The sum of the estimates for the tasks does not need to equal the estimate of the initial story.

Thus, splitting stories seems to be a team decision and there are no rules about how to split and how distribute the points, making this disaggregation a particular processs that works only for that team in that environment.

Looking for function points splitting is not a problem. No data function or transactional function should be broken because they must follow the elementary process definition: "smallest unit of activity that is meaningful to the user".

Even if a function must be broken for a technical reason, it only will be considered complete when all of the functionality is completely developed, which means delivered zero function points or all function points to the user.

But an anomalous behavior can be seen in the use of function points, in interactive and incremental projects, if the boundary of the counting just considers what is delivered in each iteration. In this case, the sums of the parts are bigger than the whole.

For example, a particular product is being built in an interactive and incremental whose two iterations have already been completed. In first iteration four features were delivered totalizing fifty function points. In the second iteration another four features were delivered, but one of these feature (and already counted with 10 function points) in first iteration were updated for technical reasons totalizing sixty function points delivered in second iteration.

The first iteration + second iteration a hundred points, but that function which was built in first iteration and updated in the second, was counted twice and this just

---

[7] www.agilemanifesto.org

happens because the boundary of the counting is not the whole product, and which are delivered in each iteration. In function points the sum of the parts could be bigger than the whole (never smaller).

This problem does not occur in story points because the cost, in points, for updating one feature is embedded in the original story.

5.4   Maintenance and Changes

According ISO/IEC 14764 identified four categories of maintenance [16]:

- **Corrective maintenance:** Reactive modification of a software product performed after delivery to correct discovered problems.
- **Adaptive maintenance:** Modification of a software product performed after delivery to keep a software product usable in a changed or changing environment.
- **Perfective maintenance:** Modification of a software product after delivery to improve performance or maintainability.
- **Preventive maintenance:** Modification of a software product after delivery to detect and correct latent faults in the software product before them become effective faults.

Agile software development considers the corrective maintenance as a bug, and this kind of problem must not be managed, but solved. Which means that must not be sized.

But adaptive maintenance (evolutive maintenance), perfective maintenance and preventive maintenance (refactoring), are considered and evaluated in agile projects as new stories. When maintenance needs to be performed, a new history is written for that specific demand.

The functional size measurement quantifies the size of business requirements. In an enhancement environment, it measures the effects of changes to those business requirements. Therefore, functional size measurement is applicable to a subset of adaptive maintenance. This includes the software functionality added, changed or deleted as well as the software functionality provided to convert data and meet other implementation requirements [8].

Function points clearly do not fit the types of corrective, perfective and preventive maintenance, fitting only a few cases of adaptive maintenance. A project that has undergone many changes may have enhanced the difference in scores between the two approaches.

5.5   One Requirement X Many Requirements

Measuring a single feature using the two techniques and compare their variation, may be the most logical path to be taken when attempting to evaluate the relationship between the two methods. And repeat this process for the all others features of the project in an attempt to increase the historical basis, would be the next step in this comparison.

In terms of story points this idea may not be the best. Cohn [9] states that the central limit theorem tells us that the sum of a number of independent samples from any distribution is approximately normally distributed.

For our purposes, this means that a team's story point estimates can be skewed way toward underestimation, way toward overestimation, or distributed in any other way. But when we grab an iteration's worth of stories from any of those distributions, the stories we grab will be normally distributed. This means that we can use the measured velocity of one iteration to predict the velocity of future iterations.

Naturally, the velocity of only one iteration is not a perfect predictor. Similarly, velocity may change as a team learns new technology, a new domain, or becomes accustomed to new team members or new ways of working. This means that to predict the behavior of the score, or the velocity, of a team is best to consider all stories delivered than each one individually.

Was also seen in the previous section that to consider the score of a feature function points can be misleading. The measure of the sum of the parts can be greater than the whole, thus sizing all features is more accurate than sizing one by one as well.

The last reason to evaluate all the features is that there may not be a perfect match between a story and a requirement. So could be difficult assign exactly which stories are equivalent to what requirements, and evaluating all iteration may bring a greater reliance to the comparison.

6 Case Study

The *Agência Estadual de Tecnologia da Informação do Estado de Pernambuco*[8], hereafter called ATI, is following the Brazilian Federal Government instruction known as the: *Instrução Normativa 04 de Maio de 2008*, hereafter called IN04, which came into force on 2 January 2009 the Department of Logistics and Technology of the Planning Ministry [17].

This instruction, in its article 14, states that the outsourcing strategy must define the understanding of the task to establish procedures and criteria for measurement of services provided, including metrics, indicators and values. With this technique Function Point Analysis has been adopted as currency in the local authority outsourcing contracts of software products.

ATI was forced to be adherent to this instruction in early 2010. Before that, since January 2009, ATI had been using Scrum as tool for contract management [17]. After the adoption of this instruction ATI continued to manage its suppliers through the scrum, but the payment of invoices should be measured based on the product delivered sized using function points.

ATI and its supplier held a planning poker meeting where it is sized in story points all demands of that sprint. But now it was necessary to conduct an estimative counting in function points required by IN04 for project planning. At the end of the sprint is still necessary to perform a counting in function points to determine the size of the product delivered and thus pay the suppliers.

The estimative counting is needed only for the allocation of project resources, which does not demand an accurate count but only an approximation of reality. But while ATI can count about 5000 story points per day, the ability to count function points is reduced to 600 function points in a day. And this estimative counting is considered "bureaucracy" being unnecessary in most cases.

---

[8] www.ati.pe.gov.br

The record of the demands is held by ATI supported by a tool called Mantis as shown in Figure 2. The functional size and story points size of each demand is stored in this tool and can be recovered directly from the MYSql database which store the Mantis database.

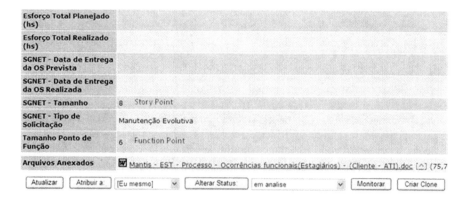

Fig. 2. Recorded data about one demand showing SP and FP in Mantis adopted by ATI

ATI intended to reduce its work performing the estimative counting at the beginning of the Sprint. Based on the idea that the functional size (FP) is a part of the product size (SP), was cogitated the possibility of creating a method of conversion between the two metrics.

The basic idea was realize a statistical correlation between the two counting results (intention of this work), and if the correlations prove strong enough, would be performed a linear regression between the two (not finished in the present moment).

To the kick off project was a selected sample of 18 sprints from February 2009 until August 2010 because this is the all period of historical basis of story points and function points contained in the database. This implies a total of 18 results (Feb 2009 - Aug 2010) for each data sample containing 2191 demands recorded.

First, will be presented the variables and their total values within a Sprint in Table 1. PH and PF represent the amount of story points and function points collected in each month respectively. The statement Fev/09 until Ago/10 represent the sprints performed (February 2009 until August 2010). The statements *Média* and *Desvio Padrão* represent the average and standard deviation respectively.

Table 1. Data from two variables in the sample

	fev/09	mar/09	abr/09	mai/09	jun/09	jul/09	ago/09	set/09	out/09	nov/09	dez/09	jan/10	fev/10	mar/10	abr/10	mai/10	jun/10	jul/10	ago/10	Média	Desvio Padrão
PH	540	437	787	593	474	648	787	758	535	480	262	373	312	506	358	819	742	469	652	554,3158	171,0065147
PF	64	41	67	51	65	130	156	159	106	91	54	45	43	71	49	90	74	66	71	78,57895	35,75583214

The first step to perform the statistical correlation should be to test the normality of the variables, SP and FP, involved in the correlation. The two variables had their normality evaluated using the Shapiro-Wilk test to determine if the correlation method, the next step, must be parametric or non-parametric [19]. The statistical tool used in this work was the R software. The results of the normality tests are found in Frame 1.

```
       Shapiro-Wilk normality test                Shapiro-Wilk normality test

data:  PH                                  data:  PF
W = 0.9519, p-value = 0.426                W = 0.8438, p-value = 0.005318
```

Frame 1. Shapiro-Wilk normality test result

The normality test to the PH variable (Story Points) was considered **normal** while the variable PF (Function Points) were considered **not normal**; hence the method of statistical correlation must be a non-parametric. The chosen one was the Spearman rank correlation [19].

The Result of the Spearman's rank correlation is shown on Frame 2.

```
        Spearman's rank correlation rho

data:  PF and PH
S = 326.2862, p-value = 0.0005989
alternative hypothesis: true rho is not equal to 0
sample estimates:
      rho
0.713784
```

Frame 2. Spearman's rank correlation result

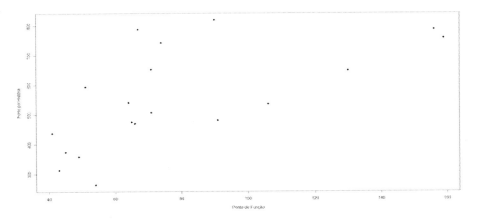

Fig. 3. Scattered Plot of Variables PH (Story Points) and PF (Function Point)

The result of the Spearman test rho (ρ) indicates the degree of linear correlation between the two variables. The value of ρ can range from -1 (negative correlation) to 1 (positive correlation) where $|\rho|$ close to zero indicates a weak correlation and $|\rho|$ close to 1 indicates strong correlation.

The value of $\rho \approx 0.7137$ means a strong positive correlation. The p-value indicates the confidence interval of the test, which is much lower value 0.05, thus indicates a large confidence interval. For visual verification of the strength of linear correlation, we have constructed a scatter plot which is shown in Figure 3.

The results shown in the scatter plot present points growing on a linear pattern, which support the Spearman's test on the correlation.

7   Conclusions

Despite the strong differences of size definition presented in function points and story points, were presented empirical evidence for a real life project realized by a Brazilian public agency, showing the correlation between functional size and number of story points which are delivered at the end of each sprint.

The strength of this correlation suggests a further distancing between the two variables studied which may come from the differences presented in section 4 of this work.

The result cannot be generalized, but it supports an idea that Product Size = Functional Size + Non-Functional Size + Environments Variables Size, Story Points = Function Points + Non-Functional Size + Environments Variables Size. This "formula" is not intended to be shown mathematically correct, but that represent that the functional size is part of the product size and finding a correlation between the whole (product size) and the piece (functional size) represents a valid proportion.

Obviously is necessary to respect the units of measurement and the reality of each organization, so the result itself is not valuable, but the method of assessment, if replicated in more environments, may prove be useful for a particular company.

7.1   Discussion of Results

Even being used to the same goal, function points and story points presents strong theoretical differences. Whereas the results of this study it is still surprising, once was observed a correlation between the functional size that is obtained accurately with impersonal method of sizing, and story points obtained purely from the experience of the team.

Especially if we evaluate this short history about this subject, starting with the Fuqua's work [7] where he performed a correlation between function points and a set of indicators used by your company, then performed the same correlation using story points and found no significant correlation between these two variables.

Although this study [7] used another function points, now known as mark II [20] which is different from official function points provided by the IFPUG. The basis of impartiality in Mark II counting method remains. The work of Jones [1] only presents the statement of the relationship between FP \ SP = 2 without more information on how the result was obtained.

It is obvious that the intention of this work was not to generalize their results, but was expected to find the same results than Fuqua [7] and close it as more empirical evidence strengthening the argument toward to "not fit".

Facing the expectations and the results, we believe that the statement raised in the Framework for Functional Sizing of IFPUG [14] where it states that product size is a combination of (quality size, technical size and functional size) or Product Size = Non-Functional Size + Environments Variables Size + Functional Size.

Of course (x)that different companies presents different "sizes" for their story points and different proportion of the impact of functional size into the product size, but the goal of this paper is to motivate how these companies can find their ratio between FP and SP.

7.2 Implications for Research and Practice

The implications of this study for practice in first place concerns to ATI itself, and the possibility for perform a linear correlation for find a conversion method between story points and function points.

Another practical implication is the description of a method that can be used by companies that are facing the same problem of the ATI and need a solution about how to assess the relationship between FP and SP within their organization. Remembering that the values found in this work will be only valid for that ATI project, but organizations can use this method in its own database and so find their own correlation.

Those that are successful, including ATI, can perform a linear regression and find a first degree equation $(y = Ax + B)$ where y refers to the number of function points, x is the amount of story points and A, B are constants. From this equation, companies can predict with a certain margin of error, which is the value of these variables from one another.

The first implication of this work in research is to present other empirical results joining a small base of scientific information about the subject and the first empirical study, not considering Jones' work [1], adopting IFPUG method.

Other implication is formally present the main differences between the two approaches in section four. Surely, there is plenty of theoretical information compiled about the subject. But still is the possibility for gathering current data from systematic reviews or systematic mapping as well as creating data from new experiments and case studies that will enrich the knowledge of the academy.

In order to present the idea that story points are related to product size and function points, or functional size, is only part of the product size. What seems clear is that the proportion between functional size and product size is different in every environment and can even be irregular within the same project.

7.3 Threats to Validity

The first group of threat validity stems from a lack of theoretical concepts consolidated about a possible correlation between the approaches. This fact may have contributed to weaken several factors in this study such as the wrong selection of the method or the pooling of demands. It is an "exploratory" study which portrays a more specific need than a company that intends to conduct scientific research. Indeed, this threat do not touch the section 5 of this work that could bring contributions if we were free of the limitations that are in the following section.

Another threat that comes from this factor is the lack of information about a demand that could help in their treatment. For example there is no way of knowing whether a demand is perfective or corrective maintenance (which could be dropped from the study because function points do not support them) or whether it is adaptive maintenance. Another problem with this group is that the number of samples (18) are still small to reach any definitive conclusion on this study.

Finally the latest threats come from the validity of the statistical method used in this work. The lack of knowledge prevents to determine which type of method is most appropriate for the conduct of case studies and experiment. For example, the statistical method used in this work and the work Fuqua's [7] were different. In this method the assumption of measuring the set of demands instead one individual (section 5.5) can bring bias to this study.

7.4 Limitation

The main limitation is the small amount of professionals who knows well the two techniques involved in this study. The impact of this work is the small number of sprints that could be counted because it was inexistent the counting of function points from September until December, which would be four more sprints for data collection.

The second limitation was not performing the linear regression to support with more strength the results of the work, although with a rank correlation of 0.71 and a high confidence interval is very difficult that there is not a valid linear regression for this correlation.

7.5 Future Work

In industry, one future work is suggested that is the discovery the first degree equation FP $(x*SP + y)$ where FP is equal to the total function points delivered after Sprint, SP represents the estimate given by points in history, x and y are constants. This time it included a regression analysis to identify the function conversion between the variables.

To academy we present, as future work, the attainment of studies using formal secondary collect data method such as systematic review or systematic mapping on the relationship between function points and story points.

Another future work is providing more empirical information about the relationship between FP and SP, to confirm the relationship Product Size = Functional Size + Non-Functional Size + Environments Variables Size.

Acknowledgments

Célio Santana is a doctoral student at the Center of Informatics of the Federal University of Pernambuco where he receives the funding from the Brazilian National Research Council (CNPq), process #141156/2010-4. The authors thank CNPq for partially funding the participation in the XP'2011 Conference.

References

1. Jones, C.: Applied Software Measurement. McGraw Hill, New York (2008)
2. Albrecht, A.J.: Measuring Application Development Productivity. In: Proc. IBM Applications Development Symposium, p. 83. GUIDE Int and Share Inc., IBM Corp., Monterey (1979)
3. ISO/IEC 14143-1:2007, Information technology — Software measurement — Functional size measurement (2007)
4. Mnkandla, E., Dwolatzky, B.: Balancing the human and the engineering factors in software development. In: Proceeding of the IEEE AFRICON 2004 Conference, pp. 1207–1210 (2004)
5. Boehm, B., Turner, R.: Balancing agility and discipline: A guide for the perplexed, 1st edn., pp. 165–194. Addison Wesley, Reading (2004)
6. Cohn, M.: Agile Estimating and Planning. Addison-Wesley, Reading (2005)
7. Fuqua, A.: Using Function Points in XP – Considerations. In: Proceedings of Extreme Programming and Agile Processes in Software Engineering, Springerlink
8. IFPUG: Counting Practices Manual V. 4.3 (2009), http://www.ifpug.org
9. Cohn, M.: User Stories Applied. Addison-Wesley, Reading (2004)
10. Glass, R.L.: Building Quality Software. Prentice-Hall, Englewood Cliffs (1992)
11. Park, R.E.: Software Size Measurement. A Framework for Counting Source Statements, SEI technical report available in
    http://www.sei.cmu.edu/reports/92tr020.pdf (last access in 03/01/2010)
12. Boehm, B., Abts, C., Brown, A.W., Chulani, S., Bradford, K.C., Horowitz, E., Madachy, R., Reifer, J., Steece, B.: Software cost estimation with COCOMO II. Prentice-Hall, Englewood Cliffs (2000)
13. ISO/IEC 9126-1: Software engineering — Product quality — Part 1: Quality model (2001)
14. IFPUG: Framework for Functional Sizing (2003), http://www.ifpug.org
15. IFPUG: Software Non-functional Assessment Process (2009),
    http://www.ifpug.org/about/
    SWNon-FunctionalAssessmentProcess_Final20-2009.pdf
    (last visit in 03/01/2011)
16. ISO/IEC 14764: Software Engineering — Software Life Cycle Processes — Maintenance (2006)
17. Department of Logistics and Technology.: INSTRUÇÃO NORMATIVA 4, 19 de maio de (2008), http://www.governoeletronico.gov.br/anexos/
    instrucao-normativa-n-04 (last access in 30/08/2010)
18. Schwaber, K., Beedle, M.: Agile Software Development with Scrum. Prentice Hall, Englewood Cliffs (2004)
19. DeGroot, M., Schervish, M.J.: Probability and Statistics, 3rd edn. Addison Wesley, Reading (2001)
20. United Kingdom Software Metrics Association (UKSMA): MKII Function Point Analysis Counting Practices Manual, Version 1.31 (Mk II FPA) (1998),
    http://www.uksma.co.uk

Empirical Investigation on Agile Methods Usage: Issues Identified from Early Adopters in Malaysia

Ani Liza Asnawi, Andrew M. Gravell, and Gary B. Wills

School of Electronics and Computer Science, University of Southampton
Southampton, SO17 1BJ, United Kingdom
{ala08r,amg,gbw}@ecs.soton.ac.uk

Abstract. Agile Methods are a set of software practices that can help to produce products faster and at the same time deliver what customers want. Despite the benefits that Agile methods can deliver, however, we found few studies from the Southeast Asia region, particularly Malaysia. As a result, less empirical evidence can be obtained in the country making its implementation harder. To use a new method, experience from other practitioners is critical, which describes what is important, what is possible and what is not possible concerning Agile. We conducted a qualitative study to understand the issues faced by early adopters in Malaysia where Agile methods are still relatively new. The initial study involves 13 participants including project managers, CEOs, founders and software developers from seven organisations. Our study has shown that social and human aspects are important when using Agile methods. While technical aspects have always been considered to exist in software development, we found these factors to be less important when using Agile methods. The results obtained can serve as guidelines to practitioners in the country and the neighbouring regions.

Keywords: Agile Methods, Factors, Barriers, Software Process.

1 Introduction

Agile methods have been increasingly adopted by organisations developing software. However in Malaysia and in the South East Asia region, we see less evidence about the current usage of the methods among practitioners [1]. This is the gap we would like to reduce. Agile methods are different from other earlier methods in that they are a set of approaches which concentrate on the collaboration of customers and developers. If these methods are to be used, we need to primarily understand what works and what does not work for the people in the country. We also need to know which factors (either social or technical) are important when using the methodologies. To answer these questions, we conducted an empirical study to understand how Agile techniques are adopted in Malaysia. We chose the early adopters, as we think this is an appropriate time to interview them while the issues and challenges are still clear in their mind. We need to mention here that this study forms part of our research; therefore the results presented here only refer to issues relating to the early adoption

A. Sillitti et al. (Eds.): XP 2011, LNBIP 77, pp. 192–207, 2011.

of Agile methods in the country. The results will help us to develop and refine our hypotheses for the next stage of our research.

In this paper, we will provide the background and motivation of our study followed by the objectives and the expected contribution. We will review the related works of our study and describe the methodology we use. We present the results, a discussion and finally the conclusion and suggestions for future work.

1.1 Background and Motivation

Our research is to investigate issues of implementing Agile methods in Malaysia. As only limited studies about Agile methods in the region can be found [2], this is the gap in the research that we would like to narrow. Lack of knowledge about Agile methods can act as a hindrance to the people who are planning to adopt it. Agile methods are sets of software processes which are dependent on how people use them [3], therefore if the method is going to be used, we need more empirical evidence for the suitability of Agile methods. However, we found inconsistencies (see section 1.2) from results referring to the suitability of Agile methods.

Furthermore, with regard to the importance of information and communication, ICT has become one of the key elements under the tenth Malaysia plan (2011-2015)[1]. However, Malaysia is still lacking in the usage of good software processes and has been identified as having problems in delivering good quality products, on time and on budget [4]. One paper described Malaysia as experiencing people-related problems when developing software [5], and that the adopters do not have a clear methodology against which to illustrate the requirements [6]. In order to adopt good practice in software development understanding the software process is critical. All of these reasons have motivated us to support the introduction of Agile methods in the country. At this stage we will identify issues related to the adoption of Agile methods. In this investigation, we aim to address three key questions:

1) How practitioners in Malaysia adopting Agile methods?
2) What are the factors that make practitioners in Malaysia using Agile Methods?
3) What are the difficulties faced by them?

1.2 Review of Related Work

Agile methods are sets of new approaches for developing software [7] which are based on practitioners' experiences [8]. The intention of the Agile manifesto is to solve the issues and problems that were found in software development [9, 10]. Agile practices are adapted from existing techniques and ideas found in the software development information field, where its usage depends on the suitability and the appropriateness of the team, organisation and project. A systematic review of empirical studies of Agile up to 2005 was conducted by Dyba and Dingsoyr [11]. Although Agile methods are considered suitable for many environments, there is, however, lack of empirical evidence to validate their suitability [11]. This is the area which we will further investigate.

---

[1] www.bernama.com/bernama/v5/newsbusiness.php?id=504844
(accessed 18 June 2010).

Software development is also about dealing with people and the organisational factor. An important aspect under the organisational factor is to consider the characteristics of projects and teams in the organisation. It is also important to understand the features and the environment within which the development is taking place. One study stated that these characteristics can also be linked to the organisational factors [12]. As mentioned by Cockburn and Highsmith [3], good communication is important in the implementation of Agile methods. However others [13] found insignificant results from the communication aspect. Agile is only suitable for specific types of software projects [14] while one study found no significant results concerning the factor of project types or nature [7]. Having identified the factors related to the people and social aspects concerned with the successful usage of Agile methods, several studies have started to investigate factors related to the organisational culture [15-18]. One study found that organisational culture plays an important role in the adoption of Agile methods [15]. Another study reported no significant findings in terms of organisational culture with adoption of Agile methods [7].

People are part of the Agile ecosystem, which is why their talents, skills, experience and communication have become the primary concerns for the success of the adoption. It is not surprising that many studies on effectiveness and adoption of Agile methods focus on people [19]. One study also confirmed the 'people' aspect as the key success factor in Agile methods [7]. In addition, from its early introduction, the method has been described as a set of approaches that concentrate on people and social aspects [3]. However, in one study, technical factors were also reported to be significant for Agile implementation [7], although not in the tools, but in the delivery strategy and Agile software practice. Nevertheless, insignificant results in technical competency have also been found [13].

Agile methods do not rely on heavy documentation as they depend on the tacit knowledge. Yet people always question how the team can adopt the methods if it does not have any documentation relating to the works they are undertaking. This is one issue that may be questioned by the early adopters of Agile methods, particularly for a country where limited study about the method can be found. One study described the creation of knowledge as a factor in the adoption of Extreme Programming, one of the Agile practices [19]. However it is not an easy task for the team to share and rely only on the knowledge they hold among themselves. One study suggested that the team should also possess the skills and should be highly motivated [20]. That is, the collective capability of the team is critical for the success of Agile [7]. On the other hand, different evidence shows that capability, professionalism and experience have actually hindered the adoption of Agile methods [12], but training [13], management involvement and access to external resources were among factors to have a positive impact on the implementation of Agile software methodology [21] . Conversely a study also found significant results in terms of technical factors [7]. We need to further investigate the inconsistent results we have reported, based on the literature studied, and to understand the relative importance of each of these factors.

1.3 Objectives and Expected Contribution

The main objective of this paper is to describe the issues and problems faced by the early adopters in Malaysia when implementing Agile methods. We should highlight here that the findings are based on a small sample, and so it might not be valid to generalise this study to the whole population in Malaysia (and so we intend to increase our sample size in future work). However the selection of respondents and the locations of the companies have helped us to generalise these results.

The contribution of our study is to reduce the gap within the adoption factors in the country and the region where scant and contradictory research about Agile methods can be found. In addition, the knowledge can help practitioners to further understand and compare the suitability of Agile methods adapting to their organisation and people.

2   The Study

In this paper, we aim to qualitatively understand how new adopters in Malaysia are using Agile methods. Qualitative data are richer in content; thus this approach increases the amount of information collected [22]. We intend to understand the factors concerned, and at the same time we seek to identify the barriers and areas of resistance relating to the adoption.

2.1 Methodology

As software development is involved with human factors, empirical study is the way to understand how software processes work. We applied a qualitative semi structured interview in this study. At this stage, the results of the interviews are used to explore the issues relating to the adoption of Agile methods in the country. The semi structured interview includes a mixture of open ended questions as '*it is designed to elicit not only the information foreseen but also unexpected types of information*' [22]. Understanding issues of Agile adoption in Malaysia is important because little knowledge exists in the country and no previous research about the topic can be found. Therefore empirical study applying the qualitative research method is suitable to look at unknown and never explored scenarios [23].

The data were collected between February and March 2010. The investigation took place in seven organisations in Malaysia involving 13 participants including project managers, the CEOs, founders and software developers. This number of respondents is considered appropriate for this kind of study [24]. Another source suggested having six to 10 subjects for interview [25]; it was also stated by adding more subjects, the research will diverge and become difficult for the researcher to draw strong conclusions.

All respondents were using Scrum method, which contrast with the findings of other researchers [11] who found XP was the most popular method. Two organisations were identified from our initial questionnaire and the rest of the respondents were known from a Scrum workshop that was held in Malaysia. It was the second workshop (10-12 March 2010) held in the country[2]. The number of participants in the second Scrum workshop has increased to approximately 100 participants while the first workshop had only about 20 participants. The interviews were recorded using a digital voice recorder and each of the interviews took no more

---

[2] http://www.asiaictpm.org/mpc_event.php?id=94

than one hour. Prior to recording the interview, we sought the respondents' consent by providing them with a form to be signed. If they agreed, then we started the recording. At the same time, the researcher took handwritten notes, which serve as a reference and can be compared with the audio recorded data.

2.3 Data Analysis

We use a 'Thematic Analysis' to analyse our data. A thematic analysis is a way of seeing things and patterns within the information collected, a process also known as pattern recognition. Codes are produced from themes which are developed through several stages [26]. We chose Thematic Analysis as it is a process used as part of many qualitative methods [26].

In order to develop themes and codes, the raw information (the data) need to be reduced. 'Reduce' here means to filter and remove any information which is not relevant to our study. We listened to the audio recordings and compared the information with the notes we took during the interview. We transcribed the information from these two sources. Only the information related to the questions was transcribed. We referred back to the questions to ensure we had transcribed the responses correctly and that we had not omitted any important information. After the transcription, the themes were identified within the subsamples. The processes and stages were repeated for all of the interviews. Once the themes within the subsamples were identified, they were then compared across subsamples. Lastly, we created codes from these themes as presented in our results section. In this paper, we will present the results by introducing the organisations we interviewed. Then the results section will describe the issues faced by the organisations in the adoption of Agile methods. We group the issues into categories such as knowledge, mind set, people, project, management, knowledge transfer, organisational structure, communication and technical aspects. These results illustrate issues related to the factors, barriers and the way practitioners in Malaysia are using Agile methods.

3 Companies' Overview

In this section, we present an overview of the companies we interviewed. Table 1 introduces a snapshot of the companies' background. All of the companies we interviewed practice the Scrum method, responding to the review undertaken by Dyba and Dingsoyr [11]. We use Agile methods and Scrum interchangeably in this section. For company A, the switch to Agile Methods resulted from the frequent changes and scope of its requirement, especially when they are implementing a government's project. An interviewee said: *"When you are implementing Scrum in a government project, you are able to deliver as per what they want at that time rather than you waiting until the whole specifications have came out and signed off only then can you deliver. Now with a small scope you can actually deliver so they can actually use it."* Company A started to use Scrum over two years ago, but with no proper training. The interviewee said that they failed to implement Scrum correctly without training but fortunately managed to do so after training.

Table 1. Summary of the Companies

Company	Types	Status of the Companies Interviewed	Company's Main Activity
A	Local Company	Fully adopting Scrum	Airport product development, critical system, r&d, middleware
B	Multinational	Fully adopting Scrum	Technology and services
C	Local Company (small and startup)	Scrum + Prototyping	Rapid web application development
D	Local company (Large)	Adopting only parts of Scrum	e-commerce
E	Local company	No longer adopting Scrum	Instrumentation and control solution-offshore and critical system
F	Multinational Company	Fully adopting Scrum	Technology and services
G	Local Company	At the very initial phase of adopting Scrum	ICT infrastructure solution

Company B started to use Scrum method when implementing a pilot project. "*It makes sense for our environment*" is one reason they continue to use it. They added "*it really help us in terms of getting the environment, and also adopting to changing of the time line, changing of the requirements in order to deliver our product in a phase by phase perspective*". The company representatives we interviewed are project managers and developers. They are very enthusiastic about using Scrum and other Agile methods. This can be seen as all developers have a positive opinion about it.

In order to save time by building their own product, company C found Agile methods to be an alternative way to develop software. Initially they started practicing Agile without any training. The CEO stressed that it was difficult to learn Agile methods before they attended training about it in March 2010. The company combines Prototyping and Scrum method to understand the requirements of users. They stated that using Prototyping at the beginning is only to understand the requirements (without involving any codes) and the implementation still takes place in an Agile environment.

Company D believes in Agile, and expressed positive opinions about it. However, the organisation does not formally practice Scrum. It only applies part of the Scrum techniques. They believe that the environment and project should be suitable before fully implementing Scrum. Lack of emphasis on documentation is described as a weakness by both project managers in the company. They believe that for one to adopt Agile, people should find ways to mitigate the risks.

In company E, Scrum was introduced by the project manager. Ineffective results from the Waterfall model was the main reason for company E adopting Scrum. The implementation using Scrum was practiced through trial and error, and it was a decision taken by all the team members. Customers do not know about the method they are using; they are only involved when they have problems and when the team needs clarification of their requirements. From here, problems can be anticipated at an early stage. The company project manager said that Agile was being practiced more in the process as they were doing tasks in order of priority and holding weekly reviews. He also added that it was difficult to introduce Agile, and that method is no longer used when he was transferred to another department. When asked about Agile methods in Malaysia, he admitted "*I never heard about any. In Malaysia, I think not many are interested. I don't know any organisations that are using Agile methods*".

Knowing the advantages Agile can deliver from its other sub-components made it easy for company F to adopt the method. Developers' satisfaction and efficiency are among reasons why they prefer to use the method. Company G is at the early stages of Agile adoption. The project manager we interviewed had just attended a workshop on Scrum methodology. Issues described by this company are to understand issues adopters face at the early stage. This is what we intend to deliver through this study.

4   Results: Issues in the Factors of Agile Adoption in Malaysia

In this section we will describe the results we obtained from the interviews. All of the companies we interviewed practice the Scrum method. This scenario contradicts that of an earlier study specifying XP as the first chosen method in Agile [17]. Scrum is a project management focus with a Scrum master and daily stand up meeting. Scrum has become the preferred method for the early adopters in our interview. All of the organisations we interviewed are still at an early phase with a maximum of two years experience. We think this is an appropriate time as the issues and challenges in adoption are still clear in their mind.

4.1   Knowledge

In our study we coded issues about education and training into knowledge. Education leans more towards understanding the concept and roles and how Agile is different from other methods. Company A emphasises education for implementing Agile. It is essential to ensure that the customers fully understand the concept or how Agile works. Agile provides opportunities for the customers, where they are also taught to relay their requirements easier. For company A, educating the customer is important: "*...if the customer understands how it is going to be done, then it is easier to follow, rather than like previously when we were using Waterfall, because people are so familiar with the Waterfall, so they thought that they can understand how Waterfall works.*" As mentioned by the interviewee from company A, Scrum is not difficult to practice because both parties (customers and internal developers) can be managed easily as a result of practicing the method.

Company C also mentioned education. From their experiences, if the customers do not understand the method, it is difficult to use Scrum; as stated, "*Malaysian customers are not familiar with Agile methods and we need to help them in this matter*". From the interviews, education of the customers in particular, and at the same time the developers', is important to ensure everyone in the team plays their roles correctly.

Training is more for the practitioners and is about how to practice the method in a right and proper way. Practicing Agile methods takes time and requires understanding.

Agile is difficult to learn by oneself and most of the practitioners we interviewed admitted that they were not using Agile correctly before they attended the training. According to most of the interviews, Scrum only provides a framework, but to make it work in a company, it requires experience. *"Dare to fail at the first development"* is mentioned by one of the developers in company B.

Internally, the training department in company A provides monthly classes for Agile development. However, they still teach the Waterfall model to their development team because at the same time they are considering customers' backgrounds before deciding to use any of the methods. A respondent from company C gave an opinion on training: *"If we can have more training here, I think the adoption of the method will be boosted. Malaysia is still in the early phase, but you know, it's just that they don't know how to use Agile because the knowledge is not here, if we learn ourselves, surely it will be harder. You see my team came back from training, they quickly learnt the method from there."*

One of the founders in company C added *"The first time we learnt Agile, we didn't know what to do, but when we go for training, they tell you what to do, you know and you confident."* Company G also thinks training is important for practitioners to understand the method. Surprisingly, we did not hear any serious issue cited in terms of training from the two multinational companies we interviewed (companies B and F).

4.2 Mind Set

Apart from knowledge, mind set is equally important for the adoption factor of Agile methods. The mind set should be from the stakeholders' perspective (for example, team members, customers, project managers and management). Agile is different in terms of its way of working and thus requires a change in mind set. In other words, those involved must be willing to change the way they work especially those who have been using different methods for a long time. This is agreed by most of the companies that were interviewed (companies A, B, C, D and F). As stated by one of the developers in company B, *"These people are stuck in the Waterfall mind set and it can lead to a poor team dynamic."*

The implementation of Scrum was initially difficult for company A when they were dealing with the government sector which is used to the Waterfall model – *"..so the first time that we implemented Agile, it was difficult because the method is not familiar to the government. The method is not familiar to them because they are so familiar with Waterfall stuff."*

One of the founders we interviewed from company C suggested that the mind set must change first in order for the environment to support Agile methods. We discovered an interesting issue in company D which stresses that Scrum is a risky method because no emphasis is placed on documentation. Both of the project managers we interviewed from this company have a background in professional management (PMP). They still believe in Scrum as a way to survive in the business; however at the same time they need documentation to be imposed in the method. To confirm, we also obtained an opinion from company C: *"In Malaysia, when you have pmi/pmp background, you are not suited to Agile, because you have been trained to be in control, so if you are out of control- conflict."*

According to company D, the mind set towards Agile methods does not only apply to the project manager but it requires the cooperation of the team and parties concerned. Although Agile is proven to be successful in many companies [27], the two project managers in company D stated that it will not be necessarily succeed in their company: *"To apply this to a business company like us, it is not necessarily successful. It is a matter of how do we change this people's mind set. It requires the whole team to change, but if we only have some that are changing, and the rest are doing it their own way, we will not be successful, because the other group is waiting for documentation and other groups want to start doing work. The whole company has to adapt to that before we can do it successfully."*

He also added: *"It can be very scary for people like us, for me, I am from the old school; I am PMP, which does not follow this kind of thing. Everything is on paper, formal. It's difficult, but I like this new method. I want to experiment, but when I go in, I realised with this method, that you need this kind of professionalism, commitment, the passion in the project. If you don't have those things, then you can't practice Scrum. In Scrum everybody should be able to get up to par, being able to carry and run that entire thing. That is a very big challenge."*

The mind set is also considered important in company C when they combine Scrum and Kanban for their development. These are combined to help manage several projects when using Scrum. *"In Kanban Scrum we do not have a time box.....-so team members must change their mind set. If before this the mind set is only to one project, but now it is multiple, which the focus can be on multiple projects."*

4.3 People

All of the organisations we interviewed mentioned the importance of people's attitude. Customers, developers and people involved in Agile must understand their roles and responsibilities. A representative in company A stated; *"We need to make sure that the product owners understand their role, so everybody in the team has to understand their role first. I think if they understand their roles, it will be easier because they understand the responsibility that they have, so that is very important."*

The two organisations we interviewed (companies C and D) shared the problems of attitude and working style in their workplace. The resistance from company D can be seen from one comment: *"What do you need in your people in Scrum? You need them to be committed, to be skilled in what they bring to the table, we don't have them. See, you can implement Scrum, but they will again refer to the boss (every time when given the tasks), then how to implement Scrum? This is one of the disadvantages, this is a core problem, when you do not go to the core problem, you will never solve it. Today you need people who are very committed, skilled, yes they are, but not enough of them, very few"*. The two project managers we interviewed from company D were from a professional management background (PMP) and used to have documentation for every task they performed.

The team members in company E waited for the project manager to start each daily meeting. If he did not, no meeting would take place that day, stated the project manager in company E. The method is no longer used following the transfer of the project manager to another department. Although there were several project managers at that time, they did not have the background of Agile methods and software engineering. The project manager we interviewed suggested the use of Agile methods was not continued as he was the one who drove the methodology in the team which might have contributed to the decision to stop using Agile methods.

The two multinational companies (B and F) that we interviewed agreed that people are the essence of doing Agile methods. *"It is up to the individual"* said one developer from company F. He believes that the developer should be independent in order to succeed with the method. Responsibility and commitment are required. One of the developers in company B suggested: *"You need the team which is very self supportive, everybody helps each other to move the whole project forward. So each of the team members should know their particular role and responsibility. The biggest thing is commitment."*

When asked what factors made the project manager in company B chose Agile methods, he replied: *"I think first thing comes to mind is team sprit. Scrum really encourages team work together and whole team commitment, that really helps team spirit, kind of like bringing everyone closer, because working in IT is more like, yeah, you deliver something, and have a fun environment, it is very important to me."*

4.4 Project

Companies A, C and E are using Agile to develop critical and safety systems, which shows that Agile is also suitable for this type of project. Identifying the complexity of the project is also being considered in company A. Besides, before deciding to use Agile, it also seeks clarification of the project. This is the most important factor for company A to adopt Scrum for their development team. However, this again depends on the product owner and the customers' understanding. Company D also mentioned the types of project, and the types of product they developed before deciding to use Agile methods.

4.5 Management Involvement

When using Agile methods, one question always arose: how to obtain management buy-in and how to get their support? In addition, concerns are always raised over how to gain the interest of the customers in using the method. All of these scenarios require management to deal them.

In most organisations, choosing a method to use is based on the decision of the management. This is particularly common in large organisations. Management should be given a clear understanding about the method. Company A also thinks that people management (for example by ensuring the product owner understands his roles) is important when adopting Agile methods. The project manager in Company B struggled initially with his own attitude to the use of Agile methods: *"For me, I do have a struggle initially changing from Waterfall to Scrum. The first thing is not really to get the management buy in, the first thing is to get myself to buy in-as a project manager role."*

The management factor is considered to be the first in practicing Agile methods from company C. Both interviewees from company C said: *"When management seriously wants to implement Agile, then adoption will be easier. Management top down is important, although we are very enthusiastic (team members), but when the top management does not believe in the method, it will not apply, and Agile cannot be practiced."*

Company D also believes management to be an important factor in the adoption of Agile methods. This can be seen from comments they have made: *"In order for us to practice it formally and successfully, implement it successfully, then we need from management right down to marketing, to understand that the methodology will be Scrum"*. Another comment which supports this statement is: *"It depends where you sit in the company, if you are in the top management, they will always go for Waterfall because they can easily see what can be delivered by man, but if you sit at the development model, you prefer to use Scrum because you want to see the product/result fast, that is why if you want to implement Scrum methodology fully, the top management must understand what is happening."*

Company G is only considering how to get customer buy-in as the management has given the decision of using the new method to the project manager. This company is only in the very early phases of implementing Agile methods.

4.6 Knowledge Transfer

Using Agile, retention of knowledge is questioned when people leave the group. This could occur due to the nature of Agile methods which does not rely on documentation. Therefore, when a person or several people move out from a group, they must ensure the next person is able to continue the work. Staff turnover is the most worrying problem shared by two project managers who we interviewed from a local company (D). They agreed that a focus on getting the product faster is one of the best contributed from Agile working's way, but the problem of staff turnover should also be mitigated. They also added that because Malaysia is experiencing this problem, full dependency on the developers should be avoided. Several comments were offered by company D regarding this issue: *"If you use Agile methods, things like Scrum, where the focus is not on documentation, you become very dependent on the developers, but in Malaysia our developers keep moving- move on and move on. If the knowledge resides in only one person, or only a few people, then you have an issue, the moment they leave your company, you're dead."*

Scrum in company D is no longer applied when the project manager was transferred as a result of this problem (no knowledge transfer). However, we did not find this problem discussed seriously in two multinational companies (B and F) that we interviewed. A project manager from company B shared that the problem of staff turnover is a common occurrence. He could not agree that the lack of documentation was the reason for not using Agile methods. As he said, people in development should be balanced and always allocate some time for documentation although the method they use does not focus on it. In addition, from his experience, he did not know of any company that is not using Agile to have a good record on documentation as claimed. Therefore, Agile methods could not be blamed for this problem.

Company A develops software for government projects. According to the representative from company A, the staff turnover rate in the government sector is high and people come in and out very often resulting in frequent changes in requirements. In order to overcome this issue, company A practices Scrum. For company A, following the Waterfall model is not suitable for this kind of situation. A group of developers from a multinational company (B) believe in having a good coding for documentation. A clean code can serve as documentation that can be easily read by new staff.

4.7 Organisational Structure

Factor such as small organisations is more suitable to practice Agile [3, 19]. From the interviews, we found similar results; that small and startup companies are more appropriate for the culture of Agile. Company D agreed that the Agile method is more suitable for a small and startup company. This is because this type of company does not have any legacies that it must follow. However it is harder to practice Agile in a large, established company. Everything must be formal and documentation must be kept within the business. That is the reason why company D has only adopted certain practices that are suitable for the company.

In relation to small and start - up companies, company C claimed to have an Agile cultural environment. This could be a strong reason for them to practice Scrum fully. They believed in the method and started to practice Agile with their own effort. *"For a small startup company like us, it is good to have the culture of Agile, because it must be reflected in our values, which our value stated that the customer always comes first, they are not always right, but come first. In line with the manifesto of Agile where collaboration is more important, we believe Agile is the best for us. My point to highlight here - culture of Agile, it is very suitable for a start - up company like us."*

One interviewee from company C stated: *"To get truly Agile especially in Malaysia, one has to change the culture, this means we as a society must be trained to be open and transparent, because Agile is about transparency, at all levels. As you see, the Malaysian working way is different, totally different, so society should change the mind set first then embed it as a culture, that's the important thing."*

It is not only the company that should provide the culture; the people or team members in the organisation should also embrace it. According to the respondent from Company C, the mind set of people practicing Agile must be changed first then the environment will adapt to that culture. Company B has similar opinions; as they said that Agile is suitable for them because it can be adapted to their dynamic culture. When asked the reason they are using Agile, one of the developers answered: *"Because it makes sense for our environment"*. One of the developers from company B added: *"In a way, the Waterfall model may not be as sufficient for a community like ours, because we are very reactive, we are very fast - paced and with Waterfall is just too rigid. Scrum gives us benefits because it is able to adapt to a dynamic culture."*

A developer in Company B said, *"Organisational structure must not be rigid"* and the founder of company C suggested that the overall structure must be supportive of the culture of Agile. The structure is not restricted to internal parties but customers also should be included in it.

4.8 Communication

Usually developers will make assumptions when they do not have enough information about the requirements, and wrong assumptions create problems later on. We found this is to be the case in companies A, B and C. Therefore, the emphasis on communication in Agile helps to solve the problem. That is why the documentation being used is essential, it is minimal but not zero.

One of the developers in company B mentioned that clear communication should be practiced when trying to introduce the methods. According to him, the project manager should also communicate the method clearly to the team members. He added that not having a clear understanding of what they are doing will attract more resistance from the team members. Instead of asking the team members to cooperate, the project manager received the objections from the team as they thought Agile practices were just wasting their time.

4.9 Technical Aspects

The companies we interviewed stated that the people factor and other social factors mentioned before are more important than the technical factor. The respondent from company B stated: *"That's why I can do Scrum without any tools"*. A comment from a project manager in B referred to technical aspects; *"Scrum is basically only a framework, and I've been thinking about how come the tools that I have been used are not really there in the framework"*. However for company C, the technical aspect must also be there to support Agile methods. It is another factor for the success of Agile methods.

Another important aspect is communication tools. This is essential when a company has more than one team and also when these teams are not co-located. In this case, communication tools are used to share information through conversation. This is usually the case in a multinational company such as companies B and F. However, the problem is amplified when there is a difference in time zones. Inconsistencies in the conference tools they use can create problems in conveying the required information.

5   Discussion

Malaysia is still in the early phases of using Agile methods, and some respondents from our ongoing questionnaire and informal discussions have indicated they had not heard of Agile methods previously. At the time this interviews were conducted, to the best of our knowledge, only two workshops about Agile methods (i.e Scrum) had been held in the country. One was in December 2009 and the second was in March 2010, in which the researcher was one of the participants. Therefore, if more training is available, it can help to increase the rates of adoption among the practitioners in the country as agreed by most of the companies. The number of participants from the second workshop has increased from the first one and there were also repeating companies or participants in the second workshop. We also perceived passive resistance, learned anecdotally from the Scrum workshop. The participants we met (from the group not using the method) did not believe in Agile methods. They attended the workshop as required by their companies, maybe because the companies had become aware of the advantages of Agile. Clear demand for the training of Agile methods can be seen from the increase in the number of participants in the workshop.

The interview results also show that training is an important factor in the correct usage of Agile methods. These interviews are probably representative of Malaysia as a whole.

We have seen that people are an important factor, as stated by most of the companies we interviewed. This is so as the core of Agile lies in the people [3]. They should be cooperative and fully committed, as in Agile, it is the people concerned who decide what they want to do in the development. Although they will know their responsibilities and roles from training or education that might be provided by the company, nevertheless, the attitude must be open and transparent at all levels. Working in Agile is a whole team effort; thus all parties involved in Agile are required to act accordingly. For instance, the product owner should be in control, and communicative, to represent what the customers need and vice versa. The people in the team should also be independent. If team members cannot be independent and are always waiting for instructions then Agile cannot be practiced. Although it was not directly mentioned by company E, we identified that team members are not committed enough and do not possess the knowledge to continue the method; thus the method was discontinued. This scenario was identified in company E.

Company A places emphasis on education and checking customers' background before deciding to use the methods. This is important as customers have a role to play in Agile methods. However, company D stressed the importance of mind set, and Agile is lacking in documentation is identified as an obvious resistance from this company. If the mindset of the traditional method is still present in a person who is practicing Scrum, it will be harder to for them to adopt the method. Agile is a way to collaborate, and if the stakeholders that involved do not participate then it is difficult to practice it. Lack of awareness or knowledge about the Agile method could be one factor causing this difficulty. These people are very familiar with the method they used before and this makes it hard for them to accept the new approach.

The participants from the workshop have also shared that it will be difficult to practice Agile with the attitude of the software practitioners they have. The question here is whether education or mindset should come first. If education or understanding is provided, then the negative resistance towards Agile methods might be reduced.

7 Conclusion and Future Work

In this paper, we investigated the issues about the adoption of Agile methods in Malaysia. The data obtained are to understand the factors and difficulties faced by the early adopters. On the basis of these initial interviews it seems the most important people factor can be classified as knowledge, mind set, commitment, management involvement, knowledge transfer, organisational structure and communication. This study will help us to generate and refine our hypotheses for the next stage of our study. It will also be used as our background in developing a model for the adoption of Agile methods in the country. Although many factors and issues have been identified from the study, we conclude that the social factors are more important to be considered when using Agile methods. While technical factors are always said to be important when developing software, however, we found these factors to be less important in our study. This is the issue that we need to investigate further in our future work.

We hope the results we obtained from this study will help practitioners not to underestimate the factors of social aspects when implementing Agile methods. We intend to conduct further survey (questionnaire and interviews) to develop and validate a model for factors predicting successful adoption of Agile methods in Malaysia. The relative importance of these factors will be quantitatively investigated in our future works. Lastly, we would like to thank all parties involved for their assistance in this study.

References

1. Sison, R., et al.: Software practices in five ASEAN countries: an exploratory study. In: Proceedings of the 28th International Conference on Software Engineering. ACM, Shanghai (2006)
2. Sison, R., Yang, T.: Use of Agile Methods and Practices in the Philippines. In: 14th Asia-Pacific of Software Engineering Conference, APSEC 2007 (2007)
3. Cockburn, A., Highsmith, J.: Agile software development: The people factor. Computer 34(11), 131–133 (2001)
4. Baharom, F., Deraman, A., Hamdan, A.: A Survey on the Current Practices of Software Development Process in Malaysia. Journal of ICT 4, 57–76 (2006)
5. Nasir, M., Ahmad, R., Hassan, N.: An Empirical Study of Barriers in the Implementation of Software Process Improvement Project in Malaysia. Journal of Applied Sciences 8(23), 4362–4368 (2008)
6. Zainol, A., Mansoor, S.: Investigation into requirements management practices in the Malaysian software industry. In: 2008 International Conference on Computer Science and Software Engineering (CSSE 2008). IEEE, Wuhan (2008)
7. Chow, T., Cao, D.: A survey study of critical success factors in agile software projects. Journal of Systems and Software 81(6), 961–971 (2008)
8. Cohen, D., Lindvall, M., Costa, P.: An introduction to agile methods. In: Advances in Computers, vol. 62, pp. 1–66. Elsevier Academic Press Inc., San Diego (2004)
9. Highsmith, J., Cockburn, A.: Agile software development: The business of innovation. Computer, 120–122 (2001)
10. Abbas, N., Gravell, A.M., Wills, G.B.: Historical roots of Agile methods: Where did "Agile Thinking" come from? In: 9th International Conference on Agile Processes in Software Engineering and Extreme Porgramming, Limerick, IRELAND. Springer, Berlin (2008)
11. Dyba, T., Dingsoyr, T.: Empirical studies of agile software development: A systematic review. Information and Software Technology 50(9-10), 833–859 (2008)
12. Krasteva, I., Ilieva, S.: Adopting an agile methodology: why it did not work. In: Proceedings of the 2008 International Workshop on Scrutinizing Agile Practices or Shoot-out at the Agile Corral. ACM, Leipzig (2008)
13. Misra, S.C., Kumar, V., Kumar, U.: Identifying some important success factors in adopting agile software development practices. Journal of Systems and Software 82(11), 1869–1890 (2009)
14. Turk, D., France, R., Rumpe, B.: Limitations of agile software processes (2002)
15. Strode, D.E., Huff, S.L., Tretiakov, A.: The impact of organizational culture on agile method use. In: 2009 42nd Hawaii International Conference on System Sciences, HICSS-42. IEEE, Big Island (2008)

16. Wendorff, P.: Organisational culture in agile software development. In: 4th International Conference on Product Focused Software Process Improvement, Rovaniemi, Finland. Springer, Berlin (2002)
17. Tolfo, C., Wazlawick, R.S.: The influence of organizational culture on the adoption of extreme programming. Journal of Systems and Software 81(11), 1955–1967 (2008)
18. Robinson, H., Sharp, H.: Organisational culture and XP: three case studies. In: Proceedings, Agile 2005. IEEE Comput. Soc., Denver (2005)
19. Bahli, B., Abou Zeid, E.S.: The role of knowledge creation in adopting extreme programming model: An empirical study. In: ITI 3rd International Conference on Information and Communications Technology (ICICT 2005). IEEE, Cairo (2005)
20. Madeyski, L., Biela, W.: Capable Leader and Skilled and Motivated Team Practices to Introduce eXtreme Programming. In: Meyer, B., Nawrocki, J.R., Walter, B. (eds.) CEE-SET 2007. LNCS, vol. 5082, pp. 96–102. Springer, Heidelberg (2008)
21. Livermore, J.A.: Factors that impact implementing an agile software development methodology. In: Proceedings of SoutheastCon 2007. IEEE, Los Alamitos (2007)
22. Seaman, C.: Qualitative methods in empirical studies of software engineering. IEEE Transactions on Software Engineering 25(4), 557–572 (2002)
23. Creswell, J.: Research design: Qualitative, quantitative, and mixed methods approaches. Sage Pubns, Thousand Oaks (2008)
24. Kvale, S.: Interviews: An introduction to qualitative research interviewing. Sage Publications, Inc., Thousand Oaks (1996)
25. Marczyk, G., DeMatteo, D., Festinger, D.: Essentials of research design and methodology. John Wiley & Sons, Chichester (2005)
26. Boyatzis, R.: Transforming qualitative information: Thematic analysis and code development. Sage Publications, Inc., Thousand Oaks (1998)
27. Schatz, B., Abdelshafi, I.: Primavera gets agile: A successful transition to agile development. IEEE Software 22(3), 36-+ (2005)

Pair Programming and Software Defects – An Industrial Case Study

Nattakarn Phaphoom, Alberto Sillitti, and Giancarlo Succi

Center for Applied Software Engineering,
Free University of Bozen-Bolzano,
Piazza Dominicani 3, I-39100 Bozen-Bolzano, Italy
{Alberto.Sillitti,Giancarlo.Succi}@unibz.it,
nattakarn.phaphoom@stud-inf.unibz.it

Abstract. In the last decade there has been increasing interest in pair programming. However, despite work has been done, there is still a lack of substantial evidence of pair programming effects in industrial environments. To increase a body of evidence regarding the real benefits of pair programming, we investigate its relationship with software defects. The analysis is based on 14-months data collected from a large Italian manufacturing company. The team of 17 developers adopted a customized version of extreme programming and used pair programming on a daily basis. We explore and compare the defect rate of the code changed by doing pair and solo programming. The results show that defects appear to be lower for the code modified during pair programming. As a consequence, we formulate a hypothesis that pair programming is effective in reducing the introduction of new defects when existing code is modified.

Keywords: Pair programming, software defects, extreme programming.

1 Introduction

There have been claims that pair programming may improve software development under several perspectives. A significant numbers of empirical studies have been conducted and results have been used in support of such claims. The apparent benefits include (a) reducing defect rate [3, 16,18, 19, 21-24], (b) improving design [4], (c) increasing productivity [11, 13, 24], (d) shortening the time-to-market [6,8, 24, 26, 27], (e) enhancing knowledge transfer and team communication [3, 5, 6, 22, 23], (f) increasing job satisfaction [3, 20], (g) facilitating integration of newcomers [9], and (h) reducing training costs [25].

However, there are also studies that do not confirm such outcomes, especially regarding productivity and cost-efficiency. The study in [15] indicates no positive effect of pair programming in term of development times. In [10], pair productivity is varied across projects. A large experiment conducted by [1] shows that neither does pair programming reduce time required to correctly perform change tasks nor increase the percentage of correct solutions. Begel and Nagappan reports in [3] the survey results from Microsoft mentioning high skepticism over pair efficiency.

In particular, the effects of pair programming on the code quality appear to be inconsistent across situations. In [1], the correctness of solutions increases when

A. Sillitti et al. (Eds.): XP 2011, LNBIP 77, pp. 208–222, 2011.
© Springer-Verlag Berlin Heidelberg 2011

junior pairs work on a complex system. In [19], the defect rate in code decreases only when pairs implement a large program. Several studies [10, 16, 23, 27] indicate positive effects of pair programming only when using a particular quality measure. Hence, its effectiveness depends on the combination of the features of the subjects, the performed tasks, and the choices of employed quality measures. The diversity of such situational variables creates inconsistency on the results from different studies. In addition, it reflects the need to replicate the studies for each situation to confirm the previous findings.

In addition, it is difficult to generalize the results of existing studies to industrial settings, especially when the representativeness of experimental settings is considered. Most of the studies were conducted in educational settings. Data coming from classroom experiments, especially inexperienced students attending an introductory computer science course, pose serious concerns as they appear very different from the data coming from industry. Students have limited programming experience and knowledge in task domain; while generally it is not the case for professional developers. Moreover, the tasks performed in the experiments are mostly small isolated development tasks. Very few studies focus on maintenance tasks [1, 28] which are an essential area in long term software projects.

To enlarge the body of evidence, our study investigates the relationship between pair programming practices and the defects of produced code in two situations: 1) when it is used for defect corrections, and 2) when it is used for implementing user stories. The analysis is based on several data sources gathering for about 14 months from a large Italian manufacturing company. The observed team has adopted XP and used pair programming on a daily basis. The differences on the defect rates between the parts of code involved during pair programming sessions and the parts not involved during pair programming are presented as the result. Due to the limitation of observational data we used, the significant results are used to form hypotheses for further study.

The reminder of the paper is organized as follows. Section 2 summarizes the related work. Section 3 discusses the research design and hypotheses. The results are explained in Section 4 and the summary of the results are presented in Section 5. The threads to validity are discussed in Section 6, and final conclusions are presented in Section 7.

2 Related Work

Although a significant numbers of studies on pair programming have been conducted, limited numbers of them investigate its effects on code quality. The purpose of our review is to explore the effects of pair programming on the quality of produced code in industrial software projects. However, several studies are excluded from the final review results presented in Table 1 as they are considered to be out of scope or not applicable to industrial contexts. The applied exclusion criteria are as follows:

1. The study is conducted in an introductory computer science course.
2. The focus of the study is on designing or testing, rather than coding.
3. The study aims at verifying the feasibility of distributed pair programming.
4. The study does not compare pair programming with solo programming.

Such criteria results in identifying ten studies presented in Table 1. The setting of the studies, the adopted quality measures are summarized along with the results. Additionally, a ratio presenting a number of hypotheses in which pairs outperform solos and a total number of tested hypotheses for each study are calculated. Refer to Table 1, *the effective case* represents this ratio.

Table 1. The summary of work in which the effectiveness of pair programming and solo programming are compared under a certain quality measure (the effective case presents a number of cases in which pairs appear to be more effective than solos / a total number of tested cases or hypotheses)

Study	Adopted quality measure	Effective cases of PP	Outcomes and comments
[27]	Score	1/2	Effects of PP on functionality and readability were tested. Pairs outperformed solos only when using the functionality measure.
[24]	Passed test cases	1/1	Pairs outperformed solos.
[10]	Defect density, several code metrics	2/3	Code implemented by PP teams did not consistently contain fewer defects. Pairs wrote more comments in code and, surprisingly, deviated the coding standard more often than solos.
[23]	Defect density, proportion of bad methods	1/2	Code implemented by pairs contained more post-release defects but had lower proportion of bad methods. However, the effects might due to the differences of the implemented use cases.
[28]	A numbers of missed change propagations	1/1	Pairs outperformed solos to implement 6 changes in open source software. The tests of significance were not performed due to the small sample size.
[12]	Dependency metrics	0/5	Different development approaches did not appear to impact the quality of design.
[14]	A number of failures	0/1	All teams worked in pairs in design phase. During the development phase, one team continued working in pair; while developers in another team work individually.
[1]	A correctness score	3/12	Pairs outperformed solos only: 1) for junior developers, 2) when working on complex tasks, 3) when juniors worked on complex tasks.
[18]	Defect density	1/1	Pairs outperformed solos.
[19]	Defect density	1/2	Pairs outperformed solos when implementing a larger program.

3 Research Design

3.1 Goal-Question-Metrics

To organize properly the empirical investigation, we used Goal-Question-Metrics (GQM) approach proposed by Basili [2]. The GQM comes with a template for the definition of the research goal, which helps avoiding ambiguities and inconsistencies [2]. Here below we defined the goal using such template. Then the relevant questions and the associated metrics followed.

Goal:

- Analyze **pair programming**
- For the purpose of **observing its relationship**
- With respect to **the defect rate in source code**
- From the point of view of **developers**
- In the context of **industrial software development projects**

Questions:

The questions to be investigated were based on anecdotal claims and empirical findings that pair programming helps to 1) reduce and prevent defects, and 2) enhance knowledge over the source code. This work searches for such evidences by analyzing pair programming practices on the parts of code modified for defect corrections and implementations of user stories.

Table 2. Questions regarding the relationship between pair programming and defects

Id	Question	Period of pair programming
Q1	Does the code contain fewer defects when developers pair program?	The whole observation period
Q2	Considering only defect-containing methods, do the methods contain fewer defects when developers pair program?	Prior to the defect detection
Q3	Considering only defect-containing methods, are the defects reduced, once developers start to pair program when working on such methods?	Once the defect correction has started
Q4	Considering only methods modified during user story implementations, does the enhance knowledge gained from previous pair programming on such methods help to prevent new defects afterwards?	Prior to the implementation of user story
Q5	Considering only methods modified during user story implementations, do the methods contain fewer defects when developers pair program when working on such methods?	Once the implementation of user story has started

To see whether *pair programming helps to reduces defects*, we have proceeded the following: 1) identify defective parts of code, i.e. defect-containing methods, 2) measure the amount of pair programming practices on such methods before the detection of the defects, 3) perform statistical analysis between pair programming *prior to the detection* and the defect density of such methods.

To see whether *pair programming helps to prevent an introduction of new defects* when existing code are modified, we have performed: 1) identify methods which were modified for the defect corrections or the implementations of user stories, 2) measure the amount of pair programming practices on such methods once the modification has started, 3) perform the statistical analysis between pair programming and the defect density.

To see whether *pair programming helps to enhance knowledge over the code*, we have performed: 1) identify methods modified for the implementation of user stories, 2) measure the amount of pair programming which has been practiced on those methods before the implementation, i.e. from the start of the observation to the start of the implementations, 3) perform statistical analysis between pair *programming prior to the implementation* and the defect density.

Table 2 summarizes the circumstances under which the particular effects of pair programming are observed and corresponding questions.

Metrics:
Percentage of pair programming (%PP). We measured the effort spent during pair programming and solo programming for methods in classes which were modified during the maintenance work. Instead of the real effort in pairs, we use the ratio as it reflects the portions of solo effort. This metric is defined by:

$$\% PP = \frac{E_P}{E_T}$$

E_P is PP effort (in seconds) spent in the method during an observation period,

E_T is the total effort (in seconds) spent in the method during the same observation period.

Defect density (DD). We used the ratio of defects per lines of code to measure the quality of code. The benefit of using the defect density, instead of the absolute number of defects, is that it is normalized and comparable among methods of different size. It is also due to the empirical evidence that a total number of defects have a pattern of relationship with lines of code. Defect density, hence, reduces such dependency which might generate bias for the analysis.

$$DD = \frac{D_T}{LOC}$$

D_T is the total number of defects found in the method, and
LOC is the lines of code of the method.

3.2 Context

The case study is based on the 14-month data collected from an IT department of a large Italian manufacturing company. The team of 17 developers, 15 veterans and 2 newcomers, adopted a customized version of XP. In particular, they used weekly iteration, pair programming, test first, user story, planning game, daily stand-up meeting, collective code ownership, and coding standard. The team was familiar with XP as such practices had been rigorously used for two years before the data collection started.

Regarding the work environment, the team was co-located, working in an open workspace where members had their own personal workstation. This helped support flow of information and team collaboration. Each desk was equipped with a personal machine, a monitor, a single keyboard, and a mouse.

As regards to pair programming, it was used spontaneously when developers found it useful and appropriate. The team had no plan on when to pair, with whom, or when to switch a role.

3.3 Data Collection

Several types of raw data were collected from the XP team, as provided in Table 3. The data was, mainly, collected from 4 data sources, including PRO Metrics (PROM), workitem tracking system, source control system, and source code.

The data related to developer activities and effort was collected by using PROM [17]. PROM is an automated tool for data acquisition and analysis. It runs on the background of developers' computers to collect a set of product and process measures. Therefore, the data was collected with very little intervention from researchers.

In this project, workitems carried out by developers were classified into 3 types, namely defects, user stories, and tasks. Possible states of the workitem were created, assigned, resolved, verified, and closed. Evidences collected during the state changes consisted of the timestamp, the person and the rationale.

In addition, PROM accesses the source control system and the source code to identify the methods in classes which were changed for each commit. This information was used to identify a list of methods changed during the implementation of workitems.

We consider the data collected from PROM reliable for several reasons: 1) developers were familiar with its interfaces and data collection process; 2) The summarized data representing the percentage of time spent on each application had been sending to developers on a daily basis for the whole observation time, and they had confirmed the correctness of the data.

It is important to mention privacy issues regarding the use of PROM, as the collected data is confidential. In this case, the developers were informed in detail about PROM and its data collection. They also had an access to their own records and team summarized data. As the tracking data was stored in a personal machine before sending to the central database, developers were able to check those records any time and decided if they should have been deleted. This action was transparent to researchers. Additionally, the participation to the study was on a voluntary basis [7].

Table 3. Six types of raw data collected during 14 months from the XP team

	Data	Source
1.	**Effort and working duration.** Effort and duration (seconds) spent on a certain method/class in source code, collected automatically by a tools running as a background process on developers' computers.	PROM [17]
2.	**PP configuration and timeframe.** Pair partners, effort, and duration in which pairs worked together on specific work, and on specific pieces of source code.	PROM
3.	**Workitem – timeframe.** Effort and duration in which a developer works on a specific workitem.	PROM
4.	**Workitem tracking information.** Details of activities (workitem), for instance status, important dates, and responsible person. We consider three types of work item, namely defects, user stories, and tasks	PROM
5.	**Change log.** Change details of committed files on the version control system.	Source control system
6.	**Method status tracking.** A status (added, modified, removed) of each method in a committed class/file on the version control system.	Source code and source control system

3.4 Mapping Workitem and Source Code

To analyze the relationship between pair programming and defects in the source code, we need to perform several steps as follows: 1) map defects and their locations in the source code; 2) identify a list of methods modified during the implementation of each workitem; 3) measure a percentage of pair programming practiced in such methods.

To measure the defect density of each method in classes, the prerequisite was to map defects and their locations in the source code. This was done by identifying a list of methods that were changed during the defect correction activity. We performed the following steps for such mapping.

1. Identify defects with the sufficient information.
2. Identify of a sequence of timeframes that developers worked on each defect.
3. Identify of a list of methods being accessed during the defect corrections.
4. Identify of a subset of methods being modified during the defect corrections.

Apart from defect corrections, we applied the same mechanism to identify a list of methods that were changed during the user story implementation and general tasks. Table 4 summarizes the amount of remaining workitem for analysis after we applied each of the 4 steps. As a result, there were 8.4% of defects with complete tracking information during defect corrections, and 8.8% of user stories with complete information during the implementation. The general tasks were related to document, rather than the code. This information was used for exploratory analysis.

Table 4. Summary of workitem-methods mapping

4 steps to map workitems and changes in source code	Remaining number of workitems		
	Defects (the total number is 464)	**User stories** (the total number is 1635)	**Tasks** (the total number is 111)
1. Sufficient tracking information was available.	430	1568	90
2.+3. It was possible to identify a list of methods that were *'accessed'* during the work.	88	274	0
4. It was possible to identify a list of methods that were *'modified'* during the work.	39 (8.4%)	144 (8.8%)	0 (0%)
Total modified methods	377	1603	0

3.5 Data Analysis

To answer the questions identified in GQM, we applied the t-test to two distributions:

- The sample of the defect density, for the methods with the percentage of pair programming equal to zero, i.e., methods were entirely involved during solo programming.
- The sample of the defect density, for the methods with the percentage of pair programming greater than zero.

The test was applied to analyze the relationship between pair programming and defect density in the source code in five situations as mentioned in GQM. If we found a significant decrease in defect density when pair programming was practiced, then we assumed that the usage of pair programming had been effective in that situation.

4 Results

For each of the five situations the t-test has been applied. The results have to be viewed as exploratory data analysis in which the role of data is of primary relevance. We do not claim the causal effects of pair programming on the quality of code in the analyzed cases. Instead, we aim to observe their relationship and to generate hypotheses for further testing.

4.1 Q1-Pair Programming and Defect Density

The purpose of Q1 is to explore the relationship between pair programming and defect density of the sample in general. As mentioned, the sample is a group of methods which were modified during the defect corrections and the implementations of user stories. They are the results of mapping mechanism explained in Section 3.4.

Fig. 1 illustrates pair programming practices and the defect density of the sample methods at the end of the observation. Out of 1859, 1388 methods (74.6%) were involved entirely during the solo programming session (%PP = 0); and 471 methods were involved, at least partly, during the pair programming (%PP > 0). The mean of defect density of the solo group is 20.38; while that of the pair group is 8.92. The differences are significant with p-value less than 0.001 using t-test.

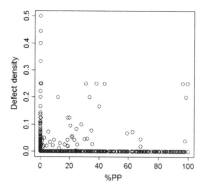

Sample	%PP=0	%PP>0
Size	1388	47
Mean (DD/KLoc)	20.38	8.92
Std. Dev.	52.75	36.27
P-Value	>0.001	

Fig. 1. The result for Q1, left: the scatter plot of %PP and the defect density, right: the result of t-test between a group of methods involved entirely during solo programming (%PP=0) and a group involved at least partly during pair programming (%PP>0), considering the measure at the *end of the observation*

4.2   Q2-Pair Programming Practices Prior to the Defect Detection

The second case considers a subset of methods analyzed in Q1. This sample is a group of methods which were modified during the corrections of 39 defects. The corrections resulted in the 412 modifications of 377 defective methods.

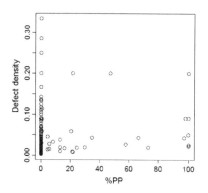

Sample	%PP=0	%PP>0
Size	380	32
Mean (DD/KLoc)	78.04	58.96
Std. Dev.	65.86	60.12
P-Value	0.09	

Fig. 2. The result for Q2, left: the scatter plot of %PP and the defect density, right: the result of t-test between a group of methods involved entirely during solo programming (%PP=0) and a group involved at least partly during pair programming (%PP>0), considering the measures at *the point the defect detection*

Fig. 2 illustrates pair programming practices prior to the defect detections of the sample and the defect density. A mean value of the defect density of the data points not involved during the pair programming is 78.04; while that of the data points involved during pair programming is 58.96. In this case, the differences are not significant at a 0.05 level.

4.3 Q3-Pair Programming Practices Once the Defect Correction Has Started

Q3 considers the fraction of pair programming on defective methods once the defect correction has started. The purpose is to investigate the relationship between pair programming and the introduction of new defects. In general it is likely that developers would introduce new defects when modifying existing source codes. This analysis allows the observation of such circumstance.

Fig. 3 illustrates this fraction of pair programming practices and the defect density. From the start of the defect corrections, 386 data points were involved entirely during solo programming; only 26 were involved during pair programming practices. The data points having zero as the defect density represent the methods in which no new defect has been found after the start of the correction.

The mean value of the defect density of the solo group is 6.96; 34 methods (8.8%) contain new defects. The mean value of the defect density of the pair group is 0.49; only one method contains new defect. Using t-test, the differences of the defect density of the two groups are significantly important; the p-value is less than 0.001.

We further analyze 35 methods in which the defects were found after the modification of the code. Out of 35, three methods contain three more defects; seven methods contain two more defects; and 25 methods contain only one more defect. Interestingly, the methods containing more than one defect were involved entirely during solo programming.

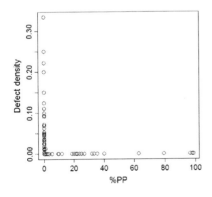

Sample	%PP=0	%PP>0
Size	386	36
Mean (DD/KLoc)	6.96	0.49
Std. Dev.	31.5	2.51
P-Value	>0.001	

Fig. 3. The result for Q3, left: the scatter plot of %PP and the defect density, right: the result of t-test for defective methods between the group involved entirely during solo programming (%PP=0) and the group involved at least partly during pair programming (%PP>0), considering the fraction of pair programming *once the defect correction has started*

4.4 Q4-Pair Programming Practices Prior to the User Story Implementation

Fig.4 illustrates pair programming practices prior to the implementations of user stories and the defect density of modified methods. Out of 1,904, 1,662 methods were involved entirely during solo programming; and 242 were involved at least partly during pair programming. The mean value of the defect density of the former is 3.42; while that of the latter is 1.28. The differences are significantly important.

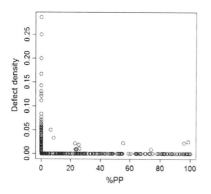

Sample	%PP=0	%PP>0
Size	1662	242
Mean (DD/KLoc)	3.42	1.28
Std. Dev.	18.72	5.66
P-Value	>0.001	

Fig. 4. The result for Q4, left: the scatter plot of %PP and the defect density, right: the result of t-test for modified methods between the group involved entirely during solo programming (%PP=0) and the group involved at least partly during pair programming (%PP>0), considering the fraction of pair programming practices prior to the implementation of a user story

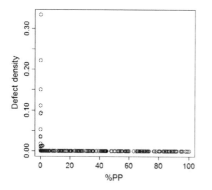

Sample	%PP=0	%PP>0
Size	1526	378
Mean (DD/KLoc)	1.03	0.72
Std. Dev.	13.4	7
P-Value	0.54	

Fig. 5. The result for Q5, left: the scatter plot of %PP and the defect density, right: the result of t-test for enhanced methods between the group involved entirely during solo programming (%PP=0) and the group involved involve at least partly during pair programming (%PP>0), considering the fraction of pair programming practices once *the implementation of a user story has started*

4.5 Q5-Pair Programming Practices Once the User Story Implementation Has Started

The last case observes the pair programming practices once the implementations of user stories have started and the introduction of new defects in code. Fig. 5 illustrates such fraction of pair programming and defect density. Out of 1526 methods involved entirely during solo programming, 21 methods contain defects which were found after the start of the implementation. Out of 378 methods involved at least partly during pair programming, 9 methods contain new defects. However, the means value of defect density of the two groups are not significantly important

5 Summary of the Results

The relationship between pair programming and the defect density in the code has been explored through Q1-Q5. Table 10 summarizes the situations in which pair programming was used and the results of t-test indicating whether defect density appears to be lower over some extend of pair programming practices. As mentioned, we do not claim the causal relationship between both variables but the results are used to formulate hypotheses.

Table 10. The summary of Q1-Q5, presenting the situations in which pair programming has been effectively used to reduce defects on the basis of t-test

Id	The situation in which pair programming was used	Have the defects been decreasing?
Q1	For implementing changes in general	yes
Q2	Prior to the defect detection	no
Q3	For the defect correction	yes
Q4	Prior to the user story implementation	yes
Q5	For the user story implementation	no

From the results, we have observed potential effective usage of pair programming and formulate hypotheses, based on the observation and the comparisons using t-test. The proposed hypotheses as follows:

- **Hypothesis 1:** Using pair programming for performing defect corrections will reduce the introduction of new defects.
- **Hypothesis 2:** The enhanced knowledge over the code through the regular usage of pair programming will reduce defects when the code has to be modified to implement new requirements or changes.

6 Validity

6.1 Construct Validity

The pair programming measure. The information regarding pair construction, duration, and pieces of source code that pairs worked with was collected automatic by PROM. We received a confirmation from developers that the tool was always activated. Therefore, we consider the measure of %PP of methods reliable. However, we could not capture the amount of pair programming practices since the creation of the methods, but during the 14-month observation. This duration is considered sufficient to reflect the actual amount of PP practice.

The quality measure. We used defect density to measure quality of methods instead of using the absolute number of defects. The possible bias of using absolute number of defects is that it is incomparable among methods of different sizes. Moreover, the empirical evidence shows a relationship between code size and defects. We avoided such issue by using defect density.

6.2 Internal Validity

The defect mapping. One of the challenges in this work was to map defects with the methods that contributed to each particular defect. Some evidences of the defect localization activities were not automatically collected by PROM. Instead, they were generated by a feature that needs to be activated manually when developers started working on the specific defects. If it was not activated then the evidences would be missing. However, we regularly asked and received the confirmation from developers regarding the activation of this feature.

The problem of confounding factors. This issue is crucial for an observational case study where researchers have no control over the subjects and their practices. In pair programming context, 2 crucial confounding factors to the effectiveness of pairs are the expertise of developers and task complexity. In our case study, the developers were professionals, 15 veterans and 2 newcomers. We found no significant effects of the two types of developers using multiple regression analysis. Task complexity depends upon the complexity of the system and the difficulty of the task. We were not able to test the effect of this factor due to the limitation of the dataset.

7 Conclusions

The contributions of this work are twofold. The first part summarizes the empirical knowledge on the effects of pair programming on the quality of produced code, as compared to solo programming. The second part presents the relationship between pair programming practices and the defect rate in different circumstances, based on the data collected over 14 months from an industrial XP team. The summary of current knowledge shows that the effects of pair programming are inconsistent across different situations. Its effectiveness depends, to some extent, upon the features of subjects, the features of performed tasks, and the choices of adopted quality measures.

In our exploratory analysis, the usage of pair programming is investigated in the context of the defect corrections and the implementations of user stories. The results shows that the defect rate in the code appears to be lower for the parts of code involved during pair programming practices than other parts. On the basis of this observation, we formulate a hypothesis that pair programming helps to reduce the introduction of new defects when existing code is modified.

References

1. Arisholm, E., Gallis, H., Dyba, T., Sjoberg, D.I.K.: Evaluating pair programming with respect to system complexity and programmer expertise. IEEE Trans. Softw. Eng. 33(2), 65–86 (2007)
2. Basili, V.: Applying the goal question metric paradigm in the experience factory. In: Proceedings of the Tenth Annual Conference of Software Metrics and Quality Assurance in Industry (1993)
3. Begel, A., Nagappan, N.: Pair programming: what's in it for me? In: ESEM 2008: Proceedings of the Second ACM-IEEE International Symposium on Empirical Software Engineering and Measurement, pp. 120–128. ACM, New York (2008)
4. Canfora, G., Cimitile, A., Garcia, F., Piattini, M., Visaggio, C.A.: Evaluating performances of pair designing in industry. J. Syst. Softw. 80(8), 1317–1327 (2007)
5. Chong, J., Hurlbutt, T.: The social dynamics of pair programming. In: ICSE 2007: Proceedings of the 29th International Conference on Software Engineering, pp. 354–363. IEEE Computer Society, Washington, DC (2007)
6. Cockburn, A., Williams, L.: The costs and benefits of pair programming, pp. 223–243 (2001)
7. Coman, I.D., Sillitti, A., Succi, G.: A case-study on using an automated in-process software engineering measurement and analysis system in an industrial environment. In: ICSE 2009: Proceedings of the 31st International Conference on Software Engineering, pp. 89–99. IEEE Computer Society, Washington, DC (2009)
8. Dyba, T., Arisholm, E., Sjøberg, D.I.K., Hannay, J.E., Shull, F.: Are two heads better than one? on the effectiveness of pair programming. IEEE Softw. 24(6), 12–15 (2007)
9. Fronza, I., Sillitti, A., Succi, G.: An interpretation of the results of the analysis of pair programming during novices integration in a team. In: ESEM 2009: Proceedings of the 2009 3rd International Symposium on Empirical Software Engineering and Measurement, pp. 225–235. IEEE Computer Society, Washington, DC (2009)
10. Hulkko, H., Abrahamsson, P.: A multiple case study on the impact of pair programming on product quality. In: ICSE 2005: Proceedings of the 27th International Conference on Software Engineering, pp. 495–504. ACM, New York (2005)
11. Lui, K.M., Chan, K.C.C., Nosek, J.: The effect of pairs in program design tasks. IEEE Trans. Softw. Eng. 34(2), 197–211 (2008)
12. Madeyski, L.: The impact of pair programming and test-driven development on package dependencies in object-oriented design — an experiment. In: Münch, J., Vierimaa, M. (eds.) PROFES 2006. LNCS, vol. 4034, pp. 278–289. Springer, Heidelberg (2006)
13. Muller, M.M.: Are reviews an alternative to pair programming? Empirical Softw. Engg. 9(4), 335–351 (2004)
14. Muller, M.M.: A preliminary study on the impact of a pair design phase on pair programming and solo programming. Inf. Softw. Technol. 48, 335–344 (2006)

15. Nawrocki, J., Wojciechowski, A.: Experimental evaluation of pair programming. In: Proc. European Software Control and Metrics Conf., ESCOM (2001)

16. Phongpaibul, M., Boehm, B.: An empirical comparison between pair development and software inspection in thailand. In: ISESE 2006: Proceedings of the 2006 ACM/IEEE International Symposium on Empirical Software Engineering, pp. 85–94. ACM, New York (2006)

17. Sillitti, A., Janes, A., Succi, G., Vernazza, T.: Collecting, integrating and analyzing software metrics and personal software process data. In: EUROMICRO 2003: Proceedings of the 29th Conference on EUROMICRO, p. 336. IEEE Computer Society, Washington, DC (2003)

18. Sison, R.: Investigating pair programming in a software engineering course in an asian setting. In: APSEC 2008: Proceedings of the 2008 15th Asia-Pacific Software Engineering Conference, pp. 325–331. IEEE Computer Society, Washington, DC (2008)

19. Sison, R.: Investigating the effect of pair programming and software size on software quality and programmer productivity. In: APSEC 2009: Proceedings of the 2009 16th Asia-Pacific Software Engineering Conference, pp. 187–193. IEEE Computer Society, Washington, DC (2009)

20. Succi, G., Pedrycz, W., Marchesi, M., Williams, L.: Preliminary analysis of the effects of pair programming on job satisfaction. In: Proceedings of the 3rd International Conference on Extreme Programming (XP), pp. 212–215 (2002)

21. Vanhanen, J., Abrahamsson, P.: Perceived effects of pair programming in an industrial context. In: EUROMICRO 2007: Proceedings of the 33rd EUROMICRO Conference on Software Engineering and Advanced Applications, pp. 211–218. IEEE Computer Society, Washington, DC (2007)

22. Vanhanen, J., Korpi, H.: Experiences of using pair programming in an agile project. In: HICSS 2007: Proceedings of the 40th Annual Hawaii International Conference on System Sciences, p. 274b. IEEE Computer Society, Washington, DC (2007)

23. Vanhanen, J., Lassenius, C.: Effects of pair programming at the development team level: an experiment. In: International Symposium on Empirical Software Engineering, pp. 336–345 (2005)

24. Williams, L., Kessler, R.R., Cunningham, W., Jeffries, R.: Strengthening the case for pair programming. IEEE Softw. 17(4), 19–25 (2000)

25. Williams, L., Shukla, A., Anton, A.I.: An initial exploration of the relationship between pair programming and brooks' law. In: Proceedings of the Agile Development Conference, pp. 11–20. IEEE Computer Society, Washington, DC (2004)

26. Phongpaibul, M., Boehm, B.: A replicate empirical comparison between pair development and software development with inspection. In: ESEM 2007: Proceedings of the First International Symposium on Empirical Software Engineering and Measurement, pp. 265–274. IEEE Computer Society, Washington, DC (2007)

27. Nosek, J.T.: The case for collaborative programming. Commun. ACM 41(3), 105–108 (1998)

28. Xu, S., Chen, X.: Pair programming in software evolution. In: Canadian Conference on Electrical and Computer Engineering, pp. 1846–1849 (2005)

Test-Driven Development of Graphical User Interfaces: A Pilot Evaluation

Theodore D. Hellmann, Ali Hosseini-Khayat, and Frank Maurer

The University of Calgary, Department of Computer Science,
2500 University Drive NW, Calgary, Alberta, Canada
{tdhellma,hosseisa,fmaurer}@ucalgary.ca

Abstract. This paper presents a technique for test-driven development of GUI-based applications, as well as a pilot evaluation. In ourapproach, user interface prototypes are created in such a way as to allow capture/replay tools to record interactions with them. These recordings can then be replayed on the actual GUI as it is being developed in a test-driven fashion. Thepilot evaluation found that developers integrated GUI tests, based on user interface prototypes,into their development process and used them as a way to determine when a feature is actually complete.Study participants felt that TDD of GUI based applications is useful.

Keywords: Interaction design, test-driven development, user interface testing, graphical user interface.

1 Introduction

Test-driven development (TDD) has proven benefits for the software engineering process in terms of increased developer confidence and increased software quality without a significant decrease in productivity [1] [2]. Over time, tests created through TDD form a regression suite that will quickly notify developers when changes to a part of the application are causing tests for any part of the application to fail. However, if tests in the regression suite are broken by changes to the underlying system that do not actually impact the application's functionality, this safety net can become a liability, with developers dismissing failing tests as "the test's fault" [3]. Unfortunately, automated GUI test suites are likely to fail erroneously, making TDD of GUI-based applications (UITDD) something of a double-edged sword[4] [3].

The difficulty of creating a suite of GUI tests before the GUI exists – as well as maintaining the suite after development of the GUI has started –is the main barrier to the uptake of UITDD. Currently, developers wishing to perform test-driven GUI development must write complex test code manually. This is especially difficult given the tight coupling between GUI tests and GUI code. In order to test a widget, automated tests need to be able to locate it reliably at runtime and interact with it reasonably in order to create a useful test. To do this, a test must make use of specific information about each widget involved in a test – such as the widget's position, type, name, or identifier. This makes GUI testslikely to break in response to changes in the

A. Sillitti et al. (Eds.): XP 2011, LNBIP 77, pp. 223–237, 2011.

system under test, even when these changes do not actually impact the functionality of the system. This is because changes to any of the characteristics used to identify widgets could prevent test code from finding the correct widget.

In order to simplify the process of UITDD, we have developed an approach that leverages the advantages of usability evaluation and user interface prototyping. By first creating a prototype of the GUI, it is possible to perform iterative usability evaluations to identify usability flaws early in the development process, before effort has been expended in development of the actual GUI. Capture/replay tools (CRTs) – tools that record users' interactions with an application – can then be used to record test scripts. These scripts can then be run against the actual GUI as it is developed, as described in Section 4.

To begin evaluating our approach, it is necessary to answer the following question: does having tests for a GUI written before the functionality of the GUI is implemented help developers? In order to investigate this question, we conducted a pilot evaluation in which a small number of participants were provided with a variety of support options, including a GUI test suite, and asked to develop the missing glue code in a sample application. This paper presents results from this pilot study, including both observations made by researchers during study sessions and participant responses to a post-survey questionnaire.

2   What Makes GUI Testing and UITDD Difficult?

In order understand this problem it is first necessary to understand the difficulties with GUI testing. GUI tests are unusually difficult to write and maintain for a variety of reasons. First, even simple GUIs are very complicated – both from the perspective of design and from the perspective of testing. Second, a GUI testshould only fail when meaningfully problematic situations are encountered, but creating such GUI tests is difficult. Third, an application's GUIis likely to change throughout the course of development, which can result in tests failing despite the fact that the features of an application are still functioning. Each of these areas is described in more detail in the following subsections. Finally, the central issue that UITDD must overcome is addressed: how can we create GUI tests easily before the GUI itself exists?

2.1   Complexity

Modern GUIs are composed of a set of user interface elements, or *widgets*. Like most classes in object-oriented systems, widgets tend to have a long chain of inheritances. For example, in the Windows Presentation Framework (WPF), the chain of inheritance between Button and the base Object class contains 8 other classes. The Button class is composed of 136 properties and 211 methods, and can fire 111 events in response to various interactions. This means that even a simple GUI has a huge number of possible user interactions, GUI states, and events. Table 1 provides an overview of the number of widgets, properties, methods, and events involved in the simple calculator application shown in Fig. 1.

Fig. 1. A calculator application

Table 1. Properties, methods, and events of user-defined widgets in application shown in Fig. 1

Widgets	19
Properties	2577
Methods	4007
Events	2108

This complexity means that the number of possible sequences of events grows exponentially with the number of steps in a test script [12]. The bug-finding potential of a GUI testsuite is determined by the number of events that are triggered and the number of states from which each event is triggered [13]. This means that there is a large amount of testing that can be done, rendering it impractical to perform comprehensive GUI testing.

2.2 Verification

A test is separated into two parts: a *test procedure* and a *test oracle*. The test procedure interacts with part or all of an application in order to generate a state that is interesting from a testing perspective. The test oracle then verifies that the system behaves as expected in response to this interaction. The effectiveness of automated tests is directly limited by the difficulty of writing useful test oracles [14]. In GUI testing, this is compounded by the fact that the more values a GUI test oracle is verifying, the higher its chances of detecting bugs [15].

An alternative to this approach would be to make use of manual testing – either scripted manual testing, in which test cases are written down for humans to perform, or exploratory testing, where humans use their knowledge and intuition to search for bugs. Since manual testing relies on human intelligence to determine whether a GUI is functioning, it avoids some of the issues associated with automated GUI testing. However, scripted manual testing takes a significant amount of time and effort to perform and exploratory testing cannot be performed in a test-driven fashion. In our approach, described in Section 4, exploratory testing combined with a CRT is used as a means to identify important paths through ExpenseManager in order to focus automated testing effort on these "interesting" subsystems.

2.3 Finding Widgets from Test Code

In GUI testing, it is necessary to look up widgets when a test is run based on information about the widgets that is recorded when a test is created. This process of looking up widgets is in large part responsible for the fragility of GUI tests. When widgets in a GUI change in ways that lead to this search missing them or returning anincorrect widget, then not only will tests of this widget break, but the resulting error can be difficult to understand. For example, in Fig. 1, if the text displayed on the widget labeled "del" is important to its proper identification, and that text is changed to "delete," this change could lead to a misidentification.

There are two ways of performing this search: *testing with object maps* and *keyword-based testing*. In the former, as much information as possible about a widget is included in the test so that a heuristic search for the desired element can be made when the test is run. Because of this, it is possible for information about widgets to change without breaking tests that rely on them. In the latter, a single, unique identifier is assigned to each widget, meaning that only this identifier needs to remain unchanged in order to a test to locate the same widget.

Even when these search methods are used, it's possible for up to 74% of test cases to be broken after modifications to an application's GUI [16] [17]. This means that most of the tests in a suite must be either fixed or recreated from scratch, which represents a significant amount of rework. The stability of a GUI is a key problem that must be addressed before UITDD becomes practical. In Section 4, we describe an approach to TDD which makes heavy use of usability evaluation in order to minimize the changes necessary to a GUI after development on the actual interface has begun.

2.4   Creating GUI Tests without a GUI

An essential requirement of TDD is that it needs to be possible to write tests before the feature being tested is implemented. In this way, developers are able to begin thinking about the design of their code earlier and avoid making mistakes in the first place. However, writing GUI tests is different from writing any other kind of test. Because of the complexity of looking up widgets, interacting with them, and verifying their behavior, GUI tests are difficult to write by handsince detailed knowledge about the implementation of the GUI isnecessary. Commonly, CRTs are used to create GUI tests. But, in order to use a CRT, a GUI must already exist and be functioning. Because of this, two alternatives exist for the creation of GUI tests without a GUI: GUI tests can be written by hand; or a way can be found to make CRTs work before a GUI is available.

Several tools exist that can simplify this process of manually writing GUI tests[18] [19]. However, creating GUI tests manually remains technically challenging. In our previous work, as described in Section 4, we have devised a method of instrumenting GUI prototypes. CRTs can then be used to record interactions with these prototypes so that tests can be rerun against the actual GUI rather than its prototypes.This makes it possible to use the recorded tests to develop the GUI in a TDD fashion.

3   Related Work

Approaches to overcoming issues described in the previous section have been proposed and evaluated. This section provides an overview of publications directly related to UITDD, but not those that bypass the GUI, including those related to the use of Model-View-Controller [20] and test harnesses [21].

Despite the wide use of design patterns like Model-View-Controller [20] to make systems more testable below the level of the user interface, GUI testing remains important given the fact that bugs originating from errors in the code of user interfaces can seriously impair the functionality available to a user. Two studies carried out on systems developed by ABB Corporate Research have shown that the number of defects originating from errors in GUI code can represent 9% of the bugs found in an application through in-house testing, but represent 60% of the bugs found in an application by customers after the release of a product [22] [23]. Of these customer-reported defects, 65% were categorized as non-cosmetic, and resulted in a loss of functionality to the user, such as inability to print from a given screen or a system crash. The amount of non-trivial bugs stemming from GUI code makes sense in light of the fact that a significant portion of an application's code – 45-60% – can be required for the creation and management of its GUI [24].

Work by Ruiz and Price has resulted in brief evaluations of the use of two approaches to test-driven GUI development: using TestNG-Abbot [18] and FEST (Fixtures for Easy Software Testing) [19]. Both of these systems provide support for manually writing programmatic tests for GUI functionality before coding the corresponding GUI. This approach requires test authors to speculate about the future implementation of the GUI, which means that once it is actually implemented, tests may need to be reconciled with this implementation. Because writing tests manually represents a significant expenditure of effort even with the support of tools like FEST, the reconciliation process may be expensive. Because this approach requires test authors to understand the technical details of a system under test, it makes it difficult for customers to understand the tests they are helping to define.

Another approach uses GTT (GUI Testing Tool) to define tests through an abstract, high-level specification language [25]. GTT combines a specification editor, which can be used to write tests before a GUI is developed, with a CRT, which can be used to create or edit tests based on interactions with an existing GUI. The main benefit to this approach is that tests defined manually or through the CRT are recorded in the same high-level language, which simplifies test maintenance after a GUI has been created. However, tests created in this fashion are difficult to understand and require intimate knowledge of the system under development.

Selenium is a web testing tool rather than a general GUI testing tool, but it has been applied to the testing of web-based systems in a test-driven fashion [3]. Selenium's keyword-based system of identification makes it easier to create and understand tests. However, the authors of the study found that tests would frequently fail even after corresponding GUI functionality had been implemented due to minor issues, such as errors identifying the desired widget or timing issues. Because of this, the team had to revise the role of tests in its process. Tests were still written before a feature was implemented for specification purposes, but these tests were generally discarded after a feature was implemented. Instead, new tests were recorded using Selenium's CRT and added to the regression suite. While this helped reduce the time spent fixing broken tests, it also removed a major benefit of TDD of GUIs: identifying when a feature is complete.

4   A Prototype-Driven Approach to UITDD

One of the main barriers to UITDD identified in the previous sections is the difficulty of using CRTs. CRTs can only be used when a GUI already exists. To address this, we propose that a prototype of the GUI be created with sufficient detail for CRTs to record tests based on interactions with this prototype. Our previous work suggests that it is possible to use tests recorded from prototypes to verify the functionality of the actual GUI as it is developed [5]. In this section, an example will be presented to describe this process. This example will be used as a basis for the pilot evaluation conducted in Section 5.

4.1 ExpenseManager

ExpenseManager is a GUI-based application for the creation, saving, modification, and totaling of expense reports, similar to those required by many organizations before they will reimburse employees for travel expenses. ExpenseManager's GUI contains three tabs: *View Totals*; *New Report*; and *Modify Report*. The View Totals tab allows users to view the total expense incurred by, paid to, and outstanding reimbursements for the entire company or for a specific individual. The New Report tab is used for creating and saving new expense reports. These expense reports consist of a name and trip number, as well as a dollar amount for transportation, lodging, meals, and conference fees. These amounts are summarized into a subtotal at the bottom of each report, and, if any reimbursement has been made, this is displayed along with the amount that remains to be reimbursed to the employee. The Modify Report tab allows users to update the amount reimbursed for specific saved reports, and changes made to reports will be reflected in the View Totals tab.

4.2 Prototyping ExpenseManager

After defining the features of ExpenseManager, a prototype of the application was created. This prototype was created using SketchFlow [6]. Prototypes are created by dragging-and-dropping widgets onto a canvas. Each canvas can be used to represent a different state of the system. Widgets can also be assigned behaviors such as transitioning to a different state. The resulting prototypes are executable, allowing test users to interact with them as though they were functional applications.

This prototype can be utilized for the purpose of usability evaluation [7] [8], specifically Wizard of Oz-like tests [9] [10] [8], in which a user is presented with a mock system and instructed to perform a task. This form of evaluation allows designers to identify potential usability flaws and refine the design of the GUI before expending effort on its implementation. Typically, this is an iterative process, involving several evaluations and revisions, until the majority of usability flaws are resolved and user satisfaction reaches an acceptable level.

A prototype of all of the functionality of ExpenseManager described in Section 4.1 was created using SketchFlow. One of the states of the SketchFlow prototype of ExpenseManager can be seen in Fig. 2, while the map of states and possible transitions involved in the prototype can be seen in Fig. 3.

4.3 Creating Tests for ExpenseManager

SketchFlow prototypes are WPF user interfaces and trigger events that can be detected through the Windows Automation API. This allows CRTs based on the Automation API to record events triggered by users' interactions with these prototypes. In this evaluation,

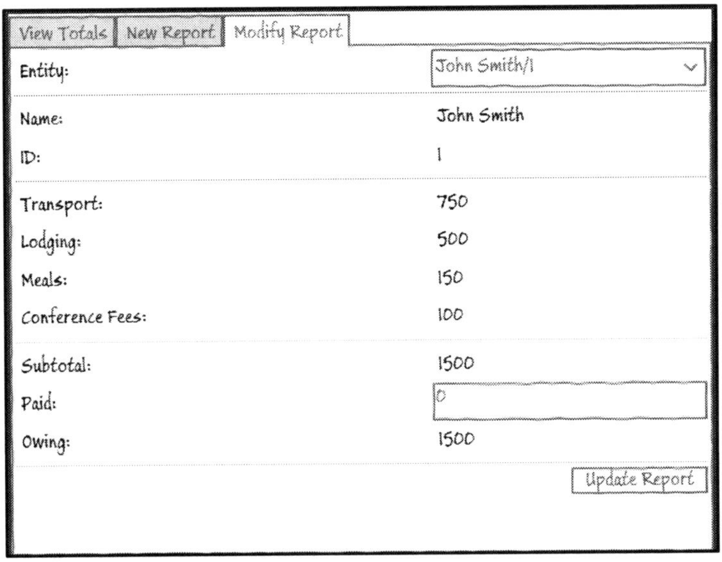

View Totals
New Report
Modify Report
Entity:
John Smith/1
Name:
John Smith
ID:
1
Transport:
750
Lodging:
500
Meals:
150
Conference Fees:
100
Subtotal:
1500
Paid:
0
Owing:
1500
Update Report

Fig. 2. One page from theSketchFlow prototype of ExpenseManager

Root
SaveReportTest1
ClearTest1
SaveMultipleTest
ModifyTest1
ModifyTest2
SaveMultiple_John
SaveMultiple_Wayne

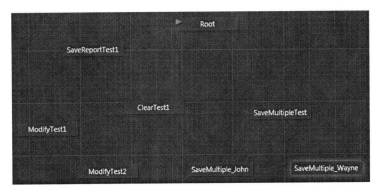

Fig. 3. State map of ExpenseManager prototype

we used LEET (LEET Enhances Exploratory Testing) to record events from interactions with prototypes of ExpenseManager [11]. LEET is based on the Automation API, and uses keyword-based identification to determine which widget to interact with for each step in the test script. This means that LEET will search for a widget with a matching keyword and then perform some action with it. Because of this, it is possible to run a test recorded from a prototype of ExpenseManager on the actual GUI as long as widgets are given the same keyword in the actual GUI as they are in the prototype. When these tests are first run against the actual GUI, they will fail – as they should in TDD – and will only pass when the actual GUI implements the same functionality expressed in the prototype. Using this approach, it is possible to go through the normal TDD cycle process of writing tests, running them, writing code, and refactoring.

For the development of ExpenseManager, four tests were recorded from the prototype verifying the following functionality: reports do not get totaled under the View Totals tab until they are saved; saved tests are still totaled under the View Totals tab even when they have been cleared from the New Report tab; saved reports modified from the Modify Report tab are also updated on the View Totals tab; and the View Totals tab is able to show both the totals for all saved reports and the totals for all reports corresponding to a specific user. It is important to stress that these tests verify that the implementation of ExpenseManager is functionally equivalent to the functionality expressed in the prototype – in other words, the tests will only be as complete as the prototypes.

5   Pilot Evaluation

We designed a pilot evaluation to determine whether our approach is actually useful to developers, given a variety of tools to assist them in development of functionality in a GUI-based application. Our results are based on the experiences of three participants recruited from the Calgary Agile Methods User Group (CAMUG) [26].

Table 3 presents some demographic information about the participants.While all participants had substantial experience with GUI development, none of the participants had previously used prototypes as part of this process. Additionally, none of the participants had experience with automated GUI testing lasting more than two years, despite having been developing GUIs for more than two years. Further, only one participant used TDD for applications he was currently developing. These points imply that the integration of the approach to UITDD described in this paper might be difficult to achieve, since participants did not have significant experience with the prerequisite techniques of GUI testing, user interface prototyping, and TDD. Despite this, participants were able to adapt to the process of UITDD.

Table 2. Quantitative Responses from Survey

	Participant 1	Participant 2	Participant 3
Experience with Testing	Over 2 Years	None	0-2 Years
Experience with GUI Testing	0-2 Years	None	0-2 Years
Experience with GUI Development	Over 2 Years	Over 2 Years	Over 2 Years
Experience with UI Prototyping	None	None	None
Uses TDD on Own Projects	No	No	Yes

5.1   Creating the Test System

First, researchers completed the development of ExpenseManager, including its GUI and event handlers, based on the tests created in Section 4. This was done to ensure that the tests provided to participants were adequate for the development of ExpenseManager. This entire process, from prototypes through to passing tests, took five hours to complete. In all, ExpenseManager's GUI is composed of 50 visible widgets, not counting those associated with the base Window object and Separators: 1 TabControl, 3 TabItems, 2 ComboBoxes, 8 TextBoxes, and 36 Labels. This version included all of the functionality described above, including a complete GUI, complete event handlers, and a complete data structure for storing reports.

Then, the researchers removed all of the code contained in ExpenseManager's 7 event handlers – the "glue code" that connects its GUI with its data structures. This means that ExpenseManager was left with a complete but nonfunctional GUI, a constructor, a data structure, and stubs for event handlers. Participants were asked to complete the implementation of this version of ExpenseManager, which requires only that they implement these missing event handlers. This simplification decreased the amount of time that would be required of participants as well as focused the pilot evaluation on the usefulness of the previously-created GUI tests to participants' development.

Participants were given one hour to complete this task and provided with several tools to aid them. First, participants were given the user interface prototype and the GUI tests created in Section 4, as well as access to Visual Studio 2010's debugger and GUI builder and the ability to ask the researcher for technical clarifications.

5.2 Observations Collected during the Study

Interestingly, all three participants entered into the same development cycle during their development of ExpenseManager. First, participants would run a single test against the prototype in order to determine which story to begin implementing next. Once they had picked a story, participants would use the GUI builder to identify the next widget involved in the story. From the GUI builder, they would then navigate to a related event handler in the code-behind and begin implementing discrete parts of a story. After changes had been made to an event handler, participants would run their implementation of ExpenseManager and manually interact with it in order to determine if their implementation met their expectations. If it did, they would then run tests against the prototype again in order to determine if their implementation also met the expectations defined in the prototype. Only after a feature was completely implemented, in their eyes, would participants then run the test against the actual GUI. A diagram of this workflow can be seen in Fig. 4.

Participants used the provided automated GUI tests as the sole indication of completeness of functionality – as soon as a test passed, participants moved on to the next feature. This could be a liability since, if the test suite for a feature is incomplete, the resulting implementation will also be incomplete. This might imply that it may be beneficial to either treat GUI tests as unit tests by testing a number of different test procedures and error conditions or ensure that the developer who is responsible for coding a given feature in a GUI is involved in creating its tests. The former would help to provide developers with more examples of how a feature is expected to function so that developers would be encouraged to implement complete solutions. The latter would encourage developers to culture an understanding of how a feature is

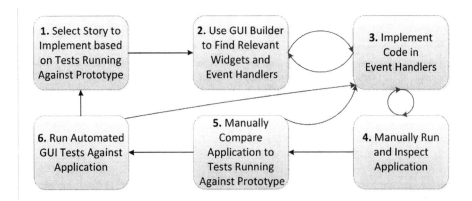

Fig. 4. Workflow for development of GUI-based application observed during studies

intended to work, which could lead to stronger implementations. However, it is possible that this could also be due to a lack of investment in the system being developed, as ExpenseManager is only a simple application.

Before code has been added to the event handlers, tests run against the application will immediately fail, without a corresponding visual indication as to which widget caused the test failure. The error message provided for this failure is not inherently understandable, and, once participants noticed this, they would tend to hold off on running tests against the application until it was mostly complete. For example, before code is added to update the subtotal of an expense report when values are added, a test might fail with the message "Assert.AreEqual failed. Expected:<750>, Actual:<0>."Notably missing from this message is the element that was expected to have a value of 750, for example. Further, it was observed that participants were unable to understand the form in which tests are recorded.

By the end of each study session, each participant had at least some of the tests passing when run against the application. A summary of which tests were passing by test participant can be seen in Table 3.

Table 3. Passing Tests by Participant

	Clear Report	Modify Report	Save Report	Save Multiple
Participant 1	✓	✗	✓	✓
Participant 2	✓	✗	✓	✗
Participant 3	✓	✗	✓	✗

It is interesting to note that Participant 1 had no previous experience with Visual Studio, WPF, or C#. Participant 1 did have significant previous experience with Java, and was able to use this, in conjunction with the resources provided during the study, to complete more features than the other participants.

When given a choice of several resources to aid in the development of ExpenseManager, developers used GUI tests to determine when stories were complete, and would not move on until the test related to a feature accessible through the GUI of the application was passing. The observations described in this subsection seem to support the idea that GUI tests used in a test-first setup serve an important role in the development process.

5.4 Observations Collected from Post-Study Surveys

After each study session was completed, the participantwas asked to fill out a survey which assessed the participant'sbackground in GUI development and testing, as well as the participant's perception of the usefulness and usability of this approach.

Table 4. Perception of Usefulness of TDD of GUIs

	Participant 1	Participant 2	Participant 3
Found TDD of ExpenseManager To Be	B. Somewhat Useful	A. Very Useful	C. Useful
Would Expect TDD of Own Work To Be	B. Somewhat Useful	A. Very Useful	B. Somewhat Useful
Would Consider Using This Approach to TDD on Own Projects	Yes	Yes	Yes

Several survey questions were also included to gauge participants' perception of the usefulness of UITDD in light of their experiences in developing ExpenseManager. The answers to these questions are recorded in Table 4. The first and second questions were ranked from A (Very Useful) to E (Useless). Despite the similarity of the first and second questions, both were asked in order to gauge the usefulness of this approach to TDD both in the current and in a broader context. These responses imply that the participants saw the potential of this approach to be of some benefit in their own work.

The first question also included a follow-up question asking participants to explain why they chose that answer. Participant 1 noted that the tests that were provided "checks for interactions/updates I may have missed during coding," but notes that the technique is "only as useful as the assertions!" This second point relates to an instance where he noticed a bug in a feature, despite the fact that the test relating to it was passing. Participant 2 responded that TDD of GUIs lets you "see functionality straight away," while participant 3 noted that running the GUI tests was "faster than running code" to verify it manually. It is interesting to note that each participant found something different of value in the approach.

Participants were also asked to rank the resources they were provided with in terms of decreasing usefulness for their development task. Their responses can be seen in Table 5, below. It is of note that participants' perception of the importance of various resources does not line up with observations recorded by the researcher during the course of study sessions as represented in Fig. 4. Instead of ranking features by frequency of use, participants seem to have ranked resources based on the value they provided to the development effort. Participants 1 and 3 noted that the UI prototype was a "standard to compare against when coding" and "captured the intent of user functionality," whereas participant 2 noted that the GUI builder "gave me names of things I needed to use." This implies that one way to immediately make this approach to UITDD provide higher value to users would be to improve the interface through which tests are run so that participants can understand the features represented by the UI tests, or to make technical details of widgets being tested more visible so that users can understand the expected details of the system they are building.

Table 5. Ranking of Available Resources

Usefulness	Participant 1	Participant 2	Participant 3
Highest	UI Prototype	GUI Builder	UI Prototype
-	Communication with Researcher	Debugger	Communication with Researcher
-	UI Tests	UI Prototype	UI Tests
-	GUI Builder	Communication with Researcher	GUI Builder
Lowest	Debugger	UI Tests	Debugger

Participants pointed out various usability issues stemming from tools used in this study. First, participants remarked on the unreadability of the error messages produced by tests generated by LEET. Participants requested that, when tests are run through Visual Studio, the error messages that result from failing tests need to be much clearer, and include contextual information about the widgets the test was interacting with when the test failed. They also suggested that, when tests are run through LEET itself, tests should also be able to pause after the last action is taken in a test script so that users can see the final state of the application. Similarly, users expressed a desire to be able to pause and step through each line of a test – similar to the way a debugger functions – rather than the current behavior, in which each step of a test executes after a set delay. Finally, users were unsure of when widgets were being interacted with by test code. A technique needs to be used to make it visually explicit that LEET is interacting with a specific widget as a test is running. These suggestions will help steer the development of LEET towards a more usable application.

In conclusion, this pilot evaluation suggests that the approach to UITDD proposed in this paper is useful for development of GUI-based applications. GUI tests were used primarily for determining when a feature was done and participants used tests as a roadmap for the completion of the application. Participants also reported through the post-experiment survey that they felt GUI tests were useful. Other major contributions of this pilot evaluation include a model describing the way developers use GUI tests, suggestions for improvement of GUI testing tools, and suggestions for improvement of this approach to UITDD.

5.5 Study Limitations

First, only three participants took part in this study. A larger subject pool would mean that opinions could be gathered from a wider group of participants with different backgrounds, which would have allowed us to draw more interesting conclusions. As it stands, this experiment can be regarded as a successful pilot evaluation that encourages setting up a more comprehensive.

Second, the time allotted for each study session was limited to one hour in order to avoid inconveniencing participants. However, it would be useful in future research to either conduct longer study sessions, multiple study sessions with each participant, or longer-term case studies. This would allow more information to be collected about the ways in which the system can be used, and improvements that can be made that only occur to participants when exposed to the system for longer periods of use.

Third, the application used for this study was, based on Table 2, too complicated for a one-hour study. Participants were unable to complete the implementation of the system in just one hour. For future controlled experiments, it would be preferable to have participants develop a simpler system. However, ultimately, this approach to UITDD must be evaluated on the development of complicated, real-world systems in order to decisively determine its real-world value.

6 Future Work

In addition to making the improvements to LEET identified in the previous section, there are several directions that could be taken to improve this approach to UITDD. First, this study should be extended to include additional participants or, ideally, case studies of long-term projects with industrial partners in order to increase the reliability and real-world applicability of its findings.

Second, LEET is also being used to support rule-based testing of GUI-based applications. In rule-based testing, short, reusable rules are defined that relate to behavior the system being developed should always (or never) exhibit. These rules are then executed after every step of a test script in order to insure that the system being developed conforms to each rule in every state accessed during the test. Due to the reusable nature of these rules, research should be done to determine how useful they will be to the process of TDD. Additionally, improvements to LEET will need to be made to eliminate distractions based on shortcomings of the tool from future research.

Finally, we hope to test our approach to UITDD on multi-touch and gesture-based interfaces, like those present in the iPhone and Windows Phone 7 mobile devices and in digital tabletops like those produced by Smart, Microsoft, and Evoluce. These interfaces pose interesting challenges in the testing, prototyping, and UITDD of touch-based interactions.

7 Conclusion

In this paper we present a pilot evaluation of an approach to test-driven development of GUI-based applications. This approach uses user interface prototyping and usability evaluation to develop a prototype of a user interface that is less likely to change than when a GUI is developed without these steps. These tests can then be run on the actual GUI of the application under development in a test-first fashion.

However, it was necessary to ask the question: will developers even find these tests useful? In order to investigate this, a pilot evaluation was conducted in which developers were presented with a variety of tools to assist them in the development of a small application, ExpenseManager. Observations were recorded by the researchers in order to observe how developers used these tests, and post-experiment surveys were used to assess the developers' perceptions of UI tests. As a result of the observations, we developed a workflow showing the way in which study participants would utilize UI tests in order to determine when they were done working on a specific feature of the sample application. Through the surveys, we were able to determine that participants seemed to feel that UITDD had benefits, and would be a useful practice. The encouraging results from the pilot study suggest that a more comprehensive study should be conducted to get significant results.

References

1. Nagappan, N., Maximilien, E., Bhat, T., Williams, L.: Realizing Quality Improvement through Test Driven Development: Results and Experiences of Four Industrial Teams. In: Empirical Software Engineering, pp. 289–302 (2008)
2. Jeffries, R., Melnik, G.: Guest Editors' Introduction: TDD - The Art of Fearless Programming. IEEE Software, 24–30 (2007)
3. Holmes, A., Kellogg, M.: Automating Functional Tests Using Selenium. In: AGILE 2006, pp. 270–275 (2006)
4. Itkonon, J., Mäntylä, M., Lassenius, C.: Defect Detection Efficiency: Test Case Based vs. Exploratory Testing. In: First International Symposium on Empirical Software Engineering and Measurement, Madrid, Spain, pp. 61–70 (2007)
5. Hellmann, T., Hosseini-Khayat, A., Maurer, F.: Supporting Test-Driven Development of Graphical User Interfaces Using Agile Interaction Design. In: Third International Conference on Software Testing, Verification, and Validation Workshops, Paris, pp. 444–447 (2010)
6. Microsoft: SketchFlow. In: Microsoft Expression,
   `http://www.microsoft.com/expression/products/`
   `Sketchflow_Overview.aspx`
7. Buxton, B.: Sketching User Experiences. Morgan Kaufmann, San Francisco (2007)
8. Barnum, C.: Usability Testing and Research. Pearson Education, New York (2002)
9. Hosseini-Khayat, A.: Distributed Wizard of Oz Usability Testing for Agile Teams. Master's Thesis, University of Calgary, Calgary (2010)
10. Wilson, P.: Active Story: A Low Fidelity Prototyping and Distributed Usability Testing Tool for Agile Teams. MSc Thesis, Univerity of Calgary (August 2008)
11. Hellmann, T.: LEET (LEET Enhances Exploratory Testing) - CodePlex.
    `http://leet.codeplex.com/` (accessed 2010)
12. Xie, Q., Memon, A.: Using a Pilot Study to Derive a GUI Model for Automated Testing. ACM Transactions on Software Engineering and Methodology 18(2), 1–35 (2008)
13. Xie, Q., Memon, A.: Studying the Characteristics of a "Good" GUI Test Suite. In: Proceedings of the 17th International Symposium on Software Reliability Engineering, Raleigh, NC, pp. 159–168 (2006)
14. Kaner, C., Bach, J.: Black Box Software Testing. In: Center for Software Testing Education and Research,
    `http://www.testingeducation.org/k04/documents/`
    `BBSTOverviewPartC.pdf` (accessed Fall 2005)

15. Memon, A., Benerjee, I., Nagarajan, A.: What Test Oracle Should I Use for Effective GUI Testing. In: 18th IEEE International Conference on Automated Software Engineering, Montreal, pp. 164–173 (2003)
16. Memon, A., Soffa, M.: Regression Testing of GUIs. In: ACM SIGSOFT International Symposium on Foundations of Software Engineering, pp. 118–127 (2003)
17. Memon, A.: Automatically Repairing Event Sequence-Based GUI Test Suites for Regression Testing. ACM Transactions on Software Engineering and Methodology 18(2), 1–36 (2008)
18. Ruiz, A., Price, W.: Test-Driven GUI Development with TestNG and Abbot. IEEE Software, 51–57 (2007)
19. Ruiz, A., Price, Y.: GUI Testing Made Easy. In: Testing: Academic and Industrial Conference - Practice and Research Techniques, pp. 99–103 (2008)
20. Burbeck, S.: Appplications Programming in Smalltalk-80: How to Use Model-View-Controller (MVC). In: How to Use Model-View-Controller (MVC), http://st-www.cs.illinois.edu/users/smarch/st-docs/mvc.html (accessed 1987, 1992)
21. Marick, B.: Bypasing the GUI. Software Testing and Quality Engineering Magazine, 41–47 (September/October 2002)
22. Brooks, P., Robinson, B., Memon, A.: An Initial Characterization of Industrial Graphical User Interface Systems. In: International Conference on Software Testing, Verification, and Validation, Denver, pp. 11–20 (2009)
23. Robinson, B., Brooks, P.: An Initial Study of Customer-Reported GUI Defects. In: Proceedings of the IEEE International Conference on Software Testing, Verification, and Validation Workshops, pp. 267–274 (2009)
24. Memon, A.: A Comprehensive Framework for Testing Graphical User Interfaces. PhD Thesis, University of Pittsburgh (2001)
25. Chen, W., Tsai, T., Chao, H.: Integration of Specification-Based and CR-Based Approaches for GUI Testing. In: 19th International Conference on Advanced Information Networking and Applications, pp. 967–972 (2005)
26. Calgary Agile Methods User Group. In: CAMUG, http://calgaryagile.com/

A Test-Driven Approach for Extracting Libraries of Reusable Components from Existing Applications

Elaf Selim, Yaser Ghanam, Chris Burns, Teddy Seyed, and Frank Maurer

Department of Computer Science, University of Calgary
2500 University Dr. NW, Calgary, AB, Canada, T2N 1N4
{esselim,yghanam,ccburns,aseyed,fmaurer}@ucalgary.ca

Abstract. In agile approaches such as Extreme Programming, time is not spent on making sure that system components can be reused in similar systems. Therefore, there is a need to investigate whether reuse can be achieved by extracting reusable assets from existing applications. This paper presents an approach that relies on refactoring and testing practices for extracting reusable assets from existing applications. The approach creates reusable APIs in a bottom-up fashion, on demand when a new application might benefit from component in an existing application. The extraction process is guided and supported by the usage examples and the testing scenarios in the existing application and the new one. The paper presents a case study, where the approach was used to extract components from the user interface of an existing application, wrap these components in an API, and use this API in the existing and new applications.

Keywords: Extracting Reusable Components, APIs, Libraries, Test-driven Refactoring, Acceptance Tests, GIS, Multi-Touch Surfaces.

1 Introduction

The lightweight software engineering practices of extreme programming (XP) were adopted to help develop software applications more quickly and so that changes during the entire software development life cycle could be accommodated more easily. XP and agile software engineering in general have become popular [5]. In XP, systems may be created using a "design-by-reuse" process by tailoring components previously extracted and added to a repository [8]. However, being committed to developing products quickly, time is not spent in a preliminary phase to design and create reusable APIs which can benefit future similar projects. "YAGNI – You Ain't Gonna Need It" is the battle cry in XP arguing against attempts to predict what might be needed in the future. In XP, software systems are developed without doing extensive research in the beginning or spending much time on requirement gathering [2]. These systems are developed simply to satisfy the current customer and what this customer really wants [16] without thinking much about the needs of future customers or how the systems can be reused.

Software reuse, on the other hand, promises to offer a number of advantages, and may require explicit support in the development process [16]. Despite the fact that

A. Sillitti et al. (Eds.): XP 2011, LNBIP 77, pp. 238–252, 2011.

reuse can reduce the development cost of new applications and also reduce the maintenance cost of these applications, XP does not aim at supporting developing software for possible future reuse or the creation of reusable components to be exploited by other applications instead of creating these applications from scratch.

In our case, our team had developed an application to support the control room operation of an electricity utility with Geographic Information System (GIS) maps on multi-touch digital surfaces. However, other applications are also in need of similar functionalities. Example applications include command and control, traffic management, analysis of agricultural and geological data...etc. Thus, our first application could provide components for similar applications designed to interact with GIS data on multi-touch devices. We found that a number of user interface elements in our application are general enough to benefit similar GIS multi-touch applications. The value of the effort spent in designing these components can be preserved by extracting them and collecting them in an API library which can support several other applications in other domains. When we started to develop a second application that supports visualizing and interacting with oil well GIS sensor data, we were motivated to start thinking about the best approach to extract this reusable API. The remainder of this paper describes a bottom-up, test-driven approach that we followed for extracting reusable APIs from the first application to support the development of the second software system.

In this paper, we propose and evaluate a systematic approach for extracting libraries of reusable components from an application and use them in new software products. The code around these components in the original application is changed as well to use the newly extracted and modified components. The approach relies on acceptance or functional tests which can help the refactoring process by planning the changes needed to be done and making sure that the resulting products match the requirements of the customer and behave as expected. Usage examples are also extracted from the original application since they help identify the appropriate use of the extracted components [23].

The remaining of this paper is structured as follows. The following section discusses some of the related work. Section 3 presents the extraction approach. In Section 4, the paper presents a preliminary case study carried out to assess the feasibility and usefulness of this approach followed by a discussion of the results in Section 5.

2   Related Work

There is a large body of literature on the concept of reuse, its approaches and techniques. Reuse approaches are commonly categorized under planned reuse [22] or opportunistic reuse [19]. Generally, planned reuse refers to the proactive treatment of reuse wherein the organization dedicates upfront planning activities specifically to plan for reuse - the software process defines what assets are to be reused and how to adapt them [22]. On the other hand, opportunistic reuse refers to the reactive treatment of reuse that happens only when the opportunity for reuse avails itself [19]. The idea we promote in this paper is an opportunistic approach in the sense that we deal with reuse only when there is a demand to provide a reusable asset to be used across a set of applications. Some work in the literature addresses the development of reusable assets as a proactive activity in which reusable asset are planned for upfront [7, 18]. Other approaches – like the one we propose in this paper – are extractive approaches that attempt to identify potentially reusable assets in existing applications and extract those assets [6, 4]. For example, Lanubile et al. [12] applied a program decomposition method to the problem of extracting reusable functions from ill-structured programs. Another approach was proposed by Ning et al. [17] which also relied on segmenting the programs into manageable pieces before the extraction process. While these methods are fundamentally different from our approach, which will be explained later, we use the same two general steps of focusing and then extracting, but we achieve the needed focus using user stories and tests.

Within the context of agile software development [13], Sugumaran et al. [21] proposed the construction of a knowledge-based framework to enable agile teams make better decisions when selecting and customizing software components for reuse. The approach, however, focuses only on how to use such a framework in an agile context but it is not clear on how to build the proposed framework within an agile context. In XP, refactoring is an essential part of the development cycle [11]. In the approach we propose, we rely on refactoring as a key activity to enhance the reusability of assets [15]. Moser et al. [16] conducted a study to assess if refactoring in agile environments improves the quality and reusability of – otherwise hard to reuse – classes. Their results support the hypothesis that continuous refactoring improves quality metrics thus promoting ad-hoc reuse of object-oriented classes. Washizaki et al. [23, 24] proposed a refactoring approach for extracting candidate reusable classes from object oriented programs and modifying the surrounding parts of the extracted parts in the original programs.

Our effort is different from the abovementioned efforts in that it takes into consideration the new user stories in order to enhance the design or/and extend the implementation of the extracted asset. The approach also leverages tests as a focusing mechanism and as a safety net. We also show how APIs can be built to enable the reuse of such components guided by the original usage instances as examples.

3 Extraction Approach

Say we have a system named S_o that has already been developed to satisfy the requirements of a given customer. S_o has been developed based on a set of user stories US_o. These user stories are translated to a set of acceptance tests AT_o. The tests interact – through a thin layer of code (aka. fixtures) – with the code units that compose the system.

The approach we suggest has the objective of maximizing reuse of the UI widgets defined in S_o to be utilized in a new application S_n such that:

(a) All ATs are passing for the system S_o. That is:
$$R(AT_i) = Pass \; \forall \; AT_i \in AT_0 \qquad\qquad (condition \; C_1)$$
where R is the result of running an AT against the system

C_1 should be maintained to be true throughout the whole process. This serves as a safety net for the old system.

(b) The new system S_n is described using the set US_n that translates to a set AT_n. The underlying functionality in S_n is initially missing (i.e. classes and methods are empty), therefore:

$R(AT_j) = \text{Fail} \ \forall \ AT_j \in AT_n$

where R is the result of running an AT against the system

This verdict is changed to become false given that a non-empty subset of AT_n will pass by reusing the code units. That is:

$R(AT_j) = \text{Pass} \ \forall \ AT_j \in AT`_n$ given $AT`_n \subseteq AT_n$ and $AT`_n \neq \emptyset$ (condition C_2)

where R is the result of running an AT against the system

We achieve this by executing the following procedure:

1. Write the ATs for S_n to verify the satisfaction of US_n.
2. Manually compare US_o with US_n to find potential reuse opportunities. Say $US_a \in US_o$ has found to be similar to $US_b \in$ to US_n.
3. Compare AT_a (that tests US_a) with AT_b (that tests US_b). This comparison yields two important pieces of information:

   a. What is common between AT_a and AT_b, since the potential API need not provide interfaces to configure common features.
   b. What is variable between AT_a and AT_b, since the potential API needs to provide a means of configuring the reused artifacts to satisfy this variability.

4. Refactor the artifacts in S_o (mainly code and possibly ATs) that are relevant to the code unit of interest based on the outcome of step 3.
5. Separate the refactored artifact into an API library. The objective of this step is to enable reuse of a single source code and avoid having redundant code in the two applications.
6. Refactor the code in S_o so that it utilizes the new design of the code (observe C_1)
7. Use the API library in the implementation of S_n (observe C_2)

To describe the extraction approach and demonstrate how it is executed, the following section presents a preliminary case study on the analysis process and the extraction steps involving two systems we built in-house.

4 Case Study

4.1 Application Context

Utilities which are heavily reliant on geospatial data have been working with paper maps unfolded on tables for a long time. Using these traditional methods causes data management tasks to be asynchronous and very tedious. Delays in updating these maps pose a safety risk for field workers that may be guided based on outdated information. More recently, utility companies are starting to adopt Geographic Information Systems technology. A GIS is used for capturing, storing, managing, analyzing, and displaying all forms of geographically referenced information. Some electrical utilities now have their own GIS data which include details of their circuits, power-lines, switches, etc. Despite their use of GIS servers to store geospatial data and GIS software tools to analyze it, some teams in the control centers of electricity companies still prefer to use large printed paper maps to assist in data management tasks such as making changes to the data and discussing and analyzing snapshots of the data to find solutions for problems. Most GIS applications are focused on supporting a single user and these teams typically work in a collaborative mode, which is why they tend to gravitate towards using large paper maps. Paper maps on a table are convenient when multiple team members are working together to achieve a certain goal since they are large enough so that everyone can see the information comfortably, subgroups can work on different maps concurrently and everyone has concurrent access to editing these maps using pens and markers.

Using the technology of multi-touch digital tables can serve as a suitable alternative for using paper maps on regular tables. They can be used for displaying and managing these large digital maps for collaborative purposes. Since interactive digital surfaces combine both the input and visual output spaces, they have a number of potential benefits. Tabletop surfaces accept a number of new types of input, including using hand gestures and tangible objects. They encourage people to work collaboratively in co-located groups [20] and the large surface area is very convenient for displaying and interacting with information. The idea behind developing the first application; eGrid, was to provide an innovative and convenient digital tabletop environment to address the needs of co-located control center teams in electricity companies. By using eGrid, teams are able to browse through, analyze and annotate GIS maps, facilitating collaboration without the need to print the maps on paper. The second application, eWell, visualizes oil well sensor data which is captured and stored in GIS form. Starting the development of this second application motivated the extraction of the API from the first application.

4.2 The First Application: eGrid

The requirements behind eGrid reflect the needs of a local electricity company. The application was designed and developed using a simple, lightweight extreme programming process which relied mainly on effective feedback for iterative product improvement. The process started by creating low fidelity prototypes such as sketches and simple demos, since "a picture is worth a thousand words" [14]. Specifying the requirements of the application was done in a number of simple and informal ways including sketches, user story lists and interview notes. Whiteboards were usually used to help focus attention and promote collaboration in the design process. [3] The demos were useful in brainstorming interface ideas but they actually did not capture the design of the interactions in this gesture-oriented application, which is why these demos were of little use in getting valuable feedback from users.

eGrid is a very user interface intensive application. It sits on top of ESRI ArcGIS API for WPF 4.0 [1]. It is developed as a multi-touch user interface for a horizontal digital table with no specific orientation. The design of the user interface elements, touch events and hand gestures were done with this target hardware platform in mind. To capture the interactivity and multi-touch capabilities of the application, more advanced prototypes were developed next; allowing eGrid to gain increased customer interest. The prototypes were developed in multiple iterations guided by frequent demonstrations to industrial partners and other interested GIS professionals. The interface and features of eGrid have been changing continuously throughout these iterations to respond to the feedback received and to add more requested features. Training and observation sessions in the control center of the electricity company were also conducted to understand more about the actual environment in which the application will be deployed. In addition, several interviews with GIS professionals were also conducted to further understand the problem domain, the extra features needed in eGrid and the general features in eGrid that can be useful to other tabletop GIS applications.

In the process of analyzing the design of eGrid and brainstorming the extraction of reusable components, two important questions had to be in mind:

(1) Which of these components are general enough to be useful in similar GIS applications?
(2) How can the design of these user interface elements be flexible enough to accommodate different application needs?

The following sub-sections describe briefly some of the components in the UI of eGrid which will be extracted and added to the API and the reason behind certain design decisions.

Background Map. This map is displayed in the background to help users keep track of trouble report locations and provide an overview on the state of the electrical grid of the city. The location envelope, i.e. the coordinates of the map, the layers, as well as the ability to interact with the map by panning and zooming will have to be changed through options.

Corner Menus. To access common application tasks which are not related to any specific map frame, an alternative was needed for the ordinary menu designs of vertical screen applications. Since the target platform is a horizontal surface, for which there is no fixed orientation, quarter pie corner menus were added to the interface. This design consumes a small area of the screen and is accessible by any user no matter where he/she is standing. When the user taps on any of the corner menus, it expands to a slightly larger quarter circle menu showing a group of icons for different functionalities.

Trouble Report Pins. Trouble reports define service outage locations and the details of the outage situation. Trouble reports are geo-referenced; each report has an exact map location and they have different severities and/or priorities similar to IT trouble tickets. The design of eGrid represents these reports as circular pins placed in their locations on the background map. Fig 1 is a snapshot of eGrid with some map frames opened. On the background map, trouble report pins are scattered in their correct locations.

Map Frames. Giving users the flexibility to work on multiple different maps at the same time or work on one big map was motivated by a number of factors. This design

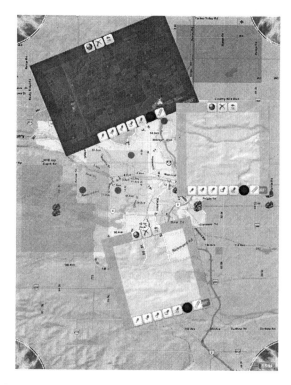

Fig. 1. An overall screen shot of eGrid with three map frames opened. The background map appears with trouble report pins.

tries to mimic the environment of the control center in which users have the flexibility to work on multiple printed maps at the same time. In addition, collaborating teams often toggle between different modes of collaboration and this design is flexible and avoids imposing any specific mode on the users. For achieving this flexibility, individual map frames were designed. Each map frame has its own layers settings. The design also allows multiple users to interact with multiple maps at the same time. A map frame can be created in a number of different ways. One option is to use a gesture composed of two consecutive finger touches that define the corners of the rectangular part of the background map which will appear in the map frame. Another option is to use a lasso gesture to define this area. Inside the frame, the map itself can be navigated using hand gestures. The design of these navigation gestures is based on the work of Wobbrock el al in their paper about user defined gestures for surface computing. [12]

4.3 The Second Application: eWell

The second application eWell is an application for the oil and gas industry. Its main target is to visualize oil well sensor data which is captured and stored in GIS form. The requirements of this second application motivated the extraction of the API from eGrid. A certain question seemed fundamental and needed an answer: which features/user scenarios fall in the intersection of the requirements of eGrid and the requirements of eWell? Or which components of eGrid should be separated into the API to benefit eWell and other applications? We found that eGrid in its current state has a lot of user interface elements which can benefit all tabletop GIS applications regardless of the domain. By trying to answer this question and based on the user stories of eGrid and the user stories of eWell, we created a list of user stories for the API user (the developer of GIS applications on multi-touch tables). The user stories also helped in brainstorming the extraction approach chosen and the granularity of the interface functions exposed.

After implementing the API and changing eGrid into an example application built on top of the API, the next question would be: which new features are needed by eWell which were not part of eGrid and thus are not yet supported by the API? And which of these features are specific to eWell and which of them can be useful for other applications? An iterative pattern is revealed here in the approach used, where new applications built on top of the API participate in enriching the API while having their own flavours at the same time. In our case, for example, for Corner Menus to be reused, the API should provide the application developer with the flexibility of changing the contents of these menus. Another example is the concept of marking some locations on the map and having more information associated with each location. This notion can be very useful in other applications as well. Therefore, trouble report pins and their associated information are generalized in the API as bookmark locations and associated notes or comments.

After a few iterations of building products on top of the API, users of the API should be able to select from various options and tailor the components to meet their specific needs.

Our case study includes the process of extracting the user interface components of eGrid which can be reused in similar applications, creating an API to include these components and using this API in both eGrid and a new application eWell. The approach presented learns from the usage examples in eGrid to guide the extraction of the API and relies on the acceptance tests of eGrid and also new acceptance tests that capture the user stories of the second application eWell. Acceptance tests are used to determine the components which can be reused in eWell and the extra features and changes that need to be done to these components. The acceptance tests are also used as a safety net in order to make sure that the refactoring steps will not change the behaviour of the eGrid and also serve the user stories of the new application eWell. The approach is iterative such that the requirements from any other new application interested in using the API can change the design of the API and add more options or variability points to the components extracted.

4.4 Example Case Study

This section includes an example of applying the extraction approach on the Map Frame widget from eGrid and reusing it in eWell.

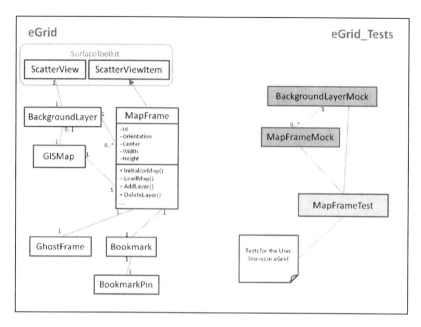

Fig. 2. A class diagram explaining the state of the design of eGrid before any extraction is done

Fig. 2 is a diagram representing part of the design in eGrid before any extraction is done. All the classes are in the user interface layer of eGrid. The implementation of the interface in eGrid was done in WPF 4.0 mostly in XAML files. Since part of the implementation was done using a markup language (i.e. XAML not C# code), it was difficult to implement the acceptance tests without creating mock versions of these classes. Mock classes have no XAML portions and they have mock implementations for the objects defined in the XAML files. The purpose of having these mock classes is to help create acceptance tests for UI code. The functionality is nearly perfectly preserved between the mock under test and the original user control. They are created only for the purpose of facilitating the creation of tests and they have to be in synchronization with the original classes at all times. The following steps are the same as the steps described in extraction approach section and will be applied iteratively on each component to be extracted.

1.   Writing Acceptance Tests for eWell

This step includes making sure that the acceptance tests of eGrid and eWell cover the scenarios related to the map frame widget. From the user stories of eWell, acceptance tests were created. Since there are no implemented classes for eWell, simple mock classes were created with no logic in them so that they can be attached to the tests. The created tests compile but fail against the incomplete mock classes. Fig 3 explains how the acceptance tests of eGrid and eWell interact with the class and mock classes in the implementation of eGrid.

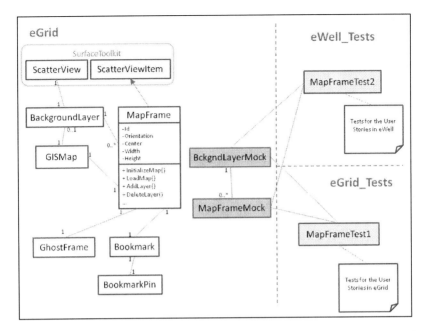

Fig. 3. A class diagram explaining how the tests of eGrid and eWell reference the classes in the implementation of eGrid

2. Comparing the User Stories of eGrid and eWell

By comparing the user stories of eGrid and eWell concerning the map frame widget, reuse opportunities can be identified. In eGrid, the main user story which relates to the map frame is: "As a user I can open a map frame using a two-point gesture. The map frame is positioned on the screen such that the two touch points are on top of two frame corners and the map displayed inside of the map frame has the same coordinates as the map area underneath the map frame". In eWell, the user story is: "As a user I can create a map frame using a single touch point. The map frame is positioned on the screen such that its center point is underneath the touch point and the map displayed inside of the map frame has the same coordinates as the map area underneath the map frame". In addition, another eWell user story is also related to the map frame widget: "As a user I can define a different default layer to be loaded into the map frame when it is first created".

3. Analyzing the Acceptance Tests of eGrid and eWell

The next step is to determine the changes to be done to the map frame widget based on the acceptance tests of eGrid and the new tests of eWell. Comparing the acceptance tests resulted in understanding the features which the map frame widget should provide. In addition, we also understood the options or variability points that the interface should provide to accommodate the differences between the scenarios in eGrid and in eWell. For example, after separating the map frame widget, changes will have to be done to handle the distinction between one and two map point instantiation methods and to handle the ability to change the default map layer.

4.   Refactoring the Map Frame Widget Based on the Analysis

After analyzing the common features and the variability between the use of the map frame in eGrid and eWell, changes have to be done to the implementation of the widget. For example, to handle two different methods for creating the map frame, we defined multiple constructors in the refactored map frame class and we added a new property to handle the URL address for the map when created.

5.   Moving the Map Frame Widget to the API Layer

In this step, the refactored map frame classes were moved into the new API layer. eGrid will use the map frame widget from the API layer just like it uses other third party components. eWell, as well as any other similar application, can use these classes from the API layer. The extraction of the component and the refactoring changes needed are not complete unless the acceptance tests in eGrid and eWell pass. These tests were combined to run against the new extracted component in the API after slightly modifying the implementation to run against the refactored map frame. The scenarios tested are semantically identical to the scenarios captured by the original acceptance tests from both applications.

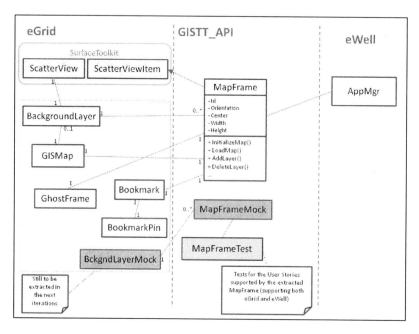

Fig. 4. A diagram explaining how the final state after extracting the MapFrame component and adding it to the API

6.   Refactoring eGrid Artifacts Which Interact with the Map Frame

Since the constructors of the map frame have changed to accommodate the extra new scenarios, changes will have to be done to all the code pieces in eGrid which interfaced with the map frame widget. For example, changing the constructors of the map frame necessitates changes in the code parts of eGrid which used these constructors. Other changes also needed to be made in order to make sure that the map frame classes absolutely encapsulate the behavior of the widget and to make sure that the interface is as simple and intuitive as possible. Needless to say that the acceptance tests of eGrid have to pass in order to make sure that the behavior has not been changed.

7. Using the Extracted Map Frame in eWell

In this step, the extracted component will be used in the new application. The usage examples found in eGrid will make it simple to use the component in eWell as well. Fig 4 explains how the MapFrame class and its associated Mock class and test is moved into an API layer and used from there in both eGrid and eWell.

5 Discussion

The proposed approach for extracting components and creating API libraries offers a number of potential benefits. First, the approach aligns better with the iterative and incremental nature of XP since it handles components on-demand, one at a time – as opposed to developing all the components in one phase. Moreover, the approach supports reuse reactively which minimizes investment upfront, and guarantees that component extraction happens only when there is a real need for a component's functionality by other applications. The opposite would be a proactive treatment where all the possibilities of reuse have to be examined and handled in the beginning facing the risk of losing this investment if the components were not actually used in other applications. Furthermore, this approach makes use of the usage examples and the acceptance tests, which are existing assets in the original application, to inform the decisions made about exposing and hiding certain features in the API.

A challenge exists, however, when the reusable components that are to be extracted are mostly user interface components. This is due to the fact that testing user interface components is sometimes tricky especially if they are designed using scripting or mark-up languages. In particular, creating acceptance tests for user interface related stories is far from trivial [10]. Usually, in user-interface intensive applications, tests do not cover the entire portion of the user interface layer which makes refactoring code in this layer risky. A partial solution has been used in this case study where mock classes have been created for user interface classes which have scripting parts. The purpose of having these mock classes is to help create acceptance tests for the user interface classes. This served as a solution for creating acceptance tests for user interface classes, however, these mock classes have to be synchronized with the original classes whenever any changes are made to them. Although we emphasized the use of acceptance tests as a safety net throughout the whole process, the proposed approach can leverage any type of tests (e.g. unit tests) to do the job. The most critical aspect is that these tests need to be automated so that the abstraction process could be done with minimal risk.

Our next step is to repeat the process by developing other applications based on the new API using the same approach. The benefit of repeating the process is to further assess the approach of using acceptance test driven extraction of user interface APIs, as well as enhance the API by generalizing it more according to the options needed by the new applications. Usability studies of the API will follow to assess how effective, valuable and useful the API is for developing GIS tabletop systems and thus how useful is the approach used in designing the API and extracting it from the scenarios of other applications.

6 Conclusions

In XP, little time is spent in gathering requirements and doing upfront design to facilitate the creation of reusable components. Refactoring can be used to extract the reusable components from existing applications. This paper presents an approach for structured refactoring to extract reusable user interface components guided and supported by the acceptance testing framework and the usage examples found in the original application.

The contribution of this research paper is twofold. First, we proposed an iterative technique for extracting reusable components and usage examples from existing applications guided by their acceptance tests. Second, we presented a case study in which we apply this technique to extract components from an existing application based on the requirements of a new application and try to assess its value and usefulness. The main conclusion of this research can be summarized as follows: extracting reusable components from existing applications can be done in an XP environment using a systematic iterative test-driven approach for refactoring. The usefulness and limitations of this approach will further be assessed through more case studies in the future.

Acknowledgments. We would like to extend our thanks to TRLabs and NSERC SurfNet for supporting the projects of eGrid, eWell and the API.

References

1. ArcGIS API for WPF and Silverlight can be found at,
   http://resources.esri.com/arcgisserver/apis/silverlight/
   (last accessed on November 29, 2010)
2. Beck, K.: Extreme Programming Explained: Embrace Change. Addison-Wesley, Reading (2000)
3. Brown, J., Lindgaard, G., Biddle, R.: Stories, Sketches, and Lists: Developers and Interaction Designers Interacting Through Artefacts. In: Proc. of the Agile Conference 2008, Toronto, Canada, pp. 39–50 (2008)
4. Burd, E., Munro, M., Wezeman, C.: Extracting reusable modules from legacy code: considering the issues of module granularity. In: Proceedings of the Third Working Conference on Reverse Engineering, pp. 189–196 (1996)

5. Cao, L., Mohan, K., Xu, P., Ramesh, B.: How Extreme Does Extreme Programming Have to Be? Adapting XP Practices to Large-Scale Projects. In: Proceedings of the 37th Annual Hawaii International Conference on System Sciences (HICSS 2004) - Track 3, p. 30083c (2004)
6. Krueger, C.W.: New methods in software product line practice. Commun. ACM 49(12), 37–40 (2006)
7. Clements, P., Northrop, L.: Software Product Lines: Practice and Patterns. Addison-Wesley, US (2001)
8. De Antonellis, V., Castano, S., Vandoni, L.: Building reusable components through project evolution analysis. Information Systems 19(3), 259–274 (1994)
9. Evoluce Table Technology available at, http://www.evoluce.com/en/ (last accessed November 18, 2010)
10. Finsterwalder, M.: Automating acceptance tests for GUI applications in an extreme programming environment. In: Proceedings of the 2nd International Conference on eXtreme Programming and Flexible Processes in Software Engineering, Villasimius, Sardinia, Italy, pp. 114–117. Addison-Wesley, Reading (2001)
11. Fowler, M.: Refactoring: Improving the Design of Existing Code. Addison-Wesley, Longman Publishing Co., Inc., Boston, MA, USA (1999)
12. Lanubile, F., Visaggio, G.: Extracting reusable functions by flow graph based program slicing. IEEE Transactions on Software Engineering 23(4), 246–259
13. Manifesto for Agile Software Development, http://www.agilemanifesto.org (last accessed on December 13, 2010)
14. Memmel, T., Reiterer, H.: Model-Based and Prototyping-Driven User Interface Specification to Support Collaboration and Creativity. Journal of Universal Computer Science 14(19) (2008)
15. Mens, T., Tourwe, T.: A survey of software refactoring. IEEE Transactions on Software Engineering 30(2), 126–139 (2004)
16. Moser, R., Sillitti, A., Abrahamsson, P., Succi, G.: Does refactoring improve reusability? In: Ninth International Conference on Software Reuse (ICSR-9), Turin, Italy, June 11-15 (2006)
17. Ning, J.Q., Engberts, A., Kozaczynski, W.: Recovering reusable components from legacy systems by program segmentation. In: Proceedings of Working Conference on Reverse Engineering, pp. 64–72 (1993)
18. Pohl, K., Böckle, G., Linden, F.: Software Product Line Engineering: Foundations, Principles and Techniques. Springer, Germany (2005)
19. Prieto-Díaz, R.: Reuse as a New Paradigm for Software Development. In: Proceedings of the International Workshop on Systematic Reuse, London (1996)
20. Shen, C., Ryall, K., Forlines, C., Esenther, A., Vernier, F.D., Everitt, K., Wu, M., Wigdor, D., Morris, M.R., Hancock, M., Tse, E.: Interfaces and Interactions for Direct-Touch Horizontal Surfaces. IEEE Computer Graphics and Applications 26(5), 36–46 (2006)
21. Sugumaran, V., Tanniru, M., Storey, V.: A knowledge-based framework for extracting components in agile systems development. Inf. Technol. and Management 9(1), 37–53 (2008)
22. Wartik, S., Prieto-Diaz, P.: Criteria for comparing reuse-oriented domain analysis approaches. International Journal of Software Engineering and Knowledge Engineering 2(3), 403–431 (1992)

23. Washizaki, H., Fukazawa, Y.: A technique for automatic component extraction from object-oriented programs by refactoring. In: Science of Computer Programming. New Software Composition Concepts, vol. 56(1-2), pp. 99–116 (April 2005) ISSN 0167-6423, doi:10.1016/j.scico.2004.11.007
24. Washizaki, H., Fukazawa, Y.: Automated extract component refactoring. In: Marchesi, M., Succi, G. (eds.) XP 2003. LNCS, vol. 2675, pp. 328–330. Springer, Heidelberg (2003)
25. Wobbrock, J.O., Morris, M.R., Wilson, A.D.: User-defined gestures for surface computing. In: Proceedings of the 27th International Conference on Human Factors in Computing Systems, CHI 2009, Boston, MA, USA, April 04-09 (2009)

An Empirical Study of Decision Making, Participation, and Empowerment in Norwegian Software Development Organisations

Bjørnar Tessem

Dept of Information Science and Media Studies,
Post box 7802, NO-5020 Bergen, Norway
Bjornar.Tessem@uib.no

Abstract. With the growth of agile software development methods we have seen an increased focus on the empowerment of software developers as a means to improving productivity and quality in software development. From other knowledge-intensive industries we also see that participation in decision making is argued to improve not only business, but also workers' job satisfaction. In this study, interviews from four different types of software development organisations in Norway are collected and analysed to get more insight in how decisions are made in software development. The four types of organisations are a) Small, in-house software teams, b) Software company with undefined development process, c) Software company using unified process, and d) Software company using scrum. The data confirm that experience is a dimension that significantly influences a developer's empowerment. But there is also clear differences between these four groups in what kind of decisions developers are participating in, and what level of participation they are admitted.

Keywords: Software development, decision making, empowerment, interview study.

1 Introduction

Empowering workers has for some time been seen as a means to increase productivity and quality in many industries and business areas. Participation in decision making in issues pertaining to workers' daily activities and even at more high-level decisions is supposed to increase job motivation, responsibility, and with that, better quality and productivity. This is currently also an influential trend in software development organisations as seen with the adoption of agile software development methodologies like scrum [1], extreme programming [2], and others. Agile methodologies are supposed to increase developers' say in not only the design and solutions but also in how projects are organised, what tasks to prioritise, and not least, the selection of work tasks in the daily work.

There are, however, very few studies describing decision making and participation in software development teams, projects, or organisations. This means that we do not

A. Sillitti et al. (Eds.): XP 2011, LNBIP 77, pp. 253–265, 2011.

have a clear map of how the developers are empowered, meaning participation in decision making, in different types of software development organisations. For instance, how much, when, and how are agile developers participating compared to developers in traditional plan-driven projects? What kind of decisions do developers participate in, and to what degree are they participating?

The study described here aims to address these questions, and presents and analyses data from semi-structured interviews with 11 Norwegian developers in 5 different software development organisations using different development methodologies. Even though organisations can be described according to many dimensions, like whether the software team is an in-house team or not, or whether they are selling to a mass-market or developing tailor-made software, I assume that there is a strong connection between their organisation and their chosen development methodology.

In the analysis I use qualitative techniques to establish a better understanding of the relationships between different development practices, as occurring in the different organisations, and developer empowerment. Further, I use the interview data to categorise each of the developers according to the methodology used, what kind of decisions they participate in (ranking from simple choices of techniques in solving a programming problem to strategic business decisions), and levels of participation (ranking from not been informed at all to being responsible for making the decision).

The initial hypothesis is that there are no differences among the developers from different software development organisations, except what one should expect occurring from personal traits like being experienced or outgoing. But as differences are found in my analysis, I suggest explanations for those differences, and discuss how much of this can be attributed to development methodology.

I start with some background knowledge from literature on decision making and participation in general and in software engineering. I continue by describing the research approach, and define categories of methodologies, decision making areas, and levels of participation. Next, in the analysis I give a short description of data, and use our interpretation of the interviews to place each developer in this landscape. In the discussion I describe the implications of the analysis, and also present a validity discussion, before I conclude.

2 Background

To clarify, by software development I mean activities necessary to significantly change the functionality of existing software or to construct new software. This includes activities such as programming, work requirements, design, testing, and project management. Included in this are many areas that require decision making, such as choosing a technical solution to a programming problem, skipping or prioritising a requirement, designing a test for a particular functionality, deciding who will work on a problem, choosing a programming language, choosing a development methodology, and so on. But work is also influenced by more strategic decisions, such as the internal organisation of a firm, or business decisions such as going into a merger with another company. With maximum empowerment an employee would also have the ability to participate in decisions normally consigned to management or owners.

In general, decision making is the process of seeing a need for making a choice of action, initiating a process towards doing that choice, and actually choosing an action among several alternatives. But one may also include the actual execution of the chosen action, and perhaps a final evaluation. Empowerment is a term used in work to indicate an employee's ability to participate in the decision making of a company. Studies in highly knowledge-intensive industries other than the software industry have shown that the empowered knowledge worker has higher productivity and is more satisfied with the work situation [3]. At the same time, in ideas like lean manufacturing [4] we find the empowerment of the blue-collar worker as a central ingredient in activities aiming to improve performance of the team and the business.

A concept such as "participation in decision making" has a wide and imprecise meaning, including anything from labour union participation at an industrial production facility to the knowledge worker's participation in strategic discussions in a small, innovative, technology firm. To get a better understanding of this term, it is useful to apply Wilkinson et al.'s [3] deconstruction of this concept into four dimensions: degree, form, level, and range of subject matter. **Degree** means how much an employee is involved in a decision. **Level** means at what level the decision takes place; is it operational or strategic or something in between? **Range of subject matter** is about what issues the decision is about; is it about where to go for lunch or is it about who to hire as the new CEO? **Form** is how participation is enacted; is it through labour unions or through individual communication with managers?

In the agile literature for professionals, empowerment has to some extent been an issue, particularly in the work on lean software development [5]. There are, however, only few scientific studies relating to these issues within general software engineering research. To summarize, there are some studies on decision making per se, and a couple oriented towards empowerment. Aurum & Wohlin [6] discuss the requirements engineering (RE) process in terms of classical decision making processes. Also placed within RE, Alenljung & Persson [7] use data from a case study to identify the matter of RE decisions, factors that affect decisions, activities in decision making, and decision processes. Zannier et al. [8] conduct an interview study on how design decisions were made. Their results indicate that design decisions are often not based on rational approaches and known best practices, particularly in unstructured design problems. A study more oriented towards the issue of empowerment is by Saarelainen et al. [9] where the issue is on how groups collaborate to make decisions on software evolution. McAvoy & Butler [10] take a critical view on empowered, agile software teams and use data from a multiple case study to discuss the role of the project manager to prevent groupthink in agile software development.

3   The Data and the Research Method

The data collected are 11 semi-structured interviews with Norwegian software developers initially collected to get an in-depth understanding of how empowered the software developers are. The interviews focused on topics such as background, work practices, collaboration, and involvement in decisions at all levels.

I have taken the conservative hypothesis that there are no differences among software developers' abilities to participate in decision making at the workplace given that they work in different organisations using different software development methodologies and given that their background is similar. For instance, it is a fairly well confirmed result from general research on empowerment at work that experience and competence are positively correlated with factors of empowerment (see for instance [11]), so I will expect to see that empowerment will be positively influenced by experience in my data.

As I am using a qualitative approach, the challenge is finding experiences, viewpoints, and anecdotes in the data that confirm or invalidate this hypothesis. At the same time it is a goal to find out whether the differences found can reasonably be explained only from experience, position, and personality, as opposed to being explained from an organisational context including the different methodologies used.

In a paper by Bygstad et al. [12] the categorization of software development organisations is according to methodology. The authors choose to use the categories "Own method", "Unified process", "Agile methods", "Microsoft Solutions Framework", and "Other methods". I have chosen to categorize the organisations I got data from in a similar way. One of the businesses defined themselves as an RUP organisation (5 interviewees), and one as a scrum organisation (2 interviewees). The rest used what I would categorize as their own, but not well defined methods. Two of the developers in this category came from different in-house development teams with only two developers, and the last two came from a software house making software for the public domain. This leaves me with data from four categories:

1. Small, in-house team with undefined methodology
2. Software house with undefined methodology
3. Software house using unified process
4. Software house using scrum

A couple of Bygstad et al.'s categories [12] remain uncovered by the data, but doing the analysis on these four categories will still give us valuable insights. As seen, I have also chosen to split data from organisations with undefined methodologies in two categories, because the work situations of the two groups are very different. It is also relevant that most software development organisations in fact fall in to the "Own method" group of Bygstad et al. [12], as in 2006, 68% of software development organisations in Norway fell in this category.

In addition to the four organisation categories, I have used Wilkinson et al's [3] dimensions **degree** and **level**. This is because the subject matters in the data I have is almost exclusively about issues relating to the development of software, as well as about a form of participation focused on the individual's involvement. Within software development, the level categories I have chosen as suitable are:

*   **Operational** – daily work practices like programming, testing, designing
*   **Resource and task allocation** – assigning people to different tasks and prioritising tasks
*   **Low-level strategic decisions** – changes in technology, methodology, work practices
*   **High-level strategic** – business decisions

Further, I use a variant of Wilkinson et al's [3] escalator of participation giving the following degrees of participation:

- No participation
- Information
- Communication
- Consultation – asked
- Consultation – suggesting
- Codetermination
- Control

Based on the data and other experiences from the software business, I chose to modify Wilkinson's original scale by splitting the *consultation* degree into two variants: Consultation – asked and Consultation – suggesting. This is based on the experience that in software development, as in many other knowledge intensive industries, decision processes are often started on suggestions from employees without management having initiated these suggestions. The ability to come up with uninitiated suggestions indicates a higher degree of empowerment than the plain consultation degree.

4   Analysis

The analysis is split into four parts, one for each of the organisation categories defined. In the analysis I have considered participation in decisions up to the level of low-level strategic decisions. In the data, there are some statements concerning high-level strategic discussions, but it seemed as if none of the interviewees had really been involved to a great extent in business-level decision processes. For instance, one of the interviewees said the following about the decision to split the software development organisation from the main corporation: *"That was a decision we were not involved in at all. There was a long time of secrecy. Then the next step was that we were informed and it was decided to establish the new company."* Another interviewee from a different company said the following on the process of creating a new business and leaving the mother company: *"I was not involved. That was at a high level. That was the chief executives."* Since my data on decisions at this level are scarce and indeed indicating that the developers are not really involved, I have chosen to omit this level from the further analysis.

4.1   Small, In-House Teams

The first two interviewees are from two different, small, in-house teams. They both worked with one other developer on their projects. One of the developers worked in what was more of a maintenance project, but also with continuous additions of functionality.

The first interviewee was responsible for developing the user interface for a small subsystem that was part of a larger system for public domain information. He came in from a leave period, and was, according to himself, forced to work with this project, and with Delphi, which was a completely new technology for him. He had more experience with other more old-fashioned technologies, and also of maintenance and systems operations, but he was not needed for that anymore. He would normally have control over the operational decisions in his work, but was to a large extent influenced by the project's customer on how the interface design should be. He would also have little say in priorities and task assignments, as well as methodology discussions and so on. At an earlier point in time the company chose to go for a unified process methodology in their larger projects, and the interviewee's statement about that was: *"Those decisions were made at a different level than mine. That is, I have the impressions that the project managers have had some to say on that. And we also have architects who are in on decisions."* It must be noted that this was the interviewee with the lowest competence among the 11 with regard to his current work tasks, and he also seemed to be a rather careful person, who would not push hard for his will. Still, he had some feeling of being empowered in personal matters, like choices for further education, and regarding being allowed to avoid working with certain colleagues.

The second interviewee in this category was far more outgoing and experienced at his work. He was maintaining and extending software for controlling hardware components delivered by the company. The developer was fully in control of all design decisions, and collaborated with one other programmer. However, when it came to priorities, he had little to say and did not want to be responsible for those decisions. If the hardware people asked for functionality he would pass them on to the product manager, who would then make the decisions: *"If they come to me, I say, go to R [the product manager]. I will talk with them and help them, but he will make the final decisions."* The interviewee was also fairly powerful in more advanced design decisions, as he often was trusted to solve complex problems related to more advanced use of the hardware. He was also heard on issues relating to IT solutions in general. But there were limitations to his participation at higher level decisions. For instance, he was not involved in process improvement activities: *"The organisation has been through such a thing. And to my disappointment the whole software development was forgotten in those matters, so we kind of live our own lives."*

Both these developers work in situations where they are able to participate in decisions only to a limited extent. Both have much to say in operational decisions, but when it comes to the next level, i.e., resource and task allocation, they are only heard (and also seem to be content with that), as they both have people who decide their priorities, seemingly in an ad hoc manner. They differ somewhat in how they participate, but this seems to be more caused by their experience and personalities than working in different companies. They are in some sense marginalized within the organisation, leaving them with little influence over their own work situation except at the operational level.

A summary of my interpretation of these two interviewee's answers is given in Figure 1. A dark grey indicates that all the developers certainly have this degree of participation at this organisational level. A lighter grey indicates that there is some degree (i.e. At least one of the interviewees can be placed here) of participation at this decision level. White indicates that this degree of participation is not found in the data.

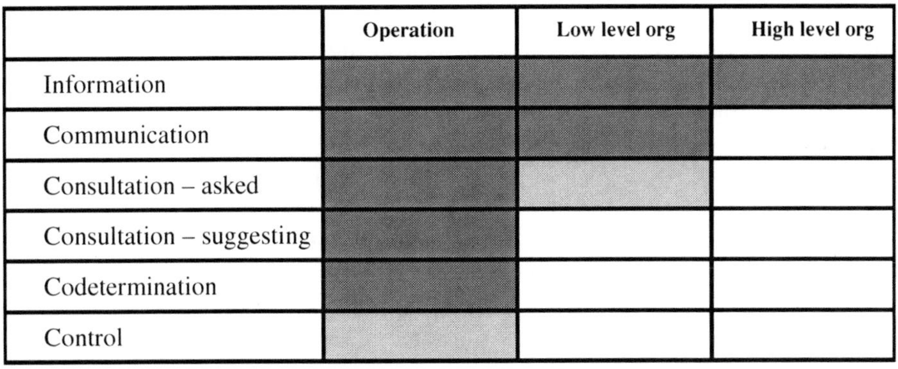

	Operation	Low level org	High level org
Information	▓▓▓	▓▓▓	▓▓▓
Communication	▓▓▓	▓▓▓	
Consultation – asked	▓▓▓	▒▒▒	
Consultation – suggesting	▓▓▓		
Codetermination	▓▓▓		
Control	▒▒▒		

Fig. 1. Participation degrees for small, in-house teams

4.2 Undefined Development Method Team

The second data set came from a software company without a defined development method. The company makes software for the public domain, i.e., a class of systems running as both stand-alone and web applications. Two interviewees were from this organisation. They were both educated to Bachelor level. One of them had been working with the company almost from its start (senior developer) and the other had been working in the company for 2-3 years (junior developer). Some of the work here was maintenance oriented, but they also continuously worked with extending their product portfolio by adding new applications and functionality. According to the senior developer there have been discussions about defining a standard development method in the company, but work practices still seemed to be quite ad hoc.

The programmers here work much on their own, and they are given much responsibility in finding the solutions. The developers work alone on projects and tasks they are assigned to, and within these projects they are to a large extent in control: *"There is little control in details. Within a task they have the freedom to choose their own solutions as long as they reach the goal."* (senior developer). The distribution of work tasks is still mainly the responsibility of managers, but to some extent bringing in opinions from the developers: *"He gets a load of things to be done, and he hands it out, and he asks us a little bit on what to do, and the time needed as well."* (junior developer). In fact, the loose project organisation gives developers more influence. For instance, when project leaders for some reason were not able to follow up on a project: *"Of course there is projects, where you have to grab hold of things. It really depends, in some external project, there has been somewhat indolent management, so you kind of have to take responsibility, otherwise nothing will happen."* (junior developer). It seems as if there is openness in the organisation towards accepting suggestions from the staff regarding changes in work practices, but the developers are not able or willing to grab that opportunity: *"It is really the team leader's responsibility to get the team into such things. Except for that we are maybe not so good at suggesting how to improve processes."* (junior developer).

To summarize, programmers in this organisation operate much on their own, having defined responsibilities within one or a few projects. Work assignments come from leaders, who suggest, inform, hear and then decide. The more experienced interviewee is really in a position to participate in that kind of decision making, whereas the less experienced is heard, but also has influence through being in an open-minded organisation where suggestions are considered. One observation here is that in this organisation it is a career path to start as a programmer with few responsibilities and then continue to low-level leadership with responsibility for resource allocation and project monitoring.

The undefined decision making procedures in this organisation seem to give developers much freedom, but with the risk of making choices that have little foundation in the organisation. The organisation thus seems to be not far above the initial level (lowest level) in the CMM hierarchy [13], facing risks of overspending, low quality, and late deliveries. My interpretation of the data is given in Figure 2. Note that we also see here that the most experienced developer is more empowered than the least experienced. This is in line with the expectations that experience would positively influence empowerment.

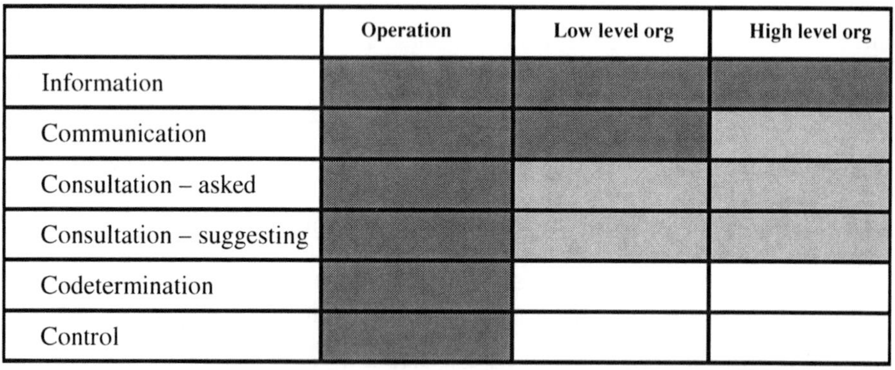

	Operation	Low level org	High level org
Information			
Communication			
Consultation – asked			
Consultation – suggesting			
Codetermination			
Control			

Fig. 2. Participation degrees for software company with undefined development method

4.3 Unified Process Development Method

The third category in this research is represented by a company that makes controlling software for embedded systems. This company use an adapted version of RUP (Rational Unified Process) as their development methodology, and hence is classified as being a unified process-company. From this company, I got 5 interviews with developers having different roles in the RUP: one architect, one requirements analyst, one test manager, one technical project leader, and one programmer.

Three of these employees, the architect, the requirements analyst and the technical project leader had extensive experience. All of these three participated to the codetermination level in low-level organisational decisions. They were allowed to do prioritizing of tasks and resource allocation. These three also participated in higher level, long-term decisions: *"I come with suggestions about who is best suited to implement those parts. But it is really in collaboration with the project manager. I and the project manager have a close collaboration and discuss matters, so that is a dialogue."* (Architect about prioritization). *"As an architect I think further, what is appropriate in half a year, one year, with a long term perspective."* (Architect on system configurations).

The developers in this company were allowed some freedom outside their defined roles, but mainly stuck to their defined work tasks. In these tasks they all had full control of their work. Of course they got suggestions from their colleagues, but they really had to ask for support if they needed it. *"They are pretty much left to themselves, that they have to find a solution [...] But the culture here is very open and you can go and ask, and it is ok not to know."* (Requirements analyst about the programmers work).

As for the less experienced interviewees they were heard in priorities and higher level decisions. For instance, one of them said about project manager meetings on assessments and priorities: *"They took decisions at a higher level then, kind of. About what should be cut or had to be done."* (Less experienced programmer). But then he also refers to local project assessment meetings and said: *"But we did priorities also, and in these assessment meetings we agreed on what should be done, somehow. But at the bottom it is the project manager who has to take that decision."* The test manager said: *"The project manager typically has a meeting where testers and programmers inform, how far we have come, what status is, and some suggestions on what is going happens, and then the project manager meets those who can make decisions, and then it is decided there."*

To summarize, this is an organisation where everybody has a large degree of participation in lower level decisions, but also where the experienced people participate to a large extent in higher level decisions. The organisation has a flat structure open for suggestions, but final decisions are often left to project managers or higher level managers, and meritocracy is quite visible. As the programmer said about meetings: *"Some feel most comfortable within particular areas. Where as others, those who know the most are also those who talk in those meetings. Then it is also personality types. But I really think it is quite flat. We are a quite flat hierarchy."* A summary of the organisation is given in Figure 3.

4.4 Agile Development Method

I interviewed two developers from a company using scrum as their development methodology. This organisation delivers software development services to different industries, but mainly to the financial industry, and had switched from undefined ad hoc approaches to scrum two years before these interviews were done. The two developers were also not very experienced, so in contrast to the other organisations there is a lack of breadth in experience represented in my data here, which again lead to some uncertainty in the conclusions. Both developers worked as programmers, including testing and bug fixing. One of them was at the time only working with bug fixing, as they had a team doing that in relation to an upcoming production release.

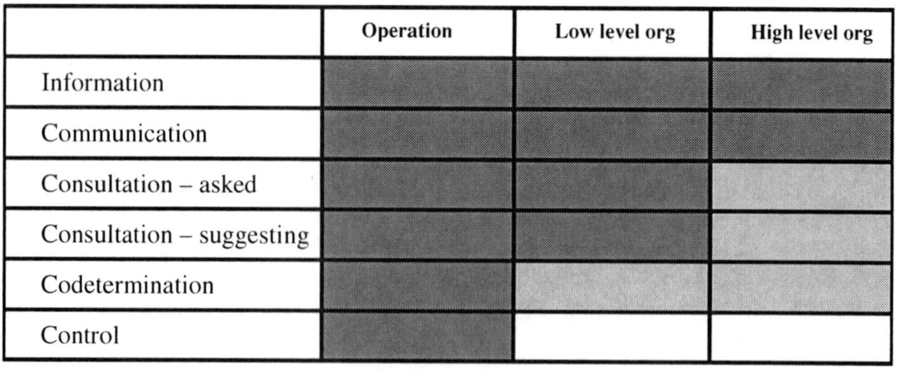

	Operation	Low level org	High level org
Information	▓	▓	▓
Communication	▓	▓	▓
Consultation – asked	▓	▓	░
Consultation – suggesting	▓	▓	░
Codetermination	▓	░	▓
Control	▓		

Fig. 3. Participation degrees for developers working in a unified process organisation

They both describe the typical scrum development practices with daily meetings and iteration meetings. Developers work mainly alone, but pair up with others when they need to do designs or have difficult problems they need to be helped with: *"And then we tell a little bit about the problem, and then someone says 'ok I can help you with this' and then we go together when we are finished with the meeting."* (Developer on daily scrum meetings).

During iteration planning, estimation is done using planning poker [14], and work is distributed by consensus: *"Everyone is involved there. Everyone has their opinion, and those with highest and lowest number must tell why and tell why they think the task is difficult or easy and such things. Then it is the planning poker again and we have an approximate number. Everyone agrees in the end. Then we go through the tasks and thus are the tasks distributed and everyone must choose their task to work with."* (Developer on iteration planning). One of the developers had the responsibility to distribute tasks that needed immediate attention. Occasionally the customer company would call with problems, and this developer would then assess whether it was something to be put on the backlog or forwarded to another developer. In the last case, the interviewee would also be responsible for choosing the right person, using knowledge about people's specialities.

There is much acceptance for personal initiatives, and good solutions are given credit: *"What I really think was good, was that it was valued. My colleagues said 'This was cool. We haven't seen this before.' Those things are nice, when you get recognition for the things you make."* (Developer about responses after introducing a new approach to web testing).

The two also participate in more high level decisions such as how resources are to be allocated in the future: *"And then we sat in this room everyone from this project and discussed jointly these matters, some were going into management projects and stuff, those with the most experience. And there were questions about what we would prefer, what we expected and so on. And I thought that was very constructive as everyone could tell and everyone could hear. No sneaking in the corridors,"* (Developer about reassignment of jobs after project ending).

To summarize, both these developers are very much empowered in their organisations. They have full control of their own work, they suggest solutions and participate in lower level decisions, and are consulted on higher level decisions. It seems as if decision making processes suggested in agile methodologies are complied with in this organisation. The result is that these two developers are very satisfied with their work and also have high degrees of participation at the three levels discussed here. The analysis is summarized in Figure 4.

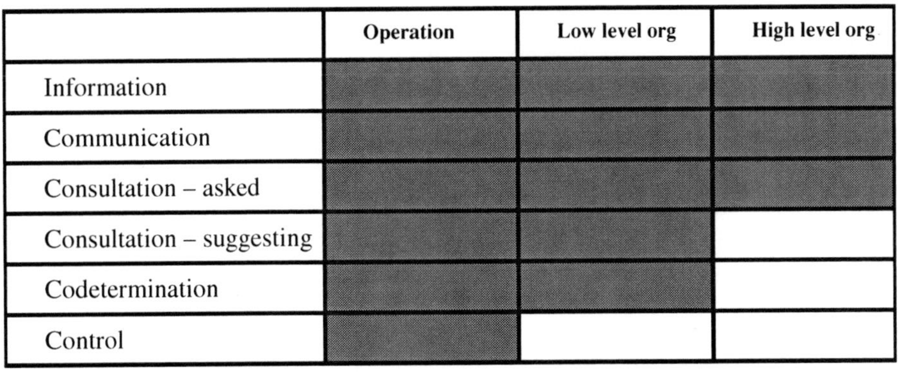

	Operation	Low level org	High level org
Information			
Communication			
Consultation – asked			
Consultation – suggesting			
Codetermination			
Control			

Fig. 4. Participation degrees for developers working in a scrum organisation

5   Summary and Discussion

From the interview data I collected there is clear evidence that there is a difference in the ability to participate in the four different types of software development organisations. The darkest areas of Figures 1-4 indicate degrees of participation for the least empowered and least experienced, whereas the lighter areas indicate participation for the most empowered, but also the most experienced. From this we see a very strong association between experience and empowerment within each organisation category. That is, within the organisation categories, experienced people were more empowered (except perhaps for the scrum company where I have no data from the most experienced developers). Further, if we control for experience, developers in small, in-house teams are generally the least empowered. Organisations with undefined methods are somewhat less empowered than developers working in unified process teams, and developers working in agile teams are the most empowered. Note particularly that the two inexperienced agile developers were almost as empowered within their organisation as the most experienced of the unified process organisation. Most likely this difference comes from the fact that empowerment is more institutionalized in agile methodologies.

Another finding is the meritocracy found in particularly the undefined methodology and unified process organisations. In both those organisations the experienced developers said that they had a few people they would preferably ask if they had some issues to discuss. Of course there is a rational explanation behind this, because it saves time, and that you most probably will not get any interesting answers from other colleagues. However, there is also the risk of missing good ideas, and also the risk of making some of your colleagues less satisfied with work as they are kept out of decision making processes.

Melnik and Maurer [15] reported that there is a correlation between job satisfaction and empowerment among software engineers, and that empowerment is also associated with agile methodology. The last point is confirmed by this study, but it also implies that for the software developer, working in agile teams should be more attractive. Certainly we see that working in small, in-house teams is a situation where developers would probably be less content with their work situation than elsewhere.

When considering validity of qualitative data, there is nothing in the scientific method saying that you have to work with numbers and statistical analyses. However, the analytical approach you have to use when analysing qualitative data poses validity threats of a different kind than what is found in quantitative methods. For instance, with a survey you have the problem of whether the respondents really understand the concepts you use, and you have to give introductions and pose questions in a way that diminish the risk of misunderstanding. In an interview study you will in fact have good control of this as you will, through the recordings or transcripts of the interview, be able to uncover misunderstandings and disagreements about how concepts are understood, and through the interview you can guide the interviewee to the correct understanding. A quite different issue that we find in qualitative research is that the analysis instrument is the researcher's mind, and objectivity can, for instance, only be verified by means such as having other researchers look at the same data and agreeing with the conclusions.

Another point is whether I, with only 11 interviews, can draw general conclusions. I believe that it is correct to assume that from these data we can reject the initial, conservative hypothesis that there is no difference between the organisation categories. We have a fairly representative group of developers, with differing experiences, except for in the agile company. Further, the interviews uncover significant differences in how empowered the developers are in the different organisations, as given in Figures 1-4. It is, of course, not obvious that this follows from the teams' methodologies (or lack of methodologies), but I will still argue that it is defendable to draw this conclusion as the data here come from what we could call typical representative organisations of their category, as they seem to behave in the way you would expect such organisations to behave, either because they behave as prescribed (for UP and scrum) or because they have properties normally found in that kind of organisation (for the undefined methodology software company and the small, in-house teams). A tentative conclusion (which should be considered in light of the validity threats mentioned) is that organisations that spend time to reflect on methodology choice, and choose a systematic approach to software development, will obtain higher levels of empowerment among its employees, and enjoy the positive organisational consequences that follow from empowerment.

6 Conclusions

In this research I set out to investigate whether there is a difference in empowerment among developers in different types of software development organisations. The findings indicate that there is a difference. The data verify that the decision participation and empowerment vary in software teams and there are clear indications that this can be attributed to different organisations and the methodologies chosen. It does not seem to be tempting for a software developer to work in small, in-house teams because they have less influence on their own work than in other software development organisations. This comes in addition to the lack of a specialist environment giving the possibility to bring in other developers' knowledge in difficult problem solving situations. The data indicate that agile teams seem to be the most empowered, at least at the decision levels investigated here. The explicit institutionalization of participation found in agile organisations seems to have a clear effect on empowerment.

References

1. Schwaber, K.: Agile project management with Scrum. Microsoft Press, Redmond (2004)
2. Beck, K., Andres, C.: Extreme programming explained: Embrace change, 2nd edn. Addison-Wesley, Reading (2004)
3. Wilkinson, A., Gollan, P.J., Marchington, M., Lewin, D.: Conceptualizing Employee Participation in Organizations. In: Wilkinson, A., Gollan, P.J., Marchington, M., Lewin, D. (eds.) The Oxford Handbook of Participation in Organizations, pp. 3–25. Oxford University Press, Oxford (2010)
4. Womack, J., Jones, D., Roos, D.: The machine that changed the world: The story of lean production. Harper Perennial, New York (1990)
5. Poppendieck, M., Poppendieck, T.: Lean software development; An agile toolkit. Addison-Wesley Professional, Reading (2003)
6. Aurum, A., Wohlin, C.: The Fundamental Nature of Requirement Engineering Activities as a Decision-Making Process. Information and Software Technology 45, 945–954 (2003)
7. Alenljung, B., Persson, A.: Portraying the practice of decision-making in requirements engineering: a case of large scale bespoke development. Requirements Engineering 13, 257–279 (2008)
8. Zannier, C., Chiasson, M., Maurer, F.: A model of design decision making based on empirical results of interviews with software designers. Information and Software Technology 49, 637–653 (2007)
9. Saarelainen, M.-M., Koskinen, J., Ahonen, J.J., Kankaanpää, I., Sivula, H., Lintinen, H., Juutilainen, P., Tilus, T.: Group decision-making processes in industrial software evolution. In: International Conference on Software Engineering Advances (ICSEA 2007). IEEE, Los Alamitos (2007)
10. McAvoy, J., Butler, T.: The role of project management in ineffective decision making within agile software development projects. European Journal of Inforamtion Systems 18, 372–383 (2009)
11. Spreitzer, G.M.: Psychological empowerment in the workplace: Dimensions, measurement, and validation. The Academy of Management Journal 38, 1442–1465 (1995)
12. Bygstad, B., Ghinea, G., Brevik, E.: Software development methods and usability: Perspectives from a survey in the software industry in Norway. Interacting with Computers 20, 375–385 (2008)
13. Paulk, M.C., Curtis, B., Chrissis, M.B., Weber, C.V.: Capability Maturity Model, Version 1.1. IEEE Softw. 10, 18–27 (1993)
14. Grenning, J.: Planning poker. Renaissance Software Consulting (2002)
15. Melnik, G., Maurer, F.: Comparative analysis of job satisfaction in agile and non-agile software development teams. In: Abrahamsson, P., Marchesi, M., Succi, G. (eds.) XP 2006. LNCS, vol. 4044, pp. 32–42. Springer, Heidelberg (2006)

A Case Study in Agile-at-Scale Delivery

Alan W. Brown

IBM Rational software
alanbrown@es.ibm.com

Abstract. Many individuals and teams involved on projects are already using agile development techniques as part of their daily work. However, we have much less experience in how to scale and manage agile practices as part of a concerted effort of improvement across an integrated supply-chain for enterprise software delivery. In this paper we discuss the scalability of agile approaches through a detailed case study in agile adoption. In the context of this example we examine how "agility-at-scale" is applied, describe the key scaling factors and their impact on agility, and review some of the rollout and deployment issues that can limit the adoption of agile approaches in practice.

Keywords: agile software delivery; software process; enterprise IT.

1 Introduction

The past few years has seen wide adoption of agile software development approaches in many parts of the software industry. Driven by demands for more software more quickly, many organizations looked to understand the practices in use by high-performing teams to see how they could be replicated. Similarly, those high-performing teams tried to shake off the overly constraining processes that they believed were hampering innovation and creativity. From this emerged a series of principles for agile development, most famously captured in the so-called "Agile Manifesto" [1], and a series of development practices that encapsulate those principles [2,3].

A majority of the work around agile software delivery has focused in the software development area, with new approaches and techniques for accelerating coding and testing, understanding requirements changes, and coordinating code-test-build activities. However, a broader perspective on agile software delivery is also important. For many organizations a shift of thinking is taking place that covers all aspects of their enterprise software delivery challenge. They are looking to apply agile approaches in all aspects of their delivery.

In this paper we discuss that broader view of agility. In particular, we consider the change in enterprise software delivery thinking that agility requires, and focus on the ways in which this agility can be scaled and adopted from a software factory viewpoint in an enterprise software delivery organization. This discussion is based on a detailed case study in "agility at scale" deployment at a large European bank.

A. Sillitti et al. (Eds.): XP 2011, LNBIP 77, pp. 266–281, 2011.

2   Agility at Scale

In the adoption of agile practices to enterprise software delivery, the context in which ideas and approaches are applied can have significant impact on their utility and value [4]. Although the key principles may remain consistent, their application in practice can vary widely.[1] In particular, many challenges must be addressed in understanding the complexity of the enterprise software delivery environment in which agile thinking is applied.

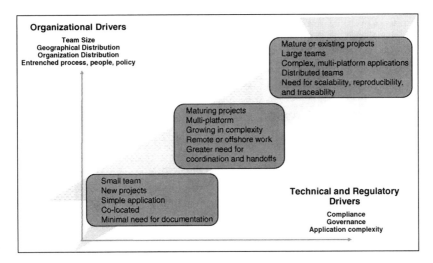

Fig. 1. The Context for Agile Delivery in 2 Dimensions

As illustrated in Figure 1, it is helpful to highlight the context for agility in two dimensions: Organizational drivers and Technical/Regulatory drivers. These dimensions help to understand the implications of increasing complexity on the way agility can be applied in practice.

At the bottom left of the diagram, where the organizational and regulatory/technical aspects are least complex, we typically see co-located teams with small numbers of developers building applications of limited complexity and minimal deployment risk. Many of the initial agile ideas and approaches began in this context, and techniques such as "extreme programming" find their majority of use in this context.

In the middle of the diagram increasing complexity forces teams to address additional concerns, including:

- Larger team sizes requiring more coordination and transparency into planning and progress;

- Distributed teams supported by remote access, outsourced partnerships, and varied access to artifacts and system knowledge.

---

[1] To quote Albert Einstein, "In theory, theory and practice are the same. But in practice, they are not!".

- Complex or mission-critical applications requiring more attention to analysis, architecture and testing procedures.
- Multi-platform deployment environments often requiring more extensive and rigorous testing, management of multiple variants, and enhanced support mechanisms.

In the top right of the diagram, the most complex situations, we see teams that face an increasing number of issues, including:

- Very large team sizes, teams of teams, and more complex management structures forcing additional attention to coordination and management. At this level, there is an increasing need to standardize best practices to avoid reinvention and miscommunication across artifacts and processes.
- Distributed and global development, requiring attention to many technical, organizational, and cultural issues as the teams interact to cooperatively delivery the solution.
- Compliance needs for domains in which regulatory controls require audits based on process conformance and regular collection of development information from multiple data sources.
- Very complex applications that may include safety-critical or mission-critical components, and hence require complex test environments, dedicated test teams, and careful attention to analysis and architecture properties (e.g., recovery, fault tolerance, security monitoring, etc.).

In summary, we note that complexity issues in enterprise software delivery can have significant impact on the adoption of agile approaches. As a consequence, agile strategies will typically need to be evaluated, tailored, and perhaps combined with traditional approaches to suit the particular context.

3 Agile at Scale Delivery at ABC Bank[2]

The banking and financial markets are under increasing pressure to be competitive, respond more quickly to change, and be more transparent in their governance practices. In a fiercely competitive market, ABC Bank is finding that it is essential that it realizes synergies from a period of active acquisitions and mergers, solidifies its market value by strengthening weakly positioned services in key customer segments, and enhances customer satisfaction in comparison to key competitors in several key market areas.

ABC Bank is the largest universal bank in its country, and the second largest in the region, managing over $500B in assets. It is part of the ABC Bank Group offering a wide range of financial services, including insurance, mortgage finance, asset management, brokerage, real estate and leasing services. ABC Bank is responsible for approximately 5 million retail customers and has almost 200,000 corporate, public

---

[2] Although this work is derived from actual use, we have used a fictitious name to replace the actual name of the bank.

and institutional clients. As a result, it employs of 20,000 employees across Northern Europe. In addition, over the past decade the recent business climate has pushed ABC Bank toward a more global approach to banking. Consequently, ABC Bank is expanding into other countries, including more than 10 acquisitions over past 20 years.

The enterprise software delivery organization for ABC Bank is tasked with timely and efficient development and delivery of end-to-end solutions with an appropriate level of quality to the different business areas (and through them to the customers of ABC Bank). That organization currently has an annual budget of about $350M allocated to developing new solutions as well as maintaining and delivering the existing portfolio of solutions (excluding infrastructure related costs). This is used to support a large portfolio of systems, with over 50,000 applications and many hundreds of concurrently executing projects to add, update, or decommission those applications. Those applications are implemented in a variety of technologies and programming languages: CICS/PL1, CICS/Cobol, J2EE, Microsoft VisualBasic/C#.

During the last couple of years, increasing the level of process maturity in the development organization has been a key focus. As a result, development projects in ABC Bank are now able to consistently achieve CMMI level 2 compliance. The stated goal is to achieve CMMI level 3 compliance within a couple of years.

4 Objectives in Adopting an Agile Approach

ABC Bank defined a set of objectives for an agile adoption approach aimed at making measured improvements in several areas. In particular, by focusing on the highest revenue generating aspects of the business, the primary objective was to achieve a substantial improvement in efficiency in the development effort, aimed at:

- Providing solutions to the business within short release cycles (<12 months but typically releases every 3-4 months for more agile projects);

- Increasing delivery flexibility to change scope as required with minimal impact on schedules and commitments;

- Managing project risks through earlier identification of problems and easier mitigation of risks;

- Delivering higher quality solutions at a cost that is the same or lower than previously seen;

- Expanding the sourcing options for projects to allow an increased use of offshore resourced.

The concepts and principles of agile software development were well known to ABC Bank. Over the past years there had been several efforts involving a number of different agile methods, a limited amount of coaching and external consulting had been contracted, and a handful of projects openly described their approaches in terms of agile processes and techniques. In fact, a small but growing grassroots agile community had been formed. This was beginning to gain visibility and influence in the organization, particularly among influential groups of users across the enterprise software delivery management team. The challenge, then, was not *whether* agile approaches should be used, but *where* and *how* agile approaches could be applied in a more controlled way to the greatest benefit of ABC Bank.

To help with this task, ABC Bank defined a focus for its agile adoption efforts by creating a shared "agile adoption charter". The basis of this charter was a series of focus areas ("do's and don'ts") to clarify how agility would be scoped and interpreted at ABC Bank. From their viewpoint, an agile project at ABC Bank should focus on:

- Delivering a potentially shippable (part of a) solution after each sprint, and after each release;
- Self-organized and highly disciplined teams;
- Collective ownership of project results by team members working across multiple disciplines;
- Close and on-going collaboration with the business (represented by the product owner);
- Continuous improvement through meaningful measures.

In particular, the previous ABC Bank experiences with agile development had also raised some concerns with people in the organizations. Perceptions existed that agility was simply a lack of governance and a way to avoid burdensome reporting practices. It was therefore essential to also be clear on what an agile project at ABC Bank should *not* focus on:

- Working without a plan;
- Producing no documentation;
- Neglecting to do analysis and design;
- Having no process for managing change;
- Avoiding managing your risks, stakeholders, or suppliers;
- Not adhering to common ABC Bank standards, terminology, and work products.

5 The ABC Bank Agile Delivery Process

Based on these needs, the basic approach at ABC Bank was to build on best industry practice, and create an agile delivery process that adapted well-known agile development methods to the ABC Bank context. In particular, as illustrated in Figure 2, the approach was to consider the approach in terms of a set of layers of concern with different scope and focus.

As illustrated in Figure 2, there are 4 layers of concern to the agile delivery approach at ABC Bank:

- *SCRUM*: The core development ideas of the agile delivery approach in ABC Bank are drawn from the SCRUM approach [5].. The limited existing experiences at ABC Bank were mostly involving use of SCRUM in small development projects, so it made sense to leverage those experiences and to use the main terminology from SCRUM as the basis on which to build. Hence, the ABC Bank agile approach reuses the familiar ideas of backlogs, sprints, scrums and the new roles of product owners and scrum masters, etc. This also opens the opportunity for ABC Bank to use a wide range of existing training materials and external consultants.

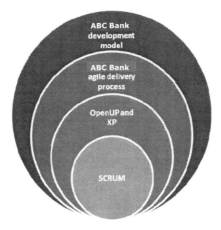

Fig. 2. The Layers of Concern for Agile delivery in ABC Bank

- *OpenUP and XP*: The core ideas of SCRUM are augmented with the broader view taken by OpenUP [6] and XP [7]. These approaches introduce a perspective based on agile practices that extend beyond development and into the broader software delivery life-cycle areas. In addition, this enabled easier adoption of agile ideas for those in ABC Bank who had a history with the Rational Unified Process (RUP), already widely deployed in the organization.

- *ABC Bank Agile Delivery Process*: The customization and packaging of the agile delivery process for ABC Bank was given its own identity (including a logo, graphics, posters, and so on). This encapsulated the specific choices of concepts, processes, and terminology for agile delivery and both expressed them in a vocabulary that was familiar, and also made them more readily identifiable to the wide range of stakeholders around ABC Bank that would be involved with the enterprise software delivery organization.

- *ABC Bank Development Model:* The final concern was to align the agile delivery processes with the pre-existing delivery model in use at ABC Bank. Not only were many projects already in-flight using existing development approaches, but also many new projects would be a blend of traditional and agile approaches. A clear relationship to the existing delivery approaches was essential.

The resulting ABC Bank agile delivery process was a balance of innovative agile techniques within the context of the traditional concepts and practices widely understood and in use in the organization. As illustrated in Figure 3, the core of the agile delivery process is the SCRUM-based ideas of backlogs and sprints, but extended in the ABC Bank delivery model.

In this delivery approach, the well-known agile techniques of backlogs and sprints are at the core. However, surrounding this is a further layer of product backlogs that help specify and define a product release. Then, at the outmost layer, the project ideas and project charter create the managed definition that is used by project management for project tracking.

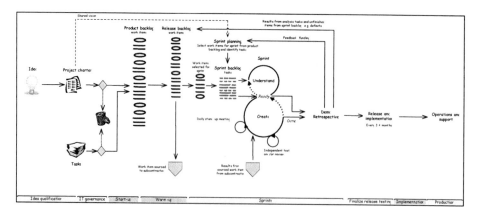

Fig. 3. The Key Elements of the ABC Bank Agile Delivery Process

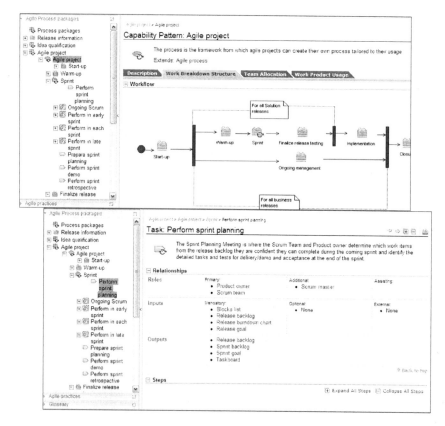

Fig. 4. An Example of the ABC Bank Agile Delivery Process

A specialized process authoring technology was used to formalize the capture, validation, and delivery of the process. This technology eased process authoring to ensure all elements had been captured effectively and consistently, and allowed validation for completeness and compatibility with the existing ABC Bank delivery processes. An example of the ABC Bank agile delivery process is shown in Figure 4.

The result, as shown in Figure 4, was a detailed process that extended their existing development process, delivered in a user-friendly common format for sharing across the organization. This level of detail proved to be invaluable in bringing common terminology and concepts to everyone involved in the program.

6 Implementing an Agile Delivery Process Workbench

Automation and support for the ABC Bank agile delivery process is essential to improve efficiency, ensure consistency, enable broad rollout to the distributed organization. The ABC Bank enterprise software delivery organization already had in place a fairly complete (and complex) tooling platform for software delivery. As illustrated in Figure 5, this platform already addressed several key areas of concern in software delivery (shown in green).

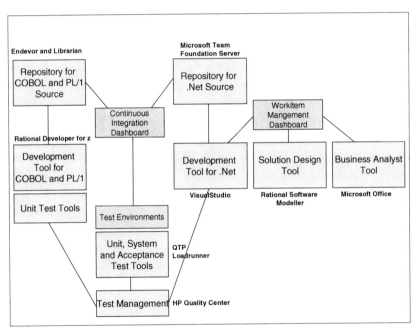

Fig. 5. Key Areas of Automation in the ABC Bank Enterprise Software Delivery Organization

Many potential candidates for additional tool support are possible. However, in-line with the incremental adoption and rollout philosophy at ABC Bank, a simplified approach to automation was sought. The primary addition for supporting the ABC Bank agile delivery process was found to be a collaborative application lifecycle management (CALM) workbench to automate team interactions and provide additional visibility into the projects and their progress [8]. The most critical additional automation targets were determined to be around work item management, continuous integration, and visibility via dashboards (shown in blue). These were considered the central coordinating elements to ensure the teams worked together effectively, communicated in real-time on the primary delivery artefacts, and improved process transparency to plan more effectively and quickly intervene when problems arise.

The rapid interactive nature of the ABC Bank agile delivery process encouraged particular attention on areas of inter-team collaboration and communication. Hence, the Rational Team Concert CALM workbench that was selected and implemented. This has provided:

- A lightweight team management platform that coordinates team members across the geographically distributed organization;

- Multi-platform support to match the heterogeneous development and delivery technologies at ABC Bank;

- Open interfaces and a simple integration approach to ease interconnection of the currently deployed tools;

- Support for agile techniques, and in particular a clear alignment with SCRUM practices.

As illustrated in Figure 6, Rational Team Concert was customized according to the ABC Bank agile delivery process. It is standard platform for all future agile delivery at ABC Bank.

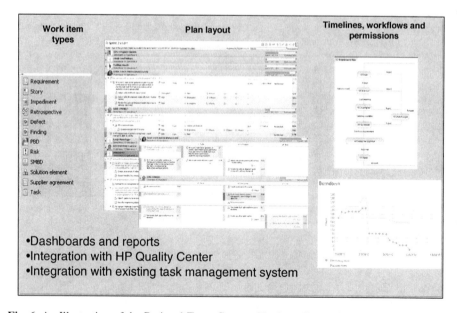

Fig. 6. An Illustration of the Rational Team Concert Platform Customized for Use in the ABC Bank Agile Delivery Process

7   Piloting the ABC Bank Agile Delivery Process

Designing and executing an effective piloting phase is particularly important in any organizational change. For the ABC Bank agile delivery process the pilot approach was carefully designed to gain as much feedback as possible across a range of different delivery scenarios, and to use the feedback to adapt the agile delivery process.

The most important initial choice was not to "invent" pilot scenarios, but to select a series of pilots from real projects that were planned or in early stages of delivery. The primary characteristics for suitable pilot project selection were defined based on the following 5 key areas:

- Project team characteristics;
- Project and task characteristics;
- Business engagement;
- Delivery or maintenance engagement;
- Stakeholder involvement and commitment.

A formal process of selection was made across different business divisions. Candidate projects were not difficult to find, as many different groups around the ABC Bank organization had either early agile development experiences, or had expressed early interest in trying out agile techniques. The result was that additional criteria were used to provide a broad set of experiences from the pilots. To achieve this, the pilots were filtered to ensure:

- Pilots covered different kind of project types and tasks (e.g. new development, extension of existing systems, maintenance, etc.);
- At least one pilot project included some degree of globally distributed team members;
- At least one pilot project included multiple teams;
- At least one pilot project involved co-operation with one or more internal and/or external vendors;
- Pilot projects cover a variety of different technology delivery platforms.

The selection and execution of 8 pilot projects involving over 100 people took place over a 9 month period, with continual monitoring and adjustment to the ABC Bank agile delivery process as a result of on-going feedback and analysis.

The main lessons from the pilot activities can be summarized as:

- The start up activities for pilot teams proved to be complex and challenging. The first pilots gave very poor feedback on the initial support they received. This resulted in a great deal more investment in coaching, education, and task transition in the early pilot stages.
- The key new role in many pilots was the Product Owner. This role was pivotal in providing a bridge between the development and project management teams. It was essential to have the right person in this task (based on skills, mindset, and attitude), and customize their training effectively.

- The pilot teams had a great deal of trouble in moving from a schedule-driven activity view of their work to one focused on work items (stories) and tasks. The shift in thinking was difficult to adopt for many people.

- Project planning and estimation altered radically, and estimation using points rather than hours required guidance and practice.

- Providing the right levels of transparency into the pilots was a difficult balance. It was important to allow the pilots some privacy to learn and experiment, but providing management information and status summaries quickly became a priority.

- Traditional project management focus had been on artifacts such as work breakdown structures and Gantt charts. This needed reinterpretation to reflect the agile approach. This was a big step for many in the organization where traditional project accounting practices had been in place for a long time.

- The enablement concept needed to be very well structured to provide the right information to the right roles at the right time. The effort required here was initially underestimated. An expert in organizational improvement was brought into the team to help redesign the enablement approach in a more structured way.

- The pilots were initially defined and managed in isolation, when much of the expected value of the agile approach was intended to be across the organization. After some readjustment, common terminology and work products were defined across all project types were critical to realize synergy and provide flexibility across the pilots taking place in enterprise software delivery organization.

- Effective rollout to the offshore teams in India was essential to demonstrate the wider applicability of the agile delivery process, and to understand the impact of an offshore model on the techniques.

8 Measuring Success

During the pilot phase, one of the key challenges that needed to be addressed concerned the best ways to measure the improvements that were expected from the ABC Bank agile delivery process. As in most organizations, in ABC Bank the theme of measurement and metrics is both complex and politically-charged. Deciding on an appropriate measurement scheme is essential, but comes with many challenges.

The decision in this case was to adopt a simple, 2 dimensional scheme for measuring the ABC Bank agile delivery project. This scheme was based on a broad range of experiences in other organizations adopting agile approaches.

As illustrated in Figure 7, two dimensions of measurement were used for the ABC Bank agile delivery process; Business-related and agile-related. The business-related measures were intended to be clear signals to the business owners that the adoption of an agile process was helping to deliver more software, more quickly, and with better quality. The agile-related measures were to be used within the agile projects and by the enterprise software delivery organization to manage and govern those projects.

	Business-related	**Agile-related**
Cycle time reduction	Time spent from project initiation to delivery of first increment Time spent from project initiation to project closure	Sprint velocity Blocking work items
Quality	Defects (severity 1 and 2) in production per 100 FPs	Defect trend
Continuous optimisation	Process maturity level	Adoption of agile practices
Productivity	Function points per man year	Sprint burndown chart Release burndown chart

Fig. 7. The Measurement Schema Used for the ABC Bank Agile Delivery Process

In addition, an informal survey approach for periodically checking on the "agile team pulse" was found to be particularly useful in regard to fine-tuning the ABC Bank agile delivery process. As illustrated in Figure 7, although this is a relatively simple and limited mechanism to monitor status of the projects, it gave immediate feedback if the projects were beginning to experience unnecessary challenges and issues.

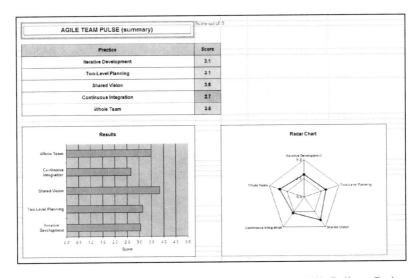

Fig. 8. A Summary of an Agile Team Pulse for a ABC Bank Agile Delivery Project

In Figure 8 we show a simple summary of an Agile Team Pulse for a ABC Bank agile delivery project. Behind each of the practice areas shown is a more detailed survey and analysis that allows greater insights in the current team perceptions.

9 Roll Out Principles

The experiences from the pilot projects were the initial steps in a broader adoption of agile delivery practices in ABC Bank. The aim of the rollout was an accelerated approach to the introduction of agile practices as broadly as possible throughout the enterprise software delivery organization. Hence, given the characteristics of ABC Bank and it history, several important rollout principles were established.

First, it was decided to prioritize system maintenance projects ahead of new development projects, but at the same time acknowledge that there is a certain "window of opportunity" for projects to switch into new practices that must be accommodated (e.g. once a project is approved and about to be initiated, or during transition of the project from delivery into production). Given the high investment in maintaining existing systems, the target distribution was two thirds of the projects adopting the agile delivery process to be carrying out system maintenance tasks.

Second, agile practice roll out should be carried across the organisation and thus not focused too heavily in one area or department. This broad approach was not only to gain wider experience of the adoption, but also to limit risk and resource bottlenecks that can occur with over concentration in some groups.

Third, it was clear that the experience from the pilots suggested that "agile readiness" and competences should be a primary determinant of when to introduce the ABC Bank agile delivery process into a project. Without an agile mindset and required skills present among all (potential) participants and stakeholders, the risks of failure increase dramatically. Similarly, essential coordination with other ongoing initiatives that impact the project must be taken into account.

To affect a broad, and accelerated rollout of the ABC Bank agile delivery process required a clear model for on-boarding new projects and supporting their transition to the new practices. The rollout model created consists of a set of enablement "trains" that start on a periodic basis. A number of "tickets" are available for each train, and to obtain a ticket required that the project passes the readiness gate.

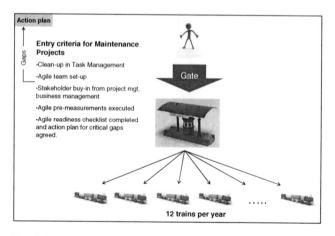

Fig. 9. The Rollout Process for ABC Bank Agile Delivery Process

As illustrated in Figure 9, a series of criteria is established to understand if the project is ready to take its place on the next agile delivery process enablement train. If the project is considered ready, a seat on the train is made available, and detailed planning for introduction of the ABC Bank agile delivery process can begin. If not, then an action plan is created to help the project prepare for re-validation.

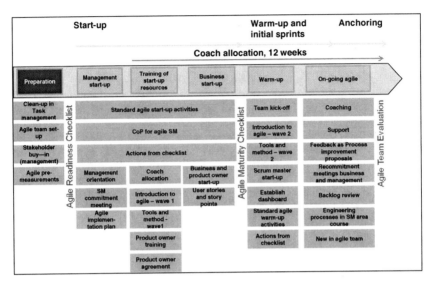

Fig. 10. A View of the Structured Enable Approach used at ABC Bank

Perhaps the most critical step in the rollout approach for the projects, are the initial enablement activities. As a result of the pilot experiences a well-structured approach to enablement was established, as illustrated in Figure 10.

As illustrated in Figure 10, there is a structured enablement program for new projects that enter the ABC Bank agile delivery process. This covers the life of the project from start up to delivery, and provides support for each of the roles needed in the process with clear measurement activities to assess progress through the process.

10 Lessons Learned

From the initial 8 pilots, a broad roll out of the ABC Bank agile delivery process in now taking place. Already over 300 people are actively engaged in delivering projects at ABC Bank using this agile delivery process, with plans for over 20 new projects and 60 maintenance teams with more than 500 new people to be enabled and productive in these approaches over the next year.

We can summarize the main lessons from this experience as follows:

- Progress requires strong management support. Given the financial and political pressures that exist, the work would have struggled for success without visibility and support from the CIO and his team.

- Intensive coaching and support for new projects is essential during the first 4-6 months. Cutting corners in these areas is very easy, but the longer term implications are severe.

- Take a broad view of enablement and awareness. In particular, training must be specialized for the development teams, business stakeholders, and management executives. Specifically, awareness training for upper-level management must also be included.

- Commitment to the adoption and rollout is critical. There will be challenges that must be addresses that require a level of faith and determination to succeed.

The focus of the agile adoption approach at ABC Bank has been on simplicity, incrementality, and structured delivery. While in practice the adoption has not been easy, it has been effective. Several lessons have been learned, in particular:

- The challenges related to adopting agile approaches are well known, however interpreting those approaches in a specific organizational context remains challenging. The relative importance of these challenges and how they should be addressed is differently for each organization. Careful customization is required. Furthermore, piloting is the best way to identify where to focus. Choose the pilots carefully, and use the feedback wisely.

- Automation helps address some of the most important challenges in scaling the rollout of agile delivery in a geographically distributed organization. A common collaborative agile workbench was an essential platform for teams to communicate and coordinate activities.

- A structured enablement concept allows for large scale deployment of a common agile delivery process in a complex, multi-platform, multi-project context.

11 Summary

Greater flexibility and time-to-market is driving many organizations toward development techniques that optimize their team interactions, and their connection with stakeholders. The resulting agile development approaches are being widely discussed and seeing broad adoption across the software industry.

In this paper we have focused on a broad view of agility as it applies to enterprise software delivery. In particular, we have examined how "agility at scale" can be realized, and provided practical guidance on adapting agility in complex enterprise software delivery organizations. The detailed illustration has emphasized the importance of many key factors in scaling agile practices for enterprise delivery.

As with many enterprises, ABC Bank has made a major commitment to agile delivery practices as a primary way to address the challenges it faces in delivering more effective enterprise systems to its business stakeholders on a more frequent basis. Furthermore, the focus for ABC Bank has been to address the challenges it faces where it is spending most of its investment effort and labor cost – in system maintenance projects.

The results have been very positive. The initial 8 pilots were able to show improvements in productivity and quality of delivered systems. They worked more closely with their business stakeholders, and created an atmosphere of mutual trust that increased their effectiveness. Roll out of the approach across the organization is in-flight, with over 300 people already using the ABC Bank agile delivery process, and more then 500 more planned for the next year.

Acknowledgements

The work described in this paper draws heavily on work by Christian Bornfeld and his team, and builds on ideas and insights from Peter Eeles, Niels Jacobsen, Annette Dalgaard, and others at IBM.

References

1. The Agile Manifesto, http://agilemanifesto.org/
2. Martin, R.: Agile Software Development. Prentice-Hall, Englewood Cliffs (2002)
3. Highsmith, J.: Agile Software Development Ecosystems. Addison Wesley, Reading (2002)
4. Kruchten, P.: Contextualizing Agile Software Development. EuroSPI, Grenoble, France, EuroSPI.net, pp. 6.1-12, (September 2010),
   http://www.ece.ubc.ca/pubs/kruchten2010contextualizing
5. Cohn, M.: Succeeding with Agile: Software Dev. using Scrum. Addison Wesley, Reading (2009)
6. An Introduction to OpenUP: The Open Unified Process (August 2007),
   http://www.eclipse.org/epf/general/OpenUP.pdf
7. Extreme Programming Pocket Guide. O'Reilly, Sebastopol (2003)
8. Collaborative Application Lifecycle Management with IBM Rational Products, IBM Redbook (2009),
   http://www.redbooks.ibm.com/abstracts/sg247622.html

A Never Ending Battle for Continuous Improvement

J.J. Zang

200 E Randolph St # 2500
Chicago, IL 60601-6501, USA
jzang@thoughtworks.com

Abstract. This paper takes the readers through a real project life path to show what went well and what didn't. The paper first lays out all the pain points of the project. Then it describes how the team has successfully handled each of the issues. The paper doesn't stop here. Instead, it digs further by taking off the veil of success as the project looks at and focuses on the areas needing improvement. The paper elaborates on how to squeeze out nonvalue-added waste through value stream mapping. It also discusses the importance of Agile "transfer", customer redefinition as well as running a true iterative iteration.

Keywords: FFM (Field Force Management); *Kaban* board; *Andon*; Push Scheduling; Pull Scheduling; Trust; Transfer; Iteration; Agile; Value Stream Map; *Kaizen*.

1 Introduction

When I was assigned to FFM project (Field Force Management) for one of the biggest international telecom companies in March, 2010, I was told I was the 7th project manager for the team and for the project. The team on the ground was completely lost and morale had hit record low. Before I agreed to take over the project, I interviewed the core team members and also spent a couple of days shadowing with each of them while they were working. The challenges the team had been facing immediately surfaced:

1. There was no scope defined
2. There was no measurement of the team capability
3. There was no "*Kanban* board"[1] (Story card board)
4. "Push scheduling"[2] mentality was pervasive
5. The trust of business stakeholders in the team was minimal
6. Most of the team members were junior with little experience and exposure to Agile methodology

---

[1] *Kanban* means "card". *Kanban board* is used to track each feature as it flows through the work flow. A *Kaban board* is usually set up by having one column for each step in the workflow. *Kaban cards*, used to signal that work needs to be done, are put in the column on the *Kanban board* that represents their current position in the workflow.

[2] Push scheduling manages systems by "pushing" a predetermined plan to the operating environment and tracking task completion against that plan.

A. Sillitti et al. (Eds.): XP 2011, LNBIP 77, pp. 282–289, 2011.

1.1 Changes Made

As a team, the first thing we did was try to understand the business purpose of the project. The FFM project was intended to reduce appointment scheduling windows, which would satisfy the call-in subscribers, as well as optimize the daily planning which would maximize the use of technician's time and save millions of gas dollars for the telecom company. Once we settled on the business goal, the team worked with our business proxy to flush out high level features. We went a little further by breaking feature sets into stories with just enough descriptions and assumptions. Keep in mind, we didn't write detailed stories and acceptance tests at that time simply because we had limited information and it was too early to put all the content into stories. Detailed analysis of each feature and story was delayed until immediately before it was developed. The reason we tried to get to the stories with some level of description was to help our developers come up with rough estimates which in return helped our business proxy prioritize the features with cost in mind. The list of feature sets with highest priority was the backlog for our first release (see Fig. 1). This list was not a surprise to the business since the proxy worked with the team through the whole process.

Epic Story ID	Epic Story Title	Sto ry ID	Story Title	Estimation Assumptions	Estimate s Pts	Priority
A	CSR/TSR able to create an install (work order)	63	Rep able to select crew in order to trigger appointment scheduleing window pops up	I. Scheduling window is empty	2	High
		188	Rep able to select an appt from the app list	I. Assuming work order ID is available II. This story also include sending the error message back to UD	3	High
		247	Rep able to confirm appoint in point server (Call API to create service order)	I. Save the data from SOA layer to Point Server II. Related to story #69, #63	5	High
B	Batch synchronization work orders between PointServe and CBS	405	FFM able to create engine to parse the definition file		5	High
		406	FFM able to read the data file for work orders		3	High
		407	import missing work orders to PointServe	I. Reuse the "create work order"	3	High
		598	Monitor batch imports to PointServe	I. Added at May 26th - Lupi email II. Split from #407	2	High
		408	Remove cancelled work orders from PointServe		2	High
	Batch synchronization service calls between PointServe and CBS	409	FFM able to read the data file for service calls		3	High
		410	Import missing service calls to PointServer		2	High
		411	Remove cancelled service calls from PointServe		2	High

Fig. 1. Feature set and story backlog with estimation and priority

Next, the team tried some experiments to corroborate the viability of architectural design, technical approach, and some large estimation numbers. The team also had a couple of iterations[3] to understand the team's capability, in another word, the velocity

---

[3] The duration of each iteration was two weeks.

per iteration. We set up a "*Kanban board*" to track each story as it flowed through the workflow[4]. We had one column for each step in the workflow. (See the picture below). Noticeably, this was repeated and iterative: almost for each iteration, the team picked technical cards such as spikes, technical debts along with feature stories.

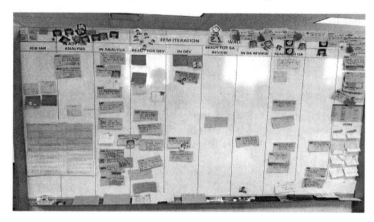

From the very beginning, we instilled the "Pull Scheduling"[5] concept into the team and worked around this concept. We had a very clear constraint – Time to market. We had to satisfy subscribers, technicians, as well as ultimately the telecom company itself from a cost saving perspective at the end of our delivery by September of 2011. The team pulled stories from the list in each iteration based on team capacity and capability. Meanwhile, our backlog list was dynamic in terms of the items in the list, the priority and the estimation based on continuous business feedback. Most important, the list with priority and estimation was frequently and clearly communicated and presented to all stakeholders.

1.2 Outcomes

What completely changed the attitude of business towards the team was our small demo at the end of each iteration. We usually demonstrated our achievements during our IPM (Iteration Planning Meeting). However, when the team found out the business couldn't make it every time, we videotaped our demo and distributed to our stakeholders. This not only won their trust quickly but more important gathered feedback from our business on a continuous basis. It took three months for the team to finish all the required features. With steady velocity and without overtime, the team actually finished the back log one iteration ahead of time. Meanwhile, the team grew more self-organizing with some leadership guidance. Everything looked good and I felt proud. You may also start wondering that you have heard this kind of story many times and what was new about it. To be honest, I thought our project was a big success until we started deployment. Suddenly I realized what we achieved was just a small corner of the iceberg, of which we had missed a huge part.

---

[4] Mary and Tom Poppendieck, *Leading Lean Software Development: Results Are Not The Point*, 2009, p. 123.

[5] Pull scheduling manages systems by managing the queue of items that should happen next; Team usually pulls an item off the top of the queue when planning work.

2 Continuous Improvement

We had 9 branches in total for the nationwide release. We adopted an incremental rollout approach due to the constraints such as the size of the branch, the readiness of the branch and the availability of rollout resources. But the main reason was we wanted to reduce our risk by first rolling out to a relatively smaller branch and then continue to the next branch based on the user feedback from the previous one. Believe it or not, it took us THREE month, equivalent to our development time, to roll out to the first branch, then another two months to the second branch. The team worked overtime and got burnt out quickly. We couldn't help wondering: What went wrong? What did we miss? But more important, what did we learn?

2.1 Too Much Waste in Deployment Process Flow

Value stream map is a diagnostic tool frequently used in lean initiatives. It draws a timeline from the moment when a customer places an order to the point when the product or service is provided to the customer. Value stream maps always begin and end with a customer. In our case, the clock started on the value stream map when customer features were submitted and the clock stopped when our product was successfully launched. Let's take a look at our value stream map below (see Fig. 2).

As you can see in Fig. 2, the process cycle efficiency is only 33%[6]. Only 1 week of the 2 months should be needed for pre production and production environment set up. Setting up environments was done by a separate infrastructure team who served more than 20 internal projects at the same time. They had different priorities than ours. Additionally, within the infrastructure team, they had different sub teams in charge of different area of set up, such as database installation, server installation, load balancer set up, and multi-casting among servers, etc. Problems fell into the cracks between sub-teams, hard-earned knowledge evaporated at handovers. This even caused cascading waste when the team tried to install the vendor application in pre-production due to the wrong configuration set up during environment set up. Before we started deployment in production, the team needed to do a final verification with integration testing of all pieces in pre-production. This took 2 weeks instead of 2 days. It was mainly because we had only one pre-production environment shared by more than 5 different teams. Instability and unavailability of the pre production environment constantly caused delay of integration testing and performance testing, with 80% waste.

Lessons Learnt: We all know dependencies are bad and that is why we have been trying our best to get rid of architecture dependencies, code dependencies and story dependencies. This holds true with team dependences too. With team dependencies, it will be so difficult to deliver even a small feature set since it requires a large amount of communication and coordination among teams. The complexity of the communication adds time and increases the likelihood of error, and the added overhead cost makes small incremental releases almost impossible. Decoupling is often the approach we use to minimize technical dependencies. This applies to teams too. Teams work better

---

[6] Process cycle efficiency (percentage) = elapsed time spent adding value/total time.

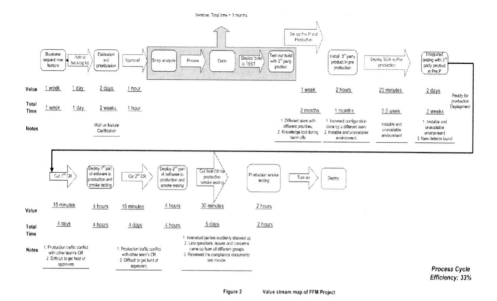

Figure 2   Value stream map of FFM Project

Fig. 2. This demonstrates the process path our software product traversed from the time when customer submitted request till the point when our product was successfully launched

if they can operate independently, without significant dependencies on other teams. Building cross-functional teams by pulling some folks from each team and embedding them in this cross-function team would help in mitigating the boundary-spanning problems.

2.2 Transfer

The root cause of the waste in the figure above was the segregation of cross function teams. Instead of working as one team to deliver the product, different teams worked on different parts or steps through the deployment process. For example, we had an infrastructure team in charge of setting up various environments for us. We then had a network team responsible for setting up routing, multicasting and load balancing. We had a third team in charge of setting up databases in all non-production environments. We had a fourth team similar to the second and the third except that they were only accountable for production environments. Different teams had their own priorities which were not necessarily aligned with each other. Each extra layer of handovers caused knowledge to be lost. But what struck me was the comment from one team lead, "Just for you to know, we don't work with Agile methodology. Because we don't think it would apply to infrastructure teams. So don't expect us to work the same way as your team does". I like how Mike Cohen put in terms of Scrum/Agile adoption, "I visualize Scrum as rocket. Pushing that rocket forward is the power of its engines. But pulling it back are the forces of gravity. If the rocket is able to push far enough, it can enter into orbit. But if it cannot, it will inevitably get pulled back to earth, right where it started"[7].

---

[7] Mike Cohn, *Succeeding With Agile: Software Development Using Scrum*, 2009, p. 37.

Lessons Learnt: The implications of Agile must be pushed far enough into other parts of the organization so that the entire team effort is not pulled back by organizational gravity. It is a relatively easy job to gain acceptance for Agile among developers, QAs (Quality Assurance), project managers, database developers, user experience designers, analysts and so on. But it is impossible for a development team to remain Agile on its own to make it successful. If the implication of using Agile is not transferred to other departments, organizationally inertia from those departments will eventually stall and kill the whole team effort.

2.3 Customer Redefinition

Customer focus is one critical Agile concept since it spans technology boundaries. When we jot down the value stream maps of our development process, we look at customer need from the time a customer has a request till that need is resolved. We step through our process that request must traverse and how long it takes to satisfy the customer. However, focusing only on the end customer is not enough. If we look at the pathway of the stream value map, we will see customers are not only the ones who pay for the system, who use the system; customers are also the ones who support the system and who may derive value from the system. When we had our retrospective after the first branch rollout, more than 50% of the feedback was about training and deployment support improvements. On the other hand, if we zoom in on the value stream map, we will notice every team on the value stream has its own immediate "customer" and "supplier". For example, the infrastructure team was our supplier in terms of providing different environments for us. At the same time, we were "customer" to the EAS team (Enterprise application team) who deployed our code to pre-production after our test. On the downstream side, we had been constantly struggling with what support our "immediate" customer (e.g. EAS team) needed from us and their definition of deployable and quality build. On the upstream side, we accepted the "not ready for use" environment with multicasting issues and then struggled to figure out what went wrong at a much later stage when we started installing our software into pre production.

Lessons Learnt: Traditional customer definition is limited to project sponsors, stakeholders or end users. We need to redefine customer to include the ones who support, maintain or derive value from the system. In our case, the support team, the training team, and the transformation teams are also our customers. Including these customers will give us a complete boundary-spanning view of our work. In addition, as complexity increases, cross-functional teams sometimes are not enough. A single team will not be able to handle the complexity, thus handovers are inevitable. With every handover, it is important to clarify the immediate customer's needs and flag whenever there is an issue.

2.4 Run a True Iterative Iteration

As you may have noticed in our value stream map or story board, our cards were labeled as "complete" in each iteration when testing was done. But the testing was done in our TEST environment, which was not an integrated testing environment. This caused huge risks and wastes at later stages. First, this left a tremendous workload of integration testing with other teams when we moved to pre production. New defects, impacts on other teams, and missing functionalities all surfaced. Second, due to the unavailability of an end to end testing environment, QAs could not have a clear load lineup for UAT verification testing till pre production. New findings, user feedback and edge scenarios all jumped onboard. The price we paid for not having a true iterative iteration was big – it took us 2 weeks instead of 2 days for our integration testing before our production deployment.

Lessons Learnt: A true iterative iteration means the development team should strive to produce a releasable application. Software needs to go through a thorough system testing including such things as end-to-end scenario testing, stress testing, UAT (User Acceptance Test), etc. to make sure that the code is ready for release. It is a mistake to delay all staging activities until the system is ready for release. It is risky not to pull the "*Andon*"[8] cord to "stop-the-line" if a true iterative iteration can't be achieved. In our case, we should have exposed the test environment problem at an earlier stage and called for attention and action instead of hoping to chase away problems with "work around".

3 Summary

Most companies are aware that continuous improvement is critical but few practice it as hard as Toyota. Feeling the pain is easy, seeing the problems is hard, but taking actions towards them is even harder. In most people's eyes, our project was a successful one since the development was completed ahead of schedule and the release was on time. But we know what we missed and where we could improve. We would like to share our lessons, our experience and our journey with others so we can all "Change for the better". Software development is a never ending battle for continuous improvement.

References

1. Poppendieck, M., Poppendieck, T.: Implementing Lean Software Development: From Concept To Cash (2006)
2. Poppendieck, M., Poppendieck, T.: Leading Lean Software Development: Results Are Not The Point (2009)
3. Cohn, M.: Succeeding With Agile: Software Development Using Scrum (2009)

Appendix

See the value stream map of FFM project on the next page.

---

[8] An *andon* is a portable Japanese lantern made of paper stretched over a bamboo framework. Toyota used the word *andon* to name the cord that worker could pull to "stop-the-line". See Mary and Tom Poppendieck, *Implementing Lean Software Development: From Concept To Cash*, 2006, p. 139.

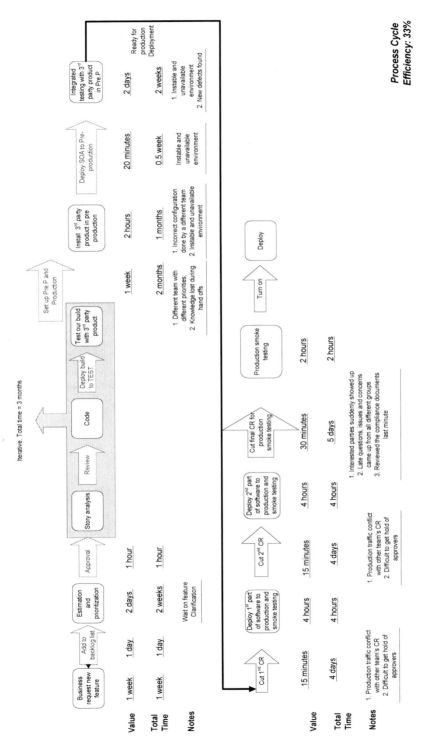

Figure 2   **Value stream map of FFM Project**

Process Cycle Efficiency: 33%

Agile Technical Management of Industrial Contracts: Scrum Development of Ground Segment Software at the European Space Agency

Rui Santos[1], Felix Flentge[1], Marc-Elian Begin[2], and Vicente Navarro[3]

[1] ESOC / ESA, Robert-Bosch-Str. 5, D-64293 Darmstadt, Germany
{Ruis.Santos,Felix.Flentge}@esa.int
[2] SixSq, c/o Jawer, Route de Pré-Bois 20, 1215, Geneva, Switzerland
meb@sixsq.com
[3] ESAC / ESA, E-28691 Villanueva de la Cañada, Madrid, Spain
Vicente.Navarro@esa.int

Abstract. ESOC[1] (the European Space Agency's Operation Centre) is experimenting with Agile and Scrum methodologies in its quest for improving productivity, enhancing project visibility and control, reducing time to market, improve software quality and increasing user satisfaction. In this article we present lessons learned from applying Agile in general and Scrum in particular to a number of projects, from applying a few Agile best practices to full Scrum. ESOC has traditionally developed its software using a waterfall life cycle mostly under Firm Fixed Price contracts, in this context using Agile brings challenges from project management, contracts and quality control perspective. Using a coaching approach, delivered by SixSq a Swiss-based company specialised in agile and Scrum coaching and development, the organisation has managed to accelerate its integration of Scrum, including industrial teams developing the software, and already yields positive results which are promising for the future.

Keywords: Agile Software Development, Coaching, Scrum, Firm Fixed Price contracts.

1 Introduction

This paper summarises the activities at ESOC (the European Space Agency's Operation Centre) to apply Scrum [1] to a number of projects developing software for ground segment systems. These activities started to address challenges ESOC faces with respect to productivity, time-to-market, costs, schedule and user satisfaction. ESOC has traditionally used waterfall-based life cycle to develop its complex software, including early and over specification of requirements. This lead in most cases to poor software quality or irrelevant set of implemented functionalities. Within the Agile ecosystem, Scrum was therefore selected to combat such issues, since Scrum provides a clear framework regarding project management, including the

---

[1] http://www.esa.int/esaMI/ESOC/

A. Sillitti et al. (Eds.): XP 2011, LNBIP 77, pp. 290–305, 2011.
© Springer-Verlag Berlin Heidelberg 2011

handling and expression of functional requirements as well as the relationship between customer and provider. However using Agile in this context brings cultural and organisational challenges. Further, these projects were executed using the Firm Fixed Price contracts where the provider comes from industry, while the customer is ESOC. Following from preliminary exploration of selected Agile best practices, a group at ESOC decided to manage a few projects using Scrum to a fuller extent. To facilitate this exploration of Scrum, a dedicated Agile coaching and consultancy project was setup with the goal of providing coaching to key ESOC staff, in order for them, the project and the contractor's team to avoid/correct pitfalls and leverage Scrum to its full potential, yet responding to the contractual constraints of ESOC's current environment. In order to make the project more effective, the key staff were coached in real-life situation, focusing on main Scrum events: planning and demo meetings, as well as the production of key artefacts such as the Product Backlog.

The paper will shortly introduce the general approach at ESOC to Ground Segment Software Developments and briefly describes the expectations for applying Scrum software development. We report on the initial attempts to integrate Agile techniques in two projects. Following from this initial and successful Agile exploration, ESOC noticed that different approaches to Agile development could be taken. In order to harmonise across projects and groups a common base was deemed necessary which lead the group to focus on Scrum since it focuses on the customer/provider relationship which seemed best suited to the ESOC context.

The introduction of Scrum was facilitated by 'live' coaching of selected Technical Officers at ESOC (ESOC staff responsible to individual projects). The paper will describe this coaching, give details on the projects that were coached and the experiences gained. Lessons learned from this experience are summarised in a dedicated section before the paper's conclusions.

2 Approach to Ground Segment Software Development

Traditionally, Ground Segment Software Development at ESOC is constrained to be based on the ECSS (European Cooperation for Space Standards) standards [1]. The aim of this process is to provide the right balance across the four aspects governing the software development lifecycle: Scope, Schedule, Cost and Quality. Up to now, ECSS has been used in a waterfall manner, following distinct development phases that end with formal reviews:

- Requirements Engineering, ending with the Software Requirements Review
- Architecture and Interface Design, ending with the Preliminary Design Review
- Design and Implementation, ending with the Critical Design Review
- Provisional and Final Acceptance Phases, ending with the Provisional Acceptance and the Final Acceptance Reviews

Sometimes, a Warranty Phase is added after the Final Acceptance. All major software developments are performed by external companies. There are two basic types of contracts:

- Firm Fix Price (FFP): fixed scope, cost and quality assuming risks in schedule.
- Firm Unit Price (FUP): fix schedule and quality assuming risks in cost and/or scope.

Usually a hybrid approach is adopted with the core of the work being done under FFP conditions with a small 'Flexibility Work Package' to cover minor changes introduced in the course of the project (usually around 10-15% of the contract volume). Despite a number of success stories, projects suffer at different degrees from requirements creep, a high management overhead, over engineered solutions, inadequate quality, long time-to-market and suboptimal user satisfaction.

Analysis of the root causes of these problems led to the identification of the following key areas for improvement in our software development process:

- Better understanding and capture of the user requirements
- Stronger involvement of end users
- Better communication with the contractors and improved visibility of the project status and measure of technical realisation
- Improved change management of software functionality
- Better risk management

The need to improve on these areas led a group at ESOC working on Ground System Software to explore the benefits that Agile in general and then Scrum in particular could bring compared to the traditional waterfall that ESOC has been using thus far.

3 Initial Adoption of Agile Techniques

This section reports on early attempts to introduce Agile best practices in waterfall projects. This early experimentation and its successes formed the basis for experimenting with 'full Scrum' and departing in selected projects from the waterfall model.

3.1 Project A – Small, Low-Risk Study

Prior to the execution of the coaching project that led to a fuller application of Scrum, ESOC explored integrating a subset of Agile practices. For this, a low-risk project was selected. The selected project was a web-based system for data-warehousing and reporting of software project management data. The web based nature of this project helped to provide continuous access to the development environment with no overhead. This access was used to support continuous reviews of the status of the project from a technical and functional point of view.

For this project, the following key changes were introduced:

- Communication: weekly meetings via teleconference / videoconference
- Visibility: direct access to the development environment (Web based app)
- Adaptability to change: incremental development and prioritisation. This caused some back and forth traffic.

Following these simple but effective changes, the results were promising. The project was delivered on time, on schedule and 90% of the requirements were delivered. Despite not being able to deliver all requirements, customer satisfaction was very high. High customer satisfaction was achieved delivering all key customer requirements even those added at a later stage in the development cycle.

One of the ideas explored with this was to split projects into two phases:

- Phase 1: FFP Contract for Requirements Engineering + Architecture and Interface Design + Functional Validation (based on a prototype)
- Phase 2) FFP Contract for Coding and Implementation + Strong Validation

While this change does not match Agile practices it has the benefit of being compatible with existing contractual practices at the European Space Agency (ESA).

The first phase focuses on consolidating the requirements baseline while using intensively prototyping with mock-ups, diagrams, etc. This phase can adapt easily to changes in an inexpensive way. The second phase starts with a better understanding of the work to be done. In some cases, for intensive user interface systems, all of the interface can be prototyped. This phase then focuses on the implementation of the requirements baseline adapting to changes through a series of iterations.

3.2 Project B – Full Ground System Software Development Project

Based on the relative success of small projects adopting Agile practises the decision was made to introduce them in a production Ground Segment Project. Communication was first talked with the introduction of several types of meetings ensuring the continuous involvement of all stakeholders. There were a higher number of technical meetings than management ones. The User representatives attended all functional related meetings. These meetings were supported by data coming from several tools deployed for this project (DOORS, Mercury Quality Center, etc). These tools supported the improvement of communication and the visibility of the status of the software to all project stakeholders. Improvement of change management was supported by all these changes as well. Functional changes were integrated from the regular feedback provided by project stakeholders.

As depicted in Figure 1 showing the amount of software change requests (SCRs) and fixes (software problem reports - SPRs) over the weeks, modifications were managed on a regular basis. This represents a clear difference with respect to the more formal approach based on a few review milestones.

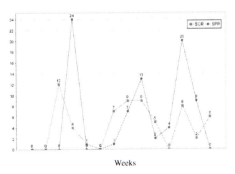

Weeks

Fig. 1. Changes and bug fixes for Project B

As a result of all these measures the project ran smoothly from the beginning with clearer visibility of schedule, cost and quality variables. Figure 2 show plots tracking cost and schedule evolution for the project. On the quality side the project also achieved the required levels of quality for its associated criticality level. Including passing a quality audit and featuring a high percentage of test coverage and number of unit tests (relative to the lines of code). Overall, the project was delivered on schedule and according to the quality requirements.

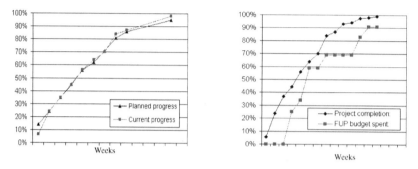

Fig. 2. Cost and schedule tracking for Project B

4   Applying Scrum to Ground Segment Software Development

In this section we briefly introduce our understanding and implementation of Scrum, followed by an overview of the coaching activities that took place to better integrate Scrum into real projects. These projects are then described, focusing on the impact from Scrum on the management of these, which will form the basis for the lessons learned section.

4.1   Scrum Overview

While the Agile eco-system is rich and diverse (e.g. Extreme Programming - XP, Scrum, Lean Development, Kanban, Core Principals), ESOC chose to focus on Scrum. Scrum has a clear model and is prescriptive of the dynamics between the customer and the provider, the emergence of functional specification (i.e. Product Backlog) and the rhythm of development (i.e. sprints). While other methods would also apply, such as XP (as well as derivatives like Test-driven development - TDD), we focused our effort on the Scrum part of the development process.

The main reasons for choosing Scrum have been:

- Client centric approach encouraging convergence towards fulfilling the real needs
- Improved project visibility
- Promotes trust between all stakeholders
- Controlled incorporation of changes
- Continuous inspection and improvement of the process
- Higher software quality
- Simpler solutions, easier to maintain and evolve
- More predictable delivery of functionality

While a complete description of Agile and Scrum is outside the scope of this paper, the following explains the main artefacts and processes involved in ESOC's implementation of Scrum. In Scrum, each iteration (called 'sprint') starts with a planning meeting. During this meeting, high-priority requirements are reviewed, analysed, decomposed into tasks and selected for the next sprint. The duration of each sprint was roughly four weeks. Each sprint ends with a sprint review, composed of two events: a retrospective and a demo. The objective of the retrospective is to review the past sprint's performance, with a focus on emulating what was particularly effective, while eliminating impediments (i.e. obstacles). For the demo, the team assembles and deploys the software and presents the implementation of the requirements selected for the sprint. Different stakeholders can be invited to this event, if necessary, including for example end-users. This is an important generator of feedback and insights, which can be fed into the requirements, and provide new data for prioritisation.

The projects that were executed and reported in this paper were FFP, where the contractor was requested to commit to the price based on a functional specification, using tabular functional, and often very detailed, requirements. This offered a real challenge since Agile in general and Scrum in particular require that functional requirements be expressed in the form of user stories. A translation effort was therefore required to build the user stories that would populate the Product Backlog. Further, since the contract was written such that the contractor's obligation was on the successful implementation of the requirements, traceability had to be maintained between the user stories and the requirements.

Scrum is often deployed inside a single organization. This model therefore requires adaptation to the reality of ESOC, with ESOC being the customer and industry providing the team. In this case, the ESOC Technical Officer takes the role of the Product Owner (PO). Further, for this to work at ESOC, the pattern of the Product Owner Proxy is recommended, whereby the consortium leader deploys a proxy of the PO. This person, who should be highly available, is then the unique interlocutor for the team, while forwarding back and forth communication asynchronously with the real PO. This is important to offload the PO, who is typically involved in several projects in parallel. It is however important to agree on the respective responsibility of the PO and the PO Proxy, especially in terms or Product Backlog ownership. There are currently no known hard rules regarding the distribution of responsibility. We should therefore explore further this aspect of Scrum in the ESOC context.

4.2 Coaching

The coaching project was designed to provide three live coaching sessions of two days duration over a period of five months. The coaching service was provided by SixSq. SixSq[2] is a small company, based in Geneve, Switzerland, specialized in agile and Scrum coaching, training and software development, as well as software process automation. Three ESA staff Technical Officers were coached. They were chosen since they were all managing a project using Agile. Each trip focused on a single individual, with shorter follow-up meetings with the other two.

The trips were timed to coincide with one of the important milestones of the project the staff were managing. For project C and D, trips coincided with a sprint demo and the planning meetings.

---

[2] www.sixsq.com

The pattern for each trip was to cut the two days into two half days around a full day. This allowed for a preparation meeting during the first half day, going through the status of the project and identifying the goals of the event the next day (e.g. demo meeting, followed by sprint planning meeting). Following that intense day, another half day was spent reviewing the event, conducting a mini retrospective to better identify what went well and what needed further work.

During each trip, a discussion took place with other stakeholders in this Scrum experimentation, including the instigator of the project, to ensure that the coaching was on track and that it was addressing the current and urgent concerns of ESOC.

A common theme between projects C and D was the need to create user stories, and map these to traditional requirements. This represented a significant effort, which was largely shared between ESOC and their respective contractors. For this aspect in particular, lessons learned and recommendations are proposed in Section 5.

4.3 Project C – Full Ground System Software Development Project

The objective of Project C (started in Q2 2009) is the development of a Data Dissemination system for operational spacecraft data. This system is an evolution of several predecessors data dissemination systems already in use by ESA missions. As any dissemination system it interfaces with several data archives for data retrieval. Of the main data archives, two were still unstable at project kick-off and eventual interface changes were foreseen during Project's C lifetime. Additionally the project uses an ESA-internal Eclipse RCP (Rich Client Platform) – based GUI (Graphical User Interface) Framework that was not stable at the time Project C started and it was clear that changes in this framework would occur and that a new version would have to be integrated in the course of Project C. The project uses also an ESA Service Management framework to serve as the basis of the project and allow for service automation and export. This framework was not fully supported and validated in Project's C OS baseline, and was still immature and unstable.

As can be seen from Project's C description above, there were several uncertainties and potential risks associated with the surrounding components. For that reason the Scrum framework has been recommended as part of Project's C Statement of Work. This Project is the second phase of the data dissemination concept approach in ESA. In the first phase (concluded two years prior to the start of Project C) a detailed software requirements specification and high level design had been prepared. As it would be expected the software requirements and design prepared at that time had to be heavily reviewed and reworked. A review of the requirements document was done prior to the Tender period, however the specification was still very extensive (i.e. trying to capture all possible scenarios) and detailed, even after the review. The requirements were also not set in the form of user stories and therefore difficult to map to test scenarios.

The very detailed (reviewed) software requirements document and design specification were included within Project's C Tender applicable documents and therefore were a reference for the bid and the FFP contract to be established. The SoW (Statement of Work) defined a delta architecture phase to consolidate the high level architecture already available which wouldn't need to follow the Agile approach, then the design and implementation would follow Scrum (where eight sprints were foreseen) and finally a final acceptance and end of warranty period where again Scrum was not mandated. Independently of the use of Scrum it was required to follow the ESA Software Engineering Standards [2][3], which as already mentioned define several milestones. The selected bidder actually proposed the extended use of Scrum to all project phases (including the delta design and acceptance phases) and a fixed timebox of 4 weeks for each sprint. This was accepted and considered highly positive by the Agency. The defined milestones were taken as constrains on the work tasks and stories to be implemented (i.e. establishing priorities according to the milestones). In the initial phase the proposed team consisted of 4 persons (not including Product Owner as this is with the Agency's responsibility). It was the first time all stakeholders were trying to use Scrum.

One of the first activities of the project consisted in defining the Product backlog. This was done by both Product Owner and Scrum Master together. Due to the complexity and low level of detail of the requirements document the mapping of the requirements into the product backlog was cumbersome and time consuming. It was also very difficult to establish product backlog items (we call them items because initially they were not formatted in a user story format) which could be mapped and used to complete the activities required for the delta design. This initial product backlog lacked several key pieces of information, such as test scenarios (or validation criteria), relative priority between items or item effort estimation. Once the first draft of the Product backlog was considered completed, the initial release plan took plan. This meeting included once again only the PO and the SM (a trend throughout the project which would be corrected only after the coaching activity). The product backlog items were assigned to different sprints, based on their dependencies and level of importance/risk. The team also agreed to have an extended Sprint 0 where the integration of all Customer Furnished Item - CFIs (and there were several as the system had multiples interfaces and dependencies) into the development environment was to be done together with the preparation of the integration and development environment of the system itself.

From this point on the Scrum deficiencies (also known as 'Scrum but...') started to grow. Please find below a list of the main ones:

- Product backlog not being managed exclusively by the Product Owner: this was due to the fact that the PO was engaged in several projects and was therefore not always available. The team (mainly the Scrum Master) was also performing updates on the product backlog (basically the principles of Product owner proxy were being used within being well defined and agreed).
- Product backlog items were not properly defined: the items were too generic and not defined in a format of a user story. This made it quite difficult to completely implement any item within the timeframe of a single sprint and to demonstrate and validate it during the review. Also the prioritization of the items in the product backlog was rarely reviewed, along with their estimation.
- There was no definition of acceptance criteria (test scenarios) or Done: there was no written and agreed definition for evaluating the product backlog items. This was done based on each individual item and the Team's perception of what needed to be done.

- Lack of Team participation on Sprint meetings: Only the Scrum master and main developer was participating in representation of the Team. This didn't allow the team to feel involved in the project and the process and also to provide their input and contribution.
- No regular daily stand-up: The Team didn't feel the need to have a regular meeting. This could be seen as side effect of the previous item, where the team was detached from the process.
- Sprint backlog not updated and inconsistent: The Team didn't define/report all ongoing tasks within the Sprint backlog and the backlog content was seldom updated.

Despite several attempts to improve and correct the process, as one would expect from the deficiencies mentioned above, the project was struggling both in terms of process, performance and results. For example, even after several sprints it was still quite difficult to have a good demonstration of work done after a sprint (i.e. Sprint Review) and especially involve the end users to collect their feedback. The meetings were becoming quite chaotic, lengthy and without concrete final outcome. The project was starting to get deviation from the expected progress (approximately a month and a half delay).

Although the project was already quite advance it was decided that coaching and training in how to adopt and use Scrum was required. This has happen initially in the form of embedded coaching and later in the form of certified Scrum training (both for the PO and the Team). The initial coaching took place in the preparation of one of the Sprint review/planning meetings (for Sprint #7). The fact that the coach was embedded into the team was very useful as the deficiencies were highlighted during the real event and corrective measures recommended (and tried during the meeting). Although it was quite an exhausting meeting and coaching process the feeling afterwards was quite positive (both from the Agency as from the contractor side), as the team finally started to realize the main advantages and reasons to use Scrum (the seed had finally been planted). The result of both types of coaching were indeed impressive, to the point that now the team is very comfortable with the process and is much more productive (and fully engaged in the project). Below are the main corrective measure taken:

- The product backlog has been fully restructured by the PO in order to contain all the key information (User story format, acceptance criteria, requirement or software problem references, relative priority, item estimation (using the reference of 1 story point equals to 1 man/day), etc). The PO is also now the single responsible for any product backlog modification.
- The "bill of rights" has been produced by the Scrum Team and defines all Scrum events for the project, the time box of all these events, the roles and responsibilities and the definition of Done applicable to any product backlog item.
- The level of inspection and transparency has been highly increased with the constant participation and review from all project stakeholder within all project events. Product and sprint backlog are fully maintained and constantly being updated.
- The Team is now participating in all events and performs a regular daily Scrum meeting.

As an example of the improvement in planning, it is now visible and clear the required effort and time to perform all remaining product backlog activities (assuming Sprint 0 as the current point in time). The picture is based on estimated velocity from the previous sprint (as past velocities were not conclusive due to the already mentioned deficiencies). This shows that if the velocity is maintained the team would have "Done" all stories in the next 5 sprints.

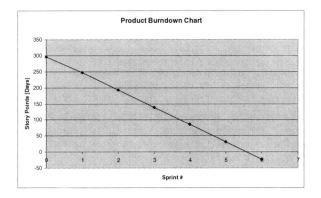

Fig. 3. Project C Product burndown chart

This allows the PO (and other management) to decide how to approach the project regarding future activities and remaining work (decisions such as extending budget or preparing a new Tender activity for the remaining work can be taken more confidently). Another very good improvement is the visibility of the work being done at each moment in time (for each sprint) and easy tracking of the progress. As an example please see below the last sprint burn down chart.

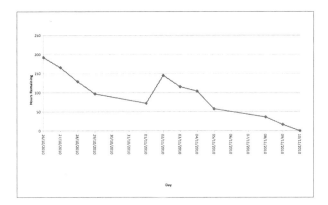

Fig. 4. Project C Sprint backlog of Sprint #1 (post Provisional Acceptance release)

Due to a team restructuring this sprint had a shorter length (2 weeks). The spike in the middle of the sprint occurred due to the fact that the Team realized they would complete all assigned activities prior to the end of the sprint and could therefore perform an additional item (despite the fact that the sprint was shorted than usual and the team was new working together). After discussing this with the PO an item was assigned (with an adequate level of priority and effort) and added to the sprint work. In the end still all assigned work has been performed.

The perception of the Team and the stakeholder regarding the project went from doubt in the fact the system would be successfully implemented and released to met customer requirements to full believe and confidence this will become/is a reality (as production and potentially releasable software is being produced every sprint with tangible results).

4.4 Project D – Full Ground Infrastructure Software Development Project

The objective of Project D is to implement certain generic GUI capabilities to be used for a variety of Ground Segment Software Systems like Mission Control Systems and systems for Ground Station Monitoring & Control. The project uses the same ESA-internal Eclipse RCP – based GUI Framework as Project C. On the other hand there has been some pressure on the schedule for Project D as there is a large ongoing Ground Station project that needs the results of Project D. The Project started 2nd quarter 2010 with an overall planned duration of 19 month (including a 6 month warranty period).

The Statement of Work that has been issued to the frame contractors gave strong indications to use a model-based approach applying Eclipse EMF (Eclipse Modeling Framework), GEF (Graphical Editing Framework) and GMF (Graphical Modeling Framework) for building an editor and rendering the graphical displays. A very detailed Software Requirements Document has been part of the Invitation to Tender. However, the Software Requirements Document had not been consolidated properly and some parts have been unclear and vague while other parts were over specified. The Statement of Work asked for two releases of the software and required the use of the ESA Software Engineering Standards [2][3] and their defined milestones. The use of Scrum with 4 weeks sprint duration was requested for the implementation phase only and the whole duration of the implementation phase for both releases has been eight month. In the proposal that has been selected an option for skipping the intermediate release and shortening the development phase to six month with four sprint deliveries (plus one 'final' delivery for preliminary acceptance) has been chosen. The proposed core team consisted of five persons.

The project started with a short architectural design phase. Even before the Preliminary Design Review the first Sprint Planning Meeting was held to plan for the implementation phase. An initial product backlog had been created by the Product Owner from the Software Requirements Document. However, an exact tracing of requirements to user stories has not been possible and test scenarios were still missing. This first meeting has been quite chaotic and took almost five hours but only half of the sprint backlog had been finalised. One main reason for that were diverging expectation regarding the Scrum approach and a lack of training. After the meeting, the Contractor decided to have a dedicated Scrum training and coaching to the Product Owner has been provided. To reduce the effort on the Product Owner the Product Owner Proxy pattern has been applied with the Contractor's Project Manager as the Product Owner Proxy. The product backlog was refined, test scenarios have been added and the main responsibility for updating the backlog slowly transitioned from the Product Owner to the Product Owner Proxy during the project.

The second Sprint Planning Meeting has been organised and performed with the coach being involved. The Product Owner prioritized the user stories according to importance and estimated difficulty in order to implement more important and more difficult ones first. The user stories were printed on paper to have something 'tangible' to arrange and write notes on it. In addition to the Product Owner, the complete Team and the coach two Technical Experts from ESOC also took part in the Sprint Planning. The most important stories were discussed and clarified with the help of the experts and were estimated in story points by the team. It is important to note that during this sprint planning design discussions took place and decisions were taken. There was a lot of work being done in parallel and the meeting was overall considered successful. This time it took four hours to complete the sprint planning. The format of this meeting was not changed for the following Sprint Planning Meetings and it could be observed that the meetings become more productive and even shorter.

While for the first Sprint Review Meeting only the Team, the PO and the Technical Experts had been invited, for the second Sprint Review Meeting several stakeholders, including section managers and end user have been invited. While the demonstration was slightly chaotic because of missing preparation, a late start and an unclear modus operandi, the result was very interesting. Users provided significant feedback during a live demo of the system. The demo lasted around 90 minutes. At the end of the coach asked everyone in the room to provide feedback on the format of the meeting and the approach in general. Overall there was a positive response and all stakeholders were very happy to see a product so early in its development and welcomed the opportunity to provide feedback. On the format of the meeting, explaining a bit better the scope of the meeting and how it fits in the overall process of the project would have helped users and observers to better understand and contribute. Taking the user feedback into account the format of the meeting has been slightly changed. Now there is a one hour well-prepared Sprint Demonstration Meeting where all the stakeholders are involved and provide their feedback. The feedback is visibly recorded and the users are informed about the decisions taken regarding the feedback they have provided. Directly afterwards a up to three hours Sprint Review Meeting were all implemented user stories are tested in detail and marked as 'Done' or rejected. This format seems to work very well for the project, the stakeholder involvement is quite high (in particular compared to the usual formal review meetings). After the Sprint Review the Sprint Delivery is given to the PO and 'tested' for a few days. Issues that are detected in the Sprint Delivery a reported as 'observations' to the Product Owner Proxy. They are either taken into account during the running sprint (there is a special user story for minor improvements) or in one of the next sprints.

One important issue that came up was the tracing of requirements because preliminary and final acceptance of the software requires validation that all requirements are covered. As it was not easily possible to trace user stories to requirements, it was decided to do this indirectly. While user stories are implemented, test cases and procedures are created in a tool that allows linking the test procedures to the requirements managed by another tool. This allows the tracking of which requirements have already been implemented and which are still missing. These test procedures will be used for the acceptance testing once the software has been finalised. For new developments without an existing Software Requirements Document it would be probably much easier to start directly with user stories.

At the same time the Software Requirements Document was continuously updated to clarify requirements, improve its structure, take user feedback into account and refine some features. Some modifications were done to allow to make better use of the chosen software technology (Eclipse EMF, GEF, GMF) because some requirements were asking for a certain implementation that would have be very difficult using this technology while slightly different and even better solutions were easily doable.

Another important point is that the Scrum approach allowed the Technical Office to have a much better technical and management visibility of the project. Advice from the Technical Experts could immediately be included in the software and the estimation of the project velocity allowed to discover a potential delay early in the project so that corrective measures could be taken.

Overall, we concluded that the Scrum approach allowed to increase the software quality by incorporating end user feedback and early test results and providing enough flexibility for continuous improvement of the Software Requirements Document. It allowed us to provide more technical expertise to the project and make better use of the chosen technology. Communication between Technical Office, Project Manager and the whole team has been improved and potential risks (delays) have been identified early and corrective measures have been taken. The iterative approach allowed to deliver an early version of the software to a dependent project and also allowed to make use of part of the software in another project.

5   Lessons Learned

This section brings together lessons learned from applying Agile in general and Scrum in particular at ESOC. Some of these lessons learned are more straightforward than others, thus addressing them will bring different levels of challenges and return on investment.

User Requirements: Functional requirements written in the form of user stories (covering both functional and non-functional types) are more expressive than traditional functional requirements. Using these provides a format with which most stakeholders can understand and engage. A transition is required such that FFP contracts are specified using this form of functional requirements. A benefit observed by projects C and D is the ability for users to engage with projects when using user stories as the functional specification for the project. Using test scenarios or acceptance criteria for each user story is an effective mechanism for scoping user stories and define the expectation from each user story. This was extensively used for projects C and D where test scenarios were used to drive the end of sprint demos and yield excellent results.

Statement of Work Template Update for Agile/Scrum: ESOC issues a Statement of Work (SoW) for each project it requires industry to bid for. Up to now, the standard template for such SoW was used, designed for waterfall, with additional information specifying that industry shall respond using Agile/Scrum. This has led to some ambiguity from bidders as to ESOC's intent. Therefore, with experience in executing Scrum projects, ESOC can now be more specific in its expectations, in terms of events, artefacts, as well as roles and responsibilities.

Scrum at ESOC: Agile relies heavily on people, their experience and knowledge. In order to scale up the number of projects executed using Agile, ESOC must build a core of staff able to take the role of Product Owners as part of their Technical Officer function inside the organisation. In order to achieve that, ESOC must extend awareness in Agile and Scrum inside the organisation and to all the stakeholders involved in the definition, execution and termination of Ground Systems Software projects. Further, it is perceived executing Scrum project requires more time from the Technical Officer compared to traditional waterfall projects (where the effort is usually much higher in terms of consolidation phase and risks). However, Scrum provides a predictable framework, where the involvement from the PO follows the rhythm of sprints. While this has not been verified at the time of writing, we predict that project conclusion is much more likely to be smooth using Scrum than waterfall, as fewer deliverables should be rejected, since most will have undergone several incremental deliveries.

User Involvement: Users have shown greater interest and willingness in participating to end of sprint demos, compared to traditional reviews. However, the part of the demo during which users are expected to contribute most should be kept short (i.e. one hour) and well organized. Providing ahead of time users with the user stories that will be demoed during the next demos meeting improves users' ability to provide feedback. This feedback is key in guiding the project towards success.

Contracts Updates: Executing Firm Fixed Price projects using Scrum brings challenges. One of these challenges comes from the fact that the customer and the provider come from distinct organisations. In order to maximise success in such situation, we found using the 'Product Owner Proxy' organisational pattern useful.

In order to take advantage of the opportunity to change requirements as better ways are discovered or the business value of items in the product backlog shift with new knowledge, we recommend exploring the possibility to implement in the ESOC FFP contract template Jeff Sutherland's "Money for nothing and changes for free" concept [4]. This means that the project will be able to embrace change within the contract, trading not yet implemented Product Backlog items (change for free) and early termination of contract (money for nothing) when the project reaches a point where the cost of the backlog items exceed their business value. The reasoning in terms of business value per user story is possible since the Team provides estimates for each user story, hence providing all the data the PO requires to evaluate the benefit to cost ratio. The exact conditions and penalties for such an early conclusion of the project must be crafted such that the provider would recover the profit that would have been made assuming a successful conclusion of the projects.

Coaching Model and Scrum Fluency: The coaching model used in the project reported in this paper was effective, in turning theory into practice. While the coaching project was primarily geared towards coaching ESOC staff in their Product

Owner role, the fact that coaching took place during planning meeting and demos also meant that the coaching extended to the project, including the team, the Product Owner Proxy and the Scrum Master. This approach also unloaded the ESOC staff from needing to specify what was expected of all stakeholders, leaving this responsibility to the coach. ESOC can only do so much in terms of Scrum, even with coaching support. It is therefore important that the team has a few experienced Scrum members, and/or that the team be trained in Scrum. Both project Teams chose this last option, with good results.

Tools: Scrum requires regular deliveries of working systems, as well as tighter communication (e.g. daily stand-up meetings). Tool support can make the delivery process much simpler and reliable, with considerable gain in time and effort. The same can be said for communication, especially when the team is distributed and/or distant from ESOC. ESOC currently uses several tools to support its software development. It is therefore important to explore how to best use current tools (e.g. requirements tracking, test scenario system) and where to introduce new tools and to what extent should tools be mandated or standardised on.

6 Conclusions

ESOC has progressed from doing Agile "only nominally" (e.g. perhaps closer to a "multiple waterfalls" approach) to really starting to leverage Agile and Scrum at a much deeper level. This brings challenges, especially at the managerial and contractual levels. There seems to be a shared, but caution, enthusiasm from industry, which must also be managed carefully during this transitional phase. Teaching and coaching the ESOC staff executing Agile projects is only one part on the path towards a more Agile organisation.

To support this transition towards Agile in general and Scrum in particular, a coaching project was setup. The specific objectives of the coaching was to help the staff identify dysfunctions and traps in the application of Agile and Scrum, and better utilise the methodology to deliver results that maximises benefit to the users, in time and within budget. This objective was achieved. The coaching format was particularly well suited to help the staff, and their contractors, to better integrate Scrum practices and experience its real benefits. The immersive formula provided a unique opportunity to prepare, observe, guide and provide feedback to the staff in their application of Agile and Scrum. As a result, all staff improved significantly in terms of their ability and confidence in executing a project using Agile in general and Scrum in particular, while also guiding their respective contractor. This resulted in a more performant and enjoyable project for all stakeholders. Since the coaching took place over real life events, it had the added benefit that the teams from industry involved in the events also improved. This was particularly evident in Project D, where the Team and ESOC formed an efficient, trusting and performing unit of work, both during Sprint 2 demo Sprint 3 planning meetings, including revealing feedback from users during the demo.

We can summarise our experience as follows. Introducing Scrum in the execution of Firm Fixed Price contracts at ESOC brings challenges. For example, Scrum might require more time from the staff responsible for these projects as they fill the role of

Product Owner. The time invested provides better guidance to the project and is generally felt as a positive aspect of Scrum. Further, this investment required by Scrum might actually pay-off in reducing the integration and stabilization phase of projects, phases that can be time consuming and particularly stressful. However, this still has to be verified in practice. The current 'hybrid' situation of having to deal with traditional functional requirements and user stories, and the mapping between them, represents a complex, cumbersome and time consuming series of tasks. While this is currently unavoidable, future projects following a more Scrum-like project definition might alleviate some of this burden.

On the other hand, Scrum brings significant benefits. For example, the quality of the delivered software system is perceived as being of a higher quality. The rhythm imposed by Scrum in producing early and regular incremental deliveries is the source of valuable feedback and an opportunity to test systems early. Regular deliveries and reviews provide non-ambiguous and analytical progress measurements to better manage the project and risks. This is a major benefit from Agile and Scrum, where potential problems can be detected early, in time for effective correction actions. Further, this early visibility into project results can be used to prioritise features and activities, to maximise the chance of success. The ability to regularly test the system produced at the end of every sprint provides an opportunity to report problems and find solutions early and gain confidence in the final results. The documentation of the system is more likely to match the system being developed, hence providing a more reliable source of information.

The rhythm imposed by Scrum also promotes clearer and better communication between the different stakeholders in general and between the TO/PO, PO Proxy and Team in particular. This is reflected by getting away from a 'us' and 'them' mentality towards a more inclusive 'us' vision of the project and its shared goals. Finally, the value and strength of the commitment the Team makes in implementing a set of user stories (prioritised by the PO) before each sprint is significant and provides both focus and transparency in terms of tasks, problems and solutions.

Acknowledgments. The authors would like to thank all the companies that were involved in the different projects for the openness and flexibility required for experimenting with new approaches to software development. In particular, we would like to mention Terma and Logica for their support and high level of commitment.

References

1. Schwaber, K.: Agile Project Management with Scrum, Microsoft (2004)
2. ECSS-E-ST-40C, Software, European Cooperation for Space Standardization (3 issue, March 6, 2009), http://www.ecss.nl/
3. ECSS-Q-ST-80C, Software Product Assurance, European Cooperation for Space Standardization (3 issue, March 6, 2009), http://www.ecss.nl/
4. Sutherland, J.: Money For Nothing And Your Change For Free: Agile Contacts. In: Agile 2008 Conference, Toronto (2008),
   http://jeffsutherland.com/Agile2008MoneyforNothing.pdf

Evolution of Longer-Term Planning in a Large Scale Agile Project – F-Secure's Experience

Gabor Gunyho[1] and Juan Gutiérrez Plaza[2]

[1] F-Secure Corporation, Helsinki, Finland
[2] F-Secure Corporation, Bordeaux, France
{Gabor.Gunyho,Juan.Gutierrez}@f-secure.com

Abstract. This article describes the experience of F-Secure on practicing a long/mid-term planning for a multi-team, multi-site project. It shows how the planning is thought to cover several iterations so a meaningful business value is potentially reached and given to the customer as well as all the procedures and artifacts used for and during the planning. The paper also describes the evolution (modifications and improvements) done on the planning process along the whole project. We also reflect on the major events of the project (such as project split) for which the project steering was enabled by the planning method.

Keywords: Agile, large-scale, planning, release train, business iteration.

1 Introduction

Being flexible and adaptable to change may be seen in contradiction with planning and estimation. In fact, when teams doing agile reach a certain maturity, they tend to stop (or at least make it very light weight) planning because it is seen that only certainty of a plan is that it is going to change.

On other hand, we have stakeholders more focusing on business, company strategy, future market demands, long term architectural evolution, etc., whom like to plan well in advance with a sufficient level of certainty. They need to make decisions that will affect the long term-future and, for that, they want to have plans and estimations so this decisions are the best possible at that moment.

There is a wide range of levels between these two extreme scenarios. One of them, which tries to bring both extremes closer, is what it is called the Agile Release Train [1]. It covers multiple layers of abstractions in all key dimensions of the project: content, timeline and organization.

This article explains what the experience of F-Secure is on using the Agile Release Train for a big, multi-team and multi-site project. It consisted of about 10 teams located in Helsinki and Kuala Lumpur and later one team from Poland. They were fairly mature in Scrum [2] and agile engineering practices[1].

2 Longer-Term Planning

Companies are looking for ways to be flexible and adaptable so they can give to the customer what they want when they need it. However, large projects, long lasting

---

[1] We refer to practices such as: shared code ownership, continuous integration, unit testing, pair programming, etc.

A. Sillitti et al. (Eds.): XP 2011, LNBIP 77, pp. 306–315, 2011.

architectures and companies' strategy require certain level of long term planning. Therefore, in order to plan for developing complex systems with lots of unknowns and dependencies, both in feature and architecture-wise, a good way of hinting the future is needed.

Firms want to be able to estimate and see the progress on a higher level of abstraction of the content (like user stories [3]) and timeline (like sprints or iterations) This enables them to make correct decisions to mitigate the impact of their mistakes, adapt to customer needs or change their strategy. Companies also want to handle inherent organizational complexity in multi-team set-ups in an optimal manner. They want to make sure that teams are aligned to a common "longer-term" objective[2].

Agile Release Train handles different level of abstractions on requirements (from a very high business level to a very low technical level), time frame (from business iterations –months- to small iterations like Sprints in the Scrum jargon –weeks-) and organizational (from multi team and site approach to single small team approach).

2.1 Agile Release Train

As other models and proposals ([4] and [5]), Agile Release Train seeks to find the balance between flexibility and planning as well as communication and understanding between business and development. It takes the best of agile practises in a team or small scale level, and adds an upper layer for "agile requirement handling" and "agile enterprise".

There are some few rules in Agile Trains:

- Periodic release dates for the solution are fixed
- Intermediate, global integration milestones are established and enforced
- Constraining these means that component/feature functionality must flex
- Shared infrastructure must track ahead
- Teams evolve to a flexible model: Design spectrum for new functionality and backup plan to ship less capable version if necessary

In Agile Trains, user stories are defined in different layers of abstraction: Epics, features and stories. They are different in definition, scope and size (see Table 1).

Table 1. Different layers or abstractions for user stories

Term	Interest	Size/Lifespan	Testable
Epic	Business	May span several GA (Generally Available) releases	No
Feature	Business, Customer, User	Generally fits in one GA release (But may also be versioned across releases)	Yes
Story	Product o wner, Team, User	Demonstrable functionality, fits in one team iteration. Otherwise – split	Yes

When the Business Iteration Planning meetings are executed, it is important to follow some advices to maximize the output and quality of the planning.

---

[2] "Longer-term" refers to a Business Iteration and no longer than that.

308   G. Gunyho and J. Gutiérrez Plaza

- Co-locate team often, at least at Release Planning
- Establish core hours, with overlap required
- Apply high cohesion and low coupling to sites (organize and reorganize around features/components) if planning is not co-located
- Do not let anyone go dark, apply daily Integration Scrums
- Establish a single global instance of project assets
- Invest in tools that support distributed, but shared view of status
- Scaling agile requires managing interdependencies among teams of developers
- Only the teams themselves can plan and manage this complexity
- Only the teams can commit to the schedule
- Systematic enterprise delivery requires an "agile release train" delivery model
- Rolling-wave Enterprise Release Planning drives release train vision and execution

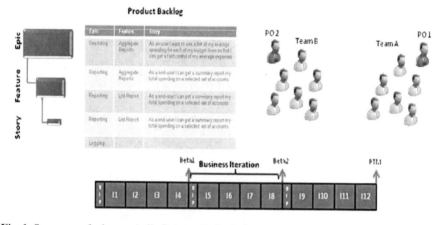

Fig. 1. Summary of what an Agile Release Train deals with: several abstractions in requirements and time, multi team configuration, single Product Owner (PO) per team, etc.

As the main metric to see if the method works (although we have also checked the feelings and opinions of the people involved in the planning; see Results section), we have used the primary metric suggested by Lean Leffingwell, creator of the Agile Release Train: *"The primary metric for agile is whether or not working software actually exists, and is demonstrably suitable for its intended purpose. This is determined empirically, by demonstration, at the end of every single iteration."*

3 Project Set-Up

The project kick-off was done in December 2009 together with the first business iteration planning (BIP) event. The first "wagon" of the "train" is marked at the end by a Potentially Shippable Increment (PSI) -later renamed to Business Iteration- of the functionality requested. It is worth noting that we follow the principle of having software that works after every sprint, however, we enforce the idea of having real business increments that can be potentially shippable after every PSI.

First Business Iteration Planning (BIP) event. The first planning was done for a timeframe of 90 days. This means 6 sprints of 2 weeks duration each (plus 1 week for retrospectives, planning the next BI, etc).

The program of the planning event was set up as follows:

- One day training on Scaling SW agility
- "Release" Planning: 2 days +1 day reserve (that had to be used after all)
- Attendants: ~120, including all functions (R&D, Product Mgmt, business, etc)
- Everybody in one single space (with the exception of those teams who could not travel to Helsinki)

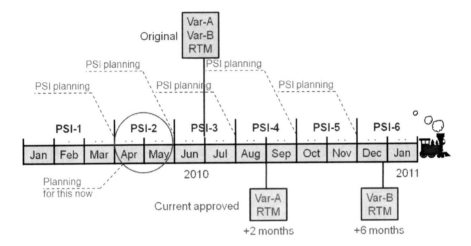

Fig. 2. Agile Release Planning "train" with its "wagons" reflecting the status after the first BIP. RTM means Release To Market, Var-A and Var-B are Variant A and B of the project.

After the first BIP (see Figure 2), we found the following items in the process by the practice or feedback from the attendees:

- Huge amount of content becomes apparent, many dependencies and risks
- Feature vs. story concept is not clear to many
- Missed 1st internal beta (4 sprints -> 5 sprints)
- Planning event can be done in 2 days (keep a 3rd day in reserve though)
- The 90-day "Business Iteration" with mid-term re-planning is not meaningful
- Change the cadence to 8-week Business Iterations with proper planning for each

The aim of the process from the very beginning was to evolve and to be improved. Therefore, based on what we found, we decided to change it for the next planning as follows:

- Draft plan review scrapped
- Adding "planning Scrum of Scrums (SoS)", short, hourly synchronization meeting attended by a team representative (usually Scrum Master)

From now on, the evolution of the following BIPs and schedule (see Figure 3) will be shown by the remarks seen during the time of the business iteration and the changes done in the process during the business iteration.

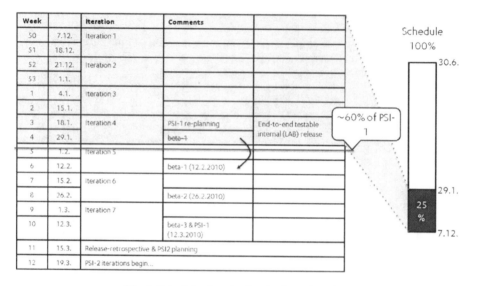

Week		Iteration	Comments		
50	7.12.	Iteration 1			
51	18.12.				
52	21.12.	Iteration 2			
53	1.1.				
1	4.1.	Iteration 3			
2	15.1.				
3	18.1.	Iteration 4	PSI-1 re-planning	End-to-end testable	
4	29.1.		beta-1	internal (LAB) release	
5	1.2.	Iteration 5			
6	12.2.		beta-1 (12.2.2010)		
7	15.2.	Iteration 6			
8	26.2.		beta-2 (26.2.2010)		
9	1.3.	Iteration 7			
10	12.3.		beta-3 & PSI-1 (12.3.2010)		
11	15.3.	Release-retrospective & PSI2 planning			
12	19.3.	PSI-2 iterations begin...			

Fig. 3. Schedule after the first business iteration

Second BIP event

Remarks:
- Beta releases: 2 of 3 successful
- Preceded by a ½ day retrospective done with Open Space [6]
- Slow feedback in development
- Improve Build System, Test Automation and reduce release effort
- "Release" Planning fixes: focus on dependencies, limit sprint load to team's capacity
- Architecture challenges: different levels of abstraction needed, establish virtual team for architects

Changes:
- Internal facilitator in charge for the event
- Imbalance between scope and velocity recognized and acknowledged
- Change project setup: Full system release June 2010 -> "Variant-A" release by August (+2 months), "Variant-B" by December (+ 6 months)
- Plan for releasing a beta (at least internal) in every sprint

Third BIP event

Remarks:

- Beta releases: 2 of 4 successful
- Stakeholders realised before the planning that: *"Based on R&D analysis of project scope and schedule it is apparent that the current roadmap is not feasible"*
- Project split on "mini-project" for downscaled "Variant-A". "Variant-B" development continues, with stages delivery; planned a basic release by October 2010 and a full release by January 2011

Changes:

- At every hour SoS and Architecture-SoS alternate
- Helpers for planning the improvement items rotate in teams
- Risk, impediment and dependency handling in short cycles (along with the SoS), and not at the end of the release planning event
- "Feature wall" (or "master wall", see Figure 4) to depict which feature will be done by whom and when, also visualizing dependencies

Fig. 4. Feature or Master wall

Fourth BIP event

Remarks:

- Beta releases: 3 of 6 successful.
- Event delayed by 1 week, time used for:
    - Hardening (bug killing)
    - Re-teaming event: moving towards more feature teams
    - Scrum Master training

Changes:

- Separate intro briefing session, including solution demo
- All input in physical tokens (all features printed)
- Improved master wall, physical visualization of dependencies
- Clear priorities for planning: "honesty over precision"
- Smoother planning in general

Fifth BIP event

Remarks:

- Period: Beta releases: 4 of 5 successful
- 1st public beta release

- "Last mile" before release
- Company restructuring
- Feature leaks (slipping content)
- Last-minute change in the planning process, decision taken by stakeholders: *"We believe the last mile before release is better executed with feature focused planning"* (see Figure 5). Note that BIP method is not abandoned, it is just not applied for the last mile of the project

Changes:
- Experienced internal facilitator not available: new internal facilitator
- New "feature planning", a step towards more "continuous planning"
- More emphasis in backlog grooming within sprints and Product Backlog preparation by Product Owners
- Release is when last good build is deemed by Product Owners as good to go
- Joint synchronization events might be held if needed

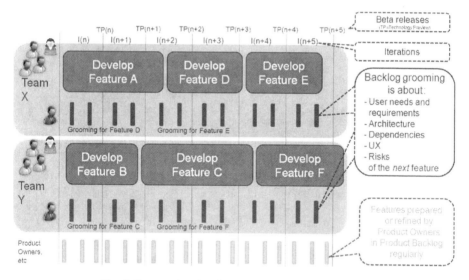

Fig. 5. Feature planning for the "last mile" before release

4   Results

If we take the primary metric stated in the Section 2.1 as a metric for the usefulness of the method, we encounter varying results.

During the first business iterations, teams were struggling with making internal releases. Software was not potentially shippable and it did not meet stakeholders' expectations. We believe the reasons behind this were twofold: lack of maturity of the teams with the method and lack of proper engineering practices for such a big number of teams working in parallel.

Teams improved considerably the Continuous Integration and Test Automation systems and tests during the following sprints and the "stop the line"[3] culture was established little by little until it became a habit. Software availability after some sprints were improved and the trend continued steadily.

If we look at it from the common goal and reacting to change point of view, release planning gave enough visibility (and early enough in time) to the stakeholders to adapt to the changes of the clients as well as the features not available on time because of different reasons. Additionally, it is worth mentioning that communication among R&D and business increased considerably during the sessions. Also concern and awareness of each others' problems.

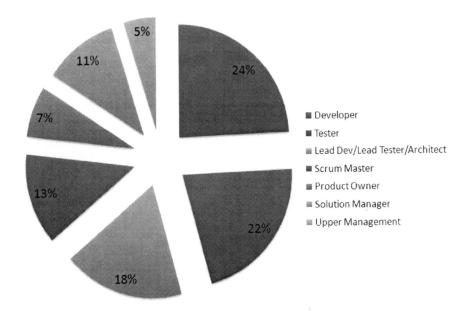

Fig. 6. Number of respondents to the survey per role

However, for many people sessions are long and tiring and despite of the advantages, people would prefer to make them much shorter or remove them.

We passed a survey for three times with different questions to see what the opinion of the people was about the release planning sessions. Unfortunately this date is only available for BIP 1, re-planning and 2. Out of the about 90 people working for the project, around 40 people responded in average. Figure 6 shows the diversity of roles in the answers.

The results of the questionnaire are good. As seen in Figure 7, more than 80% of the respondents think that release planning is good or very good. As stated before, a new questionnaire should be sent after the project is finished to validate the correctness of the figures.

---

[3] Briefly, nobody commits to the development branch (trunk in our case) until the problem is analysed. Then, the total or partial stop of the line continues until the problem is fixed. An analysis to avoid the problem in the future is done afterwards.

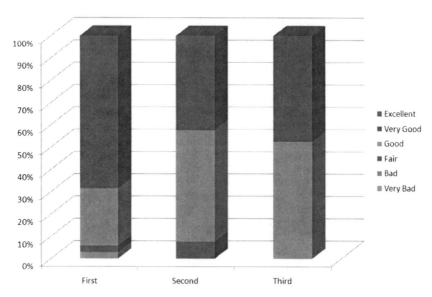

Fig. 7. Opinion about the overall usefulness of the release plannings

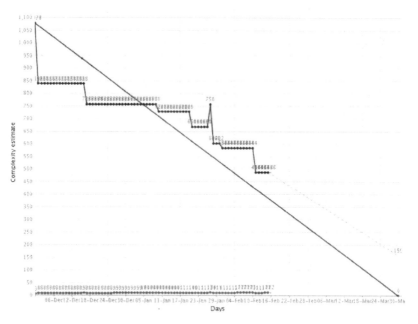

Fig. 8. Status of the project on mid of February, 2011

By the time this manuscript is written, the project is not ended yet, therefore we cannot publish the final figures and numbers. Nonetheless, in Figure 8 the status of the project as of mid of February is shown. The burndown chart in the figure shows that the remaining work might be done by the planned release date.

5 Conclusions

Our main learning is that the Agile Train concept and the BI Planning provide better visibility and steerability for business management and helps making tough decisions.

For example the initial scope (in the 1st BIP and also the 2nd) was perhaps an order of magnitude bigger, than what R&D could deliver in the expected timeframe. We just failed to see it in the first planning. But without this kind of planning events we would not have seen it, at least not as early as we did when using the BIP method. Also such tough decision like splitting the project to two (one mini-project and one main project, that one also with staged delivery and delayed release dates) would not have been possible (or would have happened much later) without the BIP. Even abandoning the BIP for the "last mile" of the project and moving to Feature planning was made possible on the foundation of (and the learning from) the BIPs earlier.

The well-know inspect-and-adapt cycle that is for the sprints in Scrum is very well applicable for the higher-level of abstraction in the planning cycle, i.e., the BI. This is valid for the BI planning method itself so evolve that too as you go. We suggest to:

- Get real feedback after almost every sprint, even if product is big
- Get help from an experienced "process master", i.e., event facilitator
- Prepare the content well and do it continuously, do not overload the system.
- Apply Scrum-of-Scrums within the BI planning, continuous handling of risks, dependencies and impediments
- Have all stakeholders (business, architects, user experience experts) available during the BIP events (we set up a "help desk" in the BIP space where these experts were sitting and supporting teams on a needed basis)
- Create a Master wall and feature coverage tracking
- Try "feature planning"

We also experienced that paying attention to Quality and the engineering practices like Continuous Integration and Test Automation is essential.

- Every bug found invokes adding a new test case to the Test Automation suite
- Never sacrifice quality
- No extra hardening outside of sprints, every sprint results in a customer beta

References

1. Leffingwell, D.: Scaling Software Agility: Best Practices for Large Enterprises. Addison-Wesley Professional, Reading (2007)
2. Schwaber, K., Beedle, M.: Agile Software Development with Scrum. Prentice Hall, Englewood Cliffs (2001)
3. Cohn, M.: User Stories Applied. Addison-Wesley, Reading (2004)
4. Larman, C., Vodde, B.: Scaling Lean & Agile Development: Thinking and Organizational Tools for Large-Scale Scrum. Addison-Wesley Professional, Reading (2008)
5. Larman, C., Vodde, B.: Practices for Scaling Lean & Agile Development: Large, Multisite, and Offshore Product Development with Large-Scale Scrum. Addison-Wesley Professional, Reading (2010)
6. Owen, H.: Open Space Technology: A User's Guide. Berrett-Koehler Publishers (2008)

Defects and Agility: Localization Issues in Agile Development Projects

Malte Ressin, José Abdelnour-Nocera, and Andy Smith

Thames Valley University, Centre for Internationalisation and Usability,
St Mary's Road, London, UK, W5 5RF
{malte.ressin,jose.abdelnour-nocera,andy.smith}@tvu.ac.uk

Abstract. It has been noted that software localization does not always fit well into agile software development. This poster aims to illustrate the relationship between the two by examining how localization issues occur in agile projects. A list of common localization issues is presented and examined as to where and why they can be caused during development and if there is a connection to agile methodologies. The poster serves as an introduction to our research in this area.

Keywords: localization, internationalization, agile, software, development.

1 Introduction

Adapting a software product for international markets is usually done in two stages: *Internationalization*, which is the process of extracting and making configurable culturally dependent elements, and *Localization*, which is the process of translating those properties for specific languages, countries or cultures [1].

Usually, the relation between the processes of development and localization are considered as strictly separate and linear, i.e. one after the other [2]. Alternatively, localization might be integrated into the development process [3].

Suggestions how to decrease localization effort through the use of new tools during the development process have been made recently [4]. Some authors specifically address issues between agile software development and localization, e.g. if a heavyweight localization process threatens to bog down lightweight agile processes [5], and how to adapt localization to iterative methodologies [6].

2 Agile Software Development and Localization Errors

Offering considerable opportunities, agile development processes also have certain limitations [7], some of which may cause conflicts with software localization. For example, localization issues might be avoided by additional documentation [1], which agile methods try to minimize. Following, common localization issues and their links to agile methodologies are listed.

Unlocalized Elements. Iterative development as well as minimal documentation and processes can lead to unlocalized elements when no formal process to identify

A. Sillitti et al. (Eds.): XP 2011, LNBIP 77, pp. 316–317, 2011.
© Springer-Verlag Berlin Heidelberg 2011

its internationalization requirements exists, internationalizing it was planned, but there was no documentation or communication to the programmers, or it was internationalized, but no localization is available because the element was added or changed after localization had begun, or it was lost due to lack of a formal process.

High Localization Cost and Effort. Changes in the product between development iterations can require re-translations of already localized elements, rendering the original efforts useless and causing additional costs. Also, missing processes and infrastructure can bind resources, in particular for extraction of internationalized elements, handover to external localizers, and building of localized resources.

Insufficient Quality. Localizers need to know the context of the elements. The proper documentation for this does not necessarily exist in agile projects. Prototypes can be a substitution if they are sufficiently stable and the localizers have access.

3 Future Outlook

This poster illustrates challenges for localization in agile software development. These serve as foundation for future research during which we will establish a broader data basis by conducting case studies about software localization in applied agile software development. Eventually, we aim for concrete suggestions to mitigate and avoid the presented issues in order to improve development of international products using agile methodologies.

References

1. Carey, J.M.: Creating global software: a conspectus and review. Interacting with Computers 9, 449–465 (1998)
2. Esselink, B.: A practical guide to localization. John Benjamins Pub. Co., Philadelphia (2000)
3. Asnes, A.: Internationalization and automation. MultiLingual 20, 22–23 (2009)
4. Ryan, L., Anastasiou, D., Cleary, Y.: Using Content Development Guidelines to Reduce the Cost of Localising Digital Content. Localisation Focus 8, 11–28 (2009)
5. Hogan, J.M., Ho-Stuart, C., Pham, B.: Key Challenges in Software Internationalisation. In: Hogan, J., Montague, P., Purvis, M., Steketee, C. (eds.) Proceedings of the Second Workshop on Australasian Information Security, Data Mining and Web Intelligence, and Software Internationalisation, vol. 32, pp. 187–194. Australian Computer Society, Inc., Dunedin (2004)
6. Trillaud, S.: Content management consultancy for MLVs. MultiLingual 20, 34–38 (2009)
7. Turk, D., France, R., Rumpe, B.: Limitations of Agile Software Processes. In: Third International Conference on eXtreme Programming and Agile Processes in Software Engineering, Alghero, Sardinia, Italy, pp. 43–46 (2002)

Prioritization of Features in Agile Product Line Engineering

Jessica Díaz*, Juan Garbajosa**, and Jennifer Pérez**

Technical University of Madrid (UPM), SYST Research Group
E.U. Informática. Ctra. Valencia Km. 7. E-28031 Madrid, Spain
yesica.diaz@upm.es, {jgs,jenifer.perez}@eui.upm.es

1 Motivation

Agile Software Development (ASD) and Software Product Line Engineering (SPLE) methodologies have proved significant benefits in software development. Although they pursue common promises (faster time-to-market, better quality and lower cost), many of their foundations are completely different. ASD focuses on requirements at hand and proposes continuous delivery of valuable software by short time-framed iterations. Instead, SPLE exploits the commonality across the products of a same family by investing on an upfront design of reusable assets (*domain engineering*) which are assembled into customer-specific products (*application engineering*).

Both methodologies require alternatives to (i) scale agile projects up to effectively manage reusability across the products of a same family, and (ii) decrease the risk of developing reusable assets that will become obsolete and not used in volatile business situations. As a result, a new approach called **Agile Product Line Engineering (APLE)** [1] advocates the integration of SPLE and ASD with the aim of addressing the lacks of both approaches when they are individually applied to software development.

Several APLE practitioners [2,3] have proposed an approach in which *domain-then-application* phases are incrementally iterated. This provides a reactive approach where reusable assets respond to current customer demands while (i) being able to iteratively, incrementally construct a flexible SPL platform and (ii) being able to deliver features to the customer in time. However, most authors agree that the applicability of agile methods in domain engineering requires more effort to meet the challenge of reducing the upfront design while being able to get closer to agile principles and values. Specifically, the following challenges have been identified:

- **C1:** How to prioritize the features[1] to be implemented in each agile iteration?
- **C2:** How to evaluate the impact of adding, modifying, or deleting features in each agile iteration? (support for C1).

---

* PhD student.

** Advisors.

[1] "A prominent or distinctive user-visible aspect, quality, or characteristic of a software system or systems".

A. Sillitti et al. (Eds.): XP 2011, LNBIP 77, pp. 318–319, 2011.

- **C3** How to specify traceability between features and architecture without entailing a great overhead? (support for C2).
- **C4:** How to specify these features in a Product Line Architecture (PL Architecture) which will evolve in each iteration? (support for C3).

2   Feature Prioritization in APLE

The aim of this thesis is to provide agile teams rationale to prioritize features to be implemented in an iteration of a APLE development (Challenge labeled **C1**), which requires dealing with challenges labeled **C2**, **C3** and **C4**.

This research started from our experience on an agile project (FLEXI ITEA2 6022 project). A subsequent work was focused on a new concept called *Plastic Partial Components (PPC)* [4]. PPCs are highly malleable components that can be partially described, what increases the flexibility of architecture design. PPCs-based architectures let reinforce some of the agile values and principles [5]. From this proposal, a new concept in software architectures, called *working architecture*, emerged. A working architecture is the architecture that is obtained along with each working product in each agile iteration.

This work [4;5] has provided an attempt to solve the **C4**. Adopting a bottom-up approach, the next research step may be to define a traceability model that establishes the relations between features (*problem space*) and architecture (*solution space*) (**C3**). The following research step may be to define a formal approach to analyze/evaluate the impact of adding, modifying, or deleting features in each agile iteration in terms of which components will be affected, which components will require refactoring, etc. (**C2**). The results of this evaluation provide useful data to facilitate the making-decision process during the prioritization of features to be implemented in each agile iteration (**C1**). Once challenges 1-4 have been dealt with, practitioners have the mechanisms to reduce the upfront domain engineering through agile practices. As a result, domain engineering and the upfront design can be reduced by an incremental, iterative agile life-cycle being able to deliver features to the customer in time.

References

1. Cooper, K., Franch, X.: Aple 1st international workshop on agile product line engineering. In: SPLC 2006, pp. 205–206. IEEE Computer Society, Los Alamitos (2006)
2. McGregor, J.: Agile software product lines, deconstructed. Journal of Object Technology 7(8), 7–19 (2008)
3. Ghanam, Y., Maurer, F.: An iterative model for agile product line engineering. In: SPLC (2) The SPLC Doctoral Symposium 2008. Lero Int. Science Centre, pp. 377–384. University of Limerick, Ireland (2008)
4. Pérez, J., Díaz, J., Costa-Soria, C., Garbajosa, J.: Plastic partial components: A solution to support variability in architectural components. In: WICSA/ECSA 2009, pp. 221–230. IEEE, Los Alamitos (2009)
5. Pérez, J., Díaz, J., Garbajosa, J., Alarcón, P.: Flexible working architectures: Agile architecting using ppcs. In: Babar, M.A., Gorton, I. (eds.) ECSA 2010. LNCS, vol. 6285, pp. 102–117. Springer, Heidelberg (2010)

Lost in Agility? Approaching Software Localization in Agile Software Development

Malte Ressin[*], José Abdelnour-Nocera[**], and Andy Smith[**]

Thames Valley University, Centre for Internationalisation and Usability,
St Mary's Road, London, UK, W5 5RF
{malte.ressin,jose.abdelnour-nocera,andy.smith}@tvu.ac.uk

Keywords: agile, software, development, localization, internationalization.

1 Introduction

Adapting software for different languages is required to gain market access by increasing product acceptance and usability, and satisfying legal requirements. This process commonly consists of two steps: *Internationalization*, i.e. the generalization of any language- and culture-specific properties and elements of the software in question, and *localization*, i.e. the specialization of said elements for specific languages, cultures and countries [1]. It is a topic with increasing relevance as new technologies enable new software uses and interaction modes, which in turn create new cultural dependencies which need to be localized, and new ways to do it, e.g. crowdsourcing [2] and machine translation [3].

Technical challenges in localization, e.g. display of foreign characters [4], have been examined within the academic community. The relationship between localization and software development processes has been mostly absent in research [5]. In practice, localization is often separated from development [6], resulting in serious issues [7] particularly in agile development. An example is the practice of simshipping, an occupational slogan for releasing all language versions of a product simultaneously [8]: this might require localization to start before development is finished, increasing the risk of unlocalized late changes.

Alternatively, localization might be positioned within development [9] and an adaption for iterative methodologies has been considered [10]. However, the requirements of agile development [11] can be in conflict with the holistic model of localizers [12]. Localization is time-consuming, expensive [13] and often done by external partners who have little access to the developers and rely on documentation and formalized processes. This is in contrast with minimal documentation and on-site presence cultivated in agile methods.

---

[*] Student.
[**] Supervisors.

A. Sillitti et al. (Eds.): XP 2011, LNBIP 77, pp. 320–321, 2011.

2 Software Localization in Agile Software Development

Our research aims to create a scientific model for applied software development by correlating theoretical predictions and practical findings. This will be used to deduce recommendations that will help developers improve their localization practices in agile projects. We will examine applied agile development and software localization by conducting case studies *in situ*, e.g. observing planning, execution and evaluation meetings. This will incorporate qualitative and quantitative data gathering and analysis in a mixed-methods approach and will be complemented by surveys, interviews and focus group sessions. Our interest lies in processes, concepts and experiences of teams developing localized software using agile methodologies. We intend to confirm issues predicted by previous experience, literature and theory, and gain a firm understanding how development methodologies are related to effort and product quality.

Further research aims to produce recommendations to facilitate localization in agile development, e.g. tool usage such as translation memory systems or machine translation, a collection of guidelines for interface design and software architecture, or templates for processes and organization.

References

1. Carey, J.M.: Creating global software: a conspectus and review. Interacting with Computers 9, 449–465 (1998)
2. Garcia, I., Stevenson, V.: Translation trends and the social web. MultiLingual 20, 28–31 (2009)
3. Yunker, J.: The end of translation as we know it. MultiLingual 19, 30–31 (2008)
4. Dr. International: Developing Internatinonal Software. Microsoft Press, Redmond (2003)
5. Stanley, J.W., Speights, W.S.: Website localization. In: Proceedings of the 17th Annual International Conference on Computer Documentation, pp. 127–130. ACM, New Orleans (1999)
6. Esselink, B.: A practical guide to localization. John Benjamins Pub. Co., Philadelphia (2000)
7. Caesar, M., Fehrenbach, C.: Management von Lokalisierungsprojekten. In: Reineke, D., Schmitz, K.-D. (eds.) Einführung in die Softwarelokalisierung, pp. 27–38. Narr, Tübingen (2005)
8. Kahler, T.: Projektmanagement in der Softwarelokalisierung: Eine Einführung. In: Schmitz, K.-D., Wahle, K. (eds.) Softwarelokalisierung, pp. 11–19. Stauffenburg, Tübingen (2000)
9. Ciarlone, L.: Evolving global product content practices. MultiLingual 20, 50–52 (2009)
10. Trillaud, S.: Content management consultancy for MLVs. MultiLingual 20, 34–38 (2009)
11. Turk, D., France, R., Rumpe, B.: Limitations of Agile Software Processes. In: Third International Conference on Extreme Programming and Agile Processes in Software Engineering, Alghero, Sardinia, Italy, pp. 43–46 (2002)
12. Hogan, J.M., Ho-Stuart, C., Pham, B.: Key Challenges in Software Internationalisation. In: Hogan, J., Montague, P., Purvis, M., Steketee, C. (eds.) Proceedings of the Second Workshop on Australasian Information Security, Data Mining and Web Intelligence, and Software Internationalisation, vol. 32, pp. 187–194. Australian Computer Society, Inc., Dunedin (2004)
13. Ryan, L., Anastasiou, D., Cleary, Y.: Using Content Development Guidelines to Reduce the Cost of Localising Digital Content. Localisation Focus 8, 11–28 (2009)

Empirical Evaluation of Agile Practices Impact on Team Productivity

Claudia de O. Melo* and Fabio Kon**

Department of Computer Science,
University of São Paulo, Brazil
{claudia,kon}@ime.usp.br

Keywords: team productivity, agile methods, empirical evaluation.

1 Motivation

Agile methods have become more popular since the early 2000s and, in some cases, can offer better results for software development projects when compared to traditional approaches. Agile methods promise to achieve high productivity and to deliver high-quality software, attracting the attention of companies, which demand ever-higher development speed and quality in their products.

The general topic of this PhD thesis is to perform an empirical evaluation of the impact of agile practices on team productivity by means of empirical studies. Regarding the current state of theory and research, more empirical evidence of effectiveness on practices recommended by agile methods are required [1]. Particularly, there are few scientific studies about the impact of agile practices on productivity. In the systematic review conducted by Dybå and Dingsoyr [1], studies just analyse the impact of agile methods on team productivity in terms of lines of code (LOC). However, software development is knowledge work which nature is more complex and harder to evaluate [2]. Measuring productivity with a richer set of metrics would help to deal with this drawback, allowing deeper analysis of the results obtained in the studies. Moreover, agile teams not always collect enough data for a consistent measurement. Therefore, we have to identify the most viable way that best fits the agile spirit in order to measure productivity.

Some recent studies discuss the main software development productivity factors [3]. All include the development method as a factor, but in a very superficial way. None of them discusses how agile methods can influence team productivity. In addition, according to Petersen [4], many studies have been conducted before the year 2000. Thus, productivity factors "need to be re-evaluated in currently operating development organizations".

2 Agile Practices Impact on Team Productivity

The goals of my PhD research are expressed by the Research Question 1 (RQ1) and better investigated through the following sub-questions (SQ):

---

* PhD student.
** Advisor.

A. Sillitti et al. (Eds.): XP 2011, LNBIP 77, pp. 322–323, 2011.

- **RQ1. How do agile practices affect productivity of agile teams?**
  - SQ1. What are the agile practices that *most* affect the productivity of teams?
  - SQ2. What are the effects of those agile practices in team productivity? What are the mechanisms behind those practices that enable productivity?
  - SQ3. What metrics are appropriate for measuring productivity in agile teams?
  - SQ4. Are there possible adaptations to promote productivity in cases where those practices have negative impacts?

To manage productivity effectively, it is important to identify the most relevant practices and develop strategies to get the most out of them. Therefone, we aim to contribute in the field by studying which practices impact on team productivity and how they impact.

We are currently performing an empirical case study [5] inside organizations, within a real environment and with real problems. Qualitative and quantitative data are being collected in Brazilian companies through interviews, direct observation and document analysis. The first objective is to gain and organize knowledge on the most perceived threats to productivity in the agile projects. The second is to identify, without preconceived ideas, which agile practices were more related, in the team's opinion, to their performance. For this reason, we are using some principles of Grounded Theory [6], a methodology for collecting and analyzing qualitative data that permit the collection of meanings, gain understanding and development of empirical knowledge. This step of the project is related to the research sub-questions SQ1 and SQ2. After this first step, we plan to conduct multiple industrial case studies to answer sub-questions SQ3-4. This allow a cross-case analysis [5] that will enable the comparison of multiple cases in many divergent ways. The idea is to use the first case studies to generate hypothesis and the other to test them, ensuring research completeness and consistency. The methodology to test the hypothesis probably will be action research, the type of study where more realistic scenarios for the research are found, which involves the investigation of concrete actions in an industrial environment.

References

1. Dybå, T., Dingsoyr, T.: Empirical studies of agile software development: A systematic review. Information and Software Technology 50(9-10), 833–859 (2008)
2. Ramírez, Y.W., Nembhard, D.A.: Measuring knowledge worker productivity: A taxonomy. Journal of Intellectual Capital 5(4), 602–628 (2004)
3. Trendowicz, A., Münch, J.: Factors influencing software development productivity - state-of-the-art and industrial experiences. Advances in Computers 77, 185–241 (2009)
4. Petersen, K.: Measuring and predicting software productivity: A systematic map and review. Information and Software Technology (2010) (in press)
5. Gerring, J.: Case Study Research: Principles and Practices. Cambridge University Press, Cambridge (2006)
6. Glaser, B.G., Strauss, A.: The Discovery of Grounded Theory: Strategies for Qualitative Research. Aldine Transaction (1967)

An Approach on Applying Organizational Learning in Agile Software Organizations

Viviane Santos[*] and Alfredo Goldman[**]

University of São Paulo, São Paulo, Brazil
{vsantos,gold}@ime.usp.br

Keywords: organizational learning, agile methods, inter-teams knowledge sharing, competitiveness.

1 Motivation

Agile software development (ASD) has been in evidence over the past years by encouraging changes on how software is developed [1]. However, agile methods strongly focus on empowering the project team in achieving its goals [2]. Little attention is given to creating insights and experiences to the organizational level [3]. Therefore, there is a challenge to overcome the barriers to scale the knowledge on the group level to the organizational level effectively [4].

Some of the problems have been bypassed through the adaptation of practices such as job rotation to increase knowledge redundancy [5], scrum-of-scrums [6], workshops [7] and communities of practice [8] to support multi-team issues.

However, they are not effective in all contexts and must be carefully adapted and tailored. For this reason, specific strategies are needed to spread useful knowledge for the organizational level [9].

In this context, Organizational Learning (OL) may be very relevant to support the generation of organizational competitive advantage, since OL helps improving organization actions through better knowledge and understanding [10].

2 Applying OL in Agile Software Organizations

The primary goal of this research is to investigate how OL can be facilitated in agile organizations to foster organizational competitive advantage.

The overall research tasks consist on analyzing assumptions [10] that contribute to facilitate OL in agile organizations; identifying practices to effectively share tacit and explicit knowledge; analyzing exploitation-exploration tension in agile organizations and proposing alternative balance solutions; proposing an OL framework for agile software organizations considering their characteristics, contextual factors and appropriated practices to address competitive advantage; and evaluating inter-teams

---

[*] PhD. Student.
[**] Advisor.

A. Sillitti et al. (Eds.): XP 2011, LNBIP 77, pp. 324–325, 2011.
© Springer-Verlag Berlin Heidelberg 2011

knowledge sharing and perceived organizational competitiveness (responsiveness, innovativeness, customer satisfaction, financial performance, software process improvement, employees commitment and satisfaction, etc).

The ongoing research is running both in academic and corporate environments. Some preliminary results are the need for (1) joining practices detected by the students in a repository (academic environment), and (2) the achievement of better understanding of the research problem (corporate environment) through an empirical study performed in a software organization that implemented the Scrum method and in an interview with a specialist on implementation of agile methods.

In the academic environment, the next steps consist in designing the participant observations and the case studies, as well as, determining the form of data collection, tools and technical analysis. After, we will execute them to collect and further analyze the evidences.

In the corporate environment, the next steps consist in establishing the companies participating in the action research; develop collaboration agreements between researchers and practitioners; plan and execute the iterative cycle of activities, including problem diagnosis, action intervention and reflective learning to propose a solution to the problem outline by applying and adjusting the proposed framework.

Finally, we aim at analyzing the qualitative evidence, consolidating the proposed framework and reporting the research outcomes to wider community and developing research publications.

References

1. Dybå, T., Dingsøyr, T., Moe, N.B.: Agile software development – current research and future directions, 1st edn. Springer, Heidelberg (2010)
2. Dybå, T., Dingsøyr, T.: Empirical studies of agile software development: A systematic review. Information and Software Technology 50, 833–859 (2008)
3. Kettunen, P.: Adopting key lessons from agile manufacturing to agile software product development – A comparative study. Technovation 29(6-7), 408–422 (2009)
4. Bjørnson, F.O., Dingsøyr, T.: Knowledge management in software engineering: A systematic review of studied concepts, findings and research methods used. Information and Software Technology 50, 1055–1068 (2008)
5. Fægri, T.E.: Improving general knowledge in agile software organizations. In: Agile Conference (AGILE 2009), Chicago, IL, pp. 49–56 (2009)
6. Srinivasan, J., Lundqvist, K.: Using Agile Methods in Software Product Development: A Case Study. In: Sixth International Conference on Information Technology: New Generations (2009)
7. Dybå, T., Dingsøyr, T., Moe, N.B.: Process Improvement in Practice: A Handbook for It Companies. Kluwer Academic Publishers, Norwell (2004)
8. Kähkönen, T.: Agile methods for large organizations building communities of practice. In: Agile Development Conference, ADC 2004. Journal Computer 37(12), 2–11 (2004)
9. Levy, M., Hazzan, O.: Knowledge management in practice: the case of agile software development. In: Cooperative and Human Aspects on Software Engineering (CHASE). ICSE Workshop, Vancouver (2009)
10. Fiol, C.M., Lyles, M.A.: Organizational Learning. The Academy of Management Review 10(4), 803–814 (1985)

Managing Uncertainty in Software Development Projects: An Assessment of the Agile Development Method Scrum

Denniz Dönmez* and Gudela Grote**

ETH Zurich
{ddonmez,ggrote}@ethz.ch

1 Motivation

In the face of uncertainties that constitute a challenge to every software development project, developers lack guidance to manoeuvre between the boundaries of flexibility and structures when choosing or amending development methods to their needs. The underlying motivation for this research was the question of how to improve the predictability and controllability while at the same time increasing flexibility, which lies at the heart of system design [1]. This is especially true in fast changing industries such as software development. In order to investigate how agile development methods, and especially the project management framework Scrum, can best support different software development endeavours it is necessary to test agile methods for their capability to establish a balance of organisational flexibility and stability, which is a fundamental challenge for organisations [2].

In software development, waterfall methods have been the predominant approach, aiming to minimise uncertainties through detailed planning. These plan-driven approaches have been discovered to yield several imperfections, and it has been pointed out that uncertainties in the development process cannot be minimised by a highly structured project management [3, 4]. As a response, agile software development methods have emerged and gained huge popularity within the last decade, influencing how software is developed worldwide [5]. Scrum, first presented by Schwaber [6], defines an agile development framework that takes a managerial approach to software development, which focusses on people rather than on processes [7]. It must be noted that the mere presence of expertise on a team is insufficient to produce high-quality work, and that expertise must be managed and coordinated in order to leverage its potential [8]. In order to fully understand agile software development its 'intrinsically collaborative nature' [9] has to be recognised and the focus of research needs to be shifted to how human and social factors affect, and are affected by, agile development methods [10]. By emphasising an evolutionary, highly collaborative and feedback-focused approach they constitute a revolution to the development process, especially in terms of planning and team organisation. However, contemporarily abounding phenomena such as the self-organisation of teams as a strategy to improve quality are not

---

* PhD student.
** Supervising professor.

A. Sillitti et al. (Eds.): XP 2011, LNBIP 77, pp. 326–328, 2011.

yet fully understood within the context of software development. A deeper understanding of evolving agile development methods in general, and management frameworks such as Scrum in particular, can be gained through research that connects theoretical frameworks with insights from company projects. This shall be achieved by drawing upon the perspectives from various disciplines including computer science, management science, and psychology.

2 Contribution

To investigate how agile teams manage uncertainties an assessment of agile development methods in general, and the Scrum framework in particular, was set out. After an investigation of software development methods and a review of the literature on Scrum, observations of daily work and meetings (stand-up, planning, review, and retrospective) in four teams of two different companies were carried out, and a first insight into the typical deployment of the Scrum framework has been gained.

It has been understood that the Scrum framework consists to a large extent of established concepts that are known to practitioners and academics. Such concepts include for example the visualisation of the workflow, or the self-management of teams. Their positive effects are seized by Scrum as they are assembled into a set of complementary elements and tools. This results in a framework that can lead to exceptionally high increases in team performance in the best case, or ineffective and uncontrolled work processes if not understood and applied properly.

In company settings it has been observed that in many situations not all of the elements suggested by Scrum are equally implementable, and some changes from traditional development approaches appear more appropriate than others. At the same time it has been observed during a project where Scrum was introduced to a team of novices that it can be implemented easier when a team is newly composed and no previous constraining structures exist.

Drawing upon these observations, subsequent research will aim to identify how Scrum works from a conceptual point of view. In order to be able to assess their impacts for the design of work systems and organisational structures, an analysis of elements that support either flexibility or structures is planned. The research also seeks to give an explanation of the links between elements of the Scrum framework and their effects on the work and organisational systems. Eventually, this research aims to establish reliable guidelines to balancing flexibility and stability in software development projects.

References

[1] Grote, G.: Uncertainty management at the core of system design. Annual Reviews in Control 28, 267–274 (2004)
[2] Grote, G.: Management of Uncertainty. In: Theory and Application in the Design of Systems and Organizations. Springer, Heidelberg (2009)

[3] Boehm, B.: Software risk management: principles and practices. Software 8(1), 32–41 (1991)

[4] Boehm, B., Turner, R.: Management challenges to implementing agile processes in traditional development organizations. Software 22(5), 30–39 (2005)

[5] Dyba, T., Dingsoyr, T.: Empirical studies of agile software development: A systematic review. Information and Software Technology 50, 833–859 (2008)

[6] Schwaber, K.: Scrum Development Process. In: Sutherland, J., et al. (eds.) OOPSLA Business Object Design and Implementation Workshop. Springer, London (1997)

[7] Moe, N.B., Dingsoyr, T.: Scrum and team effectiveness: Theory and practice. In: Abrahamsson, P., et al. (eds.) Agile Processes in Software Engineering and Extreme Programming. LNBIP, vol. 9, pp. 11–20. Springer, Berlin (2008)

[8] Faraj, S., Sproull, L.: Coordinating expertise in software development teams. Management Science 46(12), 1554–1568 (2000)

[9] Good, J., Romero, P.: Collaborative and social aspects of software development. International Journal of Human-Computer Studies 66(7), 481–483 (2008)

[10] Dyba, T., Dingsoyr, T.: What Do We Know about Agile Software Development? IEEE Software 26(5), 6–9 (2009)

Agile Testing and Critical Systems

Jørgen Bøegh[1], Juan Garbajosa[2], and Alex Rennoch[3]

[1] Beijing University of Posts and Telecommunications, No.10 Xitucheng Road,
Haidian District, Beijing 100876, China
[2] Tehnical University of Madrid (UPM), Ctra. de Valencia, Km. 7. E-28031 Madrid, Spain
[3] Fraunhofer FOKUS, MOTION, Kaiserin-Augusta-Allee 31, D-10589 Berlin, Germany
jorgen_boegh@yahoo.dk, jgs@eui.upm.es,
axel.rennoch@focus.fraunhofer.de

Workshop Description

The need to count on critical systems is growing day by day. Together with traditional domains such as medical devices, automotive, railway, aeronautical, space and telecommunications, new applications and services are coming up every day. Terms such as ubiquitous, pervasive, or autonomic computing, products under the general umbrella of smart devices or the use of large wireless sensors networks indicate a clear trend in the increase of application complexity and dependency. The dependency of daily life on computers and computer based systems is growing up at a high rate, and testing is gaining importance at the same rate.

To perform a proper testing and validation of critical systems encounter a number of problems both from a technical and from a managerial point of view, also considering that the complexity of the underlying software is growing as well. Traditionally, critical systems are normally developed according to standards like IEC 61508, MIL 882 or ED 109, and emphasis is on well defined development processes. These systems usually have contractually specified requirements, and detailed documentation of all activities is very important. This approach is radically different from the usual agile development approach where focus is on customer collaboration, frequently changing requirements, and trust in individuals more than in documented quality activities. It is therefore a widely shared impression that the agile community and the critical system community live in completely different worlds.

However, there are mutual benefits of bringing the two communities together. For example, agile testing approaches can most likely bring many advantages to critical system testing. These possibilities are currently not well understood and exploited.

The high level topics of the workshop are the following:

- Shared values and principles in testing
- Quality Management goals
- Testing strategies

The workshop brings the agile and safety critical communities together, including representatives from both industry and academia. The workshop is organized in the context of the STV (System Testing and Validation) workshops, which were initiated in the year 2002.

A. Sillitti et al. (Eds.): XP 2011, LNBIP 77, p. 329, 2011.
© Springer-Verlag Berlin Heidelberg 2011

Value-Based Software Traceability Workshop (VALSOT 2011)

Angelina Espinoza[1], Richard Paige[2], and Juan Garbajosa[1]

[1] Technical University of Madrid (UPM),
E.U. Informatica, Spain
aespinoza@syst.eui.upm.es, jgs@eui.upm.es
http://syst.eui.upm.es
[2] University of York, Department of Computer Science, UK
paige@cs.york.ac.uk
http://www.cs.york.ac.uk/~paige

Traceability defines and maintains relationships among the artifacts involved in the software-engineering life cycle. This mechanism is widely used for purposes as project visibility and accountability, and it provides an essential support for developing high-quality software systems. Traceability has traditionally been strongly influenced by software process drivers; however, during the last few years, the software process is starting to take into account new drivers. One such driver is the software product's value. The global value of a product can be understood as the perceived benefits in relation to its cost. Both business and technical areas of an organization consider the value concept as a priority, for analyzing software costs and benefits. For these purposes, a tight interaction between these two sides is fundamental.

From the perspective of traceability, the value consideration may change many assumptions. For instance, the development artifacts that are involved in traceability (requirement, user story, design items, test unit, etc) should contain the necessary information to estimate its value under a given context. Similarly, traceability items (tracing links, tasks or resources to support traceability) need also to consider the value concept. Thereafter, the traditional traceability schemes seem to be too limited for describing and tracing the value. Since, business areas are involved and interested in software value tracing, the traceability approaches need to be more streamlined than those ones more technical oriented. Additionally, the agile community advocates the advantages of lean traceability for avoiding bothersome tasks that are difficult to perform in agile contexts.

The workshop aims to provide the attendees with an opportunity to develop a common research agenda through paper presentations, brainstorming, discussion and building consensus on important directions. As outcome, a report will be produced clearly outlining 1) the research topics and challenges in terms of specific problems in the area, and (2) a summary of existing solutions for targeting these topics, based on industrial experiences and academic pilots. Finally, a main expected result is to share among participants proved approaches in organizations. The aim is to spread useful traceability schemes for value-based product management, and for efficiently supporting agile projects.

A. Sillitti et al. (Eds.): XP 2011, LNBIP 77, p. 330, 2011.

Second XP Workshop about Dealing with Usability in an Agile Domain

Ana Maria Moreno and Agustin Yagüe

Universidad Politecnica de Madrid
Madrid, Spain
ammoreno@fi.upm.es, agustin.yague@upm.es

Abstract. The Second Workshop "Dealing with Usability in an Agile Domain" is aimed to be a forum for discussing these approximations for the intersection of agility and usability. More concretely, issues regarding the implications of usability in agile environments, alternatives for integrating HCI techniques in an agile process, approaches for incorporating usability features into agile artifacts or open issues in the integration of agile and usability where discussed.

Keywords: Agile development, usability patterns, user stories, HCI.

1 Presentation

The integration of usability engineering and agile software development practices is an emerging challenge. Both the agile and the HCI community have recognized the need and the difficulties to incorporate efficient usability practices in this domain. During XP 2010 a first edition of this workshop was held with about 25 attendees, who actively participated in an interesting debate about the topic and highlighted many open issues.

XP 2011 workshop is aimed to keep on being a forum for discussing approximations for the intersection of agility and usability. Participation would be open to all XP2011 attendees.

The Workshop is scheduled in two 90 minutes sessions. First sesion will be structured around an invited talk by a representative speaker in the area and the presentation and discussion of individual position papers. Second sesion will be opened to all the attendees to propose open issues to discuss about usability & agility and will be followed by a final debate about the current practice and open issues in the integration of usability and agility.

Among our learning outcomes we find contributing to understanding the implications of usability in agile environments, exploring alternatives for integrating HCI techniques in an agile proces, opening up approaches for incorporating usability requirements into agile artefacts, or identifying open issues in the integration of agile and usability.

A. Sillitti et al. (Eds.): XP 2011, LNBIP 77, p. 331, 2011.

Author Index